THE ADVANCING WRITER

THE ADVANCING WRITER

BOOK 3

READING AND WRITING ESSAYS

Judith R. Lambert
Richland College

Harvey S. Wiener, Series Editor
Adelphi University

HarperCollinsCollegePublishers

Acquisitions Editor: Mark Paluch
Development Editor: Leslie Taggart
Project Editor: Katharine H. Glynn
Art Director/Design Supervisor: Jill Yutkowitz
Text Design: Circa 86 Inc.
Cover Design: Jill Yutkowitz
Cover Photo: Superstock Inc.
Production Administrator: Valerie A. Sawyer
Compositor: Ruttle, Shaw & Wetherill
Printer and Binder: R. R. Donnelley & Sons Company
Cover Printer: The Lehigh Press, Inc.

Dedication

To James Hall, my friend and colleague,
for your love of good writing in its many forms
for the art with which you enable students to write with enthusiasm and power
for your generous spirit in exchanging classroom visits, collaborating on assignments, and mentoring many of your colleagues
for your kindness, humor, and appreciation of fine food and spirits.
Thank heavens your smile and laugh are back, and I pray speech will follow soon. Good luck, dear friend, on your journey back.

For permission to use copyrighted material, grateful acknowledgment is made to the copyright holders on pp. 405–407, which are hereby made part of this copyright page.

93 94 95 96 9 8 7 6 5 4 3 2 1

CONTENTS IN BRIEF

CONTENTS IN DETAIL

FROM THE SERIES EDITOR

The Advancing Writer series addresses the needs of college students who require a course or a series of courses in basic writing skills. Focusing on sentence, paragraph, and essay building as well as essential grammar and usage skills for successful revising and editing, *The Advancing Writer* provides a flexible yet comprehensive program for the beginning student writer in college. Each book in the series is self-contained, student oriented, and course specific; yet the three books together represent an integrated program in written language development. Philosophy, pedagogy, and design features unify the series.

Through this series beginning college writers will learn the power of language in confronting existence and the riches in transforming their private pasts into sensory language. In celebrating personal autobiography as a major force in the basic writing program, *The Advancing Writer* series recognizes that critical thinking begins with examining the self, acknowledging individual history, and thinking about language that connects one's personal reality to the larger worlds of school, work, and society. Yet, even though the writers addressed by these texts may not have fully explored their own linguistic power, they are ripe for challenge to their intellect and creativity. Unlike other basic writing texts, *The Advancing Writer* does not exclude intellectual and creative matters for reflection and analysis by taking a ''remedial'' approach; instead, it provides college-level tasks while showing students how to analyze the decisions they confront as they think and compose.

In each book, students start by examining their own attitudes toward writing and then move on to consider a variety of strategies for prewriting, drafting, revising, and editing. Although drafts of both student and professional writing are provided for discussion of content and analysis of form, students work mainly on their own writing, revisiting earlier drafts as they assimilate new strategies for revising and editing. Students learn to consider the audience for their writing through collaborative reading, writing, and revising activities that give student writers immediate feedback as they think and compose. The series emphasizes that reading and writing are both processes to create meaning, thus promoting a holistic approach to literacy and enabling students to see how writing can help them learn about and understand their academic readings. The practice of syntax, grammar, and usage are merged with genuine rhetorical goals; activities rooted in connected discourse make clear the relations between content and form.

Students and instructors who use the three-tiered program will benefit from the regular reinforcement strategies presented throughout. The books are recursive, building on concepts introduced earlier, or anticipatory, looking ahead to skills to be developed later on, or both. Each text can be used alone; but taken as a whole, *The Advancing Writer* series is a set of interlocking tools for improving students' writing at the beginning level.

Harvey S. Wiener

PREFACE

The Advancing Writer series was created to help student writers gain conscious control of their writing and reading of sentences, paragraphs, and essays. The series provides sequential and recursive instruction with a consistent rhetorical philosophy. Emerging from student needs and concerns and grounded in current theory and practice, the series also provides consistent features of design and pedagogy. Linking autobiographical and academic writing, reading and writing, and process and product, the series encourages students to explore the connectedness of their lives, their studies, and the uses of language.

Reading and Writing Essays is the third book in the series. Its goal is to help advancing writers learn to express their ideas in essay form by engaging them in the milieu of talk and texts, both those they read and those they write. By helping students discover—and create—connections between their reading and their own experiences, reactions, and associations, advancing writers are taught to honor their own intellectual and creative powers.

There are three parts to this book. Part 1 teaches the reading and writing processes. Part 2 is an anthology of readings with ample apparatus and writing assignments. Part 3 is a brief reference handbook.

In Part 1, ''Writing and Reading Processes,'' students first review the writing process and then learn to develop and revise ideas and details for their essays. An entire chapter on the reading process helps writers become conscious of the processes they use to shape meaning as they read and suggests strategies for understanding written texts. Many commonplace metaphors and examples link the abstractions of these processes with the concrete and familiar from daily life, a strategy for demystifying the processes of reading and writing and for helping students with learning differences approach reading and writing confidently. Because my classroom research continues to reveal the emotional baggage that interferes with students' motivation, learning, and retention, Part 1 helps students recognize and address their negative self-talk and feelings to achieve the cognitive growth we aim for in college.

Part 1, ''Writing and Reading Processes,'' includes writing activities, group activities, student examples of discovery strategies, drafts, revisions, and an annotated essay to show students how to mark a text as they read. Other features are reminder boxes to summarize and reinforce concepts; boxes of strategies for easy reference, for example ''Ways to Revise''; and a summary of each chapter's lesson in ''Points to Remember About. . . .''

Part 2, "Reading and Writing Essays," presents nine writing lessons in a modes format. However, a rhetorical philosophy of composition underlies this book, and writing activities and essay assignments are designed to emphasize audience and purpose. Students can be motivated to work on the content and form of their own writing when they are engaged by the experiences and ideas of other writers; and the concept of audience, easily lost when the emphasis is on modes, becomes a strong influence on writing when frequent and structured collaboration provides a live audience throughout the entire process of writing.

The essays in Part 2 were selected with the help of colleagues and manuscript reviewers for readability, interest, and appropriateness as an example of a mode. I began by selecting readings I thought would be inspirational and provocative to students—Mike Rose's transformation from voc. ed. punk to college student; Brenda Ueland's warm and affirming belief that we all have something original and important to write; and Rosa Mathe's successful, but costly, conformity to community standards. I wanted readings with flesh-and-blood people students could recognize, care about, and model themselves after. I wanted content that would help prepare students for success in college, such as David D. Burns's advice for speaking in public. I also wanted readings that would evoke conversations about cultural differences as students recognize them in their own lives, including their classroom. I believe that such a curriculum, rather than special programs and classes on multiculturalism, promotes understanding of differences, encourages tolerance, and gently invites nontraditional students into the community of readers and writers we call college.

The apparatus for each selection is extensive to provide a range of choices for you, to implement the reading principles described in Chapter 4, and to promote critical thinking and rhetorical analysis. "Thinking Before Reading" asks students to write a few sentences in their Idea Banks (journals) to tap their prior knowledge as a way to prepare for reading. "Expanding Your Vocabulary From Reading" provides a list of words students can refer to when reading to aid comprehension. "Jotting Down Your First Responses" allows students to connect the essay to their own experiences and feelings before they focus on comprehension and analysis of an essay. The brief writing students do before and after reading is expressive writing that promotes fluency and may be used as a beginning place for their essay writing.

"Checking Your Comprehension" helps students understand the literal content of an essay. "Understanding a Writer's Patterns" focuses students' attention on form and rhetorical elements, especially those elements emphasized in a chapter's lesson. "Making Predictions and Drawing Inferences" and "Making Judgments and Thinking Critically" provide questions for higher-level thinking and reading skills. "Using New Words" individualizes vocabulary study and provides work on prefixes, suffixes, roots, and word usage.

"Responding by Writing" includes several writing assignments for specific audiences and purposes. The audience varies from classmates to student-selected audience to teacher. Some writing prompts elicit essays based on personal experience; others ask students to write about some aspect of the essays they have read. Some assignments ask students to draw from two or more essays, to use brief quotations, and to include the titles and authors of essays they have read. Others require evaluation, analysis, or comparison.

Part 3, "A Writer's Handbook," is a handbook for reference in editing or for review of grammar and mechanics. It includes examples from both student and professional writing. Although the handbook doesn't include exercises, which tend to downplay the importance of purpose and audience in editing, exercises are available separately for those who need them.

UNIQUE FEATURES OF THIS TEXT

Of primary significance is that this book is part of a series that is grounded in the same philosophy of composition, uses the same terminology, and follows a recursive sequence of instruction to develop fluency, clarity, and correctness in writing. Twelve other features distinguish this book.

1. The writing and reading processes are shown to be closely interwoven, and practice in both processes is given in Parts 1 and 2. The book frequently reminds students that recognizing the rhetorical aspects and ways of development (modes) of texts can improve their reading comprehension.
2. The rhetorical philosophy of composition underlies all writing assignments and the analysis of essays. The modes, on which this book is organized, are presented as ways of developing a point that often occur in combination and that evolve out of a writing situation.
3. Collaboration is built into Part 1 in group activities and can be continued in the reading and writing activities in Part 2. The interest other students show in what a writer has written and the collegial company of fellow students involved in similar writing and reading tasks can motivate an advancing writer. Structured interaction among peers can help students discover what they have to say, stimulate substantive revision, and provide a live substitute for the imagined audiences to whom they write. Collaboration is a natural way of learning because most students are inherently social beings, because most learning outside classroom walls takes place in a social context, and because communication is a social task. Suggestions for collaboration appear in the Instructor's Manual.
4. The instruction and apparatus pay close attention to the emotional and cognitive needs of students as learners and writers. The book encourages students to be aware of their self-image and self-talk as writers and readers and encourages the growth of metacognitive skills. This book

also emphasizes the complex processes of seeking, giving, and using feedback to make collaboration successful and improve revision. Essays throughout provide information and inspiration to student writers.

5. In Parts 1 and 2, student writings are attainable models for students at this level of proficiency and represent the interests and concerns of real students. The last essay in each chapter of Part 2 is a student essay treated in an identical way with the professional essays, a treatment that assures students of our respect for their texts.
6. The reading process taught in Chapter 4 is reinforced by the reading and writing apparatus in Part 2. "Thinking Before Reading" taps students' prior knowledge to prepare for reading and to increase comprehension. "Making Predictions and Drawing Inferences" reinforces the skills of predicting and reading to confirm or refute as well as reading "between the lines" of a text, to use Louise Rosenblatt's phrase.
7. The "Exploring Further" feature at the end of each chapter in Part 1 guides students through the reading and writing processes, first asking them to read a student essay on peer pressure from Part 2 and then recommending a series of individual and collaborative activities as they consider and shape their ideas into an essay. Students then reflect on what they have discovered about their own writing process in an essay for the instructor.
8. The essays and apparatus in Part 2 raise multicultural issues. They are intended to evoke conversations about the cultural differences in the readings and in students' experiences, including the present classroom, and to help students understand the concept of "culture." Some essay assignments elicit essays about cultural experiences to increase students' awareness of their own cultures.
9. The introduction to each rhetorical mode begins with a brief lesson on a mode as a way of developing an essay and includes examples of the mode. Some introductions include examples that are excerpts from essays in the book, intended to link the lesson with the readings in the chapter and the modes-based chapters with each other. For instance, within the lesson on exemplification is a passage from the student essay in that chapter. Within the lesson on process analysis is a passage of an essay by Burns from the chapter on exemplification. The use of the same essay in several lessons as well as remarks in the text remind students that writers combine the ways of development (the modes) when they write and that the choice of ways to develop ideas emerges from the content and the writing context.
10. Bloom's taxonomy of cognitive difficulty serves as a conceptual model for developing the apparatus. "Checking Your Comprehension" calls for recall and comprehension. "Understanding a Writer's Patterns" calls for application and analysis. "Making Judgments and Thinking Criti-

cally'' calls for evaluation as do some of the writing prompts, which also include prompts that call for analysis, synthesis, and evaluation.

11. ''Using New Words'' asks students to choose which words from each essay they want to learn and to make vocabulary cards for them. The vocabulary cards individualize vocabulary study and stress student choice in order to create the habit of word curiosity and study. Other word activities and games make vocabulary study a social rather than a solitary task, emphasizing the inherently social aspect of language study.
12. The reference handbook is flexible in the ways students can find information. Preceding the handbook is ''A Quick Guide to a Writer's Handbook,'' which provides an overview of the handbook's topics; these are keyed to the marking symbols presented in Chapter 1 for easy reference while editing. ''A Brief Table of Contents for the Handbook,'' which follows ''A Quick Guide . . . ,'' and the Table of Contents for the book can be used for locating elements for review or study. ''A Quick Guide to Punctuation'' precedes the punctuation section and provides both a review of punctuation rules and a tool for quickly finding information in the handbook.

Definition and rules are followed by multiple examples, many taken from the readings, to link the handbook with the essays and teaching material. Reminders and Review boxes continue the coaching tone of the book with hints for applying the information when editing. The handbook uses the terminology of *The Advancing Writer* series and follows the organization of Book 2 to ease the student's independent use of the reference handbook. The ancillary package includes transparencies and exercises for teaching and practice.

ACKNOWLEDGMENTS

Writing this section is an exercise in humility, for one realizes how many people are involved in the production of a book on which the author's name seems to proclaim a solitary effort. The list of contributors to this book is quite long. First I am grateful to my mentors Maxine Hairston and Elaine Maimon who opened the fascinating vistas of composition teaching to me. I am grateful to my students who continue to teach me as long as I keep asking them ''What did you learn? What helped you? What made learning hard or hurtful?''—and as long as I keep listening.

I am also grateful to my colleagues at Richland College, whose conversation about reading and writing continues to teach me and who generously provided me with samples of student papers. Thanks to James Hall, Rica Garcia, Jane Peterson, and Phyllis Dawson for student papers and for sharing so much of their teaching with me; to Ed Luter and Luke Barber for their suggestions on argumentation; and to Michael McMurray for testing the questions in Part 2 by answering them. Thanks to the reading specialists Sue Cross, Joe Cortina, Janet Elder, and Katherine Gonnet for their help with reading theory and the needs of reading students. Thanks to Ann McGee-Cooper for helping me understand the needs of students with dyslexia. For testing parts of the book, I thank students Angel Jackson and Tammy Anderson.

Three rounds of reviews have challenged and affirmed the manuscript in its development. Like my students, I sometimes recoil from, crumble at, outright reject, and denigrate the copious comments of the reviewers. Ultimately, however, I evaluate, incorporate, and adapt their responses. Their feedback has shaped and strengthened this book and taught me more about the dynamics of giving and receiving feedback and using it, and I am grateful to them. They are

Eddye Gallagher, Tarrant County Junior College
Sylvia Gamboa, College of Charleston
Carin Halper, California State University, Fresno
Jan Hausmann, Southwest State University
Rosemarie Kistler, El Camino College
Marilee McGowan, Oakton Community College
Sandra Moore, Mississippi Delta Community College
Carol Paskuly, Erie Community College
Karen Patty-Graham, Southern Illinois University
DeWayne Rail, Fresno City College
Denis Sivack, Kingsborough Community College
Barbara Thompson, Columbus State Community College
Linda Weeks, Dyersburg State Community College
Betty Jeane Wallace, Sinclair Community College

Since a book is not just written, it is produced, I thank the excellent staff of HarperCollins. I thank Jane Kinney and Consulting Editor Harvey Wiener for developing the concept of the series and guiding it from conception to birth. I thank Harvey Wiener for inviting me to participate in *The Advancing Writer* series and for teaching me much through his writing and workshops, especially about collaborative learning. A special thanks goes to Leslie Taggart, developmental editor, who has worked closely with me, coordinating the series and the reviews and responding to drafts, always with grace, support, and a constant understanding of students' needs. Thanks to basic skills editor Mark Paluch for guiding and supporting this project and to Katharine Glynn, who has the tact of an ambassador, for moving the manuscript into production. Finally, thanks to my husband Don for his unflagging support and unceasing supply of deli food.

Judith R. Lambert

A Visual Guide To

THE ADVANCING WRITER SERIES

***Editor:* Harvey Wiener** Adelphi University

BOOK 1	BOOK 2	BOOK 3
SENTENCES AND PARAGRAPHS	**PARAGRAPHS AND ESSAYS**	**READING AND WRITING ESSAYS**
ISBN: 0-06-500301-2	ISBN: 0-06-500302-0	ISBN: 0-06-500303-9
Karen L. Greenberg Hunter College, City University of New York **Peter Rondinone** La Guardia College, City University of New York	**Karen L. Greenberg** Hunter College, City University of New York	**Judith R. Lambert** Richland College

Informed by current theory and research on developmental writing, this exciting new series actively engages students in each stage of the writing process. These comprehensive texts cover all the basics of writing from sentence-level skills to composing the essay while incorporating contemporary teaching strategies, peer collaboration exercises, and grammar in the context of writing. Multicultural readings and student writing are included as bridges from personal to academic writing.

These books were developed as a series right from the start. Instructors can use the one that suits their course level, or all three for consistency across their basic writing program.

from Book 1

Finally, imagine a totally different audience: business people who were considering opening a bookstore in your town or city. What examples should you discuss if you were trying to convince these business people to open their store in your town?

How do the details that you listed to support this topic sentence *differ* for the three different audiences ______________________

____

____

____

____

Here are some questions to consider as you develop ideas and details to support your topic sentence.

QUESTIONS TO ASK YOURSELF ABOUT YOUR PURPOSE AND AUDIENCE

Who exactly am I writing for? Who would be interested in reading this paragraph?

- What are these readers like?
- How similar are they to me? Would they react as I do?
- Do I want to share my thoughts and feelings with them?
- Do I want to explain something to them?
- Do I want to persuade my readers to think or to feel or to do something? What? Why?
- How much do my readers already know about my topic?
- What else do they need to know about this topic?

REMINDER:

Good writing may have several purposes. When you w
you may also be expressing your feelings and/or trying to
ers to do or to feel or to think something.

from Book 2

Take notes as the person responds. Repeat this activity with several different readers. Then reconsider the focus, purpose, and audience for the draft and decide which of your readers' suggestions you should include in your revision. Revise the paragraph as many times as you need to in order to accomplish your purpose in writing it.

A Revision Springboard: Branching. If you decide that your draft needs additional supporting details, you can try freewriting, brainstorming, and clustering to develop new insights, ideas and details. In addition, you might try doing a form of clustering called branching to evaluate your details and to generate new ideas for your revision. *Branching* is a form of critical thinking that enables writers to analyze the relations among their ideas and details.

BRANCHING A DRAFT TO SEE PROBLEMS IN ITS DEVELOPMENT

Analyze the ideas and details in your paragraphs by doing the following:

- Write the topic sentence in a circle in the middle of a sheet of paper.
- Write each of your supporting points in its *own* circle and connect it to the main circle.
- Draw branches out from each supporting point and write in the specific experiences, examples, and reasons you used to develop each supporting point.
- Evaluate each supporting point by asking yourself whether it is clearly related to the topic sentence and is explained in enough specific detail.
- Cross out irrelevant details.
- Develop new details for the circles that do not have enough branches (enough supporting details).

Branching lets you see exactly where you do not have enough supporting details. Here is an example of a student's use of branching to determine whether a draft was developed effectively. The final version of this draft (which appeared on pages – and – in Chapter 2) is printed after the branched analysis.

1st Draft: My First College Registration

My first registration for courses at Valley Central College was a nightmare. I didn't have all the forms I needed. I was very nervous about registering. When I went to registration, the woman behind the desk told

Writing Process Emphasis

This series explores the full **writing process.** Maintaining a focus on the final product, these texts give students detailed help with prewriting, drafting, revising, and editing strategies. Book 1 emphasizes grammar and sentence-level writing. Book 2 concentrates on writing paragraphs.

Book 3 is a rhetorical reader featuring student and professional essays.

from Book 3

Responding by Writing

1. Acts of courage come in all sizes. Since the quality of courage is one we all admire, tell a story of personal courage. It may be your own or one you witnessed. It may be physical, mental, or emotional courage. Write for your classmates so they can experience the event as you did, not as disinterested spectators.
2. Tell the story of the bus incident that led to Rosa Parks' arrest from the viewpoint of the bus driver, the white man who didn't have a seat, or another black passenger. How might the event have looked from their eyes? What would they have felt and thought?
3. Create an imaginary dialogue between you and Parks or between Parks and the courageous person you described in question 1. Remember to begin a new paragraph each time the speaker changes and to use quotation marks around each speaker's words.
4. In reporting the story of her research, Ragghianti creates a portrait of her heroine Rosa Parks. Is this an effective portrait of courage? Why or why not? Remember to evaluate the article, not Rosa Parks herself. You might talk about the author's interviews with several people, her selection of Parks' past and present activities, her use of dialogue, the physical description of Parks, her use of historical facts, or anything else that makes this effective or not effective as a portrait of courage.

Momma, the Dentist, and Me

by Maya Angelou

Maya Angelou is best known for her book *I Know Why the Caged Bird Sings,* which is one of four books that make up her autobiography. Her life is the story of joyful triumph over hardship. In this excerpt from *I Know Why the Caged Bird Sings,* Angelou narrates two versions of the same incident with Momma, who is her grandmother.

Thinking Before You Read

Have you ever been treated badly by someone whose service you needed — perhaps a car salesman, personnel in a doctor's office or clinic, a teacher or other personnel in a school, a policeman or other person of authority? Write
1 about that incident in your Idea Bank. Tell what happened

Expanding Your Vocabulary from Reading

excruciating (1) intensely painful
penance (1) payment for a sin, act performed to show sor

from Book 3

help you at the current stage of drafting. Your feedback will be only as good as the questions you ask of your readers.

Your questions and concerns about your draft can help a reader look for new possibilities in a draft. First, check your understanding of the assignment (or writing situation, if you are writing for work or personal reasons). Then decide what questions and concerns you have about your draft and inform the reader about them. You should also let your reader know where you are in the writing process. Are you just getting started? Do you know some things you want to write about but can't find a focus or main point? Does the reader see your main point or thesis? Here are some questions whose answers are usually helpful to writers. They are based on the five qualities of good writing and a priority of concerns. Don't overwhelm your reader with too many questions. Choose several whose answers would help you take your draft to the next stage.

Asking for Helpful Feedback

1. Am I on the right track? Am I addressing the assignment?
2. What do you think is my thesis (main point)?
3. Have I written appropriately for my intended audience?
4. What are the strengths of this draft?
5. Is every part well-developed? Are there enough details and examples?
6. Are there any confusing or missing parts?
7. Do all of the parts have a clear connection to the thesis?
8. Is the essay well organized? Is the organization obvious to the reader?
9. What are two or three things I could do to take this draft to the next stage?

Writers are rarely helped by yes and no or right and wrong answers to these questions. If you are giving feedback, write two or three sentences to answer them. Notice that some of them can be answered by paraphrasing parts of the draft or by asking questions or by making suggestions. Even a question seems to call for a yes or no answer, such as "Am I addressing the assignment?" expand on your answer. A description of what you see the writer doing or saying is more helpful than a one-word answer to a question. For example, you have been assigned to write about a lesson you learned as a child and to use examples to explain your thesis. After reading your draft, a reader might write, "You wrote about learning to hide your Hispanic origins because of discrimination. I counted four examples." You could tell from this comment if what is coming through to your reader is what you meant. If it is not, you would know that you need to revise.

Peer Collaboration

Peer collaboration discussions ask students to work together to generate ideas, respond to drafts, and to help edit final revisions.

from Book 1

In Chapters 1 and 2, you learned how to plan and write discovery drafts of paragraphs. This chapter will show you how to evaluate, revise, and edit your drafts for the most important qualities of good writing. These qualities are described in the chart that follows.

FIVE IMPORTANT QUALITIES OF GOOD WRITING

1. Good writing has a ***focus:*** Each paragraph has a clear main point or topic sentence.
2. Good writing has adequate ***development:*** Each paragraph supports the main point with enough specific details.
3. Good writing has ***unity:*** Each paragraph sticks to its main point.
4. Good writing has ***coherence:*** Each paragraph is organized logically and flows smoothly.
5. Good writing is ***correct:*** Each paragraph has complete sentences that are relatively error-free.

Begin revising by looking for strengths in your writing—for sentences and words that you really like. Try to figure what you did to achieve these effective parts so that you can improve the weak parts. Here are additional strategies for revising:

- Ask a friend, relative, or classmate to respond to your paper.
- Reread your details: Did you provide enough relevant, specific details to support your main point?
- Add new ideas, details, and descriptive words.
- Cross out ideas, sentences, and words that do not sound logical or interesting or that are not clearly related to your main point.
- Cross out sentences or words that are repetitious.
- Use circles and arrows to indicate how sentences or words should be reorganized.
- Use scissors and tape to cut out sentences or ideas and move them to different places in the draft.

The first strategy—asking for feedback from readers—is the most important one. If you want to see how professional writers use this strategy, get a copy of the film *All the President's Men* (about the Water brought down the Nixon administration). This film profile sional writers work. In one scene, one writer (played by Du ishes a draft of a newspaper story and puts it in a bin for pu writer (played by Robert Redford) walks by the bin, picks it, and begins making changes in the story. When the Hoffm

Five Qualities of Good Writing

An emphasis on **Five Qualities of Good Writing** in every book helps students remember the important features of good writing: **"Focus," "Development," "Unity," "Coherence,"** and **"Correctness."** Student written samples are included to illustrate effective and ineffective writing.

Writer's Portfolio

Books 1,2 and 3 include a **Writer's Portfolio** that covers the rhetorical modes, always with a consideration of the writing situation, audience, and purpose.

from Book 3

For a business course in personal finance, you might be asked to keep a list of your expenditures and create categories for a budget. Division and classification is a way of organizing and simplifying diverse behaviors, information, or ideas.

ORGANIZING DIVISION AND CLASSIFICATION ESSAYS

There are many ways to divide and classify any collection of facts, ideas, items, behaviors, or expenditures. However, the categories should be consistent and exclusive. Consistency means that you decide on one system, or determining principle, for dividing and classifying and stick with it. To classify kinds of desserts, you could use the categories pies, cakes, cookies, but not pies, cakes, and chocolate because "chocolate" is a flavor and the others are not. Exclusivity means categories should not overlap. Each category should be distinct from other categories. To classify kinds of tippers in a restaurant, you could use the categories men and women, but not men, women, and business men because the category "business men" overlaps with the category "men" and excludes business women.

When using categories to make a point, writers usually announce their thinking and organizing pattern with a sentence, such as "Oppressed people deal with their oppression in three characteristic ways." Words such as ways, kinds, types, levels, categories, and groups are signals of classification and division. Writers may announce, for example, that there are "several ways to face oppression," "three kinds of discipline," "several levels of friendship," or "two groups of drivers."

Transitions. Good writers also follow an announcement of the division and classification pattern with clear transition words and phrases as they name and discuss each category. Here are some of the transition words and phrases writers use:

one way	the most	there is
the second way	the next	then there is
the third way	the last	last there is
the fourth way		

Writers may organize their categories from least to most important, from most to least effective, or from largest to smallest. However they order the categories, they help the reader stay on track by using transition phrases and by repeating key words or phrases. Here are sentences from an essay by Martin Luther King, Jr. , about the ways of dealing with oppression. Several paragraphs with discussion and examples follow each of the categories in King's essay. The transition phrase if underlined; the repeated key words are in boldface.

Integrated Reading and Writing Approach

In all three books, an integrated reading and writing approach as evidenced in the **Exploring Further** sections encourages students to respond to each other's writing and to the sample readings. In Book 3, critical reading coverage carries this approach one step further.

from Book 3

REMINDER

There are many ways to end an essay. A conclusion often echoes something in the introduction–the thesis, a key word, an image, or an incident.

POINTS TO REMEMBER FOR WRITING AN ESSAY

- Use your Idea Bank or other discovery strategies to find main point to write about.
- Write a trial thesis and test it.
- Describe your intended audience and purpose.
- Write a discovery draft.

Although you should give your best effort at each step of the writing process, don't overinvest in your discovery draft. Trying to "get it perfect" may create writer's block. Charge through with a draft and be ready for revising.

■ EXPLORING FURTHER

1. Reread "Don't Press Your Luck" on pages 0-0 and the writing you did about peer pressure for Exploring Further in Chapter 1.
2. *Group Work.* Talk about the ideas that emerged in your freewriting or group discussions about peer pressure. What struck each of you as the most important idea about each situation? Take notes about your own and your classmates' ideas.
3. *Writing Activity.* Write a trial thesis for an essay about peer pressure. Use the strategies for writing a trial thesis described in this chapter.
4. *Group Work.* Think about who needs to know what you have written. What audience would benefit and use what you have to say? Parents? Elementary school children? Young teens? College students? Voters? Teachers? Consumers? What do you want them to do or believe?
   Tell your group what your trial thesis is (the main point of your essay), and describe your intended audience and purpose. Help each other test and clarify an appropriate audience and purpose. Write down your group's comments and suggestions about your trial thesis.
5. *Writing Activity.* Write a description of the audience and purpose for your essay on peer pressure.

Writing Activity. Write a discovery draft of an essay about peer pressure in which you discuss the reasons for peer pressure and give examples. Draw on the ideas and examples of peer pressure you have read, written, and talked about. Name the person or writer whose examples you use.

CHAPTER 4

READING FOR COMPREHENSION

from Book 3

In Chapters 1 through 3 you have been reading about writing. In Chapters 5 through 13 you will be reading selections from newspapers, magazines, and books. Although this is a writing course, reading, thinking, speaking, and listening are inseparable from writing. Because the communication skills reading, writing, speaking, and listening are interrelated, you can use your stronger ones to help improve your others. For instance, your stronger communication skill may be talking to others. You can use this strength to improve your writing by talking to others as you look for ideas to write about, as you try to find a focus for your writing, and as you revise. Because communications skills are interrelated, good readers are usually good writers and the reverse. Use what you know about writing to help you read better, and use what you know about reading to help you write better.

Reading and writing, as well as the other communication activities, are skills that you can learn and improve by practice, just as you might practice juggling or skateboarding, Like juggling or skateboarding, these communication activities are part mental, part physical, and part emotional. For instance, freewriting is a physical activity that stimulates the mental activity of thinking. Reading is a mental activity that creates physical changes such as in respiration, eye movements, pulse rate, and brain activity. All of these complex activities are affected by your emotional state-how you feel and what you are about.

Earlier you read that negative self-talk creates writer's block for many people, and you looked briefly at your own. You also read how two writers use positive self-talk to create positive feelings that allow them to think and write, and you considered how you can help yourself write. Reading, too, is affected by your feelings, attitudes, and self-talk. Since reading essays is a way of learning to write, let's look at some negative messages that make it harder to read.

Contextualized Grammar Issues

Grammar concepts are discussed in relation to how they affect students' writing. Sentence-level issues are covered both in the writing and grammar chapters.

from Book 2

In Chapter 6, you practiced writing in the "first-person" point of view (*I, we*) and the "third-person" point of view (*he, she, it, they*). Most process analyses are written in a form of the "second-person" (*you*) point of view called the *imperative* ("command"). The subject of an imperative sentence is always you, but the pronoun *you* does not appear; it is "understood." For example, when Group Work activities direct you to "Form a group with two or three other students," you understand that the subject of this command is you (*"You form a group with two or three other students"*).

If all the sentences in your process analysis are imperatives, then your paragraphs or essays will sound like monotonous orders. To avoid this, try varying your sentence beginnings so that they don't all start with the verb. Here is an example:

ALL IMPERATIVES:

To cure insomnia, go to bed at the same time every night, including weekends. Wake up around the same time every morning. Develop a bedtime ritual and use it every night. Drink a glass of mild before retiring, but don't ever drink alcohol, because it disturbs sleep patterns. Finally, stop worrying about your insomnia; that will only make the problem worse. You'll fall asleep way before you die from lack of it.

VARIED SENTENCE BEGINNINGS:

Here are some tricks for curing insomnia. First, try going to bed at the same time every night and waking up around the same time every morning, including weekends. Since bedtime rituals prepare the mind to relax, develop a bedtime ritual and remember to use it every night. You might drink a glass of milk before retiring, but don't drink any alcohol because it disturbs sleep patterns. Finally, you should try to stop worrying about your insomnia; that will only make the problem worse. You'll fall asleep way before you die from lack of it.

The second version of this paragraph sounds less abrupt and more friendly and interesting than the first one. (For more information on sentence variety, see pages 122-124).

WRITING ACTIVITY 10

Write a "how-to" paragraph about one of the topics below:

- Choose a college (or a university)

from Book 2

There are two ways to correct missing-verb fragments:

1. Attach the fragment to the sentence that precedes
   (You may have to cross out the subject of the frag
   subject of the sentence to which it is being connec
2. Add a verb to the fragment.

Here are two fragments, followed by each type of correction:

Viruses as deadly as bacteria. Are responsible for many human diseases.

1. *Attach the fragments to form a sentence:*

   Viruses as deadly as bacteria are responsible for many human diseases.

2. *Add a verb to each fragment:*

   Viruses are as deadly as bacteria. They are responsible for many human diseases.

Cowpox, a virus that can have painful effects on milk cows. Does not have serious effects on humans.

1. Cowpox, a virus that can cause painful effects on milk cows, does not have serious effects on humans.
2. Cowpox is a virus that can have painful effects on milk cows. It does not have serious effects on humans.

WRITING ACTIVITY 3

Underline the fragment in each set of word groups below. Then use one of the two methods noted above to correct each fragment. The first one has been done both ways as an example.

1. The videotape is a fairly recent invention. *Only about seventy years old.*
2. The idea of storing information on a magnetic tape first occurred to Valdemar Poulson. A famous Danish scientist.
3. The videotape that Poulson created. It was a band of stretched plastic.
4. The plastic covered by a film of magnetic iron oxide.
5. The iron oxide has tiny particles in it. Particles with the ability to carry an electric current.
6. A magnetic recording head emits electric signals. These signals, which change the currents in the iron oxide particles.

Grammar Exercises

All exercises are composed of **connected discourse**: sentences (or paragraphs) that are thematically related. This puts grammar skills in the context of rhetorically sound writing. Exercise topics reflect multicultural sensitivity and span the curriculum.

WRITING AND EDITING LOG

Each time your instructor returns a piece of your writing — in your writing course and in every other course—make notes about the piece in this log. You will be able to chart progress and to identify areas that need further improvement.

Date ______________ Course ______________________________

Title of Paper ______________________________________

Strengths:

Problems and Errors:

Writing Process Log and Teacher Conference Log

These logs provide an easy format for recording the progress of students' writing.

from Book 2

Writing Activity 9

Brainstorm for five minutes about your favorite place. Write everything down that comes to your mind. If you get stuck, ask yourself the questions on page xx.

Group Work 4

Form a brainstorming group and — together — choose a problem concerning your school (for example, the registration process, placement tests, class size, or student fees). Choose one person to be the group recorder. Then take turns calling out ideas about the problem and solutions for it. Jot down a brief note about every solution that you and your classmates call out. If the group gets stuck, the recorder should read aloud the questions on page xx. When the group finishes, each person should discuss the solution he or she thinks would best solve the problem.

Writing Activity 10

Write a paragraph or two about the problem that your group discussed in the preceding activity. What is this problem? Why does it cause you (or other students) so much aggravation or trouble? What could the school's administrators, teachers, or students do to solve this problem?

from Book 1

Writing Activities, Writing Assignments, Group Work

These **writing exercises** help students develop and practice their skills and promote peer collaboration. Many are based on the readings and writing samples authored by students and professional writers of different ethnic backgrounds.

tell readers what materials they will need to accomplish the process; also define any terms that they might not understand. Finally, explain each step of the process in detail and arrange these steps in the order readers must perform them.

✔ POINTS TO REMEMBER ABOUT PROCESS ANALYSIS

1. Make sure that your process is narrow enough to explain in a paragraph or an essay.
2. Keep your purpose and your readers in mind as you brainstorm the details for you process analysis. What exactly do you want them to know? What else might they want or need to know?
3. Make your introduction interesting and briefly explain the importance or advantages of the process.
4. Describe any materials or equipment that readers will need to perform the process.
5. Define any terms that readers may not understand.
6. Explain each step in the process clearly and in detail. Also, anticipate readers' confusion or mistakes, and explain what they should *not* do.
7. Use concrete descriptive words and vivid images.
8. Make sure that your details are logically organized— in the order in which they are to be performed—and that you have included transitional words and phrases.
9. Experiment with different conclusions for your narration. Choose the ending that suits your purpose better.
10. Vary your sentence structure so that your process analysis is not a curt set of imperative commands.

from Book 2

Learning Aids

All three books in the series feature learning aids such as **"Points to Remember," "Reminders," checklists, charts,** and **boxes** that reinforce key concepts.

THE ADVANCING WRITER

PART 1

Writing and Reading Processes

CHAPTER 1

WHEN YOU WRITE

In this course you will do two kinds of writing that are defined by their purposes. One is called *expressive* writing because its main purpose is to express what you think, feel, or experience. Expressive writing is a mirror of your own thoughts and feelings. It is essentially for you, the writer, although it may be used later for another kind of writing. That other kind of writing is called *transactional.* Its basic purpose is to communicate something to someone. Do you see the difference? One is for you, the writer. The other is for a reader, a person or persons other than you.

This distinction is important because you have great freedom in expressive writing to write whatever you want in whatever way you want. You can't be wrong! Spelling, punctuation, and grammar aren't important, as long as you can read what you wrote. In this book you will often be asked to do this kind of informal writing—to recall something from your own experience, to react to something you've read, or to prepare for a class discussion. Sometimes you will use this writing as a starting device for more formal writing.

You will also be asked to do more formal, or transactional, writing. You will write essays, which are compositions of several paragraphs about a main point, in response to the readings that make up Part 2 of this book. These essays represent the kind of writing you will do in other college courses and beyond. As the writer, you will have something you want to say to others, your intended readers. These intended readers are called the audience. The audience of your writing may be your teacher, some or all of your classmates, or one or more persons beyond the class. Becoming aware of whom you are writing to (your audience) and why you are writing (your purpose) will help you develop what you have to say (your content) clearly and forcefully.

If the idea of writing essays scares you, don't worry. Your teacher, your classmates, and this book will help you get started. You'll use a series of overlapping activities for formal writing that you may have learned about in a previous writing course:

Observing or reading carefully
Jotting down what you are thinking or feeling
Talking with classmates
Using specific strategies for discovering ideas
Writing a discovery draft
Getting feedback from your classmates and teacher
Revising your draft several times
Editing the revised draft
Proofreading the final version

Do these activities of the writing process sound familiar to you? The activities do not make up a rigid series of steps but are a general plan of action to produce formal writing. You don't have to produce perfect essays in a single step and you don't have to work alone.

Now a word about the readings in this book. Because reading and writing are complementary activities and because most writing you do in other college courses will be in response to what you read, this book is designed around readings—articles from magazines and newspapers and excerpts from books. The readings will serve you in two ways: as sources of ideas and information to think and write about and as models of the several kinds of thinking and writing explored in the writing lessons in this book, for example, description, narration, comparison, and definition. We selected the readings to illustrate the main points of the lessons, but the writers wrote because they had something to say. You will write about the content of a reading and your response to it (expressive writing), and then you will write an essay (transactional writing). After you have focused on what you want to say in your essay, you can focus as you revise on the writing lesson discussed in that chapter.

Now repeat these words: "I am a writer." Does that sound strange? You must begin to think of yourself as a writer. After all, writers are only people who write, and that's you, the teacher, and the other students in this class! To be a writer, you must think and behave like a writer.

Writers often keep a journal, a place to record what they see, hear, read, or remember and what they think about these experiences. This is the expressive writing described in the beginning of this chapter. This writing is private, but you may use it later to develop writing for an audience other than yourself. There are all kinds of bits and pieces in a journal—disconnected fragments, quotations, lists, ideas, and unrelated thoughts. It is like my grandmother's sewing cabinet, full of sewing tools and leftovers from many sewing projects—

spools of thread, rolls of fabric remnants, pieces of rickrack and lace, needles, pins, scissors, and so on. The drawers were crammed full. When she needed a specific color of thread or a scrap for a new project, she'd start digging through her cabinet. A writer's journal, like my grandmother's sewing cabinet, is a place to save things for later use.

As a writer, you will keep a journal in this class. Let's call this journal an Idea Bank, a place to save your words, to try out ideas, and to record your observations. The questions and prompts that accompany the readings in Part 2 will give you some starting places for writing in your Idea Bank, but you may "ad lib." Get in the habit of writing down anything that you notice and think about, anything that takes your attention as you read, whatever you wonder about or question, and life experiences that the readings call to your memory. Look for connections between the readings and your life and between one reading and another, and write about them as they remind you of each other. In Part 2 questions before and after each essay will ask you to write in your Idea Bank. Here is an entry from Tammy's Idea Bank before she read "The Tapestry of Friendship" in Chapter 10.

What is a friend? A friend is someone I can confide in. A friend is someone I can share my hopes, dreams, and aspirations with and not be looked down on. It's someone who is totally accepting of me no matter what I look like or where I came from. A friend gives advice because he/she cares about me. A friend understands when it seems no one else can. A friend is necessary and precious—always there with a hug and a smile.

WRITING ACTIVITY 1

Begin your Idea Bank by writing about yourself as a writer. If you can, compare yourself as a writer or your writing journal to something in your experience like my grandmother's sewing cabinet.

DISCOVERING IDEAS TO WRITE ABOUT

You may think that writers always have something to write about, but that's not true. They develop strategies for discovering ideas. They read, talk to people, notice what goes on around them, and keep journals. They develop the habit of writing by writing at specific times every day, even when they don't feel like it. They also develop their own bag of tricks to get started and to keep going. You probably have some tricks that you've learned through trial and error or in other writing classes. Before you read about any strategies here, write about your own.

WRITING ACTIVITY 2

When you have to write a discussion answer on a test or an assignment in any class, how do you get yourself started? Write in your Idea Bank about at least two mental and two physical activities you go through. Tell what you do when you are stuck in order to keep writing.

My husband has a shiny red toolbox with the basic tools for hanging pictures and making simple home repairs. Occasionally he'll add a needle to pump up a basketball or a Phillips screwdriver for a screw with an "X" in the head. Different repair situations call for different tools, and different writing situations call for different discovery strategies.

If you have heard about some new strategies for getting started or continuing to write from your classmates, or if any of the strategies that follow are new to you, add these to the activities you wrote about in Writing Activity 2. Continue to add to this list in your Idea Bank throughout this course so you will have a full toolbox of discovery strategies to use.

In this section you will read about writing in an Idea Bank, brainstorming, freewriting, listing, clustering, answering the five W questions, and outlining. These are some of the *prewriting strategies* writers use before they produce a draft of a memo, report, or essay. The amount and kind of prewriting varies widely according to the kind of writing task, the writer's purpose, and the writer's work style. To make these discovery strategies work for you, set time limits, try them out several times, and use them before and during the process of producing a formal writing. Remember that no one strategy will work in every writing situation, so you will need a full toolbox of strategies.

Writing in an Idea Bank. You've already begun using one strategy—*writing in an Idea Bank, or journal.* The trick is to make writing things down a habit. To create the habit, add something to your Idea Bank every day. Write down what you observe, what interests you, and how you react (what you feel and think about what you observe). Don't dismiss your daily experiences as too trivial to record. However, notice that this type of journal is not simply a diary or log of what you did, whom you met, and what you ate. It is a place in which to record slivers of life and the quiet musings, seldom spoken, that make up your rich mental life.

IDEAS FOR WRITING IN YOUR IDEA BANK

When you write down something that takes your attention, also write down your reactions and thoughts about it.

Responses to readings, questions, and prompts in Part 2
Bumper stickers
Advertisements from billboards, radio, television, and magazines
Fragments of conversations
Jokes you hear
Comic strips and cartoons
News items from television and radio
Lyrics of songs
Significant events of the day
Quotations from books, newspapers, and magazines
Drawings and photographs from books, newspapers, and magazines
Information from another course you are currently taking
Wishes, dreams, goals, hopes
Questions about anything you hear, see, and think
Newspaper obituaries

WRITING ACTIVITY 3

Write three entries in your Idea Bank today.

Brainstorming. *Brainstorming* is a group technique for problem solving borrowed from business, but you can use it by yourself as well as in a group. You can use it to get started or to get unstuck. The goal of the technique is to generate quantity, not quality. The basic rule is to write down every idea that pops into your head or out of any group member's mouth without censoring or judging. Usually the leader writes the problem or topic on the board and records all ideas as quickly as they are generated with no discussion.

It's usually hard for people not to judge the ideas. When you are brainstorming alone or with a group, you may catch yourself or others saying "That won't work" or "That's a stupid idea" or "That doesn't fit." You may feel uncomfortable and want to quit brainstorming as soon as you have a few ideas that might work or when you don't seem to have any good ideas. You need to have patience and trust the process and yourself. You're looking for ideas to use, not fully developed and organized thoughts.

Once you have generated as many ideas as you can in the time limit or have run out of ideas, stop and evaluate them. Select the most promising ones. Try them out one at a time, knowing you don't have to keep the duds or use all the good ones. Like other discovery strategies, this strategy can be used several times during a writing assignment.

Here is Mary Ann's brainstorming as she cast her mental net widely, looking for a topic for an argumentative essay.

peer pressure

sending kids to college

coed dorms

danger of cults

weight loss and health

communication in marriage

smoking—addictive—teens

TV—advertising—children

foster care—mine—Marge

death—what to say—children affected by it

After brainstorming for possible topics, Mary Ann used other discovery strategies on two of her ideas: foster care and communication in marriage. She decided to write a draft on the marriage topic.

Here is the brainstorming Tammy did in the process of writing an essay about friendship. She did the brainstorming after she had selected the topic, had done some writing to define friendship, and had read an essay on friendship in Part 2.

My best friend Kathy

How did we become friends? started talking about the teacher in Home Ec.

How long have we been friends? since junior high—13 years

We experienced many things together from hot rollers to homework.

We have been there for each other through difficult times.

1. Death of our favorite teacher

2. Death of a friend in high school
3. Her divorce in 1992

We came from different sides of the tracks—helped us learn morals and compassion from each other.

Kathy is accepting of me just as I am.

We argue and are complete opposites right down to our toes.

Why do we remain friends?

1. Bond of trust and love developed over time
2. Shared secrets

GROUP WORK 1

With a group of four or five, brainstorm solutions for a common student problem—having enough time to keep up and do well in classes in spite of work, family, social life, and other classes.

Freewriting. Another strategy for finding or exploring a topic to write about is *freewriting*. The rules are simple. Write without stopping for five minutes about anything that comes into your mind. Don't worry about spelling, grammar, or punctuation. Don't worry about staying on a certain subject. Don't worry about sounding stupid. Just keep your pen (or computer keyboard) moving for five minutes. If you can't think of anything to write, write ''I can't think of anything to write'' until something occurs to you. The goal is to keep your pen moving. At the end of five minutes stop and read what you've written. If anything in the writing takes your attention, begin anew with that. Repeat the process several times. Students often find an idea worth writing about on the third or fourth loop, but not before.

This method works well when you don't know what to write about or when you are stuck in the middle of an essay. As with brainstorming, the trick is to suspend judgment and not to worry about wasting time or producing material you can't use. Freewriting is a discovery strategy, not a technique for producing a draft. There are two reasons this method works. The blank page is poison for many writers, and writing anything, no matter how bad it is, is the antidote for that poison. Get something down on paper. Don't wait for inspiration or expect perfection. One sage said that writing is 99 percent perspiration and 1 percent inspiration.

Another reason freewriting works for many people is a physiological one. The physical activity of generating words on a page causes electrical impulses and chemical reactions in the brain. These physical changes are both cause and effect of the mental work writing requires.

This strategy may also work well for you when you have so much to say that your thoughts are spilling all over each other, making it difficult to decide what to write. The cure for writer's block is to write! Here is Ursula's freewriting as she searched for a topic for a narrative essay.

Having the same problem as usual—no idea on what to write. Could write about the dog out there in the ravine. I am feeding him daily, since they picked up his mother. He was tiny then, last year in Dec. '91. Now he (or she?) weighs about 70 pounds. It's a nice looking dog, with a wrinkly face, but he is so timid. Disappears into his tunnels at the sight of people. I just see his head sticking out when he eats. Neither Animal Control nor the humane society or all my family have been successful in catching him. It is pitiful.

Maybe I should write about my life in Saudi Arabia, since this article is for an audience. Not that many people are interested in dogs. Well, better my life in Saudi. Not the whole $2\frac{1}{2}$ years. But some time with some *drama.* The vacation, I guess, when I was stuck in Dabai because Saudia Airline canceled the return flight. I was truly terrified, the money spent in the gold market and my re-entry visa expiring 24 hrs. later. It will be the vacation. The unique dog story later.

Listing. *Listing* is probably the most familiar way to discover what to write about when you've already chosen a topic. Some people are natural list-makers. Others detest making lists. Listing works best if you know several things you want to write about on a subject. Make a list of words or short phrases in the order that you think of them. You can organize your list after you have written it by numbering the items. There are probably several logical orders. Here is the list Alison made for her essay on using credit cards wisely.

Bills	Bank
Mark calendar 2 days before due	Endorse
Write account # on check	Account # on front
Name of company	Fill out deposit slip
Date	Back of check
Sign	Amount
Enter in register	Date

Use Discover card

Write as D in register

Write check # when bill pd.

Save money because fewer checks

Save $.29 postage on bills

Plus interest on money in bank

Pay total bill monthly

No interest

No annual fee

Cash back each yr.

Clustering. *Clustering* is a pictorial method of brainstorming or listing. To use clustering, write a key word or phrase in the center of a page, and circle it. Write related words somewhere on the page and draw lines to the circle. Each of these words may suggest related words which you should write down and attach with lines. These groups of words form clusters of ideas. Your task is to generate as many clusters as you can in your time limit. As in brainstorming, you don't have to use everything you think of. If you decide to use several clusters in writing a draft, you may want to organize them by numbering them. You may repeat this process several times before you write a draft, and you may use this strategy again if you get stuck or need to develop some part of an essay more fully.

Clustering often appeals to people who are divergent thinkers. Their thinking shoots off in many directions, like a Roman candle. People who are convergent thinkers often prefer linear strategies, such as lists or outlines.

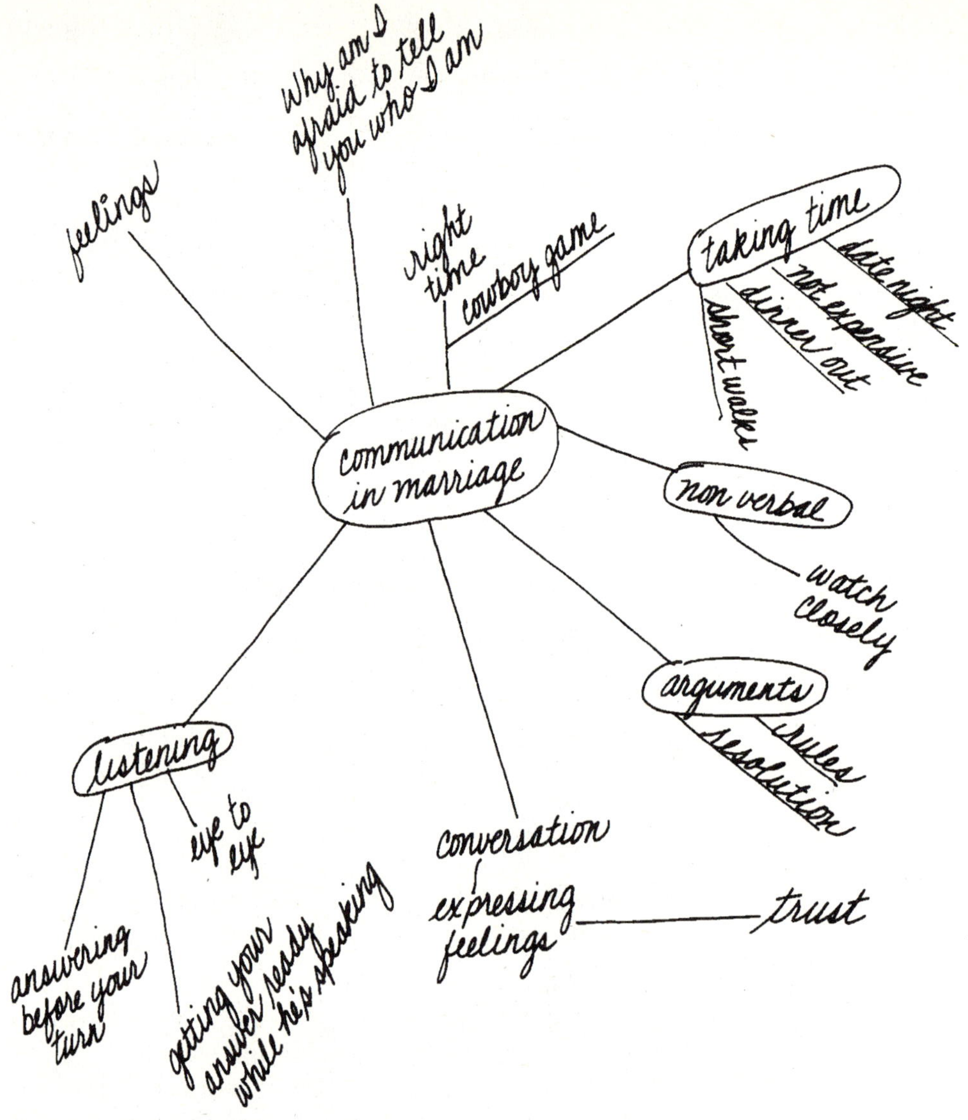

Convergent thinkers may think divergent thinkers are illogical or unorganized, but they simply have a different style of processing and organizing data. If you are a divergent thinker or a visual learner, clustering may work well for you.

After Mary Ann had discovered the topic of communication in marriage, she used the clustering above to explore that topic. As she was clustering, she began to focus on one aspect of communication that she felt wasn't typical advice. That focus emerged more strongly after she wrote her discovery draft.

The title of her finished essay was "Vocation: Romance" which suggests her emphasis on communication to keep romance in a marriage.

WRITING ACTIVITY 4

Choose *one* of the topics below. Use listing and clustering to practice with each strategy. Generate as many ideas as you can for a possible essay on the topic. Compare the two discovery strategies.

1. Describe what you consider to be a good relationship with a girlfriend, boyfriend, or spouse.
2. Describe your favorite television program.
3. Describe your ideal job or career.
4. Describe a musician or group you think is especially talented.

WRITING ACTIVITY 5

Using the same topic you worked with for listing and clustering in Writing Activity 4, do a freewriting. For this practice, write for five minutes and then read what you wrote. Choose anything that takes your attention in the writing or that your writing leads you to begin writing again. Repeat the whole freewriting process two more times.

Answering the Five W Questions. Another discovery strategy is *answering the five W questions: who, what, when, where,* and *why.* These are called the reporter's questions, and you may have learned to ask these in elementary school. They are a valuable strategy because they can generate so much specific information about a topic, so don't forget to use them. Here are Mary Ann's answers as she prepared to write her essay on communication as the key to keeping romance in a marriage.

Who? our marriage as an example; friends ask what our secret to a happy marriage is

What? dating alone, not group dates; something new; one interest of yours and one interest of mine; problems with the gang—negative humor, drop things when you're out with a group

When? once a week; when we can ship the kids out, a weekend together in a big hotel

Where? coffee shop, big hotel, picnic

Why? create romance

WRITING ACTIVITY 6

Use the five W questions on the topic you worked with in Writing Activities 4 and 5. Push yourself to give as many answers as you can to each question. You may think of two or three new ideas using this strategy, even though you've already used listing, clustering, and free-writing on the same topic. (Keep Writing Activities 4, 5, and 6 to use in Chapter 2.)

Outlining. A final discovery strategy is *outlining.* An outline is a kind of organized list, a tentative plan for a discovery draft. You can show the important supporting points for your main idea and group details, examples, and so forth under the important points.

Thesis: Main point of the essay

I. Important supporting point for thesis
  A. Support for important point I
  B. Support for important point I
    1. Support for B
    2. Support for B
  C. Support for important point I
II. Important supporting point for thesis
  A. Support for important point II
  B. Support for important point II

An outline doesn't have to be formal and detailed. Just an informal, rough outline can help you discover what you want to write, organize what you know, and show where you need to add support. It can help you block in the big picture of your essay and be a guide for writing a discovery draft. Don't invest too much time in making a perfect outline or you'll feel duty bound to follow it whether the plan works or not. Outlining works best when you know exactly what you want to say, as in an answer to an essay question on a history test you have studied for carefully.

Here's an outline of Delvora's essay "Bargain Shop Until You Drop."

I. Introduction—conversation when Toni discovered Debra's great clothes came from a thrift store
  A. Cost of her suit, silk blouse, and belt
  B. Thesis: It doesn't have to cost a bundle to look your best
II. Thrift store like a department store
  A. List of costs of slacks, blouses, skirts, suits, and jackets
  B. List of thrift stores in the area with their addresses, phone numbers, and hours
III. Tips for shopping in thrift stores
  A. Browse first to get a feel for what's available
  B. Buy at the end of a season
  C. Payment options

You have reviewed or learned about seven strategies for discovering ideas to write about. At first you may be more comfortable with some than with others, but you can become comfortable with all of them by using them several times. You will find more ideas for writing by using several discovery strategies on the same subject. You can use discovery strategies at various points in the process of writing an essay—to find a subject, to explore a subject, to narrow a subject, and to develop any part that is underdeveloped.

STRATEGIES FOR DISCOVERING IDEAS TO WRITE ABOUT

Writing in your Idea Bank
Brainstorming
Freewriting
Listing
Clustering
Answering the five W questions: who, what, when, where, why
Outlining

Advancing writers often want to skip discovery strategies because they are time consuming and jump into writing a draft. But writing isn't magic. It doesn't appear out of thin air like a magician's rabbit out of a hat. It is the product of observing and reading closely, thinking, talking, and using discovery strategies.

WRITING A DISCOVERY DRAFT

When you write an essay, you will do much reading, writing, and talking before you get to the point of writing a discovery draft. This draft is called a "discovery" draft because writing is not simply writing down what you have already thought. Writing is thinking. As you write, you make new meaning. You discover new ideas, thoughts, connections, and understandings. Have you ever felt as if you knew what you wanted to say but couldn't find the right words? Most of us have had that feeling, and it is quite frustrating. We may have a sense of what we want to say or what we mean, but our thoughts may come out in jumbled fragments of half-formulated ideas. A discovery draft moves us from the words and phrases we produced in the discovery strategies to consecutive sentences. However, even at this point in writing an essay, thinking and writing come haltingly for many of us, and we may discover some pretty fuzzy thinking and become discouraged. Students report that they often procrastinate when they feel overwhelmed or discouraged. They may say or think things like this:

"I know what I want to say, but I can't say it."
"I don't have the time."
"It's too hard. I can't write."
"I'll do it tomorrow."
"I'll do it as soon as this TV program is over."

If your discarded false starts turn into a pile of crumpled paper or you can't get started, you are probably experiencing writer's block or procrastination. An inner voice may be criticizing everything you write. In an essay in Chapter 4 entitled "The Watcher at the Gates," Gail Godwin tells about her critical inner voice. She calls it her "watcher." Another writer, Ann McGee-Cooper, calls this critical inner voice a Merciless Master. Obviously, this critical inner voice is a problem for many writers.

However, both of these writers have found ways to defeat the inner critic when it won't let them write, and you can, too. You can read Gail Godwin's essay to find out her defenses. Ann McGee-Cooper's defense is to create a Supportive Coach as a counterpart to her Merciless Master and to listen to her coach's encouraging messages. You can provide this kind of positive self-talk by telling yourself such things as

"This doesn't have to be a perfect draft."
"You can change anything you want later."

"You're just getting started. Don't be so hard on yourself."
"You can do it. Just use your discovery strategies."

When you realize you are procrastinating or blocking, the first step is to meet your watcher. The second step is to counterattack with positive messages. The third step is to set a time limit for yourself and write a discovery draft from your prewriting exercises. Write only on one side of the paper, accepting that the draft may be an embarrassing mess and knowing that you can revise.

GIVING AND RECEIVING FEEDBACK

Donald Murray, a writer and teacher of writing, reminds us that the word *revising* means "to see again." In order to revise, you must see your writing as a stranger would, not as the writer who is attached to his or her words as a parent is to a child. You may be too hard on a draft or too forgiving. You may read into a draft what you meant instead of what you actually said. You may assume your readers think as you do and so forget or misjudge their needs. To revise, you must "re-see" your draft.

To help you re-see what you have written, you need caring, informed readers to give you feedback. In this course you will receive feedback on drafts from your teacher and classmates. In order to revise effectively, you will need to learn how to use this feedback. The process of giving, asking for, receiving, and using feedback is a complicated process. You'll have help with that process in this class. When you write for other college courses, for personal reasons, or for your job, you can use this same process, but you need to understand how to make it work for you. In Chapter 3 you will learn about giving, asking for, receiving, and using feedback to revise.

REVISING YOUR DRAFT

When you revise, focus your attention on the content and organization of your essay. Add information, examples, and explanations. Delete repetitions and parts unrelated to your thesis. Reorganize sentences or paragraphs. Clarify confusing parts. Generally you should leave the grammar, spelling, and punctuation until the editing stage. After all, there's no use spending time correcting text that may be changed or deleted. In Chapter 3 you will learn about what to revise. Here are some tips for making the changes you decide upon.

WAYS TO REVISE YOUR DRAFT

Underline the main idea to be sure it is stated, and use it as a check point as you work.

(Continued)

- Number each paragraph and write in the margin what it's about. If a paragraph is too long or seems to be made up of several different clumps of sentences, mark a new paragraph break with the paragraph symbol ¶.
- Cross out repeated or unrelated words, sentences, and paragraphs.
- Use a carat (∧) to show where you want to insert some text.
- Use circles and arrows to indicate how sentences and words should be moved and added.
- Check the order of the paragraphs by reading your marginal notes about the content of each paragraph. Renumber them if you want to reorder them.
- Use scissors and tape to cut out sentences or paragraphs and move them to new places in the draft.
- Use a new piece of paper to rewrite paragraphs and sections with many changes.
- If you are using a word processor, make changes and print a new version.
- If you are handwriting or typing, make a new version.

When you are satisfied with the content and organization of the essay, you are ready to edit.

EDITING YOUR DRAFT

In this book revising and editing are separate activities, although the two activities often overlap. Separating revising and editing allows you to focus first on the content of your essays and then to focus on correctness. Here *editing* means correcting errors in spelling, punctuation, and grammar. It means making your meaning clearer for your audience by improving sentences that are too long, awkward, or otherwise difficult to follow. It means replacing general or vague words with words that capture your intended meaning more precisely. It means working at the word and sentence level.

This is a polishing stage of the writing process. After washing your car, you wax it. After mowing the yard, you trim it and sweep up. After writing and revising your essay, you edit it. You want the finished essay to "shine." You don't want to distract a reader from your meaning with errors or awkward writing. You don't want to send the message that you don't care about the reader or about what you said. Mina Shaughnessy, a revered teacher of writing, said that errors send messages you can't afford to send. So don't skimp on your effort now. Allow a good chunk of time to edit your draft.

To edit your revised draft, try these strategies. Read your draft aloud—both to yourself and to someone else. Each of these readings has a different dynamic. When you stumble or have to reread, you may need to edit a sentence or correct the punctuation. If a word sounds slightly peculiar to you, you can look for a different one. For yet a different hearing of your essay, have someone else read it aloud to you, or tape record it and listen to it.

Additionally, other students and your teacher may read the essay and mark errors on the page. Here is a list of frequently made errors with the symbols your teacher may use to mark them. Each error is followed by the page in this book on which the error is briefly discussed. For more help, use the handbook adopted by your English department.

COMMON ERRORS AND CORRECTION SYMBOLS

agr	error in agreement of subject and verb (page 343)
cap	letter should be capitalized (page 379)
cs	comma splice (page 389)
dm	dangling modifier (page 339)
frag	fragment (page 335)
mm	misplaced modifier (page 339)
¶	indent for a new paragraph
//	error in parallelism (page 340)
pl	error in number or plural noun form (page 359)
poss	error in possessive pronoun or noun form (pages 360–361)
pron	error in pronoun reference (page 353)
∧	add the omitted punctuation mark
R-O	run-on sentence (page 338)
sp	spelling error (page 377)

(Continued)

vb	verb error (page 347)
ww	wrong word (pages 369–370)

When you have edited your draft, you are ready to print a final copy on your word processor, retype it, or recopy it. Then there is one last, brief, but important step.

PROOFREADING YOUR REVISED AND EDITED DRAFT

Your final draft needs one last careful reading before you turn it over to your teacher for grading, or to your reader. Some writers are tempted to skip this proofreading step after they have worked for so long on an essay, and others simply fail to plan enough time to do it. However, strange things sometimes appear in the final printing, typing, or copying of an essay. You will be surprised and wonder "How did this happen?" Here are some common glitches you may find when you proofread.

a missing word or line, even with a word processor
one more misspelled word or punctuation error
the same word or phrase copied twice
the wrong word (*form* for *from, its* for *it's, an* for *and*).

Correcting such errors is the finishing touch on your essay. It takes more self-discipline than it does time, but it shows you care about your writing and your reader.

One way to proofread is to read from the bottom up. Begin with the last sentence and work toward the beginning of the essay. Use a ruler or blank sheet of paper to mark your place and help you focus on one line at a time. When you read this way, you pay attention to what is actually on the page, not what you meant to write. Many teachers will allow you to make neat ink corrections on your final draft rather than produce a new and perfect copy.

REVIEWING THE PROCESS OF WRITING AN ESSAY

Now congratulations are in order. Some people are very good at being kind to themselves. Others aren't and often feel overworked and underappreciated. You deserve a reward for a job well done, so be kind to yourself. Buy yourself a ticket to a concert or go to a movie. Treat yourself to a bag of Reese's Pieces. Call a friend you haven't seen for a while. But do something! You have successfully completed the process of writing.

As you write more, you can adapt the writing process to fit the kind of tasks you have and your personal style of thinking and writing. You can use the overlapping activities in the general plan for writing in many ways.

GUIDELINES FOR THE PROCESS OF WRITING

Prewriting phase
- Observing or reading carefully
- Jotting down what you are thinking or feeling
- Talking with classmates or others
- Using discovery strategies several times in the writing process

Drafting and revising phase
- Writing a discovery draft
- Giving and receiving feedback
- Revising your draft, perhaps several times

Editing and proofreading phase
- Editing the last revised draft
- Proofreading the edited draft

Use this general plan for writing during this course and for other transactional writing in college and beyond when you want to communicate in a formal way. You don't have to take expressive or private writing through the whole process. You may simplify the process for less important and less complex writing situations and use it more fully on important and difficult writing tasks.

Remember writing a good essay is not like one-step floor wax. You may be able to scrub, rinse, and wax in one step, but you can't discover ideas, draft, revise, and edit in one step. Students are often surprised by their own essays when they use this writing process effectively. You, too, may be surprised.

EXPLORING FURTHER

A section called Exploring Further follows Chapters 1 through 4. These sections are linked. For instance, you will use what you do here in Chapter 1 when you do Exploring Further in Chapter 2. The activities in these sections will give you practice in the process of reading and writing essays that you will use in Part 2 of the book.

1. *Writing Activity.* Do you ever let others influence your behavior—to eat too much, watch TV instead of studying or reading, stay up too late, spend too much money, change your opinion about another

person? Who can influence your behavior and decisions? When? Why? Write a few sentences in your Idea Bank about how easily you are or are not influenced by others.

2. *Reading Activity.* Read the student essay about peer pressure "Don't Press Your Luck" on pages 166–168.
3. *Group Work.* Discuss peer pressure. What is it? What are some examples of it? Who are your peers? Each student should give an example of peer pressure from his or her life. The incident may be from childhood or from more recent times. It may be an incident in which you influenced someone else or in which someone else influenced you to do something wrong or in poor judgment or to do something right or in good judgment.
4. *Writing Activity.* Use listing or clustering to explore a peer pressure incident or situation from your own life. It may be one you thought about as a result of the group discussion. Imagine the scene before you begin. Transport yourself mentally into the scene. See the time of day, the light, the place. Smell the smells; hear the voices and other sounds or the quiet. Feel the feelings you felt then. Make the list or cluster as detailed as you can.
5. *Group Work.* Brainstorm about the reasons for peer pressure. Why do people give in to peer pressure? What kinds of pressure are there? Take notes to use later when you write your essay.
6. *Writing Activity.* Do a freewriting about peer pressure. Write for five minutes without stopping to read or think. Let your writing lead you. You're not writing a draft yet, so don't try to be organized and don't worry about correctness. After five minutes stop and read what you have written. Underline any phrase or sentence that is strong or interesting to you. On a clean page write the underlined phrase as a starting point for another freewriting. Write nonstop for another five minutes. Let your writing wander. Explore peer pressure. After five minutes, stop and repeat the process. Do three or four rounds, writing as much as you can each time.

Save all the writing you did for these activities. You will use them at the end of Chapter 2.

CHAPTER 2

WRITING ESSAYS

What is an essay? An essay is a specific form of writing, different from a poem, short story, novel, or play. However, the term *essay* is used in a more general way to mean transactional writing—writing that communicates something to someone. It is different from a news article about something that happened or an interview with a famous person in that it not only records what has happened or what someone said; it makes a point and comments on the information or ideas. An essay is a piece of writing of varying length about a single point. It is written to inform, entertain, or convince an intended audience. Different from the writing you do in discovery strategies, which are written for yourself as audience, the essays you write in this class will be written for various audiences. You will define appropriate audiences for your essays—your classmates, your teacher, or others beyond the classroom. Because the essay is written to communicate a single point to an audience, you will want to make full use of the writing process you read about in Chapter 1.

CLEANING YOUR MENTAL ATTIC

In Chapter 1 you learned that good writing is not magic. It is something people learn to do. Yet some students cringe at an essay assignment. Their mental attic is full of fears, bad experiences, and rigid rules for writing. What's in your mental attic about writing essays?

WRITING ACTIVITY 1

Write for five minutes about what's in your mental attic about writing essays. What are you afraid of? What worries you? Why? What makes writing an essay hard for you? What rules about writing an essay do you remember?

Students sometimes say they are afraid that they won't have enough to write about or can't stay on the topic. Some fear making errors in spelling, punctuation, and grammar to the extent that they can't think of what to write. Some are afraid their ideas or writing will be laughed at. Fear of failure, in these and other forms, is shared by most of the people in your class and by many others.

Some say that rules about good writing make it hard to write. ''Never use *I*.'' ''Never use *you*.'' ''Never use contractions.'' ''A paragraph must have five sentences.'' ''An essay has to have five paragraphs: an introductory paragraph, three middle paragraphs, and a concluding paragraph.'' ''Always put a comma before *and*.''

None of the ''rules'' above is truly a rule, yet students say they have heard versions of these or others. These rigid rules often result from overlearning—applying a rule intended for a single lesson to all other writing situations—or sometimes from mislearning. Whatever the source, trying to follow faulty rules makes writing very hard.

Check out your negative feelings and rules about writing to see which are legitimate and which aren't. You may have outgrown some of your fears. You may have learned strategies for solving the problems that gave rise to those fears. Check out your rules about writing to see if they are correct.

GROUP WORK 1

Check out the fears and rules you wrote about in Writing Activity 1. Talk about these with your teacher and fellow students. Then physically wad up the paper on which these fears and rigid rules are written and throw them away!

EXPANDING A PARAGRAPH TO AN ESSAY

If you can write a paragraph, you can write an essay. A paragraph is a group of related sentences about a main idea; an essay is a group of related paragraphs about a main idea. The main idea of a paragraph is called a topic sentence;

the main idea of an essay is called the *thesis.* Both the paragraph and the essay have a beginning, a middle, and an end. You can use the writing process, including reading, talking, writing, and rewriting, to "grow" your ideas from a seedling paragraph to a flowering plant—a focused and well-developed essay.

Paragraph	=	topic sentence	+	supporting sentences
Essay	=	thesis sentence	+	supporting paragraphs

Why should you write an essay instead of just a paragraph? Some ideas can be developed adequately in a few sentences, but others are more complex and take more sentences. If you're telling how to pick a movie to go to, you might do that adequately in a paragraph. If you're writing about how to have a good marriage, you might write a whole book!

Some audiences want a paragraph, or short piece of writing, and others want a full discussion. If you're writing a response to an exam question for 10 points and are given three inches of space in which to respond, your teacher probably wants a paragraph. If your boss asks you to research copiers and recommend one to buy for the office, she probably wants a report of several pages, including an analysis of the needs in the office; the names, model numbers, costs, advantages, and disadvantages of several copiers; and a recommendation for the purchase of one particular copier with reasons for the recommendations.

Some purposes influence the length of a piece of writing. If you're describing your first job in answer to a question on a job application, you may briefly describe this job or you may tell about it fully if you wish to emphasize the range of skills you have in order to persuade a potential employer to hire you.

The length of a piece of writing depends on the complexity of the main idea, the audience, and your purpose in writing. Do you know the joke about the child who asked, "Daddy, where did I come from?" The father squirmed uncomfortably and launched into a long lecture about the birds and bees. "No," the child responded. "I meant what town did I come from." Unclear about what was being asked (the main point), the father answered with a discussion (an essay) when a single word was all that was needed.

As you write essays in this class, you should become aware of your own pattern of thinking and writing. Once you have discovered an idea you want to write about in response to your assigned readings, you may write down what you have to say and find that you have only a paragraph, not an essay. Your paragraph may be a mini essay, waiting to be developed. You may have produced one main idea and two or three sentences that support the main idea. You may have to turn each of these into a full paragraph. This kind of development is not padding or wordiness. It takes into account your purpose in writing and your intended reader's need for details, examples, definitions, comparisons, and so on—ways of communicating your full meaning.

I have learned that my writing style is to underdevelop ideas in a first draft. I find a main point and several supporting points and write a draft. A friend, commenting on the different first draft styles of my coauthor and me in an earlier book, compared us to roofers. If a shingle required nine nails, I put in five and my colleague used fifteen. In revising, we agreed upon what to add to my chapters and what to delete from hers. Now that I know my writing style, I can forge ahead with a draft, knowing I'll have a good basic draft, but that I'll need to make several additions. I don't have to worry myself into writer's block with thoughts about how long or short something is. I know I can add and develop parts when I revise, relying on my own sense of a reader's need and on the feedback I receive from colleagues.

The moral of the story about my writing style is to learn about your own writing style. Do you tend to write too much or too little in a first draft? Are you too wordy or too brief? Do you tend to wander off the path that heads to your main point or do you keep everything related in some way? Do you jump all over the place in discussing your main point and need to figure out a logical organization for what you've written? Knowing your style of thinking and writing can eliminate "ought to's" and "should have's" and free you to write, knowing you can revise and get help from others in the process.

WRITING ACTIVITY 2

Think of one word that describes your style of writing and write it down. Then draw a visual representation of your writing style—any shape or design or symbol. Finally describe your style of thinking and writing in a few sentences.

REMINDER

You can expand a paragraph into an essay. How much to write depends upon your purpose, the intended audience, and the complexity of the topic.

GOING FROM YOUR DISCOVERY STRATEGIES TO AN ESSAY

By developing the habit of writing in your Idea Bank about what you observe and read, you will practice writing what you think and you will save ideas and information you can use in your essays. Remember that writing in your Idea

Bank is writing for an audience of yourself. Be honest, thoughtful, and observant. Question what you see, hear, and read. Guess about causes, reasons, and the meanings of what you see, hear, and read. Connect facts with ideas and your life experiences with the readings. Don't be distracted by correctness, organization, or completeness. Just remember that you must write clearly enough so that you will be able to read your writing later and understand what you meant.

If your Idea Bank gives you a starting place for a draft, use other discovery strategies that you learned in Chapter 1 to explore the essay idea. Or use several strategies to find a possible topic for an essay. Then develop this topic into a trial thesis before you begin writing your discovery draft.

Here is part of Alison's entry in her Idea Bank after she read an essay in Chapter 8 called "How to Write a Personal Letter."

Keillor sounds like he really likes to write letters, and I like his humorous tone. I guess I could write something funny too. How to do something doesn't have to be serious or earth-shaking. What can I write about? It ought to be about something I know really well, maybe something I've had to learn the hard way or that some people don't know how to do, but I do. Like keep a budget or balance a checkbook or keeping your credit cards under control. Boy, I use to struggle with that one. That's it! I can write about using credit cards wisely. I can tell how to save money with credit cards. I know somebody's going to be interested in that. And earn money too. That's a good twist and a surprise to most people. I can talk about my system of keeping up with charges.

When Alison began to think about a subject for a process analysis essay, she began with a freewriting in her Idea Bank. She also talked with other students about what they were going to write about. She discarded several ideas before she settled on her credit card topic.

WRITING A TRIAL THESIS

A thesis is the main point of the essay, and everything in the essay supports or develops that one main point. Just as the topic sentence is the controlling idea of the paragraph, the thesis is the controlling idea of the essay. The thesis sentence usually appears in the introduction, although it's seldom the first sentence in an essay. A thesis is more than a topic; it is a topic *and* your opinion or attitude about the topic. It is more than a general topic; it is a narrowed topic. It allows a good reader to predict what will follow: the focus of the essay and how the writer will develop or support that focus.

Trial thesis: With the wonderful world of thrift store shopping, it doesn't have to cost a bundle to look your best.
General topic: bargain shopping
Narrowed topic: shopping for bargains at thrift stores
Opinion or attitude: Looking your best doesn't have to cost a lot.
Prediction about development of the thesis: The writer will explain what thrift stores are, describe them, and probably give specific prices and some examples of stylish, good-quality clothes.

WRITING ACTIVITY 3

The following thesis sentences are taken from essays you will read in Part 2. Read each thesis sentence. What is the general topic? What is the narrowed topic? What is the writer's opinion or attitude about the topic? What predictions can you make about the ways the writer may develop this thesis?

1. What is *macho*? That depends which side of the border you come from.
2. Now on the screen, they were at least aware of the subtle distinction between men and women as buddies and friends.
3. No matter how far I travel or how long I've been gone, this church will always be my home, the place where I grew up.
4. A child, in growing up, may meet and learn from three different kinds of disciplines.
5. When she died at the age of 94, I lost more than a good friend—I lost a mentor who inspired me to do my best.
6. He was one of the greatest scientists the world has ever known, yet if I had to convey the essence of Albert Einstein in a single word, I would choose *simplicity.*
7. It was because of my letters that I happened to stumble upon starting to acquire some kind of homemade education.
8. Pheasant hunting is actually an extremely complicated adventure.
9. That day I learned to hide my ethnic difference and to assimilate into the accepted white culture.
10. In other cultures and in our past, time had a different meaning.

You will often be asked to write a thesis before writing an essay, but you may have to revise your thesis sentence several times. You will often know what you're going to write about, but have trouble writing a one-sentence thesis. Your first attempts will sometimes be too general; they will sometimes be too specific. They may merely state a simple fact or point that doesn't require a full essay. They may not express an opinion or attitude.

Too general: My grandmother was wonderful.
Too specific: As I hold my dusty passport, I hear her soft and encouraging words, "Baby, your life is in America."
A fact: My grandmother is the reason I came to America.
Good thesis: As my guardian angel my grandmother made me feel secure, but as my grandmother she made me feel loved.

WRITING ACTIVITY 4

Evaluate the following thesis sentences. Label each *okay, too broad,* or *too specific.*

1. The first thing to remember when dealing with a RED APPLE SALE is that it only lasts for one day.
2. Whatever style of music, there are many formulas for putting music and lyric together.
3. People need a good vocabulary for success in college and for success after college.
4. I remember the day I met the good-looking, red-haired fellow who sat in the back of my history class.
5. Friendship is an important part of life.
6. Inside the stranger I had so quickly judged lay a real person who truly cared.
7. If you are going to be part of that hospital system, you must learn how to manipulate it. It's a matter of your own survival.
8. Just because you are on the bench, however, doesn't mean you can't help the team or even learn something in the process of the game.

When you read an essay, the thesis is already focused and polished, but writers often have to revise their thesis several times as they clarify their thinking through talking and writing. You will probably have to revise your thesis, too. When you are writing an essay, the first attempt to put your main idea into a sentence is called a *trial thesis.*

When you are ready to write a trial thesis, usually after using some discovery strategies, begin with a key word or phrase that expresses your topic. Then narrow (or make more specific) this topic by adding words or phrases to describe it further. Then add an opinion or attitude you have about this narrowed topic. Notice that there are many possible thesis sentences about any topic. Remember that the thesis is the main point you wish to make in your essay and that arriving at one main point, clearly stated, may take several revisions of your thesis, even after you have produced a draft. Here are some examples of narrowing and adding opinions or attitudes to a topic.

DEVELOPING A TRIAL THESIS

Topic	Narrowed Topic	Opinion or Attitude
friendship	with an adult daughter	mother must treat her as she would other close female friends

Trial thesis: Friendship between a mother and an adult daughter requires a mother to treat her daughter as she would other close friends.

Topic	Narrowed Topic	Opinion or Attitude
friendship	between men based on shared activities	contrasts sharply with women's friendships

Trial thesis: Men build close friendships on shared activities, while women build their friendships through talk.

Topic	Narrowed Topic	Opinion or Attitude
friendship	between gang members	based on fear and respect

Trial thesis: Friendship between gang members depends strongly on fear and respect.

Topic	Narrowed Topic	Opinion or Attitude
friendship	between men and women	avoids sex role stereotypes and requires mutual respect

Trial thesis: Friendship between men and women must focus on mutual respect and avoid sex role stereotypes.

WRITING ACTIVITY 5

To prepare for thesis writing, practice narrowing topics, adding your opinion or attitude about the narrowed topic, and then writing a trial thesis for each topic.

Topic	**Narrowed Topic**	**Opinion or Attitude**
love		

Trial thesis:

advertising

Trial thesis:

watching sports

Trial thesis:

Another way to develop a thesis is to use the five W questions on a topic: who, what, when, where, why? Start with the topic you want to write about and ask yourself the questions. Repeat each question until you see a thesis taking shape. For instance, you might ask "Who?" "Who else?" "Who specifically?"

General Topic: Friendship

Who? men, adult men, married men
What? activities: watch sports, run, golf, work, hunt, play pool
When? adulthood, without women or kids
Where? at work, in softball league, at church, in the neighborhood
Why? to share interests, have company, give moral support without talking about it

Trial thesis: Men's friendships grow out of shared activities.

WRITING ACTIVITY 6

Answer the five W questions for the topic below and write a trial thesis. Give several answers to each question.

General Topic: Punctuality (being on time)

Who?

What?

When?

Where?

Why?

Trial thesis:

QUESTIONS TO TEST YOUR TRIAL THESIS

What is the topic I want to write about?
What is the narrowed topic?
What is my opinion or attitude about this topic?
Who is my specific audience?
What is my purpose?

GROUP WORK 2

Choose one of your trial thesis sentences from Writing Activities 5 and 6. Help each other apply the five test questions and revise your thesis sentences.

In the section "Going from Your Discovery Strategies to an Essay," you read part of Alison's entry in her Idea Bank about using credit cards written after she had read Keillor's "How to Write a Personal Letter." She answered some questions about the essay and wrote about some things she liked to do and took pride in doing well. Here is her trial thesis: "You can use credit cards to your advantage, actually saving and earning money."

WRITING ACTIVITY 7

In Chapter 1 you practiced several discovery strategies on a topic you selected from a list. Review these prewritings in Writing Activities 5 and 6 of Chapter 1 to choose an idea for an essay. Use the questions on page 32 to help you compose a thesis.

Although defining ''thesis'' is easy, most writers struggle to put their main points into words. They often say, ''I know what I mean, but I can't say it in one sentence.'' They may write a trial thesis and then, as they write, find their draft is only partially about their thesis. Their main point may come into focus just as a dot far down a highway becomes a red Mazda sports car as it approaches. As you write thesis sentences for your essays in this course, remember the thesis writing problem and don't get discouraged. Even if it is a struggle, don't skip writing a trial thesis before writing a draft. The trial thesis serves as a valuable guide for your draft and is one of many steps in the process of bringing your main point into focus. Writers often become increasingly clear about their main point as they write, so they often find themselves rewriting their thesis after they have written a discovery draft. Writing, writing, and more writing moves their thinking along.

REMINDER

There are many possible thesis statements for every topic. To develop a trial thesis, use one of these strategies.

1. Narrow the topic with descriptive words and phrases and add your opinion or attitude about the narrowed topic.
2. Repeat the five W's until a thesis takes shape from a general topic.

DECIDING ON AN AUDIENCE AND A PURPOSE

After you have written a trial thesis for an essay, think about your purpose and intended audience. What do you want to accomplish with this essay? Who is your audience? After you think about the specific people you want to read your essay and are clear about what you want them to do, think, or feel, revise your trial thesis.

Although writers may write for the general public, they still don't expect everybody to be interested in or to benefit from a particular piece of writing.

They have a few faces in their mind's eyes, a few people whom they know well. You can develop your sense of audience and purpose for an essay by writing a description of your intended readers and what you want to happen when they read your essay. For example, you may be writing an article for people who are experienced hunters, but who have never hunted pheasants. Your purpose may be to give this audience information about the equipment needed, special problems to be prepared for, the habits of pheasants, and the steps of hunting. If, instead, you are addressing inexperienced hunters or friends of experienced hunters, you will write a very different essay, even though some of the information would be the same.

Sometimes it helps to think of a person you know who is part of your intended audience. In fact, one strategy for developing a sense of audience is to write your discovery draft to a person as though you were writing a letter, beginning "Dear So-and-so." You can drop the salutation when you revise the draft and perhaps eliminate some informalities in language, but you can keep the heightened sense of audience. A sharp awareness of your intended audience will help you use your oral skills in communicating, use your authentic voice rather than a phoney one, and select details, examples, comparisons, and information that will be effective with that person.

Now you may think that there's only one way to support a particular thesis and that a particular thesis support is just as good for one audience as for another. But that's not true. A good writer figures out what will work with a specific audience. Does a television writer write the same jokes for a family audience with school-age kids as for career people in their 20s and 30s? Does a sportscaster wisecrack about opera or the stock market? Writers of essays, too, have to tailor what they say to their specific audiences, focusing on the audiences' special interests, needs, and values.

Here is the description of audience and purpose that Alison wrote for her essay about credit cards.

Adult men and women who use credit cards but have trouble keeping their credit card balances in control. People who don't use credit cards for fear of getting too much in debt. Also men and women who are interested in saving money. My purpose is to show them the advantage of using credit cards wisely and how to do it.

Here is the description of audience and purpose that Gloria wrote for her essay "One More Foreigner, One More Stranger," which appears in Chapter 6.

Readers of a Hispanic magazine. In reading this article they will be able to relate to my experiences in school. My goal is to encourage these Hispanic readers to reach for their goals at all times. Learning to speak the English language is the first step.

WRITING ACTIVITY 8

Read the following thesis sentences and write a description of the writer's intended audience and purpose.

1. In other cultures and in our own past, time had a different meaning.
2. Why should people who can do college-level work in other subjects not be able to do college-level math as well?
3. If you are going to be a hospital patient, you must learn how to manipulate the system to survive.
4. Commercial businesses could incorporate a recycling plan since they are the main contributors of solid waste.
5. In order to move forward and achieve harmony, daughters must take the first step and attempt to be friendly with their mothers.

WRITING ACTIVITY 9

Each thesis sentence below could be developed into different essays for different audiences. To practice writing for different audiences, read each thesis sentence and make a list of points and examples for each audience.

Thesis 1: Smokers in the college should smoke only in the designated areas.

Audience 1: smokers, especially those who aren't complying with the college policy

Audience 2: nonsmokers, who are annoyed with smoke in the cafeteria

Thesis 2: The tuition hike from $75 to $90 a semester-hour is a reasonable and necessary increase.

Audience 1: students whose tuition will be increased $15 for each three-hour course they take next semester

Audience 2: taxpayers who are not students and who face tax raises from some level of government each year

Thesis 3: You should bring canned food at Thanksgiving for the homeless.

Audience 1: elementary school children in an affluent neighborhood

Audience 2: high school students in a poor neighborhood

Zeroing in on a specific audience and purpose is a very helpful strategy in writing essays. Writing a description of the audience and purpose is a helpful strategy for zeroing in on audience and purpose. It can help you find a focus for an essay, it can help you think of ideas to develop the essay, and it can help you revise. You should write a description of your audience and purpose early in the writing process, before or just after writing a discovery draft. However, you may revise your audience and purpose description during the writing process as you become clearer about what you have to write, what you want to accomplish, and to whom you want to direct your essay.

WRITING ACTIVITY 10

Select one of the trial thesis sentences you wrote in Writing Activities 5, 6, or 7. Write a description of the audience and purpose for an essay you might write.

GROUP WORK 3

Read your trial thesis and description of audience and purpose to the group. Help each other describe the audience and purpose in more detail.

REMINDER

Different audiences have different interests, needs, and values. A good writer selects support for a thesis with a specific audience in mind.

WRITING THE BEGINNING OF AN ESSAY

An essay, whether a paragraph or a book in length, has a beginning, a middle, and an end. This concept can help you understand what you read and can help you write. The beginning of an essay, usually called the *introduction,* may be one or several paragraphs or several pages, depending on the length of the essay. For essays you will write for this class, usually a paragraph will do.

Writers generally aim to accomplish these important tasks in their introductions:

Introduce the subject
Present the thesis, or main idea
Forecast the supporting points or method of developing the thesis
Hook the reader's interest

You may begin an introduction several ways—with an anecdote, a quotation, a question, a definition (although dictionary definitions have low audience appeal), a general idea which you then narrow to your thesis statement, an idea or situation that is the opposite of the thesis, or an explanation or example that shows the importance of your subject. Here are the beginnings of several essays from Part 2 in this book.

A direct quotation: "You gotta have frieeends," sang Bette Midler. But most men past the age of 30 don't have friends—not really.

An indirect quotation: They used to say Texas was hell on women and horses—I don't know why they stopped. Surely not because much of the citizenry has had its consciousness raised, as they say in the jargon of the women's movement, on the issue of sexism.

An incident: The other day an acquaintance of mine, a gregarious and charming man, told me he had found himself unexpectedly alone in New York for an hour or two between appointments. He went to the Whitney [Museum] and spent the "empty" time looking at things in solitary bliss. For him it proved to be a shock nearly as great as falling in love to discover that he could enjoy himself so much alone.

An opposite definition: Women are friends, I once would have said, when they totally love and support and trust each other, and bare to each other the secrets of their souls. . . . In other words, I once would have said that a friend is a friend all the way, but now I believe that's a narrow point of view. For the friendships I have and the friendships I see are conducted at many levels of intensity, serve many different functions, meet different needs. . . .

A general statement about the topic: There are thousands of theories about what's gone wrong with the world, but I think it comes down to one simple thing: The death of the Permanent Record.

Writers often have to write several introductions before they find a good one. They often begin with background information and long explanations because it's where they need to start. But in revising for a reader's needs, writers often pitch out the first opening and write one that will be more effective. You may write an introduction first or you may write it after you have written most of an essay.

WAYS TO BEGIN AN ESSAY

- Use an anecdote.
- Use a quotation.
- Ask a question.
- Define an important term.
- Begin with a general idea from which you narrowed your thesis statement.
- Give an example of an idea or situation that is the opposite of your thesis.
- Explain or give an example that shows the importance of your subject.

GROUP WORK 4

Look at the introductions of several essays in Part 2 and decide together which method the writer uses to begin the essay. Turn to ''Learning To See'' on pages 180–183, ''Americanization Is Tough on 'Macho' '' on page 265, and ''The Tapestry of Friendship'' on page 229.

To write an introduction to an essay, first write a trial thesis. A trial thesis is the clearest statement you can make at the time about the main point of your essay. Although you should write the trial thesis before you begin a discovery draft, you may clarify your thinking and revise this thesis as you write and rewrite. A clear thesis sentence is important because it makes what Elizabeth Cowan Neeld, a writing teacher, calls a promise to the reader. A good reader looks for this promise; a good writer provides it.

To write the introduction, you may begin by writing a trial thesis on a clean page. You might explain what thinking brought you to this thesis. You might begin with a scene or story, as many preachers or other speakers do, to interest your reader and lead up to your thesis. You might explain what the main parts of your essay are or how you intend to support your thesis. If you are writing an essay in response to a reading selection in Part 2, you might explain an idea chosen from the selection and name the title and author.

If you are stuck for an opening, just write your trial thesis sentence on the paper and come back to the introduction after you have written your essay. Introductions don't have to be written first just because they are read first!

Here's the beginning paragraph of Alison's discovery draft.

Using a credit card is not a bad thing. In fact it can save, even earn, you money. For every time that you use your credit card, it saves you writing a check. If you have duplicate checks, like I have, they cost you approximately eight cents apiece. Running an average household, I used to write about sixty checks a month. That's $4.80 a month, or $57.60 a year. You also keep your money in the bank for an extra month earning interest and if you use the Discover card they give you "cash-back" at the end of the year. Last year they paid me over $100 for using their card. I paid no annual fee and no interest. I earned more interest on my money in the bank and saved money by ordering fewer checks.

Notice that Alison opens with the idea that credit cards are bad, an idea opposite to her trial thesis: Using a credit card "can save, even earn, you money." She follows up by giving specific examples of a saving and an earning. Later you'll see that she revised her opening; she used questions to begin the final version of her essay.

REMINDER

There are many ways to begin an essay. A writer must find a way that hooks the reader's interest and leads up to the thesis.

WRITING THE MIDDLE OF AN ESSAY

The middle of your essay is sometimes called the *body*. It is the part that develops or supports your thesis. You will probably have several supporting ideas, for example, two reasons and a definition of an important term. Each of the supporting ideas may be one paragraph or several paragraphs. These supporting ideas do not have to be the same number of sentences or paragraphs. There is no rule about the length of the body.

You may write the body of an essay before you write the introduction, and you may write any part of the body first. You can connect the introduction and body later. You can rearrange and connect the parts of the body later. Feel free to begin with whatever sections are easiest for you to write.

To develop the main and supporting ideas in an essay, you may use examples, facts, statistics, quotations from authorities, and reasons—anything that supports your point and would be effective for your audience and purpose. The writing lessons in Part 2 focus on nine ways to develop your essays.

WAYS TO DEVELOP AN ESSAY

Description Use sensory details and facts to make a point.
Narration Tell what happened to make a point.
Exemplification Give examples to make a point.
Process analysis Show how something is done step-by-step.
Division and classification Make subgroups of similar ideas, people, or things from a larger, more diverse group.
Comparison and contrast Show how two things are alike and different to make a point.
Definition Explain the specific meaning of a generally understood word or phrase.
Cause and effect Analyze the causes and the effects (results) of certain events or situations.
Argumentation Convince a specific audience of a main point by using a combination of the ways of development.

None of these methods of development is new to you. You use each of them in ordinary communication, and you use them in combination, choosing them automatically. Let me give you an example. When you take a car into a garage for repair, you tell the mechanic what the problem is—a grinding noise when you start the car, a vibration when you drive 60 miles per hour, or a loss of power when you accelerate to enter the expressway. You are naming the effects of a problem and you want the mechanic to find the cause and repair your car (cause and effect). You tell what happened yesterday when you were entering the expressway (narration). To get the mechanic's attention, you use specific facts and details (description). Notice that what you wanted to say (the content) came first; how you talked about the content (ways of development) depended upon both the content and the effect you wanted to have on the listener (reader).

The writers of the reading selections in Part 2 concentrated on what they wanted to say, not on the methods of development. However, I selected these readings, with the help of editors and reviewers, to serve as examples of the kinds of development in order to help you learn the writer's craft. You will study one kind of development at a time, but when you write outside this course, you will use them in combination, and you will come to use them without thinking "Oh, I'll use narration (or description or process analysis) now."

Here is the middle of Alison's discovery draft in which she uses description, exemplification, and process analysis.

There is a technique. You can't just go out and use a credit card and save money, in fact many people end up in a lot of financial trouble. The secret is to use your credit card in place of a check, not for extra buying power, and most importantly record every transaction. It is amazing how $5, $10, $20, and $50 charges can add up! Every time I use my credit cards (I use Discover whenever possible) I record it in my checkbook register, as I would for a check, except in the space for check number I enter a D for Discover, V for Visa, GV for Gold Visa, or MC for MasterCard. This way you see the money as spent and there are no nasty surprises when your monthly credit card bill arrives. When it does arrive I write the due date on my calendar and put it in my "bills due" drawer. When you pay your credit card bill, two days before it is due (never pay your bills until they are due) go through your bill with your checkbook register and put a small check by each of the entries, and write the check number that you are paying the bill with by them. As you have deducted the amounts with each transaction you can zero out your bill.

For balancing your checkbook, look for the check for your credit card bill to clear. When it does you can go through and mark all the credit card transactions that you have written that check number by as cleared. You will have more adding to do when you balance your checkbook because there will be more transactions that have not cleared the bank. Remember, this is good, it means you have more money in the bank earning interest.

WRITING ACTIVITY 11

In Alison's draft find examples from her own experience to support her advice to her readers.

WRITING ACTIVITY 12

Find two places in Alison's discovery draft that you are unclear about or need more information about. Write a note to her as a friend and careful reader of the draft. Begin with what you liked best about the essay, and then ask questions like "What did you mean when you said . . .?" or "I didn't quite understand. . . ." Begin your note "Dear Alison." Add a closing, and sign your name.

WRITING ACTIVITY 13

Use the trial thesis and description of audience and purpose you wrote in Writing Activity 10. List possible supporting ideas for this thesis, using discovery strategies as needed. Give examples, analyze the cause or effect of an action, define important words—anything that will help you communicate your thesis to your intended reader.

WRITING ACTIVITY 14

Write a discovery draft using the trial thesis, the description of audience and purpose, and the list of ideas for an essay you wrote in Writing Activity 13.

Knowing Your Style of Thinking and Writing. In writing the body of an essay, know your own style of thinking and writing. Some writers see the big picture before their mental eyes and write the essay from beginning to end. Others seem to focus on one part and write from the inside out toward the big picture. Some go back and forth between the big picture and close-ups the way in televised football the camera zooms from the whole field of play to the quarterback releasing the ball and then back to the whole field.

If you are the kind of writer who writes an essay in pieces, use a separate sheet of paper for each paragraph. Then you can spread the paragraphs out on your desk, rearrange them, add to them, or remove them. You can even work with scissors and tape to create the essay you want. If you use a word processor, you can add or remove words or paragraphs by simply putting the cursor in the place on the screen where you want to insert or delete something. You can also move whole paragraphs or sections in your essay with a few keystrokes. These techniques can free you to write more easily, knowing that you can make changes after you have written a draft.

WRITING THE END OF AN ESSAY

The essential guideline for the *conclusion,* or end, of an essay, is that readers need some kind of closure. Sometimes just a sentence or two will do the job, especially in short essays. Often writers repeat something from the introduction to draw the readers' attention full circle from the ending to the beginning.

You may refer to something said in the introduction, recalling a key phrase, an image, or a story you used to open your essay. You may give a future orientation to your essay, speculating about the future of your ideas or challenging the reader to act in some way. You may close with an appropriate quotation or anecdote. You may repeat the thesis, usually rephrasing it somewhat, and you may summarize complex or numerous steps or points.

In general, avoid summarizing your whole essay. In the short essays you will write for this course, a summary will sound repetitious and may insult your readers. Also avoid giving advice or teaching a lesson to your readers. Keep your conclusions simple and brief. They should give the sense of "The End" without saying it.

Here is Alison's conclusion in her discovery draft.

Remember, this is good, it means you have more money in the bank earning interest. What ever you do, do not use your credit card beyond your means. If you do not have the money in the bank do not charge it. The interest on a bank loan, if needed, is a lot less than on credit cards. Pay the full amount each month and only have cards that have no annual fee and a thirty day grace period on purchases. Discover is the only one I have found that actually pays you cold, hard, cash for using it, and I use it when ever I can.

Alison closes with a warning about misusing credit cards and some final advice. However, there's still an abruptness at the very end. Something more is needed.

GROUP WORK 5

How can Alison improve her conclusion? Reread her introduction on page 39. Suggest a sentence or two that echoes her introduction, perhaps the opposing idea with which she began or her thesis.

WAYS TO END AN ESSAY

Repeat something from the introduction: key word, phrase, or image.
Use a quotation or an anecdote.
Provide a future orientation by speculating about your ideas or giving a challenge to the reader.
Rephrase the thesis.
Summarize the main points in a complex essay, especially in argumentation.

WRITING ACTIVITY 15

Look at the thesis sentences you evaluated in Writing Activity 4. Match the following sentences from concluding paragraphs with the appropriate thesis sentences. Which way to conclude an essay did each writer use?

1. If your vocabulary is limited, your ability to think and reason on a higher level will also be limited. The person who has a good vocabulary will probably do all these things well and is more apt to be successful.
2. Sitting on the bench can be used as a great learning experience. Remember, all that baseball is is not out there on the field!
3. I have given you a few pointers that will make your stay in the hospital more pleasant. I am sure that you will discover some pointers of your own. I encourage you to pass your pointers on to other patients, so that we can keep our commitment to ourselves and our survival.

4. These sale-time strategies will make for a safe and prosperous mission and hopefully prevent sale-shock the next time the RED APPLE SALE calls for a few good shoppers.
5. The stranger I have come to know takes the time to serve people with his whole heart. I guess it's true—you can't judge a book by its cover.

REMINDER

There are many ways to end an essay. A conclusion often echoes something in the introduction—the thesis, a key word, an image, or an incident.

POINTS TO REMEMBER FOR WRITING AN ESSAY

Use your Idea Bank or other discovery strategies to find a main point to write about.
Write a trial thesis and test it.
Describe your intended audience and purpose.
Write a discovery draft.

Although you should give your best effort at each step of the writing process, don't overinvest in your discovery draft. Trying to "get it perfect" may create writer's block. Charge through with a draft and be ready for revising.

EXPLORING FURTHER

1. *Reading Activity.* Reread "Don't Press Your Luck" on pages 166–168 and the writing you did about peer pressure for Exploring Further in Chapter 1.
2. *Group Work.* Talk about the ideas that emerged in your freewriting or group discussions about peer pressure. What struck each of you as the most important idea about each situation? Take notes about your own and your classmates' ideas.
3. *Writing Activity.* Write a trial thesis for an essay about peer pressure. Use the strategies for writing a trial thesis described in this chapter.
4. *Group Work.* Think about who needs to know what you have written. What audience would benefit and use what you have to say? Parents?

Elementary school children? Young teens? College students? Voters? Teachers? Consumers? What do you want them to do or believe?

Tell your group what your trial thesis is (the main point of your essay), and describe your intended audience and purpose. Help each other test and clarify an appropriate audience and purpose. Write down your group's comments and suggestions about your trial thesis.

5. *Writing Activity.* Write a description of the audience and purpose for your essay on peer pressure.
6. *Writing Activity.* Write a discovery draft of an essay about peer pressure in which you discuss the reasons for peer pressure and give examples. Draw on the ideas and examples of peer pressure you have read, written, and talked about. Name the person or writer whose examples you use.

Save all the writing you did for these activities, including your notes and your discovery draft. You will return to them at the end of Chapter 3.

CHAPTER 3

REVISING YOUR ESSAYS

Well-written essays are easy to read and understand, and they might appear to be easy to write. However, looks are deceiving. Well-written, easy-to-read essays have been revised many times. Students often frustrate themselves by expecting to write a good essay in a single sitting and are bound to be disappointed. They think things like

> "This is as good as I can do."
> "I just can't write."
> "Writing is harder for me than everybody else."
> "I don't have time to write."

They feel guilty, stupid, embarrassed, or angry at themselves and the teacher. These bad feelings create pressure. If you have had these feelings and have felt this pressure in the past, it's time for two important changes. First, change your expectations; expect to revise. Second, change your planning; allow as much time for revising as you do for using discovery strategies and writing a discovery draft.

TESTING A DRAFT AND PLANNING A REVISION

Chapter 1 gave you an overview of the writing process, including some ways to mark a draft you are revising. This chapter discusses the kinds of changes to make and the process of feedback. Since you are in charge of writing and rewriting your essays, even with feedback from your teacher and classmates, you should begin the revising phase by rereading the assignment and your draft so that you will have clearly in mind what is required and what you have done so far. Then think about the five qualities of good essays and use these to test your draft and plan your revisions.

Checklist for Evaluating the Five Qualities of a Good Essay

Focus
- Does the essay have a single thesis and a clear purpose?
- Does each paragraph relate to and help make the point of the thesis?

Development
- Given the writer's audience and purpose, are there enough details, examples, and reasons to develop each part that supports the thesis?
- Are all the details appropriate for the writer's audience and purpose?

Unity
- Does each paragraph clearly support the thesis? Are connections between the paragraph and the thesis obvious for the reader?
- Does each paragraph stick to its main point?

Coherence
- Is every sentence logically related to the ones that precede and follow it?
- Are there appropriate transitions to signal the relationships between paragraphs and between sentences within paragraphs?
- Is the essay organized clearly and logically?

Correctness
- Is the essay relatively free of errors in grammar, spelling, punctuation, and capitalization?

You will probably not be able to make all the changes you want to make in a single revised draft. Instead, you will want to revise in stages. You should establish what Roger Garrison, writing teacher and writer, has called a ''priority of concerns.'' Decide which problem should be solved first. There's no use adding details and examples if you're not doing the right assignment or reordering for better organization if some sections need to be eliminated because they don't support the thesis. The five qualities in the checklist for essay evaluation are listed in an appropriate order for revising.

Priority 1: *Focus,* with the assignment addressed and a thesis clearly stated

Priority 2: *Development,* adequate and appropriate for the audience and purpose

Priority 3: *Unity,* with all parts supporting the thesis

Priority 4: *Coherence,* with connections between sentences and paragraphs, logical organization, and clear transitions between supporting sections

Priority 5: *Correctness,* of grammar, spelling, punctuation, and capitalization.

Although the order of these concerns is not set in stone, you should set priorities because you can't revise everything in a single revision and because some problems in a draft need to be solved before others are tackled. If you are using a word processor, you can easily produce several intermediate drafts to solve a series of problems. You don't have to keep recopying or retyping.

At this point you may be saying, "I know I should revise, but I can't see what I should do to improve my draft, even with these guidelines for revising." That's where giving and receiving feedback come in. Most writers don't work alone. They get feedback from informed and interested readers, usually colleagues in the workplace. You don't have to work alone either. Readers of your drafts, both the teacher and other students in this class, can help you resee your draft so that you can revise effectively.

GIVING FEEDBACK ON A DRAFT

You can learn how to revise your draft from both giving and receiving feedback. Let's look at giving feedback first. Students are often uncomfortable giving feedback. They say things like "I don't know what to say" and "I don't want to hurt the writer's feelings." Some feel that it's the teacher's job, not theirs, to comment on other students' drafts. However, there's much for you to gain, both as a reader and as a writer, by learning to give feedback.

Colleagues who exchange drafts for feedback need to follow the same ground rules: Be honest, tactful, and supportive. Almost all people, students and teachers, are nervous about other people's reactions to their writing.

As a reviewer of other students' drafts, your job is to be a friendly, interested reader, a substitute for the intended audience. You are not a critic, teacher, or expert. You are not a grammar cop, looking for errors in spelling, punctuation, and grammar. You are not responsible for rewriting the essay of another student. You are not responsible for saying everything there is to say about the draft or for the grade on the final version.

However, you are responsible for understanding the assignment, including audience and purpose, for reading the draft several times carefully, for reporting the strengths and weaknesses of the draft, and for answering any questions the writer asks.

Writing on the draft is usually acceptable, but the writer may have trouble understanding single words and phrases. Remember teacher comments on your drafts that you didn't understand or know what to do with or felt insulted by? Help the writer avoid a similar situation by marking the draft but also writing a note of several sentences to the writer. Think about how your suggestions and insights might be given without hurting the writer's feelings. Generally, raising a question and leaving it open for the writer to decide what to do can be more easily received than saying a writer should make a particular change or simply saying something is no good. As a student you may be in a better position to communicate with a classmate about a draft than is the teacher. Don't underestimate your value.

You can give valuable feedback to classmates. In doing so, you can also gain insight into your own writing. When you read the drafts of several classmates on an assignment that you, too, are working on, you will see examples of good writing and weak writing. You'll get ideas for changes to make your draft stronger. Taking the role of reader, you'll develop a sense of a reader's needs that will help you revise. You'll also see that others struggle to write well just as you do. So there is a double payoff from giving feedback: value to the writer and value to the reviewer.

You may be thinking that you are willing to read other students' drafts, but you don't know what to say about a draft. You'll get better at giving feedback with practice. Here are some helpful ways to give feedback on a draft.

Paraphrase and summarize. Put the writer's ideas into your own words. Everyone feels good about being understood.

Ask questions. Questions show you have read carefully and want to understand.

Give your responses as a reader. What made you smile? What surprised you? What part did you like? What confused you? Where did you get lost or bogged down?

Use "I" messages. "I smiled when you said . . ." "I got lost for a minute in the part about . . ." Compare "I got lost" with "You lost me when you. . . ." "You" messages tend to sound blaming or accusing, so try to avoid them.

Suggest specific words, sentences, and ideas. Whether the writer uses them or not, your suggestions may stimulate other possibilities. Write "You might try saying . . ." or "The sentence I marked in the third paragraph might read like this: . . ."

Don't be an error finder. It's easy to become distracted from the writer's content by errors in spelling, punctuation, and grammar, but marking errors in a draft that may be extensively revised is a waste of your time and sends a demoralizing message to the writer.

Here's the feedback Ruby wrote after reading Keith's draft.

Dear Keith,

I enjoyed reading your story "The Wreck" because it was very descriptive and fast paced. The style is that of a story teller and I like the way it was written because it is close to the way you might communicate it orally to someone. It appears to me that you just weren't ready for this machine. Your dad took a big chance and lost. It also looks to me like you respected your dad's dream but apparently lost your head when you felt the car's beauty and power. You didn't seem too broken up about trashing your dad's car. Perhaps this will be a lesson that will last a lifetime.

I enjoyed the paragraph that mentioned the speed of 110 miles an hour because of the detailed, descriptive writing. I could almost see myself sitting in that car. I liked the way your parents handled the situation too.

Absence of details gets attention, but your essay could have been better with more. You could add one or two more sentences on your closing paragraph.

I think your order is acceptable. It seems fashionable these days to start at a later point in the story and then start the second paragraph with the beginning of the story. It worked well in getting the reader's attention.

Hey, I think you did great!

Ruby

WAYS TO GIVE FEEDBACK

Paraphrase and summarize.
Ask questions.
Give your responses as a reader.
Use ''I'' messages.

(Continued)

Suggest specific wording and ideas.
Avoid marking errors in spelling, punctuation, and grammar.

WRITING ACTIVITY 1

Mark the following discovery draft of a paragraph, and write several sentences of feedback to help the writer revise. The assignment was to choose a favorite television program and to analyze its intended audience by looking at the plot, characters, and sponsors (advertisers).

"My Three Sons" is a comedy centered around a widower (Steve Douglas) and his three sons Chip, 12, Robby, 20, and Ernie, 8. With the help of their Uncle Charlie, as housekeeper and jack of all trades, Steve is able to hold his family together. The show is intended for families with grade school children to college age children. The program portrays the everyday ups and downs of family life so the audience can associate the joys and hard times of their own lives. Because of its middle class American characters, setting, and plot, the comedy is obviously aimed at the largest segment of the public, which is the middle class with families.

REMINDER

Giving feedback on drafts of other students can help both the reader and the writer of the draft.

RECEIVING FEEDBACK ON A DRAFT

Now let's look at receiving feedback. For some people giving is harder than receiving feedback, but for others receiving is more difficult. Both become easier with practice. If you are one of the many students who don't want others to read your drafts and dread hearing what they say about your writing, I urge you to be courageous. If you are one of the many students who believe that only a teacher's feedback can help you, I urge you to give your classmates a chance to help. In a class evaluation at the end of the semester, my students often report that feedback from other students was surprisingly more helpful to them than was mine.

Many writers feel defensive or angry about feedback. They hear any suggestion or question as hurtful criticism. To overcome these negative feelings, you must trust the good will of your readers. Remember that a draft is a work-in-progress, and be willing to change it. Peter Drucker, a prolific writer about business, calls his discovery draft a "zero" draft. He doesn't expect much from it except to clarify his thinking, and he doesn't invest much in it so he's willing to start over and make big changes.

Although feedback is valuable to you as a writer, know that you are in charge of your essay. You must evaluate the feedback you receive. Some of it will be on target; some will not. Consider feedback as clues to things that may need changing, even if you don't accept a reader's suggestion. Feedback is not a demand; it is a gift that you may accept and act on or politely refuse.

Part of adjusting your attitude in receiving feedback is timing. You need to be detached from your draft and feedback so you can see them objectively. If you can, let the feedback cool before reading it. Don't read feedback if you are feeling vulnerable and sensitive, such as when you've just had a fight with your best friend or boss. Do read feedback when you're feeling emotionally strong. While I was writing this book, I sometimes waited a day or two after receiving my editor's or reviewers' comments on drafts of chapters before I read their feedback. In order to be open to feedback and to evaluate it intelligently, a writer needs to feel secure, capable, and objective.

Let's look at what kind of feedback helps writers. Students often ask "Is this right?" or "Is anything wrong with this draft?" They seem conditioned by years of schooling to think only in terms of right and wrong, but there are so many possibilities in a piece of writing that these two questions can't be answered. In this writing course you may be given questions to ask when you are seeking feedback. However, when you seek feedback on writing for other courses (I hope you will want to when you find out how much better you can write with feedback), you will need to tell your readers what kind of feedback will help you at the current stage of drafting. Your feedback will be only as good as the questions you ask of your readers.

Your questions and concerns about your draft can help a reader look for new possibilities in a draft. First, check your understanding of the assignment (or writing situation, if you are writing for work or personal reasons). Then decide what questions and concerns you have about your draft and inform the reader about them. You should also let your reader know where you are in the writing process. Are you just getting started? Do you know some things you want to write about but can't find a focus or main point? Does the reader see your main point or thesis? Have you already done three drafts and want help with organization? Here are some questions whose answers are usually helpful to writers. They are based on the five qualities of good writing and a priority of concerns. Don't overwhelm your reader with too many questions. Choose several whose answers would help you take your draft to the next stage.

Asking for Helpful Feedback

1. Am I on the right track? Am I addressing the assignment?
2. What do you think is my thesis (main point)?
3. Have I written appropriately for my intended audience?
4. What are the strengths of this draft?
5. Is every part well developed? Are there enough details and examples?
6. Are there any confusing or missing parts?
7. Do all of the parts have a clear connection to the thesis?
8. Is the essay well organized? Is the organization obvious to the reader?
9. What are two or three things I could do to take this draft to the next stage?

Writers are rarely helped by yes and no or right and wrong answers to these questions. If you are giving feedback, write two or three sentences to answer them. Notice that some of them can be answered by paraphrasing parts of the draft or by asking questions or by making suggestions. Even if a question seems to call for a yes or no answer, such as "Am I addressing the assignment?" expand on your answer. A description of what you see the writer doing or saying is more helpful than a one-word answer to a question. For example, you have been assigned to write about a lesson you learned as a child and to use examples to explain your thesis. After reading your draft, a reader might write, "You wrote about learning to hide your Hispanic origins because of discrimination. I counted four examples." You could tell from this comment if what is coming through to your reader is what you meant. If it is not, you would know that you need to revise.

REMINDER

Feedback from other students and your teacher gives you clues about changes you can make to improve your draft. Trust the good intentions of your readers and evaluate their feedback when you are in a positive frame of mind.

USING FEEDBACK TO REVISE YOUR DRAFT

You have been reading about the complex process of giving and receiving feedback. Once you've received feedback from several people, what do you do with it? Like giving feedback, using feedback is also a complex process that takes practice. Be sure you are emotionally ready to "hear" what your reviewers are saying. Try not to be defensive, angry, or hurt. Try not to ignore anything said. Be open to the feedback as clues to improving your draft. Although you may decide not to act on some of the feedback you receive, you may, as a result of it, be able to read your draft with fresh eyes—to re-see it so that you can revise. Remember that your reviewers may have been afraid of giving you bad feedback or hurting your feelings. Nevertheless, they have risked giving their thoughts and reactions. Although you should trust both their good will and their feedback, you shouldn't follow it slavishly, assuming they know better than you how to write your essay. You must evaluate the feedback and decide what to respond to by revising.

When you are emotionally ready to accept feedback, read all the feedback and take time to enjoy and learn from what your readers liked about your draft, what they agreed with, and what they saw as strengths of this work-in-progress. Students are often surprised that others really enjoy and are interested in what they have written. Your readers' interest feels good and gives you energy to write more.

Then, when you have taken time to recognize the strengths of your draft, you are ready to evaluate the rest of the feedback. Read it all and consider it carefully. Be sure you understand what your reviewers mean. If you don't, ask them: "Do you mean . . .?" "I thought I had explained enough. Can you tell me what would make it clear for you?" Checking on the reviewers' comments doesn't insult your reviewers; it shows you value their feedback and want to understand. Reread the assignment. Reread your draft. Reread the feedback. Try to see why your reviewers said what they did. Then decide on the two or three most important changes to make in your draft to take it to the next stage. Don't try to respond to everything that was given to you as feedback. This process is about improving your draft, and you don't have to respond to every piece of feedback. In fact, if you receive feedback from several readers, some of it may be contradictory. If so, you will need to be sure what your readers meant and why they said what they did before you decide which readers' feedback to use.

REMINDER

You will probably want to revise in stages, creating a logical priority of concerns to solve problems or weaknesses in a draft.

PRIORITY OF CONCERNS FOR REVISING A DRAFT

1. Address the writing assignment, including topic, audience, and purpose.
2. Revise the thesis to express the main idea of your essay. The thesis should include a narrowed topic and a comment about it.
3. Add details, facts, examples, reasons, and explanations to provide adequate and appropriate development for the audience and purpose.

(Continued)

4. Create unity by eliminating parts that do not support the thesis or that are repeated.
5. Reorder sentences and paragraphs so there are close, logical connections between them and so they are arranged in a logical and effective way.
6. Provide clear transitions between supporting parts.
7. Edit for correctness and style (after all revisions).
8. Proofread the revised and edited draft.

REVISING FOR ADEQUATE DEVELOPMENT

Remember that focus as expressed in a thesis is the first priority in revising. You learned in Chapter 2 to test your trial thesis after writing a draft and to revise it if necessary. The second priority of concern in revising is to check for adequate development. Because writers have a strong sense of the experiences and meanings they write about, they often underdevelop their supporting ideas. They underestimate a reader's need for facts, reasons, examples, and explanations. Some writers think their message is obvious to others because it is obvious to them.

You can test your essay drafts for adequate development and get additional ideas for thesis support by asking readers to read the draft for development. Readers can often point to parts that are strong and well connected to the thesis and to parts that are weak and poorly connected to the thesis. Remember to tell your readers where you are in the drafting process and what you want from them. Help them help you so that you will get the feedback you need.

After getting feedback from several other students, Alison understood that her readers needed more explanation and examples. Here are her revisions for additional development. Her revised essay appears at the end of this chapter.

Do you throw your money away by not using credit cards? Do you end up with enormous bills you can't pay when you do use them? You don't have to end up in financial trouble by using credit cards.

You can use them to your advantage actually

~~Using a credit card is not a bad thing.~~ In fact ~~it can~~ save*ing*, even earn*ing*, you money. ¶ ~~For~~ Every time that you use your credit card, it saves you writing a check. If you have duplicate checks, like I have, they cost you approximately eight cents a piece. Running an average household I used to write about sixty checks a month. ~~That's $4.00 a month, or~~ That's over $57.60 a year. For standard checks at five cents a piece, it works out to $36 a year. ~~This,~~ Of course, this is not the only saving you get by using a credit card. You also keep your money in the bank for an extra month earning interest, and if you use the Discover card it gives you cash back at the end of the year. Last year it paid me over $100 for using its card. I paid no annual fee and no interest. I earned ~~more~~ interest on my money in the bank and saved money by ordering fewer checks.

Even though this may not sound like much, why just give it away?

There is a technique. You can't just go out and use a credit card and save money. In fact many people end up in a lot of financial trouble. The secret is to use your credit card ~~in place~~ instead of a check, not for extra buying power, and most importantly, record every transaction. It is amazing how five, ten, twenty, and fifty dollar charges can add up! Every time I use my credit card ~~(I use Discover whenever possible)~~ I record it in my checkbook register, as I would for a check, except in the space for check number I enter a D for Discover, V for Visa, GV for Gold Visa, or MC for MasterCard. This way you see the money as it is spent and there are no nasty surprises when your monthly credit card bill arrives. When ~~it~~ my bill does arrive, I write the due date on my calendar and put it in my "bills due" drawer. When you pay your credit card bill two days before it is due (never pay your bills until they are due) go through your bill with your checkbook register and put a small check by each of the ~~entries and~~ write the check number that you are paying the bill with by ~~them.~~ each of the entries. I also As you ~~have~~ deduct~~ed~~ the amounts with each transaction, you can zero out your charge bill.

Insert picture by check book entries.

This makes it easy to see at a glance which charges are outstanding.

Insert checkbook sample

For balancing your checkbook, look for the check for your credit card bill to clear -- in the example above number 3653. When it does, you can go through and mark all the credit card transactions that you have written that check number by as cleared. You will have more adding to do when you balance your checkbook because there will be more transactions that have not cleared the bank. Remember, this is good, it means you have more money in the bank earning interest. Whatever you do, do not use your credit cards beyond your means. If you do not have the money in the bank do not charge it. The interest on a bank loan, if needed, is a lot less than on credit cards. Pay the full amount each month and only have cards that no annual fee and a thirty-day grace period on purchases. Discover is the only one I have found that actually pays you cold, hard cash for using it, and I use it when ever I can.

As I stated earlier, think of your credit card as you do a check.

Besides asking for feedback from readers, another way to strengthen the development of your essay is by changing vague and general words to more exact and specific ones. Although everyday words have rich meanings and create sensory images for writers, readers may receive only a foggy, perhaps confused, understanding from general and frequently used words. Much of the vocabulary you use comes from oral communication in which you rely on your voice, hand gestures, facial expressions, and other body language to add to your words. You can tell from a listener's reactions if you are being misunderstood, but you can't see a reader's reactions. Speakers sometimes shift responsibility for understanding to their listener when they say "You know what I mean." However, good speakers and writers take responsibility for saying and writing what they mean as clearly as possible. Because you can't use body language or your voice (volume, intonation, and pitch) as a mode of expression in writing, you have to use words more precisely and exactly.

What is a "good" hamburger? How much does a leather jacket cost if it costs "a lot"? What is a "hot" property and what is a "cool" date? What is a "kind" person or a "nice" salesclerk or a "tough" bus driver? What is an "understanding" teacher or a "demanding" father? What is an "irresponsible" kid or a "beautiful" sunset? You see the point by now. Such vague and general words are inadequate to convey to a reader precisely what it is that you see and what you think and feel about what you see. They seem to tell more about the speaker's feeling toward a person or thing than to describe the thing itself. When you write, don't count on vague and weak words to communicate your experiences. Give more information to your reader. For instance, to you a "good" hamburger may be a half pound not a quarter pound, grilled not fried, medium not rare or well done, with barbecue sauce and pickles on a sesame seed bun.

WRITING ACTIVITY 2

Describe a good meal, a bad movie, an irritating commercial, a neat date, and a frightening sound. Tell what makes these things *good, bad, irritating, neat,* and *frightening* to you by giving specific details. Remember the example of the hamburger.

If you tend to count on weak words to describe what you have experienced to a reader, you may need to add a describing tool to your writing tool kit. You can use a *sensory inventory* to help you provide more information for the reader. Use your senses (sight, hearing, taste, smell, touch, and movement) to recall specific details about the thing you are naming. Think of color, shape, size, number, and texture for sight. Think of tone, volume, and pitch for hearing. You don't have to use all the details you generate, you don't have to use details for all the senses, and you may use more than one ''answer'' to any of the senses. Here's how I might use the sensory inventory to add to my description of a good hamburger.

Sight: medium size, dark brown patty with bubbly red juice, but not shiny with grease; so I can hold it in one hand and take a bite of it
Hearing: sizzle of beef on the grill
Taste: grilled taste, tanginess of barbecue sauce and pickles
Smell: smoky meat, yeasty fresh bun
Touch: not dry, but not so juicy it drips down my chin; fresh but firm bun, not dry or mushy; crisp pickles

When you are revising to add descriptive details, you may write down your sensory inventory or simply make a mental sensory check and then select enough details from your inventory to give your reader a sharp, sensory picture.

Another way to develop vague writing into strong writing is to make your nouns specific and add details.

General	**Specific**
bug	wasp, spider, roach
car	a red 300ZX Nissan with twin turbo, a blue and white 1957 Chevrolet hardtop
flowers	roses, 102 white roses, long-stemmed red roses

Writing Activities 3 and 4 may help you remember to use specific nouns to communicate your unique experience to a reader.

WRITING ACTIVITY 3

Substitute three more specific terms for each of the underlined words in the following sentences. Make the substitutes progressively more specific.

> She enjoyed the show.
> Kids like to play games.
> Kevin has a new vehicle.
> Wanda wants to be a popular entertainer.
> Their family decided to recycle their trash.

General	Specific
show	TV program, sit com, "The Bill Cosby Show"
games	
vehicle	
entertainer	
trash	

WRITING ACTIVITY 4

Revise the following paragraph by adding sensory details, replacing weak adjectives, and changing general nouns into specific nouns.

A boy in funny clothes sat next to me in class. I thought he was weird, but he turned out to be nice. When we had to read each other's drafts, we met in the cafeteria. It was too noisy and the food smells were too much, so we went into a study area down the hall from our classroom where it was quiet.

CHECKING YOUR DRAFT FOR ADEQUATE DEVELOPMENT

Ask readers where they want to know more.
Replace weak adjectives.
Use a sensory inventory to generate specific details.
Replace general nouns with specific nouns.

REVISING FOR UNITY AND COHERENCE

When readers say an essay "flows" well, they may mean it has unity and coherence. Unity means that each paragraph in the body clearly supports the thesis with clear connections for the reader. It also means that each sentence in each paragraph supports the paragraph's main point. Coherence means that each sentence logically relates to the sentence before and after and that appropriate transitional words and phrases signal the relationship between sentences and between paragraphs. Coherence also means that the essay is logically organized—chronologically, spatially, or emphatically.

One way to check your essay for unity and coherence is to make an informal outline of your draft. Some people use an outline as an organizing plan before they write, especially if they are using information from several books and magazine articles. Some people use outlines as a discovery strategy to get themselves started writing. An informal outline can also be a quick and useful tool for checking the unity and coherence of your essay after you have written a discovery draft.

To make a quick outline, write notes in the margins near each paragraph. Tell what the paragraph *says* (content) and what it *does* (its connection to the thesis). If you have trouble writing these marginal notes, your paragraphs may not have one clear main idea or topic sentence. If you can make these notes, write your thesis on a clean page and list your notes in outline form. Because you can see the whole picture of your essay in this condensed form, you can check the support for your thesis in terms of quantity (how much) and quality (how good). You can also spot parts that don't support your thesis, parts that are repeats, and parts that need reordering. You can identify problem paragraphs that need to be split into two paragraphs or need a topic sentence.

Here's an outline of Alison's draft made from her discovery draft. She could see that her main points (I, II, III) were important supporting points for her thesis. Then she checked to see that support (A, B, C) for those main points fit. For instance, she could see that A, B, C, and D under "I. Gives reasons for using credit cards" were reasons.

Thesis: Credit cards can save, even earn, you money.

I. Gives reasons for using credit cards

  A. Cost of checks

    1. Duplicate checks—eight cents each

    2. Standard checks—five cents each

  B. Bank interest on money in the bank

  C. No costs—no annual fee or interest

  D. Cash back for using Discover card

II. Explains a technique for using credit cards
   A. Record credit card transactions in checkbook like a check
      1. Show name of credit card in place of check number
      2. Check off when credit card bill is paid
   B. Write due date of credit card bill on calendar and pay only two days before due

III. Explains how to balance a checkbook
   A. Mark off credit card transactions when check clears
   B. Count uncleared checks as earning power

IV. Gives advice
   A. Pay full amount each month
   B. Use only cards with no annual fee and thirty-day grace period

Be sure to check your draft for coherence. When you are confident that each paragraph sticks to its own main point and clearly supports the thesis, check your draft to be sure your essay has obvious transitions to keep your reader on track with you. Linking words and phrases show connections between sentences and paragraphs. They point backward or forward to other parts. They signal the relationship of ideas and make your ideas easier for a reader to follow and understand. Transitional words and phrases are common words and phrases that you use automatically. Writers, who obviously know the links between their own thoughts, sometimes leave out these important signals. Just as the children in the fairy tale left a trail of bread crumbs so they could find their way out of the dark forest, you must leave a clearly marked trail through your essay. For instance, when you "promise" a reader a series of causes, reasons, examples, events, or steps, follow through by clearly labeling each part of the series. Readers need several types of transitions to signal specific relationships.

Transitional Words and Phrases for Achieving Coherence

To signal the time-relationship of the next detail: first, second, next, then, after, before, during, as now, meanwhile, at last, immediately, finally

To signal that the next detail is an example: for example, for instance, in other words, in particular

To signal that the next detail is a consequence: thus, therefore, consequently, so, as a result, hence
To signal that the next detail is a conclusion: in summary, in conclusion, thus, on the whole
To signal that the next detail is similar or is an additional example or reason: also, in addition, furthermore, moreover, similarly
To signal that the next detail is different: on the other hand, however, nevertheless, still, but, although, even though, in contrast, on the contrary

WRITING ACTIVITY 5

Without looking back at Alison's draft, supply transitional words or phrases in the blanks. Then reread these sentences in her draft (page 57) to see what transitions she used.

I record it in my checkbook register, ____________________ I would for a check, except in the space for check number I enter a D for Discover, V for Visa, GV for Gold Visa, or MC for MasterCard. ____________________ you see the money as it is spent ____________________ there are no nasty surprises ____________________ your monthly credit card bill arrives. ____________________ my bill does arrive, I write the due date on my calendar and put it in my "bills due" drawer. ____________________ you pay your credit card bill, two days before it is due (never pay your bills until they are due), go through your bill with your checkbook register ____________________ write the check number that you are paying the bill with by each of the entries. I also put a small check by each of them. ____________________ makes it easy to see at a glance which charges are outstanding. ____________________ deduct the amounts with each transaction, you can zero out your charge bill.

There are other strategies for achieving coherence. You often use these automatically when writing your draft, but you may need to add more when you revise. One strategy for creating coherence is using pronouns carefully. You should use pronouns (*it, you, I, he, she, they, this,* and *which*) consistently, avoiding unnecessary shifts, for instance, from *you* to *he.* You should be sure that each pronoun refers clearly to a specific nearby noun. Careless use of pronouns destroys coherence; careful use of pronouns creates coherence.

Another strategy to achieve coherence is to use consistent verb tense. It's easy to slip back and forth between past and present tense (from *was* to *is,* for instance) and to throw in other verb tenses by using the helping verbs *will* or *would.* Unnecessary shifts in verb tense destroy coherence. Check your draft to see that you have used verb tenses consistently.

Yet another strategy to achieve coherence is purposeful repetition. Repeating key words helps a reader stay on track with your meaning. Purposeful repetition can create coherence. For instance, a writer may repeat an important word or phrase from the introduction in the conclusion to achieve closure and create coherence.

REMINDER

Coherence is the logical connection of one sentence to another and one paragraph with another. To create coherence, use transitional words and phrases. Be sure each pronoun refers clearly to a nearby noun and avoid unnecessary shifts in pronouns. Use consistent verb tenses. Repeat key words and phrases.

WRITING A TITLE FOR AN ESSAY

After you have revised for focus, adequate development, unity, and coherence, you should allow time for finishing touches. Writing a title for your essay is one such task. A title has two important jobs. It hooks the reader's interest and hints at something important in the essay. A good title may occur to you any time in the process of writing an essay. Often you will be almost finished revising before you can write an effective and appropriate title. One tip for writing titles is to reread your revised introduction and conclusion. Is there an image, anecdote, or key word you can use as a title? Also reread your statement of audience and purpose. There's sometimes a clue for a title there. You don't want a misleading title or an assignment label, such as ''A Comparison Essay'' or ''Book Report.'' You do want a title that is informative and interesting.

While she was writing and revising, Teresa tried several titles for her essay describing a family reunion at her grandparents' half-finished house in the mountains. Read her first paragraph and then read her list of trial titles. Which one do you think captures her emphasis in the essay?

She shivered as she pulled the blanket up tighter around her. Outside she could hear people moving to identify this strange, yet somehow familiar new world. As the fog of sleep left her mind, she decided to get dressed. She reached for her clothes, feeling the camper wobble, as it always did, no matter how long her Dad spent trying to get it level. She opened her overstuffed hard blue suitcase, telling herself that when she grew up, she would have the soft, pretty luggage like she had seen on TV. There were so many clothes, everything from swimsuits to sweatshirts. She wondered how it could be so cold at night and hot during the day.

A Temporary Hillbilly

Why I Prefer the City

City Slicker

Hillbilly Heaven??

Teresa wanted a title that captured the rustic quality of the place and the joy of the family gathering. Her choice was "Hillbilly Heaven??" Notice that the question marks after the word *heaven* suggest her positive and negative feelings about the time and place.

After you have composed an effective and appropriate title for your essay, write it without quotation marks on your draft. Use quotation marks for titles and essays only when you are writing *about* them.

WRITING ACTIVITY 6

The title of Alison's essay on using credit cards to save and earn money is "Every Penny Counts." Turn to her revised essay on pages 67–70. Reread her description of audience and purpose and her introduction and conclusion. Compose two other possible titles for her essay.

EDITING FOR CORRECTNESS

Although you may have corrected spelling and grammar problems as you worked on your draft, you still should edit your revised draft carefully. If you used a word processor, use the spelling checker. Because it won't catch all mistakes, such as using the wrong word (*its* for *it's, and* for *an, in* for *on*), you must still read the draft carefully. At this stage you should also look for any sentence problems such as fragments and hard-to-understand sentences. This is also the time to check punctuation. Make the task of editing easier by knowing what kinds of errors you typically make. Then look especially for those errors. You can use the handbook in the back of this book to help you solve some of these editing problems. Since there are so many small things to check at this stage, you can see the need for this final, careful editing of your draft after you have solved the bigger problems of focus, development, unity, and coherence.

Remember the strategies for editing and proofreading described in Chapter 1. One strategy for reading carefully is to use a ruler or sheet of paper to help you focus on one word or one sentence at a time—starting from the bottom up. Because the sense connections are destroyed by this reverse reading, you will see what is actually there instead of what you meant to write. This strategy allows you to focus just on words and sentences. Another strategy is to read your draft aloud, to someone or to a tape recorder. Yet another one is to ask someone to read your draft to you so you can hear it.

WRITING ACTIVITY 7

Read the following paragraph using the technique of reading from the last sentence to the first sentence. Find and correct all the errors. There are twelve errors.

Even though you're siting on the bench, you are still a member of the team. Do no think that you have no effect on the game because you are'nt playing. When you go on faraway road trips, their are not many fans rooting for your team. Letting your teammates know you are there for them helps out a great deal more than most people believe. Its really easy to get involved in a game from the bench. Once you get over the fact that this is your day off. The game seems shorter when you get into it, it's also a lot more fun to cheer and be happy then to sit and sulk by yourself. So whenever your on the bench jus root for your team. No matter what you think the outcome of the game still effects you an the cheering you do from the bench affects the game.

REVISING AS DISCOVERY AND OPPORTUNITY

Let revising be fun for you. Think of it as a discovery process much like a little kid seeing what can be discovered in a sand pile. Revising can be an opportunity to think more clearly and to communicate more effectively than you have in earlier drafts. Writing several drafts is normal. You can take the pressure off yourself by setting priorities for revising, giving and receiving feedback, and writing several drafts. You can reduce the stress of writing by giving up trying "to get it right" in one draft in an impossible time frame. Learn to revise effectively. Set priorities for revising, give and receive feedback, write several drafts, and allow time for revising as you write essays for this class. Your revised writing will surprise you!

GUIDELINES FOR REVISING YOUR DRAFT

Reread the assignment.
Get feedback on a draft.
Read the essay drafts of other students.
Revise for
- Focus
- Development
- Unity
- Coherence
- Correctness

Edit and proofread.

Here is the final draft of Alison's essay. Additions to her earlier draft are in boldface type.

Every Penny Counts

Alison Robertson

Audience: Adult men and women who are interested in saving money as well as those who don't use credit cards

Purpose: To inform these people about a technique to use credit cards wisely and save money

Do you throw money away by not using credit cards? Do you end up with enormous bills that you can't pay when you do use

them? You don't have to end up in financial trouble by using credit cards. In fact, **you can use them to your advantage actually** sav**ing,** even earn**ing,** you money.

Every time that you use your credit card, it saves you writing a check. If you have duplicate checks, like I have, they cost you approximately eight cents a piece. Running an average household, I used to write about sixty checks a month. **That's over** $57 a year. For standard checks at five cents a piece, it works out to $36 a year. **Even though this may not sound like much, why just give it away?** Of course, **this** is not the only saving you get by using a credit card. You also keep your money in the bank for **an** extra month earning interest, and if you use the Discover card, it gives you cash back at the end of the year. Last year it paid me over $100 for using its card. I paid no annual fee and no interest. I earned interest on my money in the bank and saved money by ordering fewer checks.

There is a technique. You can't just go out and use a credit card and save money. In fact many people end up in a lot of financial trouble. The secret is to use your credit card **instead** of a check, not for extra buying power, and most importantly, record every transaction. It is amazing how five, ten, twenty, and fifty dollar charges can add up! Every time I use my credit card I record it in my checkbook register, as I would for a check, except that in the space for check number I enter a D for Discover, V for Visa, GV for Gold Visa, and MC for MasterCard.

Check #	Date	Description of Transaction	Payment	Deposit	Balance
D	10/20	Kroger	35.40		35.40
					864.60
D	10/21	Home Depot	76.28		76.28
					788.32

This way you see the money as **it is** spent and there are no nasty surprises when your monthly credit card bill arrives. When **my bill** does arrive, I write the due date on my calendar and put it in my "bills due" drawer. When you pay your credit card bill, two days before it is due (never pay your bills **when they first arrive**), go through your bill with your checkbook register and write the check number that you are paying the bill with by each of the entries. I also put a small check by each of **them. This makes it easy to see at a glance which charges are still outstanding.** As you **deduct** the amounts with each transaction, you can zero out your **charge** bill.

Check #	Date	Description of Transaction	Payment	Deposit	Balance
D	10/20	Kroger	35.40		35.40
√		3653			864.60
D	10/21	Home Depot	76.28		76.28
√		3653			788.32
3653	11/18	Discover Card	111.68	111.68	0
					788.32

For balancing your checkbook, look for the check for your credit card bill to clear—**in the example above number 3653.** When it does, you can go through and mark all the credit card transactions that you have written that check number by as cleared. You will have more adding to do when you balance your checkbook because there will be more transactions that have not cleared the bank. Remember, this is good. It means you have more money in the bank earning interest.

Whatever you do, do not use your credit card**s** beyond your means. If you do not have the money in the bank, do not charge it. **As I stated earlier, think of your credit card as you do a check.** The interest on a bank loan, if needed, is a lot less than on credit cards. Pay the full amount each month and **have only** cards that **have** no annual fee and a thirty-day grace period on purchases. Discover is the only one I have found that actually pays you cold, hard cash for using it, **which is why** I use it whenever I can.

EXPLORING FURTHER

Find the discovery draft about peer pressure and the description of audience and purpose you wrote for Exploring Further in Chapter 2.

1. *Group Work.* Test your trial thesis. Read your discovery draft aloud to the group. Don't trade drafts at this point. Because the discovery draft is written only for the writer to use, it is often hard to read. Without any discussion, each listener should write down a sentence that expresses the main point (thesis) of the essay and give it to you. Then the group can discuss the essay, and you can take notes to use in revising.

   If what you meant is coming through clearly, you are on the right track. If they disagree among themselves and with you about your main point, you need to revise the trial thesis or the draft or both.

   All group members should read their drafts aloud and write thesis statements for all other group members.
2. *Writing Activity.* Revise your trial thesis and your draft so that they fit. Sometimes the real thesis emerges from the draft, so the writer revises the thesis to make it fit the draft. Sometimes the thesis is exactly what the writer wants to write about, but the essay got off track, so the writer revises the essay to make it fit the thesis. Usually both need revising at this stage. Make a clean copy of the revised draft.
3. *Group Work.* Exchange drafts. Write a friendly and supportive letter to the writer of the draft with your feedback. Begin by mentioning one thing you liked in this draft or one strength. Then outline the draft to help the writer check for unity and coherence. Finally tell the writer about any place you were confused, even a little, or needed more details or explanations. Remember that your questions, requests, and comments are gifts that the writer may politely refuse or gratefully use in revising.
4. *Writing Activity.* After you read the feedback on your draft from your group and after you have reread your draft, make a plan for revising. Don't get overwhelmed or confused. Just make a list of three or four things to do to improve the draft. Decide which is most important and start with that one. Tackle these one at a time, and revise your draft.
5. *Writing Activity.* Make a clean copy of your revised essay. Then edit it, reading from the last sentence to the first. Make corrections. Ask for help from your teacher if you spot a problem you can't solve with the help of a dictionary or the handbook in the back of this book.

CHAPTER

4

READING FOR COMPREHENSION

In Chapters 1 through 3 you have been reading about writing. In Chapters 5 through 13 you will be reading selections from newspapers, magazines, and books. Although this is a writing course, reading, thinking, speaking, and listening are inseparable from writing. Because the communication skills of reading, writing, speaking, and listening are interrelated, you can use your stronger ones to help improve the others. For instance, your strongest communication skill may be talking to others. You can use this strength to improve your writing by talking to others as you look for ideas to write about, as you try to find a focus for your writing, and as you revise. Because communications skills are interrelated, good readers are usually good writers and the reverse. Use what you know about writing to help you read better, and use what you know about reading to help you write better.

Reading and writing, as well as the other communication activities, are skills that you can learn and improve by practice, just as you might practice juggling or skateboarding. Like juggling or skateboarding, these communication activities are part mental, part physical, and part emotional. For instance, freewriting is a physical activity that stimulates the mental activity of thinking. Reading is a mental activity that creates physical changes in respiration, eye movements, pulse rate, and brain activity. All of these complex activities are affected by your emotional state—how you feel and what you care about.

Earlier you read that negative self-talk creates writer's block for many people, and you looked briefly at your own. You also read how two writers use positive self-talk to create positive feelings that allow them to think and write, and you considered how you can help yourself write. Reading, too, is affected by your feelings, attitudes, and self-talk. Since reading essays is a way of learning to write, let's look at some negative messages that make it harder to read.

> "I hate to read."
> "This is boring."
> "I can't understand what this guy is saying."
> "I'm just a bad reader."

These messages are ways to shut the door to understanding and learning. They create bad feelings in the reader and bad feelings about the reading. If you hear yourself thinking such negative thoughts about the reading assignments, replace them with positive messages that show curiosity and a willingness to add to what you know and to learn new things.

> "I want to know about this."
> "This is difficult reading, but I can use some new reading strategies."
> "Since I know about this, it's easy to read."

To be a better reader, cultivate positive self-talk and use what you know about writing to help you read.

WRITING ACTIVITY 1

What makes reading hard for you? What makes reading easy? Write for five minutes about each question.

GROUP WORK 1

Talk with a small group about their answers to the questions in Writing Activity 1. Think together how to make reading easy and fun for you in this course. Have a few outrageous ideas. Get beyond the obvious. Be creative and have fun brainstorming possibilities. Then select ideas to share with the class.

READING AS MEANING MAKING

The essays in this book have been chosen as models for specific writing lessons and as starting places for your essays. You aren't expected to know every word or to remember every name and fact in each selection. You are expected to read for meaning and enjoyment and to read with openness and curiosity. You should be asking "What's this about? Who is the author? Why is the author writing? What's the main point? Why is the author using this example? Or telling this story? Or explaining so much?''

You have been studying the process of writing. Now think about the process of reading. What is reading? Is it translating little squiggles on the page into words? Is it understanding one word at a time? Is it a passive process in which your eyes pass over pages of print and absorb information and facts? Researchers say that reading is the process of making meaning because you constantly interpret as you read. Your experience and knowledge affect what and how you understand what you read. Reading as the making of meaning is an interaction between the writer, the page, and you. You must be an active participant, not a passive recipient, when you read. Researchers of reading help us understand what good readers do as they read, and you can use these strategies, if you don't already, to become a better reader.

Activate Prior Knowledge. First, good readers *activate prior knowledge.* They connect the subject matter of the reading with something familiar, something from their own experience, *before* they begin reading. The purpose of Writing Activity 1 was to activate your prior knowledge about reading before you began reading this section. Why? Because people learn by connecting new information and ideas to what they already know. For instance, once you have learned how to play one song on the guitar, you can learn a new song more easily than you learned the first one.

Make Predictions. Second, good readers *predict* what the writer will say. They begin by reading the title, looking quickly over the article or book, noticing the author's name, and thinking about anything else they've read by the author or about the topic. Before they read and while they read, they make educated guesses about what will come next and what the writer means.

WRITING ACTIVITY 2

Without looking ahead, write briefly about what you predict the third mental activity of good readers will be.

Confirm or Refute Predictions. Third, good readers *confirm or refute* their predictions. They constantly and automatically check to see if they were right or wrong. They don't necessarily stop reading to do this. Just as you can listen to music and talk to a friend at the same time, good readers do at least two mental actions at once. Just as you can listen faster than someone can talk (that's why your mind often wanders), good readers can think about what they're seeing faster than they can see the words. Good readers keep their eyes moving rhythmically across lines and down a page, looking at phrases instead of single words. Good readers actively predict and confirm or refute their predictions as they read. Their minds work on two levels at the same time—understanding the content itself and thinking about the content.

Notice the Writer's Patterns. Fourth, good readers *notice the writer's patterns*—how the writer has chosen to develop the thesis. Good readers recognize the main chunks that form the essay—introduction, body, and conclusion. They recognize the beginning paragraphs (or pages) as the introduction and look for the writer's main point and purpose. They recognize the body of the essay and look for a pattern of development of the thesis. They notice whether the supporting part is a narration organized by time sequence, a series of steps that make up a process, the causes and effects of a problem, or a combination of ways to develop a supporting part. If you are functioning now as a good reader, you noticed that I am listing and describing several qualities of good readers in order to define reading and explain the mental activities of reading.

As you can see, reading is a busy mental and physical activity. If you have trouble concentrating on or understanding a reading assignment, you may not be using these active strategies of good readers. However, you can train yourself to do what good readers do.

WHAT GOOD READERS DO

Activate prior knowledge.
Make predictions.
Confirm or refute predictions.
Notice the writer's patterns.

USING THIS BOOK—READ, WRITE, TALK, COMPOSE

Although you may view the reading and writing in this course as work, I hope you will also view it as an opportunity to develop professionally and personally and to expand your potential. This book is designed to induct you into what Frank Smith, an expert on reading, calls "the literacy club." He says, "Learning is social and developmental. We grow to be like the people we see ourselves as being like." We become like the people we pattern ourselves after. "Moreover," he says, "learning is . . . not a consequence of instruction and practice but of demonstration and collaboration." In other words, you have to see whatever you are learning (whether it's dancing or writing) and do it with others, not just read instructions about doing it. As you use this book, you'll be reading the essays of others (seeing) and collaborating with classmates as you read, write, talk, and listen to each other (doing). As a member of the literacy club of this class, you will be in the company of other readers and writers, both student and professional, and you will learn from each other.

WRITING ACTIVITY 3

Write for five minutes about how you learned to do something you enjoy—dancing, canoeing, cooking, playing basketball, tuning up a car, growing tomatoes. In your mind's eye, see this activity being performed by some capable person. Then see yourself doing it. See those who helped you learn as they coached you. What do you notice about how you learn?

Ideally, you will view coming to class like coming to a stimulating and rewarding club meeting. In this classroom club you will read, talk about what you've read, write, and talk about what you've written. You will focus on the content of and conversations about the readings and writings you do. As a result of this reading, writing, and talking, you will become better at these communication activities.

Now that you've read about the reading and writing processes, you will be reading selections from newspapers, magazines, and books. These readings are grouped into nine chapters. Each chapter presents a writing lesson about a way of thinking and writing about a topic, such as description, narration, cause and effect, and process analysis, so that you can focus on one kind of development of ideas at a time. Several reading selections demonstrate each lesson. Each selection is accompanied by activities and questions to prompt your talking and writing, to help you understand the content of the essay and the writing lesson, and to suggest ideas for your essays.

Thinking Before Reading. Before you read an essay, you will be asked to write in your Idea Bank. There will be a question or suggestion that is intended to *activate your prior knowledge* to help you connect with the selection you are about to read. You may use this as prewriting for an essay you write later.

Expanding Your Vocabulary from Reading. There will be a list of words and definitions to look over before you read. Simply notice the words that are listed so that you can refer to them if you need to when you are reading. The meaning of many of these words will be clear to you as you read, but sometimes you'll need the definition to understand the sentence. There may be other words in the essay you don't know. If a word interferes with your understanding or if a word is one you want to add to your writing vocabulary, circle the word. You don't need to look up every word you don't know. However, you do need to notice words, try to figure out the meanings of unfamiliar ones from the sense of the passage, and select a few in each essay to add to your vocabulary.

Reading the Essay. As you start to read, read quickly for meaning. Read phrases, not one word at a time. If the reading is hard to understand, don't slow down. Keep moving to get a sense of the whole. Then go back and reread. If you slow yourself to a one-word-at-a-time pace, you destroy meaning. Don't stop to look up words you don't know unless they block you from understanding. Use the list of definitions if you need it. However, notice that you often can figure out the meaning of a word from the sense of the sentence.

Get into the habit of marking the text as you read. Mark words you want to learn. Mark writing techniques. For instance, if you are studying how to use examples to support a thesis and to develop supporting ideas, you might mark examples as you notice them by writing "ex." in the margin. See how this is done in the marked essay on pages 79–80.

Notice the parts of an essay (introduction, body, and conclusion) as you are paying attention to content. Look for the main point or thesis, and, as you read, check out (*make predictions* and *confirm or refute*) your perception of that thesis. Bracket or highlight the thesis and label it in the margin. As a writer yourself, notice how the writer is developing the essay—explaining, giving examples, comparing, narrating. Make marginal notes about these supporting parts to see the writer's patterns of development.

To mark what you are reading, you can underline, highlight, bracket, circle, and make marginal notes. You might color code your highlighting—pink for thesis and supporting ideas, yellow for vocabulary you want to learn, and blue for special features the lesson is describing, such as examples. Underline key words. Circle words you want to learn. Use a combination of marking techniques. There's no one right way. Create a system that is fun and helpful for you.

A MARKING SYSTEM TO USE AS YOU READ

Bracket or pink highlight for thesis and major supports
Bracket or blue highlight for the lesson's focus, for example, descriptive details
Marginal notes to label parts
Circle or yellow highlight for vocabulary or important words

Ann McGee-Cooper, a creativity consultant to business who has a reading disorder called dyslexia, tells her reading strategies.

> In areas of dyslexia or learning blocks, reading takes longer. I highlight abundantly and reread the highlighted material because I need this repetition to imprint. Another strategy I use as a dyslexic is to read a page, section, or chapter. Then I stop myself and ask, "What did that say?" I

often speak into a tape recorder. Then at the end of my study time, I can replay my summaries to help me see bigger patterns and remember. Until I learned how to enjoy the process of learning, I floundered. Before that I just thought learning was supposed to be magic and just happen!

Remember to be an active reader, whether you are a strong reader or a struggling one. Keep thinking about what you are reading as you read. Notice how much more you absorb and remember as you become an active participant in the reading process.

Jotting Down Your First Responses. After you have read an assignment, you will be asked to write in your Idea Bank. The questions that follow each selection suggest some ways to respond to what you read. What feelings or thoughts did you have in response to the content? What associations to your own experience did the content stimulate? John Schultz, another writer and teacher of writing, asks his students these questions: What did you notice about what was said (content) or the way it was said (comparisons, images, facts, events, descriptions, examples, organization, style, development, images—anything at all)? What questions or comments do you have? Writing about the assignment is like talking after a concert, movie, or book. You combine feelings, associations, questions, analysis, and comment as you talk. Write these first responses in your Idea Bank. You may use ''First Responses'' and ''Writing Before Reading'' as ideas for essays you write later.

Checking Your Comprehension. As you talk with others after you read an article or watch a movie or television program, you informally check your understanding. In this book you can check your understanding of the selections by answering the questions in the Checking Your Comprehension section following each selection. These questions will direct your attention to specific parts of the content and help you review the sequence of events, the names of characters, and other elements of the selection.

Understanding a Writer's Patterns. After each selection, a group of questions will direct your attention to the way the essay is written. Some questions will focus on the thesis, audience, and purpose of the author. Some will direct your attention to the topic of the writing lesson, for example, describing or comparing. Others will ask you to notice such things as transitions or organization.

Making Predictions and Drawing Inferences. Good readers constantly make predictions and confirm or refute them as they read. They also read between the lines. The questions in this section after each selection will help you practice those habits.

Making Judgments and Thinking Critically. The questions in this section will ask you to evaluate the effectiveness of the writer's work. For instance, you might be asked to find a passage that is strong description and to tell what makes the description effective for you. You might be asked "What if the writer changed . . . , would the essay be more or less effective?" Sometimes you'll be asked whether you agree or disagree with the writer.

Using New Words. Did you know that the best predictor of one's earning potential is the size of one's vocabulary? But money is not the main motivation for learning new words. You will want to increase your vocabulary and careful word usage in order to read more easily and with greater comprehension and to communicate more clearly in writing and speaking. Since words are important tools in communicating, you will want to work systematically at increasing your vocabulary and using words carefully. Activities in this section after each selection will help you.

There is a technique for increasing vocabulary that you can use throughout this book and with any reading you do. Create a personalized set of vocabulary cards as you go through this course. Add a few words each time you read an essay, not necessarily those from the list of definitions before each selection. Choose words you want to add to your writing and speaking vocabulary. Use small cards, perhaps index cards cut in half. Write the word you want to learn on one side of a card. Write an original sentence using the word and a definition on the other side. Don't try to memorize them. Listen and look for these words. Review them often to become familiar with them. Read them while you wait for the bus or your class to start, while you wait for your carpool or a doctor's appointment. Put them on tape and listen to them as you go to and from work or class. Review them often to make them words you can use.

Responding by Writing. Finally, following each selection there will be a section giving suggestions for writing an essay. The suggestions will be based in some way on the essay you read. Because the reading was selected to illustrate a writing lesson, you may be asked to use the specific method of development described in the lesson, such as comparison, to support a thesis.

Before you write an essay, look through your Idea Bank for ideas and do at least one of the discovery strategies you learned in Chapter 1. Then write a discovery draft. If your teacher decides to require a writing portfolio in your class, you may write discovery drafts for several assignments. Later you may select one of these discovery drafts to revise and edit. Your portfolio will include your discovery strategies, your discovery drafts, and the revised and edited essays.

Here is a sample of marking an essay as you read.

The Watcher at the Gates

Gail Godwin

Introduces the topic—the inner critic who keeps her from writing

I first realized I was not the only writer who had a restraining critic who lived inside me and sapped the juice from green inspirations when I was leafing through Freud's "Interpretation of Dreams" a few years ago. Ironically, it was my "inner critic" who had sent me to Freud. I was writing a novel, and my heroine was in the middle of a dream, and then I lost faith in my own invention and rushed to "an authority" to check whether she could have such a dream. In the chapter on dream interpretation, I came upon the following passage that has helped me free myself, in some measure, from my critic and has led to many pleasant and interesting exchanges with other writers.

quotation which defines the inner critic as the watcher

Freud quotes Schiller, who is writing a letter to a friend. The friend complains of his lack of creative power. Schiller replies with an allegory. He says it is not good if the intellect examines too closely the ideas pouring in at the gates. "In isolation, an idea may be quite insignificant, and venturesome in the extreme, but it may acquire importance from an idea which follows it. . . . In the case of a creative mind, it seems to me, the intellect has withdrawn its watchers from the gates, and the ideas rush in pell-mell, and only then does it review and inspect the multitude. You are ashamed or afraid of the momentary and passing madness which is found in all real creators, the longer or shorter duration of which distinguishes the thinking artist from the dreamer . . . you reject too soon and discriminate too severely."

Thesis

What watchers do

So that's what I had: a Watcher at the Gates. I decided to get to know him better. I discussed him with other writers, who told me some of the quirks and habits of their Watchers, each of whom was as individual as his host, and all of whom seemed passionately dedicated to one goal: rejecting too soon and discriminating too severely.

It is amazing the lengths a Watcher will go to keep you from pursuing the flow of your imagination. Watchers are notorious pencil sharpeners, ribbon changers, plant waterers, home repairers, and abhorrers of messy rooms or messy pages. They are compulsive looker-uppers. They are superstitious scaredy-cats. They cultivate self-important eccentricities they think are suitable for "writers." And they'd rather die (and kill your inspiration with them) than risk making a fool of themselves.

Examples of watchers

My Watcher has a wasteful penchant for 20-pound bond paper above and below the carbon of the first draft. "What's the good of writing out a whole page," he whispers begrudgingly, "if you just have to write it over again later? Get it perfect the first time!" My Watcher adores stopping in the middle of a morning's work to drive down to the library to check on the name of a flower or a World War II battle or a line of metaphysical poetry. "You can't possibly go on till you've got this right" he admonishes. I go and get the car keys.

ex. 1

ex. 2

Other Watchers have informed their writers that:

"Whenever you get a really good sentence you should stop in the middle of it and go on tomorrow. Otherwise you might run dry."

ex. 3

"Don't try and continue with your book till your dental appointment is over. When you're worried about your teeth, you can't think about art."

ex. 4

Another Watcher makes his owner pin his finished pages to a clothesline and read them through binoculars "to see how they look from a distance."

ex. 5

Countless other Watchers demand "bribes" for taking the day off: lethal doses of caffeine, alcoholic doses of Scotch or vodka or wine.

Ways to outsmart watchers

There are various ways to outsmart, pacify or coexist with your Watcher. Here are some I have tried, or my writer friends have tried, with success:

(1) Look for situations when he's likely to be off guard. Write too fast for him in an unexpected place, at an unexpected time. (Virginia Woolf captured the "diamonds in the dustheap" by writing at a "rapid haphazard gallop" in her diary.) Write when very tired. Write in purple ink on the back of a Master Charge statement. Write whatever comes into your mind while the kettle is boiling and make the steam whistle your deadline. (Deadlines are a great way to outdistance the Watcher.)

several examples of ea. way.

(2) Disguise what you are writing. If your Watcher refuses to let you get on with your story or novel, write a "letter" instead, telling your "correspondent" what you are going to write in your story or next chapter. Dash off a "review" of your own unfinished opus. It will stand up like a bully to your Watcher the next time he throws more obstacles in your path. If you write yourself a good one.

(3) Get to know your Watcher. He's yours. Do a drawing of him (or her). Pin it to the wall of your study and turn it gently to the wall when necessary. Let your Watcher feel needed. Watchers are excellent critics after inspiration has been captured; they are dependable, sharp-eyed readers of things already set down. Keep your Watcher in shape and he'll have less time to keep you from shaping. If he's really ruining your whole working day sit down, as Jung did with his personal demons, and write him a letter. On a very bad day I once wrote my Watcher a letter. "Dear Watcher," I wrote, "What is it you're so afraid I'll do?" Then I held his pen for him, and he replied instantly with a candor that has kept me from truly despising him.

Wow! "Fail," he wrote back.

EXPLORING FURTHER

1. *Group work.* Find the essay you revised for Exploring Further after Chapter 3. Exchange revised and edited drafts with another student in your group. In pencil edit the draft from the last sentence up. Use the dictionary and the handbook in this text when needed. Ask your instructor for help when you are unsure about an editing problem.
2. *Group work.* Exchange edited essays with another student, not the one whose essay you edited. Read this essay as you would an essay in Part 2. Mark it as you would in any careful reading. Use the marked copy of "The Watcher at the Gates" by Gail Godwin as a model.
3. *Writing activity.* Write a letter to your teacher. Explain what you have learned about reading and writing essays that you plan to use in Part 2. Give examples of what you learned and how. An honest appraisal and plan will make a more interesting report than a summary of Chapters 1 through 4.

PART 2

Reading and Writing Essays

CHAPTER 5

DESCRIPTION

USING DESCRIPTION TO DEVELOP YOUR ESSAYS

Almost every essay you write will include some description, so this is a very important writing lesson. Regarding description, we can note two kinds of advancing writers—those who supply wonderful details but do not make general statements to give their writing focus and organization and those who write in generalizations with few supporting details to develop their ideas. Generalizations, such as topic sentences in paragraphs and a thesis in an essay, control groups of sentences. They give the big picture to the reader. Details are the supporting information that paint the writer's picture in the reader's mind. They flesh out and explain the thesis and the supporting ideas. Think about vanilla ice cream without the vanilla or a movie without a sound track. An essay with just generalizations and few details is bland and soundless. There's no energy or excitement to it. A reader can get only a vague sense of the writer's experiences and meaning.

Create Vivid Description. To create good description, writers must look with concentrated attention, almost staring with x-ray vision, to notice the details that create a good description. If you're writing a lab report in chemistry class, you must observe closely every change of color, opaqueness, and odor in your test tube. If you're watching a sick child to determine when to call the doctor, you must observe any changes in color, temperature, respiration, and fluid intake. If you're watching films of the team you will play against next week, you must observe the fine points of your counterpart's speed, ability to change directions, and tendency to drop her shoulder before she swings. The skills of close observation are essential for many jobs, including the job of writing.

You can train yourself to observe closely by writing description, and you can train yourself to write good description by observing closely. Like reading and writing, observing and describing are interactive skills you can learn and develop. Here are some tips.

Use Strong Action Verbs. You can replace common verbs such as *walk* and *say* with more specific verbs that tell the reader more. You might replace "walk" with "swagger" or "amble" or "march" or "plod" or "skip." Instead of "say," you might write "shout" or "whisper" or "command" or "beg." If you find your draft is full of common verbs or weak verbs, such as *is, are, was,* and *were,* replace these with strong action verbs. Look at the verbs in italics in this passage by Garrison Keillor describing a humorous incident in his history of a mythical Minnesota town.

> After some debate, on the afternoon of the second day [of a blizzard], they *voted* to send Weiss. He was the only volunteer. They *gave* him one end of a ball of twine and out he went, the wind so strong he could hardly *stand.* He *fought* his way uphill, *missed* the path and had to *struggle* through deep drifts and thick brush, where the end of the string *tore* from his mitted hand, and he *panicked, broke* into a gallop, *ran* into the gale so fierce he couldn't *hear* himself *scream, ran, fell, ran* again, *hit* a tree, and finally *ran* full tilt into the porch of Main, which *caught* him at the knees, and *dragged* himself to the door and *crawled* in. (Garrison Keillor, *Lake Woebegon Days*, page 49)

Notice how much of the action and description is created by these strong verbs. Notice, too, that these verbs are simple past tense, not verb phrases with helping verbs, such as *would, is, was, were, has been,* and *have been.*

REMINDER

Avoid too many *be* verbs (*am, are, is, was, were*). Use strong action verbs. Use present or past tense (simple tenses without helping verbs) when you can. Write sentences with people and things doing the action of the verbs.

Use Specific Nouns. You studied using specific nouns and sensory details in Chapter 3 to revise for adequate development. Remember that words have many possible meanings. To communicate as clearly as possible with your reader, use the most exact word you can.

From General to Specific

animal	bird	eagle	golden eagle
fun	game	video game	Pac man
music	rock	soft rock	Phil Collins
food	dessert	cake	carrot cake

Look at the specific nouns (in italics) as Keillor's description continues. Read it, then look away, and recall as many of these objects as you can.

> He lay on the *floor,* too tired to move. He noticed the strange *light* in the cold *chapel,* as if he were *underwater,* a luminous predawn *light,* and saw a faint *corona* around the *window* above the *pulpit.* And then he heard *breathing* that was not his own, and stood up, and saw the *bear* sitting in the *doorway* to the *gallery,* and he turned away and fouled his *pants* and sat down. (page 49)

REMINDER

Readers remember specific, rather than general, nouns. To create a strong sensory experience for the reader, use specific nouns.

Use a Sensory Inventory. You learned in Chapter 3 to use your senses to help you focus on a wide range of specific details. You can use this sensory inventory as a prewriting strategy and as a revision strategy. Notice that the sense of movement, sometimes listed as a sixth sense, has been added here.

Sight: color, shape, size, number, movement
Hearing: volume, tone, rhythm, tempo, pitch
Smell: fresh, stale, piney, floral, sweaty
Taste: sweet, sour, salty, bitter, bland
Touch: rounded, smooth, ridged, sandy, pebbly
Movement: still, jerky, smooth, fast, plodding

Remember that your inventory is likely to contain more details than you want to use. Select those that add to the images and feelings you want to create in the reader's mind and that accomplish your purpose. Read the rest of Keillor's description below and notice which senses he draws on to create this vivid scene.

> The bear made no movement toward him and no sound except for its breathing, which was rough like a rasp of sandpaper. Spit fell from its mouth and froze into a pale milky beard. Its eyes were dim green

> coals. It was an immense bear, or seemed so to him who had never seen a bear, and staring at it, he could not move where he sat, not even to scratch his nose. The bear seemed to hold him in the power of its evil gaze and in the musky odor of bear. He sat, thinking no thought but that his death was close at hand. (page 49)

The bear's breathing ''like a rasp of sandpaper'' is a hearing detail. Its spit which froze ''into a pale milky beard,'' its eyes which were ''dim green coals,'' and its ''evil gaze'' are seeing details. The ''musky odor of bear'' is a smelling detail. Several moving details emphasize the stillness of the fear-filled moment: the ''bear made no movement,'' ''he could not move where he sat,'' ''the bear seemed to hold him.''

REMINDER

Take an inventory of sensory details when you describe a person, place, object, or event to re-create your experience as closely as you can for your reader. Select only those details that support your main point or mood.

Use Comparisons. Use comparisons to make the unfamiliar familiar and the abstract concrete. Good writers often use very colorful language. Intentionally or not, they often use figurative language to make their writing more powerful and vivid. They use figurative language, such as comparisons using *like* and *as*; metaphors, which are implied comparisons; and personification, which attributes life to inanimate objects or human qualities to animals. For instance, in the sample paragraph on page 86, both the storm and the porch are adversaries of Weiss. Instead of writing that Weiss ran into the porch, Keillor writes the porch ''caught him at the knees,'' as though the porch were a person, capable of physical action.

In the second paragraph the strange light in the cold chapel is likened to light seen underwater and ''a luminous predawn light.'' Both comparisons create an eerie mood.

In the third paragraph the bear's breathing is ''rough like a rasp of sandpaper.'' Its frozen spit looked like ''a pale milky beard.'' Its eyes looked like ''dim green coals.'' These comparisons create vivid details that allow us to experience a terror similar to Weiss's.

Organize Your Description with a Plan. Usually, an organizational pattern for your description will emerge as you write. The content and your purpose will create it for you. But sometimes you have to create it consciously, often in revising a draft. Here are two kinds of organizational patterns.

Time	Space
past, present, future	top to bottom
childhood, adulthood, old age	left to right
immediate, short term, long term	inside to outside
	person, family, social group

Keillor used time, the chronology of the event, to organize the description of Weiss and the bear.

Use Transitional Words. As you are revising descriptions, help your reader follow the organization of your description by providing transitional words. Transitional words that signal you are using time as an organizing pattern are these:

next	during	meanwhile
then	as	immediately
now	after	finally
before	at last	

In organizing by space you might use these words:

inside	beneath	as you enter
outside	beside	behind
on top of	next to	around

In organizing by contrasting details, you might use these words:

still	although
but	in contrast

REMINDER

Organize details logically, and give readers enough transitional words and phrases to make your organizational pattern clear to them.

The two parts of writing good description are observing and expressing. Don't underestimate a reader's need for details. Your readers need many details to understand fully what you experience through your senses, what you feel through your emotions, and what you think with your intelligence.

POINTS TO REMEMBER ABOUT DESCRIPTION

Observe closely.
Select only details that support your main point.
Use strong action verbs.
Use specific nouns.
Use sensory details.
Use comparisons.
Organize details logically.
Use transitional words.

The Flight of Eagles

N. Scott Momaday

This selection is from Momaday's Pulitzer Prize winning book *House Made of Dawn.* A member of the Kiowa tribe, Momaday has written several books about the tales and history of his people. He also writes contemporary stories about the problems of living in both Native American and the dominant cultures.

Thinking Before Reading

Beauty in nature moves many people and explains, in part, why so many enjoy hunting, fishing, hiking, or taking a walk. What in the natural world moves you with its beauty? Write a few sentences in your Idea Bank.

Expanding Your Vocabulary from Reading

Note: The number in parentheses following each word is the number of the paragraph of the reading in which the word first occurs.

erratic (1) uneven
dumb (1) mute, without words
cavorting (2) playing
hovered (2) floated as though suspended
feinting (2) moving in a misleading way
writhing (2) twisting as though in struggle

buoyed (2) held up by
hackles (2) stiff neck feathers
carrion (2) dead and decaying flesh
mote (2) speck of dust

1 Then he saw the eagles across the distance, two of them, riding low in the depths and rising diagonally toward him. He did not know what they were at first, and he stood watching them, their far, silent flight erratic and wild in the bright morning. They rose and swung across the skyline, veering close at last, and he knelt down behind the rock dumb with pleasure and excitement, holding on to them with his eyes.

2 They were golden eagles, a male and a female, in their mating flight. They were cavorting, spinning and spiraling on the cold, clear columns of air, and they were beautiful. They swooped and hovered, leaning on the air, and swung close together, feinting and screaming with delight. The female was full-grown, and the span of her broad wings was greater than any man's height. There was a fine flourish to her motion; she was deceptively, incredibly fast, and her pivots and wheels were wide and full-blown. But her great weight was streamlined and perfectly controlled. She carried a rattlesnake; it hung shining from her feet, limp and curving out in the trail of her flight. Suddenly her wings and tail fanned, catching full on the wind, and for an instant she was still, widespread and spectral in the blue, while her mate flared past and away, turning around in the distance to look for her. Then she began to beat upward at an angle from the rim until she was small in the sky, and she let go of the snake. It fell slowly, writhing and rolling, floating out like a bit of silver thread against the wide backdrop of the land. She held still above, buoyed up on the cold current, her crop and hackles gleaming like copper in the sun. The male swerved and sailed. He was younger than she and a little more than half as large. He was quicker, tighter in his moves. He let the carrion drift by; then suddenly he gathered himself and stooped, sliding down in a blur of motion to the strike. He hit the snake in the head, with not the slightest deflection of his course or speed, cracking its long body like a whip. Then he rolled and swung upward in a great pendulum arc, riding out his momentum. At the top of his glide he let go of the snake in turn, but the female did not go for it. Instead she soared out over the plain, nearly out of sight, like a mote receding into the haze of the far mountain. The male followed, and Abel watched them go, straining to see, saw them veer once, dip and disappear.

Jotting Down Your First Responses

1. Tell what happened in this scene in two or three sentences.
2. What images do you recall? Why?

3. Would you have stopped to watch the eagles? Why or why not?
4. If the reading selection reminded you of something you have seen, describe that scene or event briefly.

Checking Your Comprehension

1. Why does Abel crouch behind the rock?
2. What kind of eagles are they? What kind of snake is it?
3. What ritual are they performing?
4. How large was the female eagle?
5. What was the size and age of the male eagle?
6. What does the male do after the female drops the snake?

Understanding a Writer's Patterns

1. What is the implied thesis of this selection?
2. From whose point of view do we see the flight of the eagles?
3. What is the organizing pattern of this description?
4. Find these transitional words that add coherence: *but* (2 times), *then* (3 times), *at first,* and *instead.* Read the sentences before and after the transitional words, but omit the transitions. What change do you notice?
5. Strong verbs make this a powerful description. Circle all the verbs that show movement.
6. What specific nouns describe the female's flight?

Making Predictions and Drawing Inferences

1. Where does this scene take place? Why do you think so?
2. Why does the eagle drop the rattlesnake?
3. Why are there only two eagles?
4. Why do the eagles fly off?
5. What does this description of the flight reveal about Abel?
6. How long does this incident last?
7. What reasons might Momaday have had to write about this brief incident?

Making Judgments and Thinking Critically

1. Close your eyes and "see" the incident. Did this passage leave a strong image in your mental sight? What do you "see"? What sensory details, action verbs, specific nouns, or other techniques did Momaday use to create this strong effect on you?
2. Good description depends on close observation. Do you think Momaday has seen an incident similar to the one his character Abel sees? Why or

why not? If you had been with him viewing such an incident, would you have seen what he saw?

Using New Words

1. Here are some pairs of words: the word Momaday used and a substitute. For each pair read his sentence with the substitute. Why did he make the word choice he did? What is gained or lost with the substitute word?

Momaday's Word	Substitute Word
veering (paragraph 1)	flying
buoyed (paragraph 2)	supported
drift by (paragraph 2)	drop
sliding down (paragraph 2)	flying

2. Select five verbs from the reading that are completely unfamiliar to you but that you want to add to your writing and speaking vocabulary. Write original sentences using them.
3. As suggested in Chapter 4, make a vocabulary card for each of these verbs with the word on one side and a definition and an original sentence on the other side. Review the cards often to add these words to your vocabulary.

Responding by Writing

1. Describe a scene that you respond to with strong emotion—awe, admiration, gratitude, anger, tenderness, fear, disgust, joy, sadness, reverence, violence, dread. The scene you describe should be as brief as the one you read about here, just two or three minutes—at a concert, in the grocery store, in the park, at a doctor's office.
2. Describe your most treasured possession. Let your passion for this article leak out for the reader.
3. Observe two children playing a video game or dress-up, two people talking on the bus or in a bar, or any other interaction between two people or animals for no longer than five minutes. Write a vivid description of that encounter for an audience of this class.
4. Write an essay about the importance of powerful description in writing to make a point. Why is it needed? When is it needed? How does a writer create strong description? Use examples from Momaday's essay. Be sure to cite the author's name and the title of the selection (in quotation marks) in your discussion.

Be Careless, Reckless! Be a Lion! Be a Pirate! When You Write

Brenda Ueland

Brenda Ueland wrote, edited, and taught for more than seven decades. This selection is a chapter from *If You Want to Write.* In it you can see her kindness, intelligence, and humor as a person and as a teacher and learn more about writing description.

Thinking Before Reading

When you are learning to do something, do you respond better to being told what you do right or what you do wrong? Besides school-related learning, think about learning experiences in sports, music, jobs, and favorite activities. Write a few sentences in your Idea Bank about what helps you learn—praise and encouragement or error finding and correction.

Expanding Your Vocabulary from Reading

rollicking (6) joyful, playful
cocoon (6) case from which a butterfly or moth must escape after it is transformed from its larva stage
reckless (7) daring, without fear
timid (11) shy, afraid
glib (12) superficial, easy but shallow
whitecaps (20) waves that have broken into white foam
glacier (24) mountain of frozen snow and ice

1 Now I want to tell some things I have learned about writing from my class.

2 Though everybody is talented and original, often it does not break through for a long time. People are too scared, too self-conscious, too proud, too shy. They have been taught too many things about construction, plot, unity, mass and coherence.

3 My little brother wrote a composition when he was twelve and almost every third sentence was: "But alas, to no avail!" That is the sort of thing that everybody does for many years. That is because they have been taught that writing is something special and not just talking on paper.

4 Another trouble with writers in the first twenty years, is an anxiety to be effective, to impress people. They write pretentiously. It is so hard not to do this. That was my trouble.

5 For many years it puzzled me why so many things I wrote were preten-

tious, lying, high-sounding, and in consequence utterly dull and uninteresting. It was a regular horror to read them again. Of course they did not sell either, not one of them.

6 The explanation of this I learned from my class. Again and again after a few weeks of a kind of rollicking encouragement, they would all—even those whose work seemed hopelessly dull, trite, angular and commonplace—they would break through this, as from a cocoon, and write suddenly in a living, true, touching, remarkable way. It would happen suddenly, overnight. They would break through from composition-writing, theme-writing, to some freedom and honesty and to writing with what I call "microscopic truthfulness."

7 What made them do this? I think I know. I think I helped them to do it. And I did not do it by criticism, i.e., by pointing out all the mediocrities in their efforts (and so making them contract and try nervously to avoid all sorts of faults). I helped them by trying to make them feel freer and bolder. Let her go! Be careless, reckless! Be a lion, be a pirate! Write any old way.

8 Francesca helped me to understand this. When giving violin lessons she never tells a child that he is playing a bad note. Why do that? He knows it himself. All are trying to get nearer and nearer to the true pitch, to perfection, anyway. Why fix their attention on the avoidance of mistakes? It just tightens them up, contracts them, and makes them dislike lessons. Moreover, when they are thinking so vividly about the bad notes that they are warned to avoid, they play them again and again, just as a man learning to ride a bicycle goes into the tree he is afraid of. To play a note *truly,* as the simplest person knows, your mind must be on the true note, your Imagination hearing it as you *want* to play it.

9 I found that many gifted people are so afraid of writing a poor story that they cannot summon the nerve to write a single sentence for months. The thing to say to such people is: "See how *bad* a story you can write. See how dull you can be. Go ahead. That would be fun and interesting. I will give you ten dollars if you can write something thoroughly dull from beginning to end!" And of course no one can.

10 Try this yourself. It is a relief and you see then how you are not dull at all. It is just as guilty people who are always trying to be so good, should try to be very bad and resolve to stick to it. They would find then how natural it comes to them to be good and would not strain after it, which makes them hypocrites, though in a nice way.

11 Well, when I told the timid people in the class to see how badly they could write, it would give them the courage to venture a few little sentences. And since everybody who is human cannot say a sentence without revealing something—something mild or violent or waggish in their souls—or without having something fine in it, I would point this out. Courage would expand and they would gradually write more.

12 To show you how people's writing expands under encouragement I will tell you of some of my pupils. And what happened to these few, happened to all of them, except, as I said, to those to whom writing is an easy, glib, superficial babbling. For these are apt to give it up soon, before they break through the shell of glibness to what is true underneath.

13 Sarah McShane (I will call her) is Irish and unmarried and perhaps thirty. She is plainly and humbly dressed and because of her pallor and wide cheekbones and slanting eyes, she looks Chinese in a very beautiful way. She is so shy though that she cannot look at you directly. But when she talks she cannot keep her sad face immobile but has to smile widely and reluctantly every now and then, from both humor and bashfulness. She is a stenographer and works for nine hours a day in the sub-basement of a department store.

14 The first writing she showed me was a fat, little notebook about an inch and a half thick. It was filled with neat typing. ''Four Days in Glacier Park'' by Sarah McShane, 1935.

15 The first sentence was:

> ''There's always something fascinating about a passing freight train—the big, black engine with the ugly, bony arm on its side, the string of boxcars with sometimes a munificent supply of tramps sitting on the top, the heavy oil tanks, and bringing up in the rear, the stove-piped caboose. One and all, from youth to old age, will stand and watch it in silence and with interest.''

16 Well, as soon as I read: ''the big, black engine with the ugly, bony arm on its side,'' I knew that she could write. She could see and describe things. What she saw and felt, she put down. She did not have the impulse (as those of us who are much better educated) to put down what she felt and then think: ''No, it must be fancier than that, like: 'The engine like the charging steed of the prairies.' Or plainer, like: 'The engine with its high wheels.' ''

17 What she felt, what struck[1] her—''the ugly, bony arm on its side''—she put that down. That was a good beginning. I told her what a graphic description these few words were.

18 As I read along a little I came to this:

> ''The new air-conditioned train was a curiosity in itself—no cinders, no smoke, no stifling air—instead an even, cool, clean atmosphere. The interior was painted a delicate green, a bath- or bedroom shade. There were new silver racks for the suitcases, small, delicate, white lights for the nighttime, and soft, easy parlor-chair seats for the passengers. A de luxe layout it was indeed.''

[1] She didn't *try* to be struck. It just quietly happened. Another person would be quietly struck by something else.

19 From this I could see (and tell her) that she had a simple, open eye and noticed everything with quiet pleasure and put it down just as she saw it. And she had a quiet enthusiasm. She liked pretty colors: ''delicate green,'' ''silver.'' And this naïve truthfulness and enthusiasm, love for things, showed that there was a great deal of poetry and creative power in Sarah McShane, and that she was a simple and good person (which would also show in her writing and shine through it) and she chose simple, short and poetic words the way the poets in Ireland do. She was Irish and had a soft and very beautiful voice. That, I saw at once, meant that she could write too.

20 In the fat notebook she told everything that she noticed: what time trains pulled in and out, the towns passed.

> ''Familiar things slid by us as we chugged along from one Twin City to the other. Smokestacks and tanks; houses and trees; gaudy signboards; the big flour mills; the Mississippi River—all rolled by in panoramic review.
>
> ''Out at Wayzata,[2] Lake Minnetonka, a cold blue in color, lay stretched to the left, shivering in rolling whitecaps. Mirrored in its waters was the sun's golden face, haloed in an effect of glittering color.''

21 I like this description very, very much: ''shivering in rolling whitecaps.'' That was just right, because she told it as she felt it and so I felt it too. ''The sun's golden face haloed in an effect of glittering color.'' I liked that too. I like it now as I write it.

22 She told of the hotels they stayed in.

> '' 'How can I stay here,' I thought the minute I stepped inside the door. . . . The rough woodwork gave the room a cold, woodsy, rainy-day touch. . . . Martha was more easily pleased. She plunked herself down in the wicker chair and pulled off her shoes.

23 From this fine sentence I saw and knew then all about Martha.

> ''For dinner that first evening we had fruit compote, chicken okra (soup) with a heaped dish of crackers, grilled sirloin, a little bell-shaped cup with a ball of something in it, mashed potatoes, buttered peas, creamed onions, celery, buns and coffee, and for dessert, butterscotch ice cream and cake.''

24 Yes, she could write because she told everything simply, as it was, and didn't put on airs.

[2] This told me much about Sarah McShane. She worked in a sub-basement and was glad to see Wayzata, a commonplace little town fourteen miles from home. She felt joy and gratitude. This especially meant she could write. ''Enthusiasm is the All in All,'' said Blake. I must tell you this often.

"After studying the glacier, we spent some time watching the mountain goats on the rocky crags of the peaks. With the human eye we could only faintly make them out—white specks moving around. One lady, the wife of the big man, had a pair of field glasses, and she let us look through them.

"After I had looked through them, for a long time, she asked, 'Did you see the goats?'

" 'Yes.' I was merely being polite.

"But I didn't see the goats. I didn't see anything. All I saw was the blurred, watery surface of the lens. I have never been able to see any more than that through field glasses."

25 The class burst out laughing when I read this.

26 "You see you are funny too," I said to Sarah McShane. "See how they are all laughing? You write wonderfully well, and you have humor too!" She reddened with delight.

Jotting Down Your First Responses

1. Would you like to have Brenda Ueland as your writing teacher? Why or why not?
2. Ueland says that many students need to break out of their cocoons to write well. What is wrapping you up, like a cocoon, and keeping you from writing with fun and vigor?
3. What does Ueland mean "Be a lion, be a pirate!"? If you were giving this writing advice, what words might you use instead of "lion" and "pirate"?

Checking Your Comprehension

1. According to Ueland, what keeps people from writing with their natural talent and originality?
2. Where did she learn about writing?
3. What does the writer mean by writing with "microscopic truthfulness" (paragraph 6)?
4. According to Ueland, what happens when violin players or writers focus on mistakes?
5. What kind of treatment does Ueland believe helps people expand their writing?
6. Describe Sarah McShane.
7. What was the title of Sarah's notebook?
8. What qualities did Ueland admire in Sarah's writing?

Understanding a Writer's Patterns

1. What is Ueland's thesis?
2. Who is the intended audience? How do you know?
3. In Chapter 3 you learned about using your senses to develop an essay with details. Sarah, Ueland's student, used sight, hearing, smell, taste, and touch to write description. Find three examples of each sense in Sarah's writing (paragraphs 15, 18, 20, 22–24).
4. Sarah also used the sense of movement. Look at her writing again to find five action verbs that show movement.
5. Figurative language is powerful because the implied comparisons create mental pictures that we can see and feel. What two things are being compared in Sarah's phrases "the big, black engine with the ugly, bony arm on its side" (paragraph 15) and "the sun's golden face" (paragraph 20)?
6. Rewrite Sarah's sentence "Mirrored in its waters was the sun's golden face, haloed in an effect of glittering color." Use plain, literal language, removing the figurative language. Which do you like better and why?

Making Predictions and Drawing Inferences

1. What kind of school was Sarah attending? How do you know? Would you like to be a student there? Why or why not?
2. What was Ueland's philosophy of teaching?
3. How do you know Ueland had a sense of humor?
4. Ueland says she knows all about Martha from just two sentences in Sarah's writing. Read paragraph 22. What kind of person do you think Martha is? Why?
5. Why did Sarah write in her notebook?
6. How do you think Sarah responded as a person and as a writer to Ueland's comments about her writing?

Making Judgments and Thinking Critically

1. Did you like Sarah's writing? Why or why not?
2. Evaluate Ueland as a writing teacher. What actions or qualities make her a good or poor teacher? How would these actions or qualities affect your learning to write?
3. Did you like Ueland's writing? Why or why not?

Using New Words

1. Select any five lively verbs from the reading. Write an original sentence using each. For fun, try to use all five in one paragraph.

2. Select three words that you want to remember and be able to use. Make a vocabulary card for each word. Write the word on one side and a definition and an original sentence on the other. Review the cards often to add the words to your vocabulary.

Responding by Writing

1. Write a description of a vehicle, appliance, or other manufactured object that fills you with awe or deep appreciation, as Sarah wrote about the train engine. Possibilities: a special car, plane, motorcycle, skateboard, CD player, television set, escalator, tractor, household appliance. Try to create the strong feeling you have through vivid details and strong verbs.
2. Following Ueland's challenge to students, rewrite the description of a vehicle or appliance: ''See how *bad* a story you can write. See how dull you can be.''
3. Write a description of a scene from your past, recent or remote, that is full of people, energy, and high feelings, such as a concert, a family reunion, or a crowded department store on the first day of a sale. Before you write, identify the feeling or impression you want to come through your writing to an audience of your classmates.
4. Write an essay in which you evaluate Ueland's descriptive skills. Your thesis might be something like this: ''Be Careless, Reckless! . . .'' is (or is not) a strong piece of descriptive writing.

   In your essay give the author's name and the title of her essay. Use her full name the first time you refer to her; after the first reference you may use her last name alone. (Remember this rule as you write about other authors this semester.) Punctuate the title with quotation marks when you mention it in your essay. When you discuss Ueland's description, quote several phrases or sentences. Enclose quotations inside pairs of quotation marks.

Love, Brenda

George Sheehan

Runner, writer, and doctor, George Sheehan has written several books on running and life and writes a monthly column called Viewpoint for *Runner's World* in which this article appeared. Notice that it is a description of Brenda Ueland, the author of ''Be Careless, Reckless!''

Thinking Before Reading

Have you ever had a low point in your life—a time of difficult decisions, changes, or problems with your health, job, money, or relationships? Who raised your spirits? How? Write in your Idea Bank about the person and the kind of encouragement you received or would have liked to receive.

Expanding Your Vocabulary from Reading

mentor (1) trusted adviser or teacher
mysticism (3) belief in spiritual things
erudition (3) knowledge
disheveled (6) unkempt, untidy
amuck (6) crazy
valorous (9) brave
longevity (9) long life
benevolent (9) kind, of good will

1 One of the joys of my life was receiving letters from Brenda Ueland. When she died at the age of 94, I lost more than a good friend—I lost a mentor who inspired me to do my best. During the last 10 years of her life, Brenda sent messages that saw me through the bad days writers always have.

2 At precisely the time I needed help the most, this remarkable woman, whom I never met, would write me a note filled with praise and passion. And I would be rejuvenated. Her last letter I treasure the most.

3 "Dear, Dear Doctor Sheehan," she wrote. "I love you and the glory, the fire, the impassioned mysticism, the divine generosity and helpfulness, the erudition, the nobleness, the 18th-century grace and beauty of your columns.

4 "I am astonishingly old and have always felt an intense, loving responsibility for you. I am your coach and teacher, watching you carefully and alert every moment for your true path. *Avanti!* Forward! True love, Brenda."

5 Who would not have his head turned by such a letter? And surely it tells you more about Brenda than about me. In her early days, Brenda was known as a "free spirit." She was born, she said, with a genetic defect—"no herd instinct." She left the herd early and lived in Greenwich Village, where she studied art and began her career as a writer. She married a divorced man, had a child and then divorced her husband. She was a single working parent in the 1920s, a half-century before it became commonplace.

6 At times she flaunted her difference. "I was the first woman in the western world to have all my hair cut off," she wrote. "Wherever I went, a sea of white faces turned to gaze. That is just what I liked." She also was the first to escape from garters and corsets by wearing pants. In her 80's, she took an opposite tack, although she still dressed eccentrically. She explained it by

writing, "If I did not wear torn pants, orthopedic shoes, frantic disheveled hair—that is to say, if I did not tone down my beauty—people would go mad. Married men would go amuck."

7 But Brenda didn't tone down the youth and beauty of her mind, and she gave freely of it in her letters. "We—yourself and I—" she wrote, then 88, "are in such burning agreement about everything—Soul and Body, walking, running, Beauty, God's sweet air."

8 She also wrote about her own exercise. "People ask me how much I walk every day around Lake Harriet [3 miles]. I say, 'Once for the body, once for the soul.' " When she could, she preferred to run. "There is something easier about running, more limber, because it is more like dancing. It's more interesting, too. Perhaps, prehistorically, it was our normal gait."

9 Of course, she was an expert on aging. "I follow all you say about running, marathons, racing, suffering, grim battles, the will, the victories. I apply these things to myself, to the valorous rear-guard action against old age. I don't care a button about longevity. Mere longevity is a bore from hell. But I want to be very clear, benevolent, useful and active, and avoid, if possible, the muddy hideousness of old age."

10 In one letter she recalled the beginning of her addiction to exercise: "I discovered this in 1913. I was a jovial, too-fat girl of 22. A great man and a great walker said to me, 'Walk to your newspaper every day. Eat no lunch and walk home.' I did so. Nine miles a day. Laziness gone. Thyroid working. Tireless, sound sleep, good figure emerging, energy, red cheeks, ideas, reckless daring, taking cheerful high dives into the Unknown."

11 That will be the way I will remember Brenda. Wherever she is now (and she believed firmly in the hereafter) she is most certainly as she always was—filled with reckless daring, taking high dives into the Unknown.

Jotting Down Your First Responses

1. From this description of Brenda Ueland, do you think you would have liked her? Why or why not?
2. This article is a eulogy, a public statement to praise the achievements or character of a person who has recently died. What kinds of things would you like to be remembered for?
3. As you read this selection, if you thought of someone, living or dead, whom you particularly admire, write a praising description of that person.

Checking Your Comprehension

1. Where did Sheehan get the quotations he uses in this article?
2. What does the phrase "to have your head turned" mean? Why did Ueland's letter turn his head (paragraph 5)?

3. What does it mean to say that Ueland was a free spirit? What did Ueland mean when she said she had no ''herd instinct'' (paragraph 5)? What actions show this character trait?
4. What did Ueland look like as a young woman? As an old woman?
5. What were her goals for old age?
6. What did Ueland do? What life actions does Sheehan select to show what kind of person Ueland was?

Understanding a Writer's Patterns

1. What is Sheehan's thesis?
2. What is his purpose? Who is his audience?
3. Why is ''Love, Brenda''an appropriate title?
4. ''Taking cheerful high dives into the Unknown'' (paragraph 10) is Ueland's metaphor for the way she lived. What does she mean by ''high dives'' and ''the Unknown''? What is the implied comparison? What are some examples of ''high dives into the Unknown'' from her life?

Making Predictions and Drawing Inferences

1. Read the first sentence. What predictions can you make about the article?
2. How did Brenda Ueland know George Sheehan?
3. What activity did Sheehan and Ueland have in common?
4. What character traits, other than her free spiritedness, do her actions reveal?
5. In paragraph 6 Ueland says she cut off her hair. What does that example tell you about the time period in which she was a young woman? What does it tell you about her?

Making Judgments and Thinking Critically

1. Sheehan's monthly column where this article was first printed is called ''Viewpoint.'' Columns called Viewpoint are opinion pieces. Is this description of a person an opinion piece? If so, what is Sheehan's viewpoint (opinion) about Brenda Ueland?
2. Is this an effective eulogy (speech or article of praise for the dead)? Why or why not?

Using New Words

1. Choose five words from the essay that you want to know. Write original sentences using them or, following Ueland's advice to be bold and have fun, write a paragraph using all five words.

2. Choose three words you want to add to your speaking and writing vocabulary. Make vocabulary cards for these three words so you can review them quickly and frequently. Write the word on one side of the card and a definition and an original sentence on the other. Use your waiting times throughout the day to review your vocabulary.

Responding by Writing

1. Write a description of a person you know well who has a strong personality—either someone you like or don't like. Think of qualities of mind and spirit as well as those of appearance and behavior. Try to capture the person on paper so that an audience of classmates has a strong impression of the person and understands how you feel about this person and why.
2. Write a letter with energy and passion, like Brenda's, to encourage someone whom you may or may not know personally.
3. Write a description of a person who loves his or her job, hobby, or volunteer work. Interview this person to find out why he or she loves the work or hobby and take notes. You might ask these questions: What is your job (hobby) like? How long have you had it? How did you get started doing it? What do you like about it? What skills or experiences prepared you for it? What skills or abilities did you develop from this job or hobby? What kind of person is good at this job or hobby?

   Although you will paraphrase or summarize most of what your subject says, quote the exact words of the person at least once, either a phrase or a complete sentence. Use quotation marks before and after the exact words of the speaker.
4. Write an essay about Brenda Ueland. Use both "Be Careless, Reckless! . . ." and "Love, Brenda" for your description. Remember to use the titles of the articles and the names of the authors in your essay. Use quotation marks to punctuate the titles and quotations. Use at least one brief quotation from one of the two articles. Before you begin, decide if you would have liked her or not and let that opinion of her come through.

First United Methodist Church

Lynn Kleifgen

Lynn Kleifgen is a full-time wife and mother and a part-time student. She wrote the following essay to an audience of classmates to re-create for them a place from her childhood that remains a powerful visual and emotional image for her.

Thinking Before Reading

Think of a place from your childhood that is a mental photograph for you. It might be your grandmother's living room, the front stoop of the first place you remember living, or the skating rink where you spent every Saturday morning. Write a few sentences in your Idea Bank about this place and why it has remained a vivid memory.

Expanding Your Vocabulary from Reading

dominate (3) command attention to
regal (3) elegant, royal
diminish (3) lessen
stifle (5) squelch, hold down
cascading (6) spilling over or flowing over as in waterfalls
bind (7) tie together
awe (7) reverence, deep respect
caresses (8) touches gently

1 There is a little country church in a little town not far from here. People driving past, if they notice it at all, might think it a quaint old building, the type of old country church you would expect a congregation to have built around the turn of the century. For that is exactly what it is—a little Methodist church built about 1900 in Cedar Hill, Texas, my hometown.

2 When most people think of home, they think of the place their parents live. This is true for me. But I also have another home, a home where I am always loved and nurtured and safe. No matter how far I travel or how long I've been gone, this church will always be my home, the place where I grew up.

3 Warm autumn colors dominate the three regal arches of stained-glass, which are the most striking feature of the old white clapboard church. A large bell-tower rises above the heavy oak double-doors of the entrance. Inside, it is a combination of smooth cream-colored walls accented with warm oak Victorian trim and pews. The choir loft rises above and behind the altar which is recessed into the front of the church. It is not an unusual design for that period, but not being unusual does not diminish in any way the charm and character of this old church. In its long history, it seems to have absorbed personality from each person who walked through its heavy oak doors.

4 My first memories of this church are as a small child, sleeping in pews taller than my head, of pillars rising forever skyward to meet the towering ceiling, of people standing, then sitting, then standing again. What place is

this? It's awfully odd. It wasn't until I was much older that these memories came back, when suddenly I recognized from a child's point of view, that the strange place from my childhood was my family's favorite pew.

5 When I was a teenager, the place to be was in the back. That's where we could talk and laugh and giggle—until I felt my mother's glare all the way from the choir. Her glare couldn't reach that far in ordinary buildings. What power assisted her here? From the back, you could also see Mrs. Flyrr in the choir, nodding and dozing all during the sermon. It was hard to stifle our giggles. I could never understand why she didn't fall completely out of her chair. Some unseen hand surely took pity on her and kept her sitting upright. The back was certainly a fun place to be.

6 Sunday evenings were my Granny's favorite time because we sang lots of hymns. She was always there in the fourth pew, right side. In the winter, this southern window turned the sunlight cascading through the stained-glass into ribbons of golds and reds and blues which seemed to be loving fingers which stroked and caressed her hair. Together we would sing, *Blest Be the Tie That Binds,* while the ribbons of color danced across the hymnal she held in her hand. Oh, how she loved to sing! Her voice still rings across the pews and calls to me, "hon-nee," and I still can see the tears that were in my Dad's eyes, the day they laid her at the altar. Now the ribbons seem sad when they dance across the empty pew and there are tears on the windows though most people think it is the evening dew.

7 Like my mother and my sister, I was married in this church. On a brisk and cool November afternoon with autumn leaves swirling around our feet, we gathered in its sanctuary to bind our lives together. It is impossible to describe the feeling of walking down that aisle where so many others had walked. I felt thankful for those before me whose lives had made mine possible and in awe of how my life would affect those coming later. As we started down the aisle, a surprising peace came over me. Along with my Dad, the church was holding my hand.

8 Through happy times and sad times, this little building has always been there. Never changing, always constant, it is a part of our family, it is part of me. I like to return to the church when no one else is around, to spend some time together, my old friend and I. I walk among its pews and hear the organ's music. The sunshine through the windows still caresses Granny's pew. The altar still rings with laughter from little girls dressed as angels and boys draped in shepherds' robes. And my heart overflows with love when I recall the many special times this church and I share. This place binds us all together, and we know we are not alone.

9 In ancient times, people believed the world was flat and the sun revolved around the earth. Today some believe that God doesn't appear any more like he did in Biblical times. As I sit in the church and feel its warmth, I wonder how they could be so blind.

Jotting Down Your First Responses

1. As you read, what additional details did you remember about the place you wrote about in your Idea Bank?
2. What details do you recall from Kleifgen's description? Why?
3. If you could be any place you could imagine, what would this ideal place be? Describe this fantasy.

Checking Your Comprehension

1. What place is described by Kleifgen? Where is it?
2. Why is this place important to her?
3. What are three features of the outside of the building?
4. What are three features of the inside?
5. What did Kleifgen recall from her viewpoint as a child?
6. What two memories did she recall from her teen years?
7. What person is most strongly remembered in connection with this place? What details does Kleifgen provide about this person?
8. What event did she recall from her adult memories of this place?
9. What does Kleifgen do when she returns to this church?
10. Why does she like to return?

Understanding a Writer's Patterns

1. The thesis of this essay is implied rather than stated. Write a thesis statement for the essay that captures Kleifgen's topic and her opinion or attitude about the topic.
2. In paragraph 3 Kleifgen describes the appearance of the church. What organizational pattern does she use?
3. The rest of the description follows another organizational pattern. What is it?
4. What effect does the repetition of two images—windows and ribbons—have in paragraph 6?
5. The image of windows is repeated from what earlier paragraph? What effect does this repetition have?
6. Because Kleifgen describes a place over a period of time, there are transitional phrases that emphasize time in paragraphs 4, 5, 6, and 7. What are they?
7. Make a list of sensory details in paragraph 6.
8. Action verbs strengthen Kleifgen's description. ''Ribbons of color'' (paragraph 6) do two things; what are the two verbs that express these actions?
9. Sunlight (paragraphs 6 and 8) does two things. What are the two verbs that express these actions?

10. Look at the last three sentences in paragraph 8, beginning "The altar . . ." List six action verbs.

Making Predictions and Drawing Inferences

1. Reread the first paragraph of the essay. Recall what you expected to follow in the essay. What did you correctly predict? What was different from what you expected?
2. How old do you think Kleifgen is? Why?
3. What is Kleifgen's definition of home?
4. What are three sentences that tell or suggest how she feels about this place? Do these sentences give a consistent feeling about the church?
5. In the last paragraph what does Kleifgen "see" and why are others blind?

Making Judgments and Thinking Critically

1. Would this description of a place be as effective if the people were omitted from it? Why or why not?
2. If Kleifgen gave a more detailed picture of the church at one time instead of describing the church over time, would the place be more or less vivid to you? Why?
3. Is this description more like a photograph or a videotape recording? Explain.

Using New Words

1. In paragraph 8 substitute synonyms for *caresses, overflow,* and *binds.* Do the substitutions change the meaning of the sentences in any way? Explain.
2. Choose three words from this essay you want to add to your writing and speaking vocabulary and make vocabulary cards for them. Write a word on one side of the card and a definition and an original sentence on the other side.

Responding by Writing

1. Write an essay describing a place with special meaning to you, perhaps the place you wrote about in your Idea Bank before reading. Write for an audience who also knows this place, someone you know well. Select details that support and reveal this meaning to your audience. Review the patterns for organizing description in the first part of this chapter to help you organize the details you select.

2. Write an essay for an audience of this class, who do not know the place you described in #1 and who do not share any experience about this place with you. Consider using people, action verbs, specific nouns, and comparisons to heighten the description for this audience.
3. If you have read several descriptive essays in this chapter, decide which you think has the most vivid description. (This may or may not be the essay whose topic you like best.) Write an essay for an audience of your teacher telling which essay has the most vivid description. Support your thesis with examples from the essay. Quote phrases and words more than whole sentences. Use the title and author in your thesis sentence. Use quotation marks to punctuate the title and the quotations.

CHAPTER

6

NARRATION

USING NARRATION TO DEVELOP YOUR ESSAY

Narration (telling a story about something that happened) is the most frequent way, besides description, to explain to others. You may tell what happened at work when your friend was fired, at the doctor's office as the nurse drew a blood sample, or at the record store while you waited in line. You have a purpose in telling these stories; perhaps you want your listener to feel angry about the firing, sympathize with your illness, or support your demand for service. You tailor the story to your specific listener and purpose. For example, if you want to tell someone why you are late, you might tell briefly about your wait in line at the record store. But if you want your listener to share your sense of frustration at your long wait and to support your decision to complain to the manager about the service, you might give a longer version with many details about indecisive customers and bumbling clerks. Your purpose would guide which version of the story you tell.

In writing, too, you frequently can use narration to explain. For one thing, you are experienced at telling stories; you can draw on that oral experience as you write narratives. For another thing, you can count on readers' interest because, like listeners, readers enjoy stories too. Consider the popularity of television sitcoms, movies, and magazines with stories about the lives of famous people. Narration has strong reader interest and draws on your strength as an oral storyteller.

WRITING NARRATION

In writing, you will have several uses for narration. The topic, audience, and purpose will help you decide when to use narration. You can use a brief story, or anecdote, at the beginning of an essay to introduce the topic, lead into the thesis, and hook the reader's interest. You can use brief narratives within an essay to support a point you are making. You can also use essay-length narratives to develop a single point or feeling. The readings in this chapter are of this third type.

When you decide to use a narrative to explain, use some of the discovery strategies in Chapter 1 to recall an appropriate story and the facts and details you need to develop your narrative. You might use brainstorming to recall a story. Then you might use the five W questions to discover specific content. Whether you are writing brief or extended narratives, you can use what you know about writing description and the following guidelines to write vivid narratives.

Focus on Purpose. Focus on your purpose and select important events and details that contribute to that purpose, and leave out the rest. When you have decided what story you will use in an essay, you face some important decisions. You can't tell everything and have an effective narrative. Have you ever listened to people who give too much information or wander off into side stories when they tell a story? Did you feel impatient and want to say something like ''Go on! Go on! Get to the point!'' Such storytellers lack a focus around which to select the details they include. An effective narrative has a focus, and the writer must have a clear sense of purpose to create that focus. When you use narration, be sure to have a point clearly in mind. Then select only those details and only that information that contribute to the mood of the story, the impression you want to make on the reader, or the point you want to support.

In a passage in *Lake Woebegone,* Garrison Keillor focuses on ''the pleasure of hearing a rotten tomato hit someone in the rear end.'' All of the narrative facts and descriptive details contribute to sharing that pleasure with his readers.

> On this morning in August when I am thirteen, it's hot by ten o'clock. I poked along over the Post Toasties as long as I could, then mother sent me out to pick tomatoes. Rudy and Phyllis were already out there. I picked one and threw it at a crab apple tree. It made a good *splat.* The tree was full of little crab apples we'd have to deal with eventually, and a few of them fell. My brother and sister stood up and looked: what did you *do*? we're gonna tell. (page 135)

Keillor has set the scene. We know when and where the story takes place: a hot summer morning in the country. We know the writer's attitude from his poking over his cereal and chucking a tomato at the crab apple tree: he's feeling reluctant about doing his chore. We also know his brother and sister and he are feeling crabby with each other. We can predict from the wonderful sound detail "splat" that we'll hear more of that sound in this story. In just a few well-chosen details and actions, Keillor has set the tone of the story. He has a clear focus and purpose—to amuse his readers with a story of a sibling squabble and its sometime pleasure.

REMINDER

An effective narrative has a clear focus related to the writer's purpose. The writer selects only events and details that contribute to that focus and that help accomplish that purpose.

First Person Point of View. Use first person "I" when it is appropriate. Where does a writer find narratives to use in writing essays? You may use stories you have heard or draw from your own experiences. You may have been the observer or a participant in the story. In either case, you may write in the third person "he" or "she" or in the first person "I." You decide what point of view would be most effective in your essay.

First person "I" accounts are often the strongest writing students do and they have strong reader appeal. Notice the strong personal voice with the "I" as Keillor continues his narrative.

> I picked the biggest tomato I saw and took out a few more crab apples. Then I threw a tomato at my brother. He whipped one back at me. We ducked down by the vines, heaving tomatoes at each other. My sister, who was a good person, said, "You're going to get it." She bent over and kept on picking. (page 135)

The "I" tells us that this is clearly Keillor's story, told from his point of view. If the story were told by his mother, the focus and tone of the narrative might be angry and parental. If the story were told by a passing neighbor, the focus and tone might be detached and mildly amused. Either spectator to the event would use the third person "he" to tell the story, and Keillor could have told the story from the third person point of view. If he had done so, the story would read like this: "*He* picked the biggest tomato and took out a few more crab apples. Then *he* threw a tomato at *his* brother." Notice how the first person "I" account of the story has more energy and humor than the third person account with "he."

REMINDER

First person ''I'' is appropriate and effective in many writing situations. It is often the most direct and powerful way to write a narrative.

Use Consistent Verb Tense. Use verb tense consistently in a narrative; avoid unnecessary shifts in tense. In a narrative verb tense is important. You may use present tense or past tense to tell about a past event. Some present tense verbs are *run, hear, remember, dance, hike,* and *wash.* The past tense forms of these verbs are *ran, heard, remembered, danced, hiked,* and *washed.*

Notice the tense of the verbs in the next part of Keillor's narrative.

> What a target! She *was* seventeen, a girl with big hips, and bending over, she *looked* like the side of a barn.
>
> I *picked* up a tomato so big it sat on the ground. It *looked* like it had sat there for a week. The underside *was* brown. Small white worms *lived* in it. It *was* very juicy. I *had* to handle it carefully to keep from spilling it on myself. I *stood* up and *took* aim, and *went* into the wind-up, when my mother at the kitchen window *called* my name in a sharp voice. I *had* to decide quickly. I *decided.* (page 135)

These verbs are all in the past tense, but the story could be told in the present tense, as though it is happening right now. ''The underside *is* brown. Small white worms *live* in it. It *is* very juicy.'' Either is correct. However, whichever you decide to use in your narrative, be consistent. Shifts in tense can cause your readers to lose the story line or become confused about the chronology of events.

REMINDER

Avoid unnecessary shifts in verb tense because readers can become lost easily. When you are revising and editing, check your verbs for consistency of tense.

Use Dialogue. Use dialogue to tell the exact words of a speaker. To focus on an intense moment in your story, give the exact words of a speaker. To bring your narrative to life and avoid confusion when there are two speakers or important conversational content, use dialogue rather than paraphrasing the speakers' words. Compare these two sentences:

> My sister, who was a good person, said that I was going to get in trouble.
> My sister, who was a good person, said, "You're going to get it."

The second sentence, as Keillor wrote it, directly quotes the speaker instead of paraphrasing the speaker's words. In the following passage, he again chooses to use dialogue to heighten a dramatic moment instead of writing "Mother yelled to my sister. . . ." Notice the force of directly quoting a speaker's words.

> A rotten Big Boy hitting the target is a memorable sound. Like a fat man doing a bellyflop, and followed by a whoop and a yell from the tomatoee. She came after me faster than I knew she could run, and I took off for the house, but she grabbed my shirt and was about to brain me when Mother yelled "Phyllis!" and my sister, who was a good person, obeyed and let go and burst into tears. I guess she knew that the pleasure of obedience is pretty thin compared to the pleasure of hearing a rotten tomato hit someone in the rear end.

When you write dialogue or use direct quotations, remember to identify the speaker's words clearly by putting quotation marks around them. When you are relating a conversation between two or more persons, begin a new paragraph each time a new speaker starts to speak.

REMINDER

Dialogue brings a narrative to life and reduces confusion about who said what to whom.

ORGANIZING A NARRATIVE

Narratives are easy to organize because in essays the events in the narrative usually follow a straightforward time sequence—from the beginning to the end, from the past to the present. In conversation or informal writing, you may loop back to an earlier event, signaling with something like "Oh, I forgot to tell you . . ." or "Oh, yes, before that . . ." In fiction, a writer may begin a story at one point, flashback to an earlier time, and tell the story bringing the readers up to the beginning place of the story. In essay writing, however, you should put events or information in a chronological order.

Use Transitions. Use transitions to show time sequence. In addition to putting events in chronological sequence, you should give your readers clear signs about the sequence. You will often provide such verbal signs for your readers without thinking about them. However, in revising check your draft closely for places where the time sequence might slip away from your reader. Provide clear connections in each sentence to the idea, event, or information that came before. To signal the time relationship of events in a narrative, use transitional words, such as

first	after	immediately
next	before	finally
then	meanwhile	at last

These words provide coherence so that a reader can follow your narrative easily.

POINTS TO REMEMBER ABOUT NARRATION

Decide on a focus or main impression you want to create.
Select only those details that develop your focus.
Use first person "I."
Be consistent with verb tense, usually present or past tense.
Use dialogue.
Organize your narrative chronologically.
Use transitions to show time order of events.

"I Wanted To Be Treated Like a Human Being"

Maria Ragghianti

Rosa Parks, whose act of personal courage sparked the civil rights movement in the 1950s, had been a heroine of Maria Ragghianti's adolescence. Years later Ragghianti has the chance to find out what kind of person Rosa Parks was then and is now and what really happened that day. This is her report.

Thinking Before Reading

Have you ever taken a risk for something or someone you believed in? Have you ever stood up to a parent, teacher, boss, or peers to right a wrong? Write in your Idea Bank about the incident or about a time you wish you had stood up for your belief.

Expanding Your Vocabulary From Reading

poised (1) without embarrassment or self-consciousness
regal (1) with the dignity of royalty
modesty (1) absence of self-importance
aura (1) distinctive air or quality
bigotry (2) prejudice, intolerance
figurehead (3) leader in appearance only
daunt (4) intimidate, discourage
contradictions (5) opposing statements or situations
catalyst (17) an action that sparks a later event
vanguard (20) leading position in a trend or movement

1 I first met Rosa Parks in New York City in 1986 at a high-powered gathering of feminist and political leaders. My impression remains vivid. She was poised, even regal, yet there was a distinct modesty and an aura of spirituality about her.

2 Thirty-six years ago, on a bus in Montgomery, Ala., Rosa Parks refused to give up her seat to a white man, defying a Southern tradition of decades. To appreciate that act we have to remember that the mid-1950s were a time when the Ku Klux Klan was in its heyday, when the 1954 Supreme Court ruling against segregation in the schools had fanned the bigotry of white supremacists, and when lynchings of blacks in the Deep South were being widely reported. If the precise moment of the birth of the Civil Rights movement can be isolated, it may be said that it was from this one woman's singular, irreducible act of courage.

3 As an adolescent, my youthful idealism had been fired when I read about Rosa Parks. Our brief introduction that evening in 1986 rekindled my imagination: Who was Rosa Parks, really? Who was she then? Who is she now? How could someone so apparently shy have been bold enough to challenge a whole system embedded in racism? Was she a figurehead for the Civil Rights movement—perhaps, as some have argued, only a plant for the NAACP, someone whose act was part of a master plan designed to foster a call for the desegregation of public transportation? Or was she the authentic heroine of my youth? I wanted to find out for myself.

4 My search finally ended late last year in Detroit. It had not been easy to find her, and it was even harder to fit into her schedule. At the age of 78, Rosa Parks maintains a level of activity that would daunt someone half her age. We met outside a church where she was appearing, and the voices of children filled the air.

5 I was struck by the curious blend of seeming contradictions that she presented. She is grandmotherly in appearance, her hair a silvery crown, yet

she retains the grace of a young woman. Rather than the imposing physical presence that one might expect, she is petite and slim. And she is soft-spoken—so soft-spoken that one must lean toward her to hear her words.

6 I asked her about that fateful day, a Thursday. Had she known when she got up that morning what lay ahead? Had there been a plan?

7 "I wasn't planning to be arrested at all," she said. "I would rather not have been arrested, of course. I had a full weekend planned. It was December, Christmastime. It was the busy time of year [she was a tailor's assistant in a men's clothing store in Montgomery and secretary of the city's branch of the NAACP], and I was preparing for the weekend workshop for the Youth Council."

8 She turned slightly, and an almost wistful expression crossed her face. Then, I was startled by a revelation that she offered almost offhandedly. Suddenly, she was talking about *another* day, *another* time, *another* bus—but the same driver.

9 "The same driver, back in 1943, had evicted me from the bus," she said. "It was not about a seat that time. He wanted me to get off the bus and go around and get back on. I wouldn't do it."

10 In those days in the South, black people were expected to board the front of the bus, pay their fare, then get off and walk outside the bus to reboard on the back. But the back was already crowded, she explained—standing room only—and she couldn't help but notice that black passengers were standing even on the back steps of the vehicle. It was apparent that it would be all but impossible to reboard at the back. Besides, it was no secret that bus drivers sometimes drove off and left black passengers behind, even after accepting their fares. Rosa Parks spontaneously decided to take her chances. She paid her fare in the front of the bus, then walked down the aisle, hoping to unobtrusively find a spot as close to the back as she could get.

11 "When he saw what I was doing," she said, "he got up and ordered me to get off the bus. He wanted me to go around to the back door and get back on. When I refused, he came back and grabbed my coat sleeve—not my arm, just the sleeve. I didn't really resist at that point. But I wasn't going to get off and go around. My purse fell, and one or two things fell out. I picked them up, even though I was afraid he would attack me physically. He was livid with anger."

12 She was evicted from the bus that day but not arrested. For 12 years, she never forgot what that driver looked like. "I saw him occasionally when I was waiting for the bus," she said, "but I didn't ride the bus if he was driving." But on Dec. 1, 1955, she was in a hurry. She had a lot of things to get done. When the bus came, she got on without paying attention to the driver.

13 It is clear that what happened next was not part of a preplanned strategy. "I had had enough," she stated simply. "I wanted to be treated like a human being."

14 The bus already was crowded when she boarded. "There was a [black] man sitting next to the window," she recalled. "I sat next to him. There were two [black] women across the aisle. We went through one stop without being disturbed. But at the second stop, a [white] man got on and had to stand. He was not saying anything at all, not a word, but the bus driver noticed him." Immediately, the driver ordered the four black passengers to surrender their seats so the white man could sit down. The man beside Rosa Parks stood up after the driver spoke a second time.

15 "The driver said, 'Y'all make it light on yourselves,' " she remembered. "The two women moved then, but I moved next to the window. He asked me to move. I said, 'No.' Several people [all black] got off the bus." She does not comment on the obvious: Only the black passengers were fearful of what might happen next.

16 "When the [two] policemen came on the bus and wanted to know what was wrong, the driver pointed to me and said, 'That one won't stand up.' I asked, 'Why do you all treat us this way?' One of the policemen said, 'I don't know—the law is the law.'

17 "I stood up. One took my purse, the other my shopping bag. I got in the back of the police car." She was taken to City Hall, booked, fingerprinted, jailed and fined. Her arrest and subsequent appeal were the catalyst for a year-long boycott of the city's buses by blacks, who made up 70 percent of their riders. The boycott, which brought Martin Luther King Jr. to national prominence, ended when a Supreme Court order declared Montgomery's segregated seating laws unconstitutional.

18 Fred Gray, who defended Rosa Parks at the time, is still practicing law in Tuskegee, Ala. I asked him what it was like to represent her. "Mrs. Parks was very easygoing and cooperative," he recalled. "She was a lovely person to work with."

19 I had been unable to shake my impression of her as shy, and I asked whether he agreed. "Reserved," he said. "Not really shy. She's forceful."

20 Little has been written about Rosa Parks' life outside of the bus boycott. Her husband, Raymond Parks, was an activist at a time when to be one was to invite danger. He was in the vanguard of those who fought for the release and vindication of the Scottsboro Boys, nine black youths who had been convicted on trumped-up charges of raping a white woman in 1931. He and Rosa were married in 1932, and he encouraged her to become involved in the NAACP in the early '40s.

21 Although they never had children, Rosa Parks always has been committed to children. Today, she spends much of her time at the Rosa and Raymond Parks Institute for Self Development. Founded in Detroit in 1987, the institute is a nonprofit foundation that focuses on the "average" child, the one who often comes out on the short end of social programs. Mrs. Parks and the institute's board members believe it is the average child who may profit most

from the lessons of history and from programs designed to foster awareness and involvement. The institute also provides scholarships for youths.

22 Perhaps the most unusual of the many programs the institute offers (co-sponsored with other Michigan groups) is the Reverse Freedom Tour, an annual event that brings together teenagers from the Deep South and the North and takes them by bus on a cross-country trip that retraces major landmarks of Civil Rights history—including the site in Montgomery where Rosa Parks refused to get off the bus. The tour's highlight is a retracing of the Underground Railroad, the route of escaped slaves, both in the U.S. and Canada.

23 Tamica Mingo, 17, whose dream is to work in television, recalled how Rosa Parks had joined them on the Reverse Freedom Tour. "She never got tired of us," Tamica said, "She was willing to answer all the questions we had."

24 "Even now," Tamica added, "Mrs. Parks doesn't think of herself as a heroine. She did it because it was right. She doesn't see herself as the Mother of the Civil Rights movement, but *I* see her as that. All children do."

Jotting Down Your First Responses

1. What admired person would you like to meet and interview? Under what conditions can you see yourself seeking this person and interviewing him or her? What would you ask?
2. If you met Rosa Parks, what would you want to know?
3. What do you think you would have done if you had been on that bus in Montgomery, Alabama, in 1955 with Rosa Parks?

Checking Your Comprehension

1. Why did Maria Ragghianti want to find Rosa Parks?
2. Where was Mrs. Parks and what was she doing?
3. What did she look like?
4. What surprised Ragghianti when Rosa Parks began to tell her about that famous day?
5. Two incidents involving Rosa Parks and the same bus driver occurred twelve years apart. What happened in the first incident?
6. What happened in the second incident?
7. What did the blacks of Montgomery do to protest her arrest?
8. What significant events followed?

Understanding a Writer's Patterns

1. What is the writer's thesis?
2. What do you think is her purpose in writing this article?

3. What contrast does Ragghianti set up in paragraphs 1 and 2? Why is this contrast important?
4. From paragraph 3 (part of the introduction) you can predict what information the article will have. How does the writer let the reader know what to expect?
5. This article is a narrative account of Ragghianti's finding and talking with Rosa Parks. Within this story there is another story. What is it? Within that story is another story. What is it?
6. In paragraph 16, among other places, Ragghianti uses dialogue. Rewrite that short paragraph without dialogue. Which do you like better? Why?
7. Ragghianti concludes her article with what Parks is doing now. In paragraphs 21 through 24 Ragghianti moves from the Parks Institute for Self Development to a specific program to a specific person. Why does she end with a quotation from that person?

Making Predictions and Drawing Inferences

1. Why did Ragghianti select the title she did? Where did the title come from?
2. Sometimes our heroes and heroines are different from what we expect. How do you think the writer felt about Mrs. Parks after she interviewed her? How would you describe the tone of the article?
3. What experiences might have prepared the quiet Mrs. Parks to defy the law?

Making Judgments and Thinking Critically

1. Would you describe Parks's act as a criminal act or an act of civil disobedience? (Civil disobedience is breaking a law and being willing to take the consequences in order to show that the law is unjust and to create change.) Explain your answer.
2. Was Parks courageous or merely in a hurry? Explain.
3. Is it necessary to have thought carefully about the consequences of one's action to be called courageous? What is courage?

Using New Words

1. Substitute synonyms for the italic words in the following sentence: "She was *poised,* even *regal,* yet there was a distinct *modesty* and an *aura* of spirituality about her." Is the rewritten sentence longer or shorter? More precise in meaning or less? Does the size of one's vocabulary affect one's ability to express one's exact meaning? Why or why not?

2. Choose three words from the article that you want to add to your writing and speaking vocabulary. Make vocabulary cards for them. Write the word on one side of a card and a definition and original sentence on the other side.
3. Review your personal set of vocabulary cards. Compare your set of cards with that of someone else in this class to notice the difference in your choice of words to learn.

Responding by Writing

1. Acts of courage come in all sizes. Since the quality of courage is one we all admire, tell a story of personal courage. It may be your own or one you witnessed. It may be physical, mental, or emotional courage. Write for your classmates so they can experience the event as you did, not as disinterested spectators.
2. Tell the story of the bus incident that led to Rosa Parks's arrest from the viewpoint of the bus driver, the white man who didn't have a seat, or another black passenger. How might the event have looked from their eyes? What would they have felt and thought?
3. Create an imaginary dialogue between you and Parks or between Parks and the courageous person you described in question 1. Remember to begin a new paragraph each time the speaker changes and to use quotation marks around each speaker's words.
4. In reporting the story of her research, Ragghianti creates a portrait of her heroine Rosa Parks. Is this an effective portrait of courage? Why or why not? Remember to evaluate the article, not Rosa Parks herself. You might talk about the author's interviews with several people, her selection of Parks's past and present activities, her use of dialogue, the physical description of Parks, her use of historical facts, or anything else that makes this article effective or not effective as a portrait of courage.

Momma, the Dentist, and Me

Maya Angelou

Maya Angelou is best known for her book *I Know Why the Caged Bird Sings,* which is one of four books that make up her autobiography. Her life is the story of joyful triumph over hardship. In this excerpt from *I Know Why the Caged Bird Sings* Angelou narrates two versions of the same incident with Momma, who is her grandmother.

Thinking Before Reading

Have you ever been treated badly by someone whose service you needed—perhaps a car salesperson, a nurse in a doctor's office or clinic, a teacher or other personnel in a school, a police officer or other person of authority? Write about that incident in your Idea Bank. Tell what happened and how you felt.

Expanding Your Vocabulary from Reading

excruciating (1) intensely painful
penance (1) payment for a sin, act performed to show sorrow or regret for a sin
bailiwick (1) person's area of authority
calaboose (7) jail
contemptuous (29) full of scorn or disgust for
enunciated (29) spoken precisely and clearly
vernacular (34) everyday speech of a locality, often nonstandard or substandard
concoct (42) put together ingredients, create
obliterated (43) wiped out completely
snippity (49) annoying, uppity
retributive (50) vengeful

1 The angel of the candy counter had found me out at last, and was exacting excruciating penance for all the stolen Milky Ways, Mounds, Mr. Goodbars and Hersheys with Almonds. I had two cavities that were rotten to the gums. The pain was beyond the bailiwick of crushed aspirins or oil of cloves. Only one thing could help me, so I prayed earnestly that I'd be allowed to sit under the house and have the building collapse on my left jaw. Since there was no Negro dentist in Stamps, nor doctor either, for that matter, Momma had dealt with previous toothaches by pulling them out (a string tied to the tooth with the other end looped over her fist), pain killers and prayer. In this particular instance the medicine had proved ineffective; there wasn't enough enamel left to hook a string on, and the prayers were being ignored because the Balancing Angel was blocking their passage.

2 I lived a few days and nights in blinding pain, not so much toying with as seriously considering the idea of jumping in the well, and Momma decided I had to be taken to a dentist. The nearest Negro dentist was in Texarkana, twenty-five miles away, and I was certain that I'd be dead long before we reached half the distance. Momma said we'd go to Dr. Lincoln, right in Stamps, and he'd take care of me. She said he owed her a favor.

3 I knew there were a number of whitefolks in town that owed her favors. Bailey and I had seen the books which showed how she had lent money to

Blacks and whites alike during the Depression, and most still owed her. But I couldn't aptly remember seeing Dr. Lincoln's name, nor had I ever heard of a Negro's going to him as a patient. However, Momma said we were going, and put water on the stove for our baths. I had never been to a doctor, so she told me that after the bath (which would make my mouth feel better) I had to put on freshly starched and ironed underclothes from inside out. The ache failed to respond to the bath, and I knew then that the pain was more serious than that which anyone had ever suffered.

4 Before we left the Store, she ordered me to brush my teeth and then wash my mouth with Listerine. The idea of even opening my clamped jaws increased the pain, but upon her explanation that when you go to a doctor you have to clean yourself all over, but most especially the part that's to be examined, I screwed up my courage and unlocked my teeth. The cool air in my mouth and the jarring of my molars dislodged what little remained of my reason. I had frozen to the pain, my family nearly had to tie me down to take the toothbrush away. It was no small effort to get me started on the road to the dentist. Momma spoke to all the passers-by, but didn't stop to chat. She explained over her shoulder that we were going to the doctor and she'd ''pass the time of day'' on our way home.

5 Until we reached the pond the pain was my world, an aura that haloed me for three feet around. Crossing the bridge into whitefolks' country, pieces of sanity pushed themselves forward. I had to stop moaning and start walking straight. The white towel, which was drawn under my chin and tied over my head, had to be arranged. If one was dying, it had to be done in style if the dying took place in whitefolks' part of town.

6 On the other side of the bridge the ache seemed to lessen as if a white-breeze blew off the whitefolks and cushioned everything in their neighborhood—including my jaw. The gravel road was smoother, the stones smaller and the tree branches hung down around the path and nearly covered us. If the pain didn't diminish then, the familiar yet strange sights hypnotized me into believing that it had.

7 But my head continued to throb with the measured insistence of a bass drum, and how could a toothache pass the calaboose, hear the songs of the prisoners, their blues and laughter, and not be changed? How could one or two or even a mouthful of angry tooth roots meet a wagonload of powhitetrash children, endure their idiotic snobbery and not feel less important?

8 Behind the building which housed the dentist's office ran a small path used by servants and those tradespeople who catered to the butcher and Stamps' one restaurant. Momma and I followed that lane to the backstairs of Dentist Lincoln's office. The sun was bright and gave the day a hard reality as we climbed up the steps to the second floor.

9 Momma knocked on the back door and a young white girl opened it to show surprise at seeing us there. Momma said she wanted to see Dentist

Lincoln and to tell him Annie was there. The girl closed the door firmly. Now the humiliation of hearing Momma describe herself as if she had no last name to the young white girl was equal to the physical pain. It seemed terribly unfair to have a toothache and a headache and have to bear at the same time the heavy burden of Blackness.

10 It was always possible that the teeth would quiet down and maybe drop out of their own accord. Momma said we would wait. We leaned in the harsh sunlight on the shaky railings of the dentist's back porch for over an hour.

11 He opened the door and looked at Momma. “Well, Annie, what can I do for you?”

12 He didn't see the towel around my jaw or notice my swollen face.

13 Momma said, “Dentist Lincoln. It's my grandbaby here. She got two rotten teeth that's giving her a fit.”

14 She waited for him to acknowledge the truth of her statement. He made no comment, orally or facially.

15 “She had this toothache purt' near four days now, and today I said, ‘Young lady, you going to the Dentist.’ ”

16 “Annie?”

17 “Yes, sir, Dentist Lincoln.”

18 He was choosing words the way people hunt for shells. “Annie, you know I don't treat nigra, colored people.”

19 “I know, Dentist Lincoln. But this here is just my little grandbaby, and she ain't gone be no trouble to you . . .”

20 “Annie, everybody has a policy. In this world you have to have a policy. Now, my policy is I don't treat colored people.”

21 The sun had baked the oil out of Momma's skin and melted the Vaseline in her hair. She shone greasily as she leaned out of the dentist's shadow.

22 “Seem like to me, Dentist Lincoln, you might look after her, she ain't nothing but a little mite. And seems like maybe you owe me a favor or two.”

23 He reddened slightly. “Favor or no favor. The money has all been repaid to you and that's the end of it. Sorry, Annie.” He had his hand on the doorknob. “Sorry.” His voice was a bit kinder on the second “Sorry,” as if he really was.

24 Momma said, “I wouldn't press on you like this for myself but I can't take No. Not for my grandbaby. When you come to borrow my money you didn't have to beg. You asked me, and I lent it. Now, it wasn't my policy. I ain't no moneylender, but you stood to lose this building and I tried to help you out.”

25 “It's been paid, and raising your voice won't make me change my mind. My policy . . .” He let go of the door and stepped nearer Momma. The three of us were crowded on the small landing. “Annie, my policy is I'd rather stick my hand in a dog's mouth than in a nigger's.”

26 He had never once looked at me. He turned his back and went through

the door into the cool beyond. Momma backed up inside herself for a few minutes. I forgot everything except her face which was almost a new one to me. She leaned over and took the doorknob, and in her everyday soft voice she said, "Sister, go on downstairs. Wait for me. I'll be there directly."

27 Under the most common of circumstances I knew it did no good to argue with Momma. So I walked down the steep stairs, afraid to look back and afraid not to do so. I turned as the door slammed, and she was gone.

28 *Momma walked in that room as if she owned it. She shoved that silly nurse aside with one hand and strode into the dentist's office. He was sitting in his chair, sharpening his mean instruments and putting extra sting into his medicines. Her eyes were blazing like live coals and her arms had doubled themselves in length. He looked up at her just before she caught him by the collar of his white jacket.*

29 *"Stand up when you see a lady, you contemptuous scoundrel." Her tongue had thinned and the words rolled off her well enunciated. Enunciated and sharp like little claps of thunder.*

30 *The dentist had no choice but to stand at R.O.T.C. attention. His head dropped after a minute and his voice was humble. "Yes, ma'am, Mrs. Henderson."*

31 *"You knave, do you think you acted like a gentleman, speaking to me like that in front of my granddaughter?" She didn't shake him, although she had the power. She simply held him upright.*

32 *"No, ma'am, Mrs. Henderson."*

33 *"No, ma'am, Mrs. Henderson, what?" Then she did give him the tiniest of shakes, but because of her strength the action set his head and arms to shaking loose on the ends of his body. He stuttered much worse than Uncle Willie. "No, ma'am, Mrs. Henderson, I'm sorry."*

34 *With just an edge of her disgust showing, Momma slung him back in his dentist's chair. "Sorry is as sorry does, and you're about the sorriest dentist I ever laid my eyes on." (She could afford to slip into the vernacular because she had such eloquent command of English.)*

35 *"I didn't ask you to apologize in front of Marguerite, because I don't want her to know my power, but I order you, now and herewith. Leave Stamps by sundown."*

36 *"Mrs. Henderson, I can't get my equipment . . ." He was shaking terribly now.*

37 *"Now, that brings me to my second order. You will never again practice dentistry. Never! When you get settled in your next place, you will be a vegetarian caring for dogs with the mange, cats with the cholera and cows with the epizootic. Is that clear?"*

38 *The saliva ran down his chin and his eyes filled with tears. "Yes, ma'am. Thank you for not killing me. Thank you, Mrs. Henderson."*

39 *Momma pulled herself back from being ten feet tall with eight-foot arms*

and said, "You're welcome for nothing, you varlet, I wouldn't waste a killing on the likes of you."

40 *On her way out she waved her handkerchief at the nurse and turned her into a crocus sack of chicken feed.*

41 Momma looked tired when she came down the stairs, but who wouldn't be tired if they had gone through what she had. She came close to me and adjusted the towel under my jaw (I had forgotten the toothache; I only knew that she made her hands gentle in order not to awaken the pain). She took my hand. Her voice never changed. "Come on, Sister."

42 I reckoned we were going home where she would concoct a brew to eliminate the pain and maybe give me new teeth too. New teeth that would grow overnight out of my gums. She led me toward the drugstore, which was in the opposite direction from the Store. "I'm taking you to Dentist Baker in Texarkana."

43 I was glad after all that I had bathed and put on Mum and Cashmere Bouquet talcum powder. It was a wonderful surprise. My toothache had quieted to solemn pain, Momma had obliterated the evil white man, and we were going on a trip to Texarkana, just the two of us.

44 On the Greyhound she took an inside seat in the back, and I sat beside her. I was so proud of being her granddaughter and sure that some of her magic must have come down to me. She asked if I was scared. I only shook my head and leaned over on her cool brown upper arm. There was no chance that a dentist, especially a Negro dentist, would dare hurt me then. Not with Momma there. The trip was uneventful, except that she put her arm around me, which was very unusual for Momma to do.

45 The dentist showed me the medicine and the needle before he deadened my gums, but if he hadn't I wouldn't have worried. Momma stood right behind him. Her arms were folded and she checked on everything he did. The teeth were extracted and she bought me an ice cream cone from the side window of a drug counter. The trip back to Stamps was quiet, except that I had to spit into a very small empty snuff can which she had gotten for me and it was difficult with the bus bumping and jerking on our country roads.

46 At home, I was given a warm salt solution, and when I washed out my mouth I showed Bailey the empty holes, where the clotted blood sat like filling in a pie crust. He said I was quite brave, and that was my cue to reveal our confrontation with the peckerwood dentist and Momma's incredible powers.

47 I had to admit that I didn't hear the conversation, but what else could she have said than what I said she said? What else done? He agreed with my analysis in a lukewarm way, and I happily (after all, I'd been sick) flounced into the Store. Momma was preparing our evening meal and Uncle Willie leaned on the door sill. She gave her version.

48 "Dentist Lincoln got right uppity. Said he'd rather put his hand in a

dog's mouth. And when I reminded him of the favor, he brushed it off like a piece of lint. Well, I sent Sister downstairs and went inside. I hadn't never been in his office before, but I found the door to where he takes out teeth, and him and the nurse was in there thick as thieves. I just stood there till he caught sight of me.'' Crash bang the pots on the stove. ''He jumped like he was sitting on a pin. He said 'Annie, I done tole you, I ain't gonna mess around in no niggah's mouth.' I said, 'Somebody's got to do it then,' and he said, 'Take her to Texarkana to the colored dentist' and that's when I said, 'If you paid me my money I could afford to take her.' He said, 'It's all been paid.' I tole him everything but the interest been paid. He said, ' 'Twasn't no interest.' I said, ' 'Tis now. I'll take ten dollars as payment in full.' You know, Willie, it wasn't no right thing to do, 'cause I lent that money without thinking about it.

49 ''He tole that little snippity nurse of his'n to give me ten dollars and make me sign a 'paid in full' receipt. She gave it to me and I signed the papers. Even though by rights he was paid up before, I figger, he gonna be that kind of nasty, he gonna have to pay for it.''

50 Momma and her son laughed and laughed over the white man's evilness and her retributive sin.

51 I preferred, much preferred, my version.

Jotting Down Your First Responses

1. What do you think you would have done if you were Dr. Lincoln? Momma?
2. Is it easier for you to stand up to someone in authority or power in your own behalf or in behalf of someone else? Explain.
3. There are many kinds of prejudice. Recall an incident in which you were the subject of prejudice. Or, recall an incident in which you acted with prejudice or in which you were part of a group that acted with prejudice. Write about the incident in your Idea Bank.

Checking Your Comprehension

1. In what town did Angelou and her grandmother live?
2. What are two reasons Momma took Angelou to see Dr. Lincoln?
3. How did Angelou prepare for her visit to the dentist?
4. What three places on the way to the dentist seemed to diminish the pain of her toothache?
5. When Momma and Angelou arrived at the office, what did Momma tell the young white girl who answered the door?
6. What was Dr. Lincoln's first response to Momma's request?

7. What did Momma remind Dr. Lincoln of?
8. What was his second response when she pressed him to treat her granddaughter?
9. What fantasy did Angelou have about Momma's conversation with Dr. Lincoln behind the closed door?
10. Where did they go to have her teeth pulled?
11. What actually happened in Momma's conversation with Dr. Lincoln?

Understanding a Writer's Patterns

1. What is Angelou's purpose in narrating this story? Who do you think her audience is?
2. What are the advantages of using first person to tell the story?
3. In part of the story Angelou narrates the story. In paragraphs 11 through 25 she uses dialogue and lets the characters tell the story. Why does she change to dialogue?
4. What are two other places where she uses dialogue to tell the story? Why?
5. Angelou uses figurative language. Explain the following comparisons and why she uses them: "the pain was my world" (paragraph 5), "choosing words the way people hunt for shells" (paragraph 18), and "brushed it off like a piece of lint" (paragraph 48).

Making Predictions and Drawing Inferences

1. In paragraph 3 Angelou describes her pain as "more serious than that which anyone had ever suffered." Is that what she thinks as an adult or what she thought as a child? How do you know?
2. Why did Momma and Angelou go up the back stairs (paragraph 8) to see the dentist?
3. Why is Angelou humiliated by her grandmother's use of her first name only (paragraph 9) with the young white girl?
4. Why didn't the dentist notice Angelou with her swollen face wrapped in a towel (paragraph 12)?
5. What does the second "Sorry" (paragraph 23) reveal about the dentist?
6. Why was Momma's face "almost a new one" (paragraph 26) to Angelou?

Making Judgments and Thinking Critically

1. What does Angelou mean when she says that the bright sun "gave the day a hard reality" (paragraph 8)?

2. Was Dr. Lincoln's policy not to treat colored people peculiar to him or similar to other white doctors and dentists in Stamps?
3. Do you know of other policies or laws, then or now, that support prejudiced behavior?
4. Was Momma's belated interest on her loan to Dr. Lincoln fair? Legal? Revengeful?
5. The pain of the toothache is a vehicle for Angelou to reveal another deep pain. What is it?
6. Is this narrative an effective way to discuss an issue such as prejudice and its effects? Explain.

Using New Words

1. Paragraph 4 contains a description of Angelou's pain. Rewrite the sentences beginning "I screwed up . . ." and ending "frozen to the pain." Substitute synonyms for *screwed up, unlocked, jarring, dislodged,* and *frozen.* Change other words in the sentences to make your substitutions work. Compare Angelou's sentences with the reworked ones. What do you notice about word choices?
2. Choose three words from this selection to add to your set of vocabulary cards. Write the word on one side of a card and a definition and an original sentence on the other side.

Responding by Writing

1. In many regions, cities, and neighborhoods (or schools) of the United States, each religious, age, racial or ethnic group has its own culture. To show some aspect of your cultural past, write a narrative essay about something you liked or didn't like about a place you've lived. It could be the great comedy clubs of a city, street games you played as a kid, the kindness with which old people were treated. Write this essay for your classmates, who have not experienced this cultural aspect.
2. Write a narrative about an event from your childhood for your classmates. It may be something humorous or serious. Be sure you know what main feeling or impression you want your readers to understand so they will know the importance of this event to you.
3. Recall an incident in which you stood up to someone in authority or power. Perhaps your answer to question 2 in Jotting Down Your First Responses will help you begin. Write a narrative about this event for an audience of your classmates.
4. Write about an incident in which you were the subject of prejudice or in which you acted with prejudice. (See your answer to question 3 in Jotting Down Your First Responses.) Decide what you want your audience of classmates to understand; this is the focus for your essay.

"I Just Wanna Be Average"

Mike Rose

Mike Rose grew up in a Los Angeles ghetto, not really expecting to go to college. Because of a mix-up of test scores, he was placed in a vocational program in school. Then one teacher stimulated his interest in learning. This selection from his book *Lives on the Boundary* tells part of the story about his joining the "literacy club." It's a story about his transformation from punk to professor at UCLA (University of Los Angeles).

Thinking Before Reading

Think about how you came to be in college. Were there people who inspired you or helped you? Write in your Idea Bank about what or who influenced you to attend college.

Expanding Your Vocabulary from Reading

erratic (3) inconsistent, wandering
pedagogy (3) teaching method
quantitative (3) of or pertaining to numbers; mathematical
finessing (3) artfully moving around
impenetrable (6) not understandable
attribute (6) to regard as causing
shroud (6) a cloth used to wrap a body for burial
arteriosclerosis (7) a disease in which thickening and hardening of the arteries interferes with the circulation of the blood
suppuration (8) pus from wounds
adept (8) skilled
indifference (9) attitude of having no interest
barbs (10) cutting or biting remarks
incipient (11) in an early stage
ministrations (12) acts of serving or aiding

1 My own deliverance from the Voc. Ed. world began with sophomore biology. Every student, college prep to vocational, had to take biology, and unlike the other courses, the same person taught all sections. When teaching the vocational group, Brother Clint probably slowed down a bit or omitted a little of the fundamental biochemistry, but he used the same book and more or less the same syllabus across the board. If one class got tough, he could get tougher. He was young and powerful and very handsome, and looks and physical strength were high currency. No one gave him any trouble.

2 I was pretty bad at the dissecting table, but the lectures and the textbook were interesting: plastic overlays that, with each turned page, peeled away

skin, then veins and muscle, then organs, down to the very bones that Brother Clint, pointer in hand, would tap out on our hanging skeleton. Dave Snyder was in big trouble, for the study of life—versus the living of it—was sticking in his craw. We worked out a code for our multiple-choice exams. He'd poke me in the back: once for the answer under *A,* twice for *B,* and so on; and when he'd hit the right one, I'd look up to the ceiling as though I were lost in thought. Poke: cytoplasm. Poke, poke: methane. Poke, poke, poke: William Harvey. Poke, poke, poke, poke: islets of Langerhans. This didn't work out perfectly, but Dave passed the course, and I mastered the dreamy look of a guy on a record jacket. And something else happened. Brother Clint puzzled over this Voc. Ed. kid who was racking up 98s and 99s on his tests. He checked the school's records and discovered the error. He recommended that I begin my junior year in the College Prep program. According to all I've read since, such a shift, as one report put it, is virtually impossible. Kids at that level rarely cross tracks. The telling thing is how chancy both my placement into and exit from Voc. Ed. was; neither I nor my parents had anything to do with it. I lived in one world during spring semester, and when I came back to school in the fall, I was living in another.

3 Switching to College Prep was a mixed blessing. I was an erratic student. I was undisciplined. And I hadn't caught onto the rules of the game: Why work hard in a class that didn't grab my fancy? I was also hopelessly behind in math. Chemistry was hard; toying with my chemistry set years before hadn't prepared me for the chemist's equations. Fortunately, the priest who taught both chemistry and second-year algebra was also the school's athletic director. Membership on the track team covered me; I knew I wouldn't get lower than a *C.* U.S. history was taught pretty well, and I did okay. But civics was taken over by a football coach who had trouble reading the textbook aloud—and reading aloud was the centerpiece of his pedagogy. College Prep at Mercy was certainly an improvement over the vocational program—at least it carried some status—but the social science curriculum was weak, and the mathematics and physical sciences were simply beyond me. I had a miserable quantitative background and ended up copying some assignments and finessing the rest as best I could. Let me try to explain how it feels to see again and again material you should once have learned but didn't.

4 You are given a problem. It requires you to simplify algebraic fractions or to multiply expressions containing square roots. You know this is pretty basic material because you've seen it for years. Once a teacher took some time with you, and you learned how to carry out these operations. Simple versions, anyway. But that was a year or two or more in the past, and these are more complex versions, and now you're not sure. And this, you keep telling yourself, is ninth- or even eighth-grade stuff.

5 Next it's a word problem. This is also old hat. The basic elements are as familiar as story characters: trains speeding so many miles per hour or shadows

of buildings angling so many degrees. Maybe you know enough, have sat through enough explanations, to be able to begin setting up the problem: "If one train is going this fast . . ." or "This shadow is really one line of a triangle . . . ." Then: "Let's see . . ." "How did Jones do this?" "Hmmmm." "No." "No, that won't work." Your attention wavers. You wonder about other things: a football game, a dance, that cute new checker at the market. You try to focus on the problem again. You scribble on paper for a while, but the tension wins out and your attention flits elsewhere. You crumple the paper and begin daydreaming to ease the frustration.

6 The particulars will vary, but in essence this is what a number of students go through, especially those in so-called remedial classes. They open their textbooks and see once again the familiar and impenetrable formulas and diagrams and terms that have stumped them for years. There is no excitement here. *No* excitement. Regardless of what the teacher says, this is not a new challenge. There is, rather, embarrassment and frustration and, not surprisingly, some anger in being reminded once again of long-standing inadequacies. No wonder so many students finally attribute their difficulties to something inborn, organic: "That part of my brain just doesn't work." Given the troubling histories many of these students have, it's miraculous that any of them can lift the shroud of hopelessness sufficiently to make deliverance from these classes possible.

7 Through this entire period, my father's health was deteriorating with cruel momentum. His arteriosclerosis progressed to the point where a simple nick on his shin wouldn't heal. Eventually it ulcerated and widened. Lou Minton would come by daily to change the dressing. We tried renting an oscillating bed—which we placed in the front room—to force blood through the constricted arteries in my father's legs. The bed hummed through the night, moving in place to ward off the inevitable. The ulcer continued to spread, and the doctors finally had to amputate. My grandfather had lost his leg in a stockyard accident. Now my father too was crippled. His convalescence was slow but steady, and the doctors placed him in the Santa Monica Rehabilitation Center, a sun-bleached building that opened out onto the warm spray of the Pacific. The place gave him some strength and some color and some training in walking with an artificial leg. He did pretty well for a year or so until he slipped and broke his hip. He was confined to a wheelchair after that, and the confinement contributed to the diminishing of his body and spirit.

8 I am holding a picture of him. He is sitting in his wheelchair and smiling at the camera. The smile appears forced, unsteady, seems to quaver, though it is frozen in silver nitrate. He is in his mid-sixties and looks eighty. Late in my junior year, he had a stroke and never came out of the resulting coma. After that, I would see him only in dreams, and to this day that is how I join him. Sometimes the dreams are sad and grisly and primal: my father lying in a bed soaked with his suppuration, holding me, rocking me. But sometimes the

dreams bring him back to me healthy: him talking to me on an empty street, or buying some pictures to decorate our old house, or transformed somehow into someone strong and adept with tools and the physical.

9 Jack MacFarland couldn't have come into my life at a better time. My father was dead, and I had logged up too many years of scholastic indifference. Mr. MacFarland had a master's degree from Columbia and decided, at twenty-six, to find a little school and teach his heart out. He never took any credentialing courses, couldn't bear to, he said, so he had to find employment in a private system. He ended up at Our Lady of Mercy teaching five sections of senior English. He was a beatnik who was born too late. His teeth were stained, he tucked his sorry tie in between the third and fourth buttons of his shirt, and his pants were chronically wrinkled. At first, we couldn't believe this guy, thought he slept in his car. But within no time, he had us so startled with work that we didn't much worry about where he slept or if he slept at all. We wrote three or four essays a month. We read a book every two to three weeks, starting with the *Iliad* and ending up with Hemingway. He gave us a quiz on the reading every other day. He brought a prep school curriculum to Mercy High.

10 MacFarland's lectures were crafted, and as he delivered them he would pace the room jiggling a piece of chalk in his cupped hand, using it to scribble on the board the names of all the writers and philosophers and plays and novels he was weaving into his discussion. He asked questions often, raised everything from Zeno's paradox to the repeated last line of Frost's "Stopping by Woods on a Snowy Evening." He slowly and carefully built up our knowledge of Western intellectual history—with facts, with connections, with speculations. We learned about Greek philosophy, about Dante, the Elizabethan world view, the Age of Reason, existentialism. He analyzed poems with us, had us reading sections from John Ciardi's *How Does a Poem Mean?,* making a potentially difficult book accessible with his own explanations. We gave oral reports on poems Ciardi didn't cover. We imitated the styles of Conrad, Hemingway, and *Time* magazine. We wrote and talked, wrote and talked. The man immersed us in language.

11 Even MacFarland's barbs were literary. If Jim Fitzsimmons, hung over and irritable, tried to smart-ass him, he'd rejoin with a flourish that would spark the indomitable Skip Madison—who'd lost his front teeth in a hapless tackle—to flick his tongue through the gap and opine, "good chop," drawing out the single "o" in stinging indictment. Jack MacFarland, this tobacco-stained intellectual, brandished linguistic weapons of a kind I hadn't encountered before. Here was this *egghead,* for God's sake, keeping some pretty difficult people in line. And from what I heard, Mike Dweetz and Steve Fusco and all the notorious Voc. Ed. crowd settled down as well when MacFarland took the podium. Though a lot of guys groused in the schoolyard, it just seemed that giving trouble to this particular teacher was a silly thing to do.

Tomfoolery, not to mention assault, had no place in the world he was trying to create for us, and instinctively everyone knew that. If nothing else, we all recognized MacFarland's considerable intelligence and respected the hours he put into his work. It came to this: The troublemaker would look foolish rather than daring. Even Jim Fitzsimmons was reading *On the Road* and turning his incipient alcoholism to literary ends.

12 There were some lives that were already beyond Jack MacFarland's ministrations, but mine was not. I started reading again as I hadn't since elementary school. I would go into our gloomy little bedroom or sit at the dinner table while, on the television, Danny McShane was paralyzing Mr. Moto with the atomic drop, and work slowly back through *Heart of Darkness,* trying to catch the words in Conrad's sentences. I certainly was not MacFarland's best student; most of the other guys in College Prep, even my fellow slackers, had better backgrounds than I did. But I worked very hard, for MacFarland had hooked me. He tapped my old interest in reading and creating stories. He gave me a way to feel special by using my mind. And he provided a role model that wasn't shaped on physical prowess alone, and something inside me that I wasn't quite aware of responded to that. Jack MacFarland established a literacy club, to borrow a phrase of Frank Smith's, and invited me—invited all of us—to join.

13 There's been a good deal of research and speculation suggesting that the acknowledgment of school performance with extrinsic rewards—smiling faces, stars, numbers, grades—diminishes the intrinsic satisfaction children experience by engaging in reading or writing or problem solving. While it's certainly true that we've created an educational system that encourages our best and brightest to become cynical grade collectors and, in general, have developed an obsession with evaluation and assessment, I must tell you that venal though it may have been, I loved getting good grades from MacFarland. I now know how subjective grades can be, but then they came tucked in the back of essays like bits of scientific data, some sort of spectroscopic readout that said, objectively and publicly, that I had made something of value. I suppose I'd been mediocre for too long and enjoyed a public redefinition. And I suppose the workings of my mind, such as they were, had been private for too long. My linguistic play moved into the world; like the intergalactic stories I told years before on Frank's berry-splattered truck bed, these papers with their circled, red B-pluses and A-minuses linked my mind to something outside it. I carried them around like a club emblem.

14 One day in the December of my senior year, Mr. MacFarland asked me where I was going to go to college. I hadn't thought much about it. Many of the students I teach today spent their last year in high school with a physics text in one hand and the Stanford catalog in the other, but I wasn't even aware of what "entrance requirements" were. My folks would say that they wanted me to go to college and be a doctor, but I don't know how seriously I ever

took that; it seemed a sweet thing to say, a bit of supportive family chatter, like telling a gangly daughter she's graceful. The reality of higher education wasn't in my scheme of things: No one in the family had gone to college; only two of my uncles had completed high school. I figured I'd get a night job and go to the local junior college because I knew that Snyder and Company were going there to play ball. But I hadn't even prepared for that. When I finally said, "I don't know," MacFarland looked down at me—I was seated in his office—and said, "Listen, you can write."

15 My grades stank. I had A's in biology and a handful of B's in a few English and social science classes. All the rest were C's—or worse. MacFarland said I would do well in his class and laid down the law about doing well in the others. Still, the record for my first three years wouldn't have been acceptable to any four-year school. To nobody's surprise, I was turned down flat by USC and UCLA. But Jack MacFarland was on the case. He had received his bachelor's degree from Loyola University, so he made calls to old professors and talked to somebody in admissions and wrote me a strong letter. Loyola finally accepted me as a probationary student. I would be on trial for the first year, and if I did okay, I would be granted regular status. MacFarland also intervened to get me a loan, for I could never have afforded a private college without it. Four more years of religion classes and four more years of boys at one school, girls at another. But at least I was going to college. Amazing.

Jotting Down Your First Responses

1. In what ways were you like or unlike Rose as a high school student?
2. If you experienced the kind of change in attitude and action that Rose did, describe the change and tell how it happened.
3. Who was your most influential teacher or other adult in your school experience? Describe the person and his or her importance to you.
4. Do you think you would have liked Jack MacFarland? How would you have responded if you had been in his class?

Checking Your Comprehension

1. In what class did Rose surprise his teacher by scoring 98s and 99s? Why was the teacher surprised?
2. How did the surprised teacher discover that Rose was misplaced and what did he do?
3. What courses did Rose's track team membership help him pass?
4. In what academic area was Rose weakest?
5. According to Rose, how do students like him react when faced with algebra and word problems they can't do? (paragraph 5)
6. What feelings do such students often have? (paragraph 6)
7. What happened to his father in his junior year?

8. What teacher motivated Rose and excited him about learning?
9. How did that teacher hook Rose into reading again?
10. What effect did Rose's grades on essays have on him? (paragraph 13)
11. What preparations had Rose made for college? Why? (paragraph 14)
12. How did MacFarland help Rose attend college?

Understanding a Writer's Patterns

1. Many narratives are composed of a collection of related events or scenes that the author selects out of a vast reservoir of memory. Rose selects four events to compose this narrative. The first is the discovery by his biology teacher that he is misplaced in Voc. Ed. (paragraphs 1–3). What are the other three? What is each narrative and in what paragraphs does each occur?
2. Even though this selection is a collection of narratives, there is an implied thesis. What is it?
3. Narratives contain both people and action, but they also contain description. Description is the author's way of heightening something important so the reader will notice it. Recall a narrative scene from the selection. What sensory details or facts have set this in your memory? Write these down. Read part of the scene aloud and find other details. Add these to your list.
4. Rose laces the four narrative sections together with two sections in which he discusses something brought up by a narrative. What are those two discussion sections? Use paragraph numbers to indicate each section.
5. Narratives are often arranged chronologically, or in time order. Authors often give verbal clues to help the reader follow the pattern of events. Near the beginning of each of the four narrative events, Rose uses a phrase to signal something about time. What are these phrases? Give the paragraph number of each.

Making Predictions and Drawing Inferences

1. What does Rose mean by ''Poke'' (paragraph 2) and why does he repeat the word?
2. In paragraph 2 what is the significance of the terms *cytoplasm, methane, William Harvey,* and *islets of Langerhans*?
3. What feeling does the student have who says this ''is ninth- or even eighth-grade stuff'' (paragraph 4)?
4. What club did MacFarland establish? Who could join? What did they have to do to join?
5. What would Rose's future have been like if MacFarland had not acted in his behalf?

Making Judgments and Thinking Critically

1. Is Rose's success, as described in this narrative selection, a result of luck or effort? Explain.
2. What changes in his social life might have occurred when Rose changed from vocational to college preparatory classes? In the way he spent his time? In his attitudes?
3. What was the turning point in Rose's life? Do you think he recognized it at the time? Why or why not?
4. Why was the chapter from which this selection taken entitled "I Just Wanna Be Average"? Why is the title in quotation marks?

Using New Words

1. Choose three words from this selection to add to your reading and writing vocabulary. Make vocabulary cards for them. Write the word on one side of the card and a definition and an original sentence on the other side.
2. Rose has an extensive vocabulary. How do you think he learned so many words? Where has your vocabulary come from? Where or from whom do you learn new words?
3. Why does Rose compare the hopelessness of some students to a shroud in the phrase "a shroud of hopelessness" (paragraph 6)?
4. What is an "oscillating bed" (paragraph 7)?
5. What does *accessible* mean in "making a potentially difficult book accessible" (paragraph 10)?
6. What does *indomitable* mean in "the indomitable Skip Madison" (paragraph 11)?

Responding by Writing

1. Since you are beginning a college education, you may have recently been through decisions and changes in your goals and commitments similar to those that Rose describes. Using the writing you did in your Idea Bank or in the "Jotting Down Your First Responses" section as a starting place, write a narrative about your transformation to college student. Choose several scenes or events that show this change or decision. Write for an audience of this class. Your instructor may ask you to read this narrative aloud in small groups.
2. Write about another important decision you have made, one that took a long time to make. Write for an audience of this class.
3. Write an essay about someone you know who has struggled to be independent, to overcome an obstacle, to start a new life, to achieve a personal goal, or to adjust to a new culture. Use more than one event or

narrative scene to show the person's courage and effort. Write for an audience of this class.

4. Besides entertaining us, narratives can teach us about human nature and about other cultures. If the narratives you've read in this chapter have given you a new insight about others, write an essay using that idea as a thesis. Develop your essay with information from the selections you have read in this chapter. Write for an audience of your teacher.

   Use the title and author of the selection or selections. Put quotation marks before and after each title you use. Write the full name when you first refer to an author. Use only the last name in following references.

One More Foreigner, One More Stranger

Gloria Cruz

Gloria Cruz is an ambitious and determined student who is aiming for a business degree. She works and goes to school part time. She wrote this essay for readers of a Hispanic magazine. Her purpose was to encourage them to reach for their goals. She wanted them to see learning to speak English as a first step.

Thinking Before Reading

Everyone feels isolated and cut off from everyone else at some time. Think about a time when you felt alone. What situation caused this isolation? How did you overcome it? Did anyone reach out to you? Write a few sentences about this situation in your Idea Bank.

Expanding Your Vocabulary from Reading

hesitant (1) moving slowly because of uncertainty
burlesque (2) mocking, making to look ridiculous
repetitive (3) repeated until boring
mastered (5) learned completely
composure (6) appearance of being calm and unmoved by strong emotions
cherishing (6) holding as valuable
barrier (7) wall or obstacle intended to prevent one's exit or entrance

1 "Say b-i-t-c-h," said one of the many students who surrounded me on my second day of school one hot September day seven years ago. With a slow and hesitant movement of my tongue and lips I finally managed to pronounce

the word. The group of students became hysterical with laughter. I could not understand why they laughed. It was hard for me to imagine what I could possibly have said that could be so amusing. Knowing only the meanings to the words ''pencil'' and ''table'' did not better the situation. ''Was what I had said really that funny, or were they laughing at me,'' I thought to myself. I was horrified at the thought of this and became panic-stricken. I could feel the tears rush to my eyes while the blood rushed to my head. I tried to keep from crying, but it was absolutely useless. Suddenly the hot September day became like a cold day in winter.

2 With tears running down my face I stood still surrounded by the group of students. They saw me crying, but it was as if they couldn't see the tears. Immediately they all began to yell out words and phrases they wanted me to pronounce. The only thing my mind could translate to Spanish was their burlesque laugh. They were definitely laughing at me. Once more I asked myself, ''Can they not see the fear in my eyes, or the pain in my heart?'' They were not the ones who appeared to be different and felt out of place: I was. (No, they couldn't possibly see this.)

3 I refused to serve as a freak show to anyone, so I decided to avoid people at school completely. Everyday activities became repetitive. I went to school alone, ate lunch alone, and came home alone. Lunch and breaks were always the toughest moments. Many times I wished that one of the kids would at least make the effort to talk to me. I waited and waited only to be disappointed.

4 I enjoyed listening to the language. Everything about it sounded mysterious. When I sat alone during my lunch hours I use to pretend I was among the group of students. Under my breath I mumbled nonsense which sounded foreign to my ear. Time passed and after eight months of attending ESL (English as a Second Language) I learned to speak English. After that incident during my first week in school my desire to learn the language quickened.

5 By the time I got to high school I had mastered the language as well as any American student. During my sophomore year I became aware of a shy Vietnamese girl in my math class who reminded me of myself seven years ago. I first became aware of her because everyday after roll call the boys in our class purposely mispronounced her name. Her name was simply Namm, but the guys chose to substitute the N for every word in the alphabet. One day I heard one of the boys ask her, ''Do you know how to cuss in Vietnamese?'' She simply sat still and ignored his question. She appeared so terrified and confused, just like me seven years ago. How could others not see this! On numerous occasions I tried to communicate with her, but her only response was silence. Then one day to my surprise, she said, ''Thank you, you are much kind.'' Her English was broken, but as she struggled to pronounce each word correctly, a single tear rolled down her cheek.

6 I had never sensed such sincerity from any one person. I tried to keep my own composure. As I reached to give her hand a gentle squeeze, the single

tear fell on my hand. I grasped her hand, cherishing a feeling I never wanted to lose. Memories came flooding back of my own experience. I wanted to comfort her by telling her not to worry because it all goes well. My Vietnamese friend had finally broken the barrier. English would no longer be the obstacle it once was. She was on her way to much bigger things.

7 Today I can honestly say that through experiences as a foreigner in an American school I became a stronger individual. I realized that kids can be cruel, but more importantly, I learned that determination, not tears helps you reach your goals. I believe it is important for all people to cope with, understand and appreciate the value of fairness regardless of one's race or language. When a foreigner comes into this wonderful land the first barrier he is faced with is the language; however, this will not be the only obstacle. America offers many opportunities to all people who are determined, and I plan to achieve my goals regardless of what the obstacles are because I refuse to be just another foreigner, or just another stranger.

Jotting Down Your First Responses

1. If it had been you who was made fun of by the students because of your inability to understand and speak English, how would you have reacted that day?
2. Would such treatment by others have made you give up or made you more determined to learn? Explain.
3. Did Cruz's narrative remind you of a situation in your life in addition to the one you wrote about before reading her essay? What was it?

Checking Your Comprehension

1. What did the students want Cruz to do?
2. What English words did she know at that point?
3. What did she do in response to their requests?
4. How did she feel?
5. As a result of that incident on her second day of school, what did she do?
6. What decision did she make about learning English?
7. What did she listen to during lunch every day? Why?
8. How did she learn English? How long did it take?
9. In high school what did Cruz do to befriend a lonely Vietnamese girl? How did the girl respond to Cruz for a while?
10. What did the Vietnamese girl do that showed she was ready to change?
11. What barrier did Cruz and the Vietnamese girl face?
12. What effects did Cruz's experiences as a foreigner have on her in the long run?

Understanding a Writer's Patterns

1. What is Cruz's thesis? Where does she state it?
2. How does Cruz support her thesis?
3. How does Cruz begin this essay? Why?
4. Find four direct quotations in the essay. What are they?
5. Cruz's pattern of development is to write some facts and details of the narrative and then some of her thoughts and feelings about the events. In paragraphs 1 and 2, which sentences give facts and details of the narrative?
6. Which sentences in paragraphs 1 and 2 tell her thoughts and feelings?
7. What details in paragraphs 1 and 2 make the narrative vivid for you?
8. In paragraphs 4 and 5 underline ten words or phrases that signal the time sequence of the narrative. (Turn to the lesson at the beginning of this chapter if you would like a reminder of some of these.)

Making Predictions and Drawing Inferences

1. Why did Cruz move her tongue and lips "with a slow and hesitant movement" (paragraph 1)?
2. Why did the students laugh?
3. Although it was a hot September day, it felt "like a cold day in winter" (paragraph 1). What was Cruz feeling? Why did she use a contrast about the weather to tell about this feeling?

Making Judgments and Thinking Critically

1. The essay begins with a direct quotation and the action of the narrative. Would an introduction with background information have been more or less effective? Explain.
2. Would the essay have been strengthened or weakened if Cruz had omitted the narrative about the Vietnamese girl? Explain.
3. Do you think the acts of the students toward Cruz and the Vietnamese girl were isolated and unusual incidents? How do you explain the attitudes and behavior of the students toward the girls?

Using New Words

1. Without looking back at the essay, what specific words do you recall? Write them down. Now find these words in the essay. Why did you recall these words? As a writer, what does this show you about your own word choice?
2. Make vocabulary cards for three words from this essay that you want to add to your writing and speaking vocabulary. Write the word on one side of a card and a definition and an original sentence on the other side.

Responding by Writing

1. Write a narrative essay about foreigners, either from the perspective of a foreigner or a United States native. You may draw on your experiences from work, school, neighborhood, or other parts of daily life. Decide on your focus and write a description of your audience and purpose before you write a draft of the essay.
2. Write a narrative essay about a barrier you have broken through or an obstacle you have overcome in your life. You may use what you wrote in your Idea Bank before or after reading Cruz's essay. Let the narrative make your point; keep the explaining to a minimum. What group of people face an obstacle similar to the one you have overcome? Let them be the audience for your essay. Write a description of your purpose and audience before you write a draft of the essay.
3. Write an essay about an experience you have had with language—perhaps a speech you had to make, an important letter or report you had to write, an interview with your child's teacher or with an employer. The situation may have had a successful or unsuccessful outcome. It may have been painful or joyful. Use both narration and description to reveal this incident to an audience of this class.
4. Ordinary people often develop courage and determination when they face difficult times in life. If you agree, write an essay using this statement as a thesis. Use support from two essays you have read in this chapter. Be sure to include the author and title of both essays to give the source of your support. Write to an audience of this class.

CHAPTER

7

EXEMPLIFICATION

USING EXAMPLES TO DEVELOP YOUR ESSAYS

Using examples, like describing and narrating, are everyday activities for you. Without thinking about it, you describe, narrate, and give examples when you talk. You may also describe, narrate, and give examples automatically when you write, but the lessons in this book should help you focus on using these ways of developing an essay *intentionally* when you write. You will use examples as often as you use narration and description, usually combining these ways of thinking and explaining. Examples appear in almost every essay, and you will need to use them in all of yours. You may think of using examples as another tool to place in your toolbox of writing skills.

Why use examples? You use examples basically because readers like them and need them to understand what you really mean. You use examples to make writing livelier, to explain a point, and to shore up an argument. In Chapter 3 you studied revising. One way to strengthen your writing is to replace general words (such as *meal*) with specific words (such as *spaghetti, spinach salad, garlic bread*) and to add details (such as *spaghetti with clam sauce*). Another way to strengthen your writing is to make general sentences, such as "That's a good restaurant," more specific by giving examples.

What do you mean by "a good restaurant"? You can explain what you mean by giving an example, "We had a great meal there Saturday night." But that one sentence is probably not enough for a reader to understand or believe you. You need to add specifics about the meal. "That's a good restaurant. We had a great meal there Saturday night. The sauce for the spaghetti was full of fresh clams, the spinach in the spinach salad with croutons was fresh, and the garlic bread was hot and crisp. We had to wait only thirty minutes to be seated and the service was fast. My water glass never got more than half empty before the server filled it, and she brought us more hot garlic bread whenever we ran out.'' All these examples communicate what you mean by ''a good restaurant.''

Giving examples to explain a general statement is based on the same principle as replacing general words with specific words. To see how the principle works for a reader, read the following passage quickly and then ask yourself ''What is a ritual?''

> We are constantly performing rituals. . . . All are repeated structured practices, some consciously designed in detail, some more consciously performed than others, and some emerging spontaneously. Each ritual is a repeated, coherently structured, and unified aspect of our experience. In performing them, we give structure and significance to our activities, minimizing chaos and disparity in our actions. (Lakoff and Johnson, *Metaphors We Live By,* pages 231–232)

Now read the passage as the authors wrote it, with the examples included.

> We are constantly performing rituals, *from casual rituals, like making the morning coffee by the same sequence of steps each day and watching the eleven o'clock news straight to the end (after we've seen it already at six o'clock); to going to football games, Thanksgiving dinners, and university lectures by distinguished visitors; and so on to the most solemn prescribed religious practices.* All are repeated structured practices, some consciously designed in detail, some more consciously performed than others, and some emerging spontaneously. Each ritual is a repeated, coherently structured, and unified aspect of our experience. In performing them, we give structure and significance to our activities, minimizing chaos and disparity in our actions.

Did your understanding of rituals deepen after reading the version with examples? Which version was easier to read? Which version was more interesting to you? Undoubtedly, the examples in the second passage make the definition of ritual clearer, easier to read, and more interesting. Notice that the authors provide examples of several kinds of rituals—personal rituals, social rituals, and religious rituals. For some categories, they provide several examples.

With this experiment in mind as you write, remember that readers need many specific examples to understand exactly what you mean. Even when you are being perfectly clear (as the writers were in the first passage about rituals), examples make the meaning sharper and deeper. Readers need abstract words and general words, such as *meal* and *rituals,* made concrete and specific.

Use Different Kinds of Examples. Examples may be single words, phrases, anecdotes, or extended anecdotes from a paragraph to a whole essay in length. When you write, you can use examples from your general knowledge, from reading, and from personal experience.

In the passage about rituals Lakoff and Johnson use examples that are words or phrases to make the general term specific, from ''ritual'' to ''casual ritual'' to ''making morning coffee.'' To see the principle of going from general to specific (which you learned about in Chapter 3) as a way to strengthen your writing, look at this chart.

General	Specific	More Specific
rituals	casual rituals	making morning coffee
		watching the late news
	social rituals	going to football games
		going to Thanksgiving dinner
		going to lectures by distinguished professors

General words are code words with rich meanings locked in the mind of the writer. When you write in code, readers cannot understand these rich meanings. They understand you only in a vague way. Your job as a writer is to translate your code of general words into specific words and examples.

Another kind of example is a typical situation or incident, rather than a specific one. Here is an excerpt from Amy Jones's essay on peer pressure, which appears later in this chapter.

> Another example is your best friend stays the night and your parents are out for the evening. Your friend decides it would be cool to take out their car which neither of you know how to drive. Depending on how good friends you are or how much you value what this person thinks of you, you might end up taking out the car and possibly wrecking it, hurting yourselves or someone else. It's very easy to allow a friend's opinion to cloud your judgment of right and wrong.

Jones identifies the example with the words ''Another example is,'' giving a clear transition with *another* and keeping the reader on track with her definition of peer pressure. Notice that the example she gives is a typical, not a specific, incident.

Another kind of example is the anecdote, a brief story about something that happened on one specific occasion. Here's part of an anecdote Jones uses to define peer pressure.

> Another instance involving a good friend of mine might help you understand where I'm coming from. His name was Rob Talkington, an actor on his way up. You see, we attended the same arts high school together where we studied acting. He was in the top ten percent of our class and by far the most handsome. He was new to our school and doing all he could to make friends. I'm afraid he tried a little too hard one night. There was a major party some friends of mine were having. There was a great deal of alcohol and a bit of marijuana, as is generally found in the majority of high school parties. Rob had made a really good friend in particular, named Matt. He was known to drink in excess at every party he attended. On this particular night there was a game being played called "quarters." Rob didn't really want to play at first, but the crowd innocently, in their own stupidity, egged him on. . . .

The anecdote continues for two more paragraphs, but you can see that Jones is telling a story about a particular incident as an example of peer pressure. Anecdotes are often just a few sentences long, but Jones decided to extend this anecdote with details because she knew the story would interest her intended audience (junior high school students) and make a strong impression on them.

Select Examples That Fit Your Audience, Purpose, and Point. Would junior high students be hooked with stories about high school students? Probably. Jones drew on her personal experience with peer pressure because she believed these examples would have more impact on her audience of junior high school students than information from psychologists or other experts in human behavior. She knew they understood the dictionary definition of peer pressure, but she wanted them to understand the concept on a deeper, more personal level because her purpose was to encourage them to be independent and to think for themselves.

Lakoff, a linguist, and Johnson, a philosopher, are university professors. Are the examples of rituals they used technical or hard to understand? Do you think they were writing a scholarly article for their fellow professors to read? No, they were writing for the general public. Because the public, not other professors, is their audience, they use examples from everyday life.

The kind and number of examples you choose depend on the subject matter, your purpose, and the particular audience you are addressing. For instance, if you are writing about rituals for a sociology paper, you would probably draw on examples from the textbook, unless the assignment specified that you should use only personal experience. You may use examples from your general knowledge, from personal experience, or from your reading. Selecting examples that will make your point and work with your audience is part of your job as a writer.

ORGANIZING EXAMPLES

Although examples are used in every kind of essay and range from single words to extended anecdotes, there is one basic guideline for organizing them that you can use: A general statement or opinion usually comes before the example. Again, it's the pattern of going from general to specific. If a writer forgets to provide the general statement first, the reader is left to wonder what the example means. Perhaps you've had the experience of listening to a friend tell a story and wondering "Why is he telling this story?" When you asked, the speaker told you he'd had a lucky day and the story was an example of his good luck. Once you knew what he was trying to tell you about, the story made more sense and was more interesting.

Provide Transitions. A writer should provide clear transitions that link the examples to the general statement. Examples are easily marked with transitional words and phrases that help the reader follow the organization of the essay. For instance, Jones's essay has a clear organization that is easy to follow. Her thesis (the general statement) appears in the introduction; the body is made up of three examples, which are clearly linked to the thesis by transitional words or phrases.

> *General statement:* The sad part of it is most people will worry too much about what their friends think, instead of realizing that if these people were truly their friends they wouldn't expect them to do something they don't agree with.
> *Example 1:* *For example,* when I was in seventh grade, there was this girl named Jenifer Reiger. . . .
> *Example 2:* *Another example* is your best friend spends the night. . . .
> *Example 3:* *Another instance* involving a good friend of mine might help you understand. . . .

When the phrase *for example* or *for instance* begins a sentence, use a comma after it, as in example 1. Notice that in examples 2 and 3 there is no comma after the words *example* and *instance* because each is the subject of the sentence, not part of a parenthetical phrase. When *such as* is used to introduce one or more examples, place a comma before and not after it: *There are different kinds of rituals, such as casual, social, and religious ones.*

POINTS TO REMEMBER ABOUT USING EXAMPLES

Use many examples because readers need them.
Use different kinds of examples: words or phrases, anecdotes, extended anecdotes.
Select examples that fit your audience, purpose, and main point.
State the general idea or opinion that your example explains before you give the example.
Connect examples with the general idea they explain with transitional words and phrases.

My Friend, Albert Einstein

Banesh Hoffmann

Banesh Hoffmann is a mathematician, physicist, author, and professor. He worked with the famous physicist Albert Einstein, whose theory of relativity and quantum theory of light revolutionized science.

Thinking Before Reading

What kind of person do you imagine when you think of a brilliant scientist? What does he or she look like? Act like? Sound like? How does this person treat other people? Would you like to be around this person? Write your responses in your Idea Bank.

Expanding Your Vocabulary from Reading

essence (1) essential nature or being
awry (3) askew, twisted to one side
prodigy (5) person with exceptional abilities
physics (6) the study of matter and energy and the interaction of the two in the fields of acoustics, optics, mechanics, atomic structure, and others
recalcitrant (9) stubbornly resistant to being managed
fathom (10) get to the bottom of in order to understand
trifle (19) something of little importance
whimsical (23) playful

1 He was one of the greatest scientists the world has ever known, yet if I had to convey the essence of Albert Einstein in a single word, I would choose

simplicity. Perhaps an anecdote will help. Once, caught in a downpour, he took off his hat and held it under his coat. Asked why, he explained, with admirable logic, that the rain would damage the hat, but his hair would be none the worse for its wetting. This knack for going instinctively to the heart of a matter was the secret of his major scientific discoveries—this and his extraordinary feeling for beauty.

2 I first met Albert Einstein in 1935, at the famous Institute for Advanced Study in Princeton, N.J. He had been among the first to be invited to the Institute, and was offered *carte blanche* as to salary. To the director's dismay, Einstein asked for an impossible sum: it was far too *small.* The director had to plead with him to accept a larger salary.

3 I was in awe of Einstein, and hesitated before approaching him about some ideas I had been working on. When I finally knocked on his door, a gentle voice said, "Come"—with a rising inflection that made the single word both a welcome and a question. I entered his office and found him seated at a table, calculating and smoking his pipe. Dressed in ill-fitting clothes, his hair characteristically awry, he smiled a warm welcome. His utter naturalness at once set me at ease.

4 As I began to explain my ideas, he asked me to write the equations on the blackboard so he could see how they developed. Then came the staggering—and altogether endearing—request: "Please go slowly. I do not understand things quickly." This from Einstein! He said it gently, and I laughed. From then on, all vestiges of fear were gone.

5 Einstein was born in 1879 in the German city of Ulm. He had been no infant prodigy; indeed, he was so late in learning to speak that his parents feared he was a dullard. In school, though his teachers saw no special talent in him, the signs were already there. He taught himself calculus, for example, and his teachers seemed a little afraid of him because he asked questions they could not answer. At the age of 16, he asked himself whether a light wave would seem stationary if one ran abreast of it. From that innocent question would arise, ten years later, his theory of relativity.

6 Einstein failed his entrance examinations at the Swiss Federal Polytechnic School, in Zurich, but was admitted a year later. There he went beyond his regular work to study the masterworks of physics on his own. Rejected when he applied for academic positions, he ultimately found work, in 1902, as a patent examiner in Berne, and there in 1905 his genius burst into fabulous flower.

7 Among the extraordinary things he produced in that memorable year were his theory of relativity, with its famous offshoot, $E = mc^2$ (energy equals mass times the speed of light squared), and his quantum theory of light. These two theories were not only revolutionary, but seemingly contradictory: the former was intimately linked to the theory that light consists of waves, while the latter said it consists somehow of particles. Yet this unknown young man

boldly proposed both at once—and he was right in both cases, though how he could have been is far too complex a story to tell here.

8 Collaborating with Einstein was an unforgettable experience. In 1937, the Polish physicist Leopold Infeld and I asked if we could work with him. He was pleased with the proposal, since he had an idea about gravitation waiting to be worked out in detail. Thus we got to know not merely the man and the friend, but also the professional.

9 The intensity and depth of his concentration were fantastic. When battling a recalcitrant problem, he worried it as an animal worries its prey. Often, when we found ourselves up against a seemingly insuperable difficulty, he would stand up, put his pipe on the table, and say in his quaint English, "I will a little tink" (he could not pronounce "th"). Then he would pace up and down, twirling a lock of his long, graying hair around his forefinger.

10 A dreamy, faraway and yet inward look would come over his face. There was no appearance of concentration, no furrowing of the brow—only a placid inner communion. The minutes would pass, and then suddenly Einstein would stop pacing as his face relaxed into a gentle smile. He had found the solution to the problem. Sometimes it was so simple that Infeld and I could have kicked ourselves for not having thought of it. But the magic had been performed invisibly in the depths of Einstein's mind, by a process we could not fathom.

11 Although Einstein felt no need for religious ritual and belonged to no formal religious group, he was the most deeply religious man I have known. He once said to me, "Ideas come from God," and one could hear the capital "G" in the reverence with which he pronounced the word. On the marble fireplace in the mathematics building at Princeton University is carved, in the original German, what one might call his scientific credo: "God is subtle, but he is not malicious." By this Einstein meant that scientists could expect to find their task difficult, but not hopeless: the Universe was a Universe of law, and God was not confusing us with deliberate paradoxes and contradictions.

12 Einstein was an accomplished amateur musician. We used to play duets, he on the violin, I at the piano. One day he surprised me by saying Mozart was the greatest composer of all. Beethoven "created" his music, but the music of Mozart was of such purity and beauty one felt he had merely "found" it—that it had always existed as part of the inner beauty of the Universe, waiting to be revealed.

13 It was this very Mozartean simplicity that most characterized Einstein's methods. His 1905 theory of relativity, for example, was built on just two simple assumptions. One is the so-called principle of relativity, which means, roughly speaking, that we cannot tell whether we are at rest or moving smoothly. The other assumption is that the speed of light is the same no matter what the speed of the object that produces it. You can see how reasonable this is if you think of agitating a stick in a lake to create waves. Whether you wiggle the stick from a stationary pier, or from a rushing speedboat, the waves,

once generated, are on their own, and their speed has nothing to do with that of the stick.

14 Each of these assumptions, by itself, was so plausible as to seem primitively obvious. But together they were in such violent conflict that a lesser man would have dropped one or the other and fled in panic. Einstein daringly kept both—and by so doing he revolutionized physics. For he demonstrated they could, after all, exist peacefully side by side, provided we gave up cherished beliefs about the nature of time.

15 Science is like a house of cards, with concepts like time and space at the lowest level. Tampering with time brought most of the house tumbling down, and it was this that made Einstein's work so important—and controversial. At a conference in Princeton in honor of his 70th birthday, one of the speakers, a Nobel Prize-winner, tried to convey the magical quality of Einstein's achievement. Words failed him, and with a shrug of helplessness he pointed to his wristwatch, and said in tones of awed amazement, "It all came from this." His very ineloquence made this the most eloquent tribute I have heard to Einstein's genius.

16 We think of Einstein as one concerned only with the deepest aspects of science. But he saw scientific principles in everyday things to which most of us would give barely a second thought. He once asked me if I had ever wondered why a man's feet will sink into either dry or completely submerged sand, while sand that is merely damp provides a firm surface. When I could not answer, he offered a simple explanation.

17 It depends, he pointed out, on *surface tension,* the elastic-skin effect of a liquid surface. This is what holds a drop together, or causes two small raindrops on a window pane to pull into one big drop the moment their surfaces touch.

18 When sand is damp, Einstein explained, there are tiny amounts of water between grains. The surface tensions of these tiny amounts of water pull all the grains together, and friction then makes them hard to budge. When the sand is dry, there is obviously no water between grains. If the sand is fully immersed, there is water between grains, but no water *surface* to pull them together.

19 This is not as important as relativity; yet there is no telling what seeming trifle will lead an Einstein to a major discovery. And the puzzle of the sand does give us an inkling of the power and elegance of his mind.

20 Einstein's work, performed quietly with pencil and paper, seemed remote from the turmoil of everyday life. But his ideas were so revolutionary they caused violent controversy and irrational anger. Indeed, in order to be able to award him a belated Nobel Prize, the selection committee had to avoid mentioning relativity, and pretend the prize was awarded primarily for his work on the quantum theory.

21 Political events upset the serenity of his life even more. When the Nazis

came to power in Germany, his theories were officially declared false because they had been formulated by a Jew. His property was confiscated, and it is said a price was put on his head.

22 When scientists in the United States, fearful that the Nazis might develop an atomic bomb, sought to alert American authorities to the danger, they were scarcely heeded. In desperation, they drafted a letter which Einstein signed and sent directly to President Roosevelt. It was this act that led to the fateful decision to go all-out on the production of an atomic bomb—an endeavor in which Einstein took no active part. When he heard of the agony and destruction that his $E = mc^2$ had wrought, he was dismayed beyond measure, and from then on there was a look of ineffable sadness in his eyes.

23 There was something elusively whimsical about Einstein. It is illustrated by my favorite anecdote about him. In his first year in Princeton, on Christmas Eve, so the story goes, some children sang carols outside his house. Having finished, they knocked on his door and explained they were collecting money to buy Christmas presents. Einstein listened, then said, ''Wait a moment.'' He put on his scarf and overcoat, and took his violin from its case. Then, joining the children as they went from door to door, he accompanied their singing of ''Silent Night'' on his violin.

24 How shall I sum up what it meant to have known Einstein and his works? Like the Nobel Prize-winner who pointed helplessly at his watch, I can find no adequate words. It was akin to the revelation of great art that lets one see what was formerly hidden. And when, for example, I walk on the sand of a lonely beach, I am reminded of his ceaseless search for cosmic simplicity—and the scene takes on a deeper, sadder beauty.

Jotting Down Your First Responses

1. What surprised you about Albert Einstein as a person or as a scientist?
2. What traits do you most admire in Einstein? Why?
3. Have you ever been in awe of someone, as Hoffmann was of Einstein, and talked with that person? How did you feel? What happened?

Checking Your Comprehension

1. What word describes the essence of Einstein, according to Hoffmann?
2. Why does Hoffmann go to see Einstein?
3. What did Einstein do that wiped out Hoffmann's fear of the great man?
4. What kind of student was Einstein?
5. What was Einstein's first job?
6. What did Einstein do when he was concentrating on a problem?
7. What did Einstein mean by the credo ''God is subtle, but he is not malicious''?

8. What musical instrument did Einstein play?
9. What everyday example does Hoffmann use to explain the assumption about the speed of light?
10. Why do your feet sink into dry sand or submerged sand, but do not sink into damp sand, according to Einstein?
11. Why did Einstein come to the United States?
12. What two theories is Einstein famous for?
13. What was so unusual about his holding both theories?

Understanding a Writer's Patterns

1. Look at the last sentence of paragraph 1. Hoffmann "promises" in his thesis to focus on two qualities of Einstein—his sense of simplicity and his feeling for beauty. Does Hoffmann fulfill his promise to you the reader? Explain. Does everything that follows add to your picture of a man who loves simplicity and beauty? If not, what doesn't seem to fit?
2. Hoffmann blends anecdotes from his own experience with Einstein, anecdotes he has heard about Einstein, and a little information about Einstein's life and his contribution to science. Scan the essay and list three personal experience anecdotes. What character trait is each one an example of?
3. Scan the essay again and list three anecdotes Hoffmann heard about Einstein. What character trait is each one an example of?
4. What words in the first sentence of paragraph 24 inform the reader that the writer is concluding?
5. What key word does the writer repeat in the conclusion?
6. In the conclusion what two references to earlier content in the essay link the ending with the middle?

Making Predictions and Drawing Inferences

1. Why does Hoffmann entitle this essay "My Friend, Albert Einstein"? What hints does the title give about the kind of picture Hoffmann will draw of this famous scientist?
2. How did Einstein's mind work? What was typical of his thinking habits? Do you have any of these habits of the mind? Explain.
3. In paragraph 4 why was Einstein's request to go slowly both "staggering" and "endearing"?

Making Judgments and Thinking Critically

1. If Hoffmann had left out the personal experience anecdotes, how would that have changed your picture of Albert Einstein?
2. What distinguishes a genius from an ordinary thinker?

3. Why do you think Hoffmann and Einstein became friends? What qualities of each contributed to the friendship?
4. Hoffmann begins with a general statement about Einstein in the first and last sentences of the opening paragraph. Would another opening be more effective? Why or why not?

Using New Words

1. Choose two words from the reading selection to add to your writing and speaking vocabulary. Make a vocabulary card for each one. Write the word on one side of the card and a definition and an original sentence on the other.
2. Find the following words in the reading and define them from the sense of the sentences in which they appear: *carte blanche* (paragraph 2), inflection (paragraph 3), staggering (paragraph 4), and vestiges (paragraph 4). Sometimes you may need to read two or three sentences or reread a sentence several times in order to define a word.
3. The words below end in *-ly* because they work as adverbs in the sentences in which they appear. Find the words in the paragraphs indicated and tell what words the adverbs modify. (Reminder: Adverbs modify verbs, adjectives, or other adverbs.)

Adverb	**Word Modified**
characteristically (3)	adjective *awry*
quickly (4)	
gently (4)	
intimately (7)	
suddenly (10)	
invisibly (10)	
deeply (11)	
smoothly (13)	
peacefully (14)	
completely (16)	

4. Give the noun and adjective forms for each of the adverbs in question 3. (Reminder: Nouns often end in *-ness* or *-ity*. Adjectives often end in *-tle*, *-ate*, *-ible*, *-ful*, or *-ic*.)

Adverb	Noun	Adjective
characteristically	characteristic	characteristic
quickly		
gently		
intimately		
suddenly		
invisibly		
deeply		
smoothly		
peacefully		
completely		

Responding by Writing

1. Write an essay that develops a portrait of someone you know well. It may be someone you admire or dislike from your past or present, from your home, work, school, or social life. Decide on the main impression you want readers in this class to have about this person. Write a trial thesis. Select only information and anecdotes that are examples of the qualities you are emphasizing. Use at least two examples. Remember, examples often begin with "one time" or "once."
2. Write an essay for an audience of this class comparing the two portraits of people you have read: "Love, Brenda" in Chapter 5 and "My Friend, Albert Einstein." Include three or four points of comparison as you discuss these two essays. For example: (a) Both writers emphasize a quality in the person they particularly admire. (b) Both use examples (especially anecdotes) to bring a vivid sense of the person to the page. (c) Both use personal experiences with the person. Your thesis might be something like this: "Love, Brenda" and "My Friend, Albert Einstein" bring two famous people to life in a warm and personal way. Be sure to use the titles of the essays and the authors' names. Remember to use quotation marks to punctuate the titles.
3. In a general encyclopedia or a biographical reference book read the entry on Albert Einstein. Does the reference book or the essay give you a better sense of the person? Which is more informative? Which is more interesting? How would you describe the difference between the two

sources? Why are they different? Write an essay explaining the differences between the two sources for an audience of your teacher.

4. Which of the two essays, "Love, Brenda" and "My Friend, Albert Einstein," do you think is the stronger description of a person? Why? Give several reasons and examples from the essays. Use at least two quotations to help explain your choice. Remember that you are evaluating the quality of the description of the personality, not the person being described. Write an essay to your teacher.

Notions and Nations of Sweat

Diane Ackerman

Author of five books of poetry and several books of nonfiction, Diane Ackerman is currently a staff writer for *The New Yorker.* This selection is taken from her book *A Natural History of the Senses* (1990).

Thinking Before Reading

Make a list of memories of smells. Recall both pleasurable and repugnant smells and their effects on you. Write these in your Idea Bank.

Expanding Your Vocabulary from Reading

anthropologist (1) one who studies the physical, social, and cultural development of human beings
predatory (1) preying on other animals for food
pungent (1) sharp, acrid
anecdotal evidence (1) support by brief stories of incidents as opposed to scientific research and experiments
antimacassars (1) lacy napkinlike coverings for chair and sofa backs and arms
puberty (2) stage of reaching sexual maturity

1 In general, humans have a strong body odor, and anthropologist Dr. Louis S. B. Leakey thinks our ancestors may have had an even stronger odor, one that predatory animals found foul enough to avoid. Not long ago, I spent some time in Texas, studying bats. I placed a large Indonesian flying fox in my hair, to see if it would get entangled, as the old wives' tales warned. Not only did it not tangle, it began to cough gently from the mingling smells of my soap, cologne, saltiness, oils, and other human odors. When I put it back in its cage, it cleaned itself like a cat for many minutes, clearly feeling soiled by the

human contact. Many plants—like rosemary or sage—have evolved pungent odors to repel predators; why not animals? Nature rarely wastes a winning strategy. Of course, some humans have much stronger odors than others. Folk wisdom says that brunettes "smell different" from redheads, who smell different from blondes. There's been so much anecdotal evidence about different races having distinctive odors—because of diets, habits, hairiness or lack of it—that such claims are difficult to discount, even though the topic scares most scientists, who are understandably concerned about being called racist. There hasn't been a great deal of research into national and racial odors. In any case, one culture doesn't "smell" better or worse than another, just different, but that may be why the word "stinking" so often appears as an adjective in streams of racial abuse. Asiatics don't have as many apocrine glands at the base of hair follicles as occidentals do, and as a result they often find Europeans ripe-smelling. A strong body odor among Japanese men is so rare that at one time it could disqualify them from military service. This is also why there is so much scenting of the room and air in Asian life, and much less scenting of the body. Pungent odors are absorbed by fats: If you put an onion or cantaloupe in the refrigerator with an open tub of butter, the butter will absorb the odor. Hair also contains fat, which is why it leaves grease stains on pillows and antimacassars. It absorbs smells, too, like smoke or cologne. The hairiness of Caucasians and Blacks makes them very sweaty compared to Asians, but colognes simmer in their oil and warmth like votive candles.

2 Body odor comes from the apocrine glands, which are small when we're born and develop substantially during puberty; there are many of them scattered around our armpits, face, chest, genitals, and anus. Some researchers conclude that a large part of our joy in kissing is really a joy in smelling and caressing each other's face, where one's personal scent glows. Among far-flung tribes in a number of countries—Borneo, on the Gambia River in West Africa, in Burma, in Siberia, in India—the word for "kiss" means "smell"; a kiss is really a prolonged smelling of one's beloved, relative, or friend. Members of a tribe in New Guinea say good-bye by putting a hand in each other's armpit, withdrawing it and stroking it over themselves, thus becoming coated with the friend's scent; other cultures sniff each other or rub noses in greeting.

Jotting Down Your First Responses

1. What sharp memories of experiences associated with smell do you have? Recall a place that is associated in your memory with a smell—a basement, kitchen, movie theater, funeral home, library, church or synagogue. Or recall a person whom you associate with a particular smell—cigar smoke and your grandfather, garlic and a neighbor, leather and a

friend. Or, think about a smell that always brings to mind an incident in your life.
2. Do you ever judge a person or place by its smell? Give an example.
3. Which are your dominant senses—sight, hearing, touch, taste, or smell? Which do you rely on the least?

Checking Your Comprehension

1. What did the Indonesian flying fox do after Ackerman removed it from her hair? Why?
2. Why has nature given some plants a pungent odor?
3. What causes different races to have different odors?
4. Why is "You stinking ——" a familiar insult by children and bigots?
5. When Ackerman describes Europeans as "ripe-smelling" compared to Asiatics, what does she mean?
6. What food absorbs pungent odors in your refrigerator? Why?
7. Why does hair absorb smoke and cologne smells?
8. What part does smell play in kissing, according to some researchers?

Understanding a Writer's Patterns

1. What is the implied thesis of the essay?
2. Ackerman's experiment with the flying fox did not support the old wives' tale predicting the fox would become entangled in her hair. Instead, it provided an example to support Dr. Leakey's theory. What is this theory?
3. Ackerman gives three examples to support her claim that "one culture doesn't smell better or worse, just different." What are they?
4. What examples does Ackerman give to support the conclusion that kissing and smelling are related?

Making Predictions and Drawing Inferences

1. Before you read the essay, what did you think the essay would be about from reading the title?
2. Why would an anthropologist study smells?
3. What effects does the hairiness of Caucasians and Blacks have on colognes? Why?
4. According to Ackerman, "Folk wisdom says that brunettes 'smell different' from redheads. . . ." What is folk wisdom and what contrasting source of information is she implying?
5. Since the apocrine glands, which cause body odor, develop during puberty, what can you infer about the body odor of children?

Making Judgments and Thinking Critically

1. Ackerman makes a distinction between smelling good or bad and smelling different. Do you agree with this distinction? Why or why not?
2. Why are scientists afraid of being called racist if they do research about racial or national differences?
3. What attitudes and values do the gigantic sales of perfumes, air fresheners, and deodorants in the United States reflect?

Using New Words

1. Choose three words to add to your set of vocabulary cards. Write each word on one side of a card and a definition and an original sentence on the other side.
2. Go through all your vocabulary cards, pronouncing the words aloud until you are comfortable saying them.
3. The suffix *-logist* indicates a person who studies a specific field of knowledge. For instance, an anthropologist (from *anthropo,* meaning ''human being'') is one who studies the physical, social, and cultural development of the human race. Join the root forms below with the suffix *-logist* to form the words that mean a person who studies the particular field of knowledge indicated by the root. Write the words and practice reading them aloud until you are comfortable saying them.

   bio: life and living organisms
   pharmaco: composition, effects, and uses of drugs
   geo: origin, history, and structure of the earth
   psycho: mental processes and behavior of humans
   socio: origins, organizations, institutions, and development of human society
   musico: history and features of music
   cardio: diseases and functioning of the heart

Responding by Writing

1. Write an essay about the smells of your family or ethnic, racial, or regional heritage (Southern, New England, Swedish, German, Jewish, coastal, Midwestern). Write for classmates from a different background to let them ''visit'' this part of your past.
2. Just as people favor their right hand or their left, they seem to have preferred senses. Decide which is the sense you use most and write an essay about your preferred sense. Give examples showing that you rely on this sense.
3. Write an essay about Ackerman's use of examples in this essay. Has she used enough? Has she chosen effective examples? What kinds of exam-

ples does she use? Use the title (in quotation marks) and the writer's name so that your audience will know which essay you are discussing. After you have written a draft, write a title for your essay, but don't use Ackerman's title for the title of your essay.

How To Relax in a Crowd

David D. Burns

David D. Burns, M.D., is a practicing psychiatrist and a professor of psychiatry at the University of Pennsylvania School of Medicine in Philadelphia. This selection, condensed from his books *The Feeling Good Handbook* and *Intimate Connections,* was published in *Reader's Digest.*

Thinking Before Reading

Do you enjoy speaking or performing in front of a group or do you avoid such situations? Do you speak out easily in a classroom or meeting or do you avoid offering your opinions and asking questions? In your Idea Bank describe your feelings and their effect on how well or easily you speak in group situations.

Expanding Your Vocabulary from Reading

anxiety (1) worry, fear
incapacitating (6) paralyzing
phobias (6) deep-seated fears that alter behavior
shrinks (10) slang term for professionals who treat mental or emotional problems
frankness (11) openness about one's thoughts and feelings
gibberish (18) nonsense
slight (25) act of disrespect or discourtesy
therapists (26) psychiatrists, psychologists, social workers, and others trained to treat mental and emotional problems
reframing (26) thinking about a problem as an opportunity instead of a dead end

1 Recently I was invited to lecture on anxiety to several hundred mental-health professionals in Boston. My talk was scheduled to follow those of a number of prominent psychiatrists. When my turn came, I was especially

nervous because the speaker before me had been particularly impressive and charming.

2 As I approached the podium, my heart pounded and my mouth went completely dry. *What am I doing here?* I asked myself.

3 Making matters worse, my presentation partly dealt with fear of public speaking. To calm myself, I tried an unconventional tactic. I asked the audience, "How many of you feel nervous when you give a speech?" Nearly every hand went up. "Well, that's *exactly* how I feel right now!"

4 The audience responded with laughter. I relaxed and was able to move into my presentation.

5 At times, we all find ourselves in situations that make us nervous. Perhaps you're afraid of saying foolish things at a cocktail party, stumbling over a presentation at work or having your mind go blank on a test.

6 For some of us, the anxiety is so severe that it is incapacitating. A 1984 National Institute of Mental Health (NIMH) survey estimated that two to four million Americans are handicapped by social phobias in their personal and professional lives. Although the NIMH study focused on severe disorders, nearly everyone has experienced mild forms of social anxiety.

7 Over the years, my work with hundreds of patients has taught me that anyone can increase his or her social confidence, even in the most stressful situations. Here are a few simple but helpful tips:

8 *1. Take off the false front.* When my wife and I moved into a new neighborhood, our daughter began playing with a girl who lived nearby in a mansion. One night, clad in jeans and an old T-shirt, I stopped by to pick up my daughter. Sue, the friend's mother, who was dressed like a model out of *Vogue,* invited me into a large hallway filled with expensive antiques and oil paintings. It was like a museum.

9 I felt very awkward. Noticing my uneasiness, Sue asked if something was wrong. I had the urge to deny how I felt but instead confessed, "I'm not used to being in such a fancy house."

10 "Why, I didn't think *shrinks* ever felt insecure," she said with a laugh.

11 I believe my openness made us both feel more comfortable. Denying how I felt would only have added to the tension and made me appear phony. As with the Boston speech, I was frank about my insecurities. Such frankness is a good way to bring others closer to us.

12 *2. Tackle your fears one step at a time.* While affiliated with Penn State University, psychologist Michael J. Mahoney and gymnastics coach Marshall Avener investigated the impact of anxiety on gymnasts at the 1976 U.S. Olympic Team trials. Who do you think experienced more anxiety before competition—the athletes who went on to win, or those who ended up losing? The researchers discovered that both groups were equally anxious. What distinguished the winners from the losers was how they coped.

13 Less successful athletes dwelled on their fears, arousing themselves to states of near panic as they imagined a disastrous performance. The winners

typically ignored their anxiety, concentrating instead on what they had to do: *Take a deep breath,* or *Now reach up and grip the bar.* They controlled their fears by breaking the task down into a series of small steps. This technique will work with anything you have to accomplish.

14 Penny was referred to me three days before her first law-school final. "I'm so panicky, I can't understand a single sentence in my books," she told me. "I know I'm going to flunk. I might as well just drop out."

15 Anxiety creates the myth that we can't function properly. Penny needed to learn that even under pressure she could still work effectively. The first step was to find ways to make the test seem less threatening. Since Penny was afraid that her mind would move too fast to read even the instructions properly, she agreed to read everything word by word. If she ran into a difficult question, she would try to paraphrase it.

16 More important, I convinced Penny that no matter how nervous she became, she should keep her pencil moving for the entire two hours of the test. I told her she was not allowed to waste any time questioning herself.

17 "What if I can't think of anything meaningful to put down?" she asked.

18 "Put down anything," I said, "even if it's gibberish."

19 Two weeks later Penny came back with her exam grade—an A. Her experience shows how vitally important it is not to give up when you're nervous. Write that first sentence of a report or take that first stroke in a swim race. Once you start, you'll find you can do much better than you thought.

20 *3. Imitate Johnny Carson.* Many of us are forced to talk to people in uncomfortable situations. Maybe it's your new boss at a company party or your future in-laws. What do you say when your mind goes blank?

21 Make the other person the focus of the conversation. Johnny Carson brings out the best in his guests simply by trying to learn as much as possible about them. You can use the same approach by asking a few questions: "How did you get interested in such-and-such?" or "Will you tell me more about it?"

22 All most people want is for you to pay attention to them. Psychiatrists and psychologists make handsome livings just by nodding their heads knowingly and asking a few questions. If they can get away with it, so can you.

23 *4. Turn anxiety into energy.* Everybody gets nervous before performing in public, whether making a business presentation or acting in a school play. The trick is to let your nerves work for you.

24 I've been interviewed many times on television, and the experience used to make me extremely anxious. One patient told me she was surprised at how stiff and awkward I appeared. As soon as I got on the air, I'd freeze up and lose my spontaneity. People gave me advice, but nothing worked. The harder I tried to relax, the more nervous I got.

25 Eventually, I stumbled across a solution. On one talk show, the producer had arranged a debate between another psychiatrist and me. During the opening

segment, my fellow guest erroneously suggested that I was just an ''author'' and not a researcher. Angered by the slight, I decided to stop worrying about being a courteous, charming guest. Instead, I focused on presenting my ideas with the force and conviction they deserved. Suddenly I felt energized and found myself loving every minute of the show. I also got some of the most positive feedback I've ever received.

26 Therapists call this concept positive reframing, which means viewing a problem differently—as ''good'' rather than ''bad.'' You reduce anxiety by believing in yourself and having the courage to express your feelings. Once I used my nervousness—that extra jolt of adrenaline—as a form of energy, I was able to come on strong and ''sock it to 'em.''

27 5. *Stop comparing yourself.* One of our biggest social cripplers is the fear of not measuring up. Perhaps you feel you won't impress others because they are more confident, successful, intelligent or attractive than you. Such thinking is wrong-headed. The secret of doing well with others is accepting yourself.

28 When I was a college student, I kept a journal filled with private memories. Some were painful recollections from childhood—times when I felt hurt, confused, lonely and insecure. I described fragments of dreams and intensely personal feelings of anger and hatred, as well as things I enjoyed such as magic stores and coin shops.

29 Then a terrible thing happened. After dinner one night I realized that I had left my journal in a coat room outside the campus dining hall. Terrified that somebody might read it and find out the truth about me, I raced back, only to discover that it was gone.

30 Weeks passed, and eventually I gave up hope of ever finding it again. A month later, I was hanging up my jacket in the same place when I saw my brown, tattered journal, just where I'd left it. Nervously I flipped through the pages and found that a stranger had written this entry: ''God bless you. I am a lot like you, only I don't keep a diary, and I'm grateful to know there are others like me. I hope things turn out well for you.''

31 Tears came to my eyes. It had never dawned on me that anyone could know my inner feelings and still care about me.

32 No matter what you're like—whether you're rich or poor, insecure or outgoing, brilliant or average, attractive or plain—some people like you and others couldn't care less. *Nobody* gets accepted by everyone. But far more people will be attracted to you if you accept yourself.

Jotting Down Your First Responses

1. What surprised you about the writer's fear of public speaking?
2. What's one idea for speaking to a group that you can use?

3. Do you compare your appearance, grades, job success, athletic performance, or financial state with others? What are the advantages or disadvantages of these comparisons?

Checking Your Comprehension

1. What kind of doctor is David Burns?
2. In the introduction Burns describes a speaking situation where he felt scared. What was the topic of his speech?
3. What does Burns mean by ''social phobias,'' ''social anxiety,'' and ''social confidence''?
4. In an anecdote Burns describes picking up his child at a neighbor's mansion and feeling uneasy. Why was he uneasy?
5. How did he overcome the uneasy feeling?
6. What did Mahoney and Avener's study of gymnasts on the 1976 Olympic Team trials reveal about anxiety?
7. How did Penny overcome test anxiety?
8. What strategy for overcoming social anxiety is based on Johnny Carson's interview style?
9. In a TV debate how did the writer use his anger in a positive way? What do therapists call this behavior?
10. Why was Burns terrified when he lost his journal?

Understanding a Writer's Patterns

1. What strategy does Burns use in the introduction?
2. Who is the intended audience of the article? How do you know?
3. What sentence in paragraph 7 seems to be the best statement of the writer's thesis?
4. Why does Burns use the statistic ''two to four million Americans are handicapped by social phobias'' when the article is about social anxiety?
5. Burns gives five tips for handling social anxiety, such as the fear of public speaking. List all five tips in a column, leaving room for two more columns.
6. In the second column note one example Burns used to explain each tip.
7. In the third column identify the kind of example he used: personal experience with his own fear, professional experience as a doctor, general example that many people might have experienced, or research.
8. What words in paragraph 8 indicate that Burns is using an example?
9. What words in paragraph 24 show that he is using a general example of his nervousness about speaking in public?
10. What words in paragraph 25 show that Burns is shifting to a more specific example?

11. What words in paragraph 28 show that he is using a specific example?
12. Does the final paragraph conclude the section about tip 5 or does it conclude the whole essay?

Making Predictions and Drawing Inferences

1. Why is Burns qualified to write about the fear of public speaking?
2. In paragraph 9 Burns's hostess recognizes his uneasiness. What do you think he did that revealed his feelings to the woman?
3. In paragraph 13 Burns gives an example of something a winning gymnast might say to himself or herself. What idea for dealing with stress does this example explain?

Making Judgments and Thinking Critically

1. Each tip begins with a brief directive (a statement that tells you what to do). Evaluate each one by reading the discussion and examples that follow. Can the way any tip is stated be improved to be more helpful and appropriate? If so, which ones?
2. Suggest more helpful and appropriate substitutes for the tips you identified as needing improvement.
3. Does the conclusion give you a sense of closure? Why or why not? Write a sentence or two to add to the conclusion.

Using New Words

1. Make vocabulary cards for two words you want to add to your writing and speaking vocabulary. Add these to your set of vocabulary cards.
2. Write the antonyms (opposites) of the following words: *incapacitating, denying, frankness, slight, anxiety.* Before you use the dictionary, try to figure out the meaning of the words by reading the sentences in which they appear in the essay, and then try to think of words that mean the opposite.
3. Identify the strong action verbs in each tip. Replace them with weaker verbs; use *do, don't, use,* and *be* when you can. Which verbs are more effective? Why?

Responding by Writing

1. Write an essay about a difficult situation you learned to cope with by breaking it down into a series of small steps, as Burns reports that the Olympic athletes in the study did. Write for an audience of classmates. Use examples, both general and specific.
2. Write an essay about your fear of speaking in public. (a) Explain what kind of situation is difficult for you and how fear affects your perfor-

mance in that situation. Give examples. (b) What strategies from Burns's article might help you overcome this fear? How and when might you put these ideas into practice? Write to an audience of this class. Use the title of the article and the name of the author in your essay.

3. Fear of speaking in a group is a common fear, but speaking in public is only one of many stressful situations that make people nervous and anxious, especially in college. Think of another anxiety-producing situation in which one or all of Burns's coping tips might help you. In an essay explain what the anxiety is, give examples, and tell how you might apply Burns's tips. Write for an audience of classmates.
4. If you have read at least two essays in this chapter, write an essay to an audience of your teacher in which you discuss the value of examples in writing. Your thesis might be something like: Examples are used in almost every essay because they hook a reader's attention and help a reader understand more deeply.

   Try answering these questions about the essays in this chapter before you begin. How much did examples help you understand a writer's point or emphasis? What kind of example seemed to be most effective with you? How many examples did each writer use? How often? Use your answers as notes. Then use listing or clustering to discover additional ideas for the essay.

   Refer to all the essays you read in this chapter. Be sure to mention the authors' names and the essays' titles. Use quotation marks to punctuate the titles.

Don't Press Your Luck

Amy Marie Jones

Amy Marie Jones divides her time between college classes and work. Her immediate goal is to earn a degree in film. She wrote this essay as a speech to be delivered to junior high school students. She felt that her age as a young college student and her personal experience would give credibility to her discussion of peer pressure with that audience.

Thinking Before Reading

No matter how old we are, our peers influence us all in some areas of our lives—the clothes we wear, the cars we drive, how we spend our leisure time, how we vote, and so on. Write a few sentences in your Idea Bank about an area of your life in which you are sometimes influenced by peer pressure.

Expanding Your Vocabulary from Reading

coerce (2) use pressure or threaten someone into an action
blacktop (2) area paved with asphalt, or the paving material itself
confronting (2) coming face to face with
humiliation (2) shame, feeling without pride or dignity
opted (2) chose
egged (4) urged on with taunts or dares

1 Hello, my name is Ms. Jones and I'd like to thank you for giving me the opportunity to come and speak to you today. The reason I'm here today is to talk to you about peer pressure, something I'm sure each of you is dealing with. It may have been alcohol or drugs or maybe it was lying to your mom about where you were going to be so that you could stay out all night. I remember what it was like when I was your age, always trying to fit in with the crowd. The sad part of it is most people will worry too much about what their friends think, instead of realizing that if these people were truly their friends they wouldn't expect them to do something they don't agree with.

2 My definition of peer pressure is when the majority of a crowd or a close circle of friends attempts to coerce you into something that you either don't agree with or just don't want to do. For example, when I was in seventh grade, there was this girl named Jenifer Reiger. We didn't exactly get along. She was spreading all sorts of rumors about me that were not true. I admit I didn't like it, but I wouldn't say they were life-threatening. On this one day while we were standing outside on the blacktop, my friends pointed out the fact that she was standing alone. Jenifer was a small, frail, almost granny-weak kind of girl and, well, I wasn't. I allowed them and my foolish pride to talk me into confronting her, which I knew could only lead to a fight. Instead of fighting I decided to give her the option to simply apologize to me. There she stood bravely trembling before me, helpless, but soon the feelings of pity were quickly erased with the opening of her mouth. Anger and humiliation came back with all the familiar rudeness that I had fallen victim to. With tears falling one at a time from her eyes, she opted not to apologize, leaving me with only one thing to do. At that moment my confidence lent me the courage not to fight, but to merely turn to my friends and say "Everyone has their own opinion." As I walked proudly away, she followed me and meekly uttered, "I'm sorry." I never spoke to her again. Although my friends felt I had let them and myself down, I felt victorious. Each of us must face our own Jenifers in life.

3 Another example is your best friend stays the night and your parents are out for the evening. Your friend decides it would be cool to take out their car which neither of you know how to drive. Depending on how close you are as friends or how much you value what this person thinks of you, you might end

up taking out the car and possibly wrecking it, hurting yourselves or someone else. It's very easy to allow a friend's opinion to cloud your judgment of right and wrong.

4 Another instance involving a good friend of mine might help you understand where I'm coming from. His name was Rob Talkington, an actor on his way up. You see, we attended the same arts high school together where we studied acting. He was in the top ten percent of our class and by far the most handsome. He was new to our school and doing all he could to make friends. I'm afraid he tried a little too hard one night. There was a major party some friends of mine were having. There was a great deal of alcohol and a bit of marijuana, as is generally found in the majority of high school parties. Rob had made a really good friend in particular, named Matt. He was known to drink in excess at every party he attended, although he was not alone. On this particular night there was a game being played called "quarters." I'm sure many of you have heard of this. Well, Rob didn't really want to play at first, but the crowd innocently, in their own stupidity, egged him on. Rob's and Matt's ride to the party had also decided to join in on the great party fun.

5 A few hours and three cases of beer later, the party began to wind down. On their way home the three of them were in a terrible car accident. The driver was thrown clear of the car and got off with a broken arm and a DWI on his driving record. Rob and Matt were not so lucky. They were both admitted to an emergency room. Matt had received extensive damage to his face and legs. All of his injuries were repairable by plastic surgery. Rob's injuries were minor as far as cuts and bruises go, but he has permanent brain damage. He is no longer able to walk, talk, dress, or feed himself.

6 We all continued to go and see him for a few months. That was seven years ago and we've all gone on with our lives and made new friends. How could you forget about a friend? You don't forget, you just grow up. You don't stop caring, you just start learning to take care of yourself. Rob would have wanted us to go on. The fact is we were just kids. I can't speak for everyone else, but I learned a great deal from that incident. I learned to make my own decisions because only you know what is right for you.

7 In today's society what other people think is held too highly. Deciding what's important, such as a person's values and ideals, morally speaking, is sometimes good to worry about, but to allow somebody's or a group's opinion to decide for you what clothes to wear or what car to buy is not right. A person should not be made to feel inferior because of their financial status.

8 So the next time someone tries to talk you into doing something that you don't want to do or, for any reason, don't agree with, think of my friend Rob and remember. The people you are so desperately trying to impress won't be around forever. The ones that are still around are the ones who allow you to make your own decisions. I know you feel that you are old enough to know what is right for you. All I ask is that you make your decisions wisely. New friends are easy to find—just give it a week.

Jotting Down Your First Responses

1. As you read, did you recall peer pressure on you during your own junior high or high school days? What happened?
2. Have you ever put pressure on a peer to act in some way he or she didn't want to? What happened?
3. In what areas do you experience peer pressure now?

Checking Your Comprehension

1. According to Jones, why are junior high students likely to have a problem with peer pressure?
2. What did Jenifer do that made Jones angry?
3. Why did Jones confront her?
4. What details does Jones use to describe her friend Rob?
5. What details does she give about the party?
6. What happened to the driver? To Matt? To Rob?
7. What is the request Jones closes with?

Understanding a Writer's Patterns

1. Reread paragraphs 1 and 8. What is the writer's implied thesis?
2. What two definitions of peer pressure does the writer use?
3. What phrases introduce each major example in the essay?
4. Jones creates a pattern by looking at peer pressure in three different ways. Look at paragraphs 6, 7, and 8. What is that pattern?
5. In the body of the essay Jones focuses on content. In paragraphs 1 and 8 she focuses on audience. What pronouns show this focus on the audience?

Making Predictions and Drawing Inferences

1. Why does Jones assume that all of the audience is dealing with peer pressure? Do you agree with her?
2. Was her choice of audiences an appropriate one? Why or why not?
3. Why did Jones's friends feel she let them down when she confronted Jenifer? Why did she feel victorious?
4. Why does Jones include the paragraph about people in general (paragraph 7) when she is addressing junior high school students?

Making Judgments and Thinking Critically

1. Do you think Jones's speech would be effective with a junior high audience? Why or why not? If yes, what part of the speech would be most interesting to them? Why?

2. Since the audience probably knows what peer pressure means, why does Jones spend the whole speech developing a definition of the phrase by giving three examples?
3. What are the three main examples that compose the body of the essay? Which one is a general example? Is it more or less effective than the other two specific examples?
4. What other kind of information would be effective in a speech about peer pressure to a junior high audience? What else could Jones have used for support?
5. Consider the title of the essay. Why do you think Jones chose that title? Is it an effective title? If not, suggest a better title.

Using New Words

1. Make at least one new vocabulary card for your personal set of cards. Write the word on one side and a definition and an original sentence on the other.
2. Select ten words in your vocabulary set that sound ''pretty'' or that you like to say. Review these words and practice them aloud so that you can use them easily in conversation when you want to.
3. What are the noun forms of these verbs: *coerce, confront, opt, threaten, apologize?*
4. What are three frequently used noun suffixes (endings) in the nouns you wrote in question 3?

Responding by Writing

1. Write an essay about an abstract idea, such as confrontation, pride, humiliation, apologies, anger, confidence, courage—an abstract noun, like *peer pressure* from Jones's essay. Decide upon an audience who needs to hear what you have to say for some reason. Decide what point you want to make and what you want the audience to do, feel, or think. Use examples, narration, and description to develop your essay. Avoid being preachy and giving advice.
2. Write an essay about peer pressure to an audience of your peers. Before you write the essay, write down why you are writing to them about this topic, what you want them to do, and what point you want to make. Choose examples appropriate to your audience to develop the essay.
3. Change the audience for the essay you wrote in question 2 to one much younger or much older than you. Rewrite the essay, adapting the examples you used or changing them to be appropriate to your new audience.
4. Write a letter to Jones about her essay. Begin by telling her what you think she did well. Tell her what you understand her to be saying (paraphrase and summarize). Then tell her where you think she needs more details and information to strengthen her essay.

CHAPTER

8

PROCESS ANALYSIS

USING PROCESS ANALYSIS TO DEVELOP YOUR ESSAY

When you tell someone how to register for classes, refinance a home mortgage, program frequently called numbers into a telephone, go from your house to the nearest gas station, discipline a two-year-old child, use a data base in the library to search for information; when you explain how summer storms build up; or when you report the procedure you used in a chemistry experiment, you are using process analysis. You are telling how to do something by analyzing the sequence of steps that make up the process. You are breaking the whole process into manageable tasks and putting those tasks in a logical order. Narration focuses on *what* happens. Causal analysis, which you will study later, focuses on *why* something happens. Process analysis focuses on *how* something happens.

People write process analysis essays for two main reasons: to give directions for someone to follow or to inform someone how something happens. Like other ways of developing essays—description, narration, and exemplification—process analysis may be the main way a writer develops a piece of writing or it may be only one of several ways. When you use process analysis to develop an essay, notice the following important features.

Identify the Level of Knowledge and Needs of Your Audience. The audience is especially important in writing process analysis. As a writer, you must have a sharp sense of what your intended readers already know, what they don't know, and what they may feel as they go through the process you are describing. For instance, if you're giving a newcomer to town directions to your apartment, you must give more detailed information than you would to a friend who knows your neighborhood but hasn't been to your home. You might say, "There are two streets named Crestover. Turn right on Crestover Court, not Crestover Lane." You must anticipate trouble spots, such as intersections where three streets come together, and explain more fully about them. You might say, "Don't worry if you miss the turn. You can make a U-turn at the next intersection." Remember that your audience is reading your essay to find out something they don't already know.

Here is part of the introduction from "How To Relax in a Crowd" by David D. Burns, M.D. He begins with a narrative to introduce his subject and hook his audience's interest. Who do you think his intended audience for the article is? Why?

> Recently I was invited to lecture on anxiety to several hundred mental-health professionals in Boston. My talk was scheduled to follow those of a number of prominent psychiatrists. When my turn came, I was especially nervous because the speaker before me had been particularly impressive and charming.
>
> As I approached the podium, my heart pounded and my mouth went dry. *What am I doing here?* I asked myself.
>
> Making matters worse, my presentation partly dealt with fear of public speaking. To calm myself, I tried an unconventional tactic. I asked the audience, "How many of you feel nervous when you give a speech?" Nearly every hand went up. "Well, that's *exactly* how I feel right now!"
>
> The audience responded with laughter. I relaxed and was able to move into my presentation.
>
> At times, we all find ourselves in situations that make us nervous. Perhaps you're afraid of saying foolish things at a cocktail party, stumbling over a presentation at work or having your mind go blank on a test.

Burns has introduced the subject of fear about public speaking and other public, or social, situations. Although he begins with a story about himself, he uses examples of other problem situations to connect with his intended readers—people who get nervous when the spotlight is on them in a public situation.

REMINDER

A sharp sense of what your audience knows and doesn't know is especially important in writing process analysis.

Make a Statement That Gives an Overview of the Process. A process analysis, whether it is a whole essay or part of one, should begin with a general statement of what is being analyzed and for what reason. This statement may be the essay's thesis or a topic sentence introducing the analysis within the essay. The statement lets a reader of process analysis know right away what the big picture is. This ''big picture'' sentence gives the reader a context for what is to come. It gives an overview so that the reader has a mental hatrack on which to hang all the information that follows. Burns's thesis for ''How To Relax in a Crowd'' here is:

> . . . anyone can increase his or her social confidence, even in the most stressful situations. Here are a few simple but helpful tips:

As a reader, you know now that what follows in this essay will be how to relax when you speak and perform in public. The thesis sentence gives you an overview of the content of the essay.

REMINDER

When you write process analysis (how to do something), be sure to include a statement that gives your readers an overview so that all the information that follows will make sense to them.

Use Specific Details and Vivid Description. In writing process analysis, you'll need the writing skills you developed in earlier chapters—using specific words instead of general ones, providing sensory details, organizing logically, and using examples. Readers of process analysis need more than a few plain facts; they need details, description, and examples. Dr. Burns's essay, which appears in Chapter 7, shows how a writer uses many examples to develop an essay—even a process analysis essay.

It's easy to underestimate a reader's need for specific information. Can you remember trying to follow someone's directions and having a bad time of it? You probably understood everything said, but needed more information. If you know how to program your telephone answering machine, it's easy and you may need only a few prompts to remind you of the process. For instance, ''Next, record a greeting'' is enough if you already know how, but if this is your first answering machine, such a prompt won't mean anything to you. You need more specific information about each step. You need a full-blown explanation with diagrams.

As you are providing details and examples to explain what to do, you should also do some troubleshooting. If you are giving directions for a physical process (rather than a mental one such as in ''How To Relax in a Crowd''), you should list the tools and materials the reader will need to follow the directions. You should spot places in the process where your audience, who is less informed about this process than you, might easily become confused, and you should explain special words or names that your audience might not know. For instance, you might warn a friend, as in the earlier example, that there are two streets named Crestover as she looks for the turn to your street or you might explain the technical term ''Record Greeting'' button.

> **REMINDER**
> A good process analysis includes early in the essay a list of materials needed to follow the process, definitions of special terms, and special explanations for potential trouble spots.

ORGANIZING A PROCESS ANALYSIS

Another important part in writing process analysis is organizing information in the sequence in which the reader needs it, especially when you are giving directions. For example, in face-to-face conversations you can correct your directions if you forget something, but in written directions you confuse your reader if you give information in the wrong order.

Break the Process into Several Major Steps and Put These into a Logical Sequence. Then organize the details, examples, explanations, and minor steps around these major divisions of the process. A long list of small steps or details is confusing and hard to follow.

Provide Many Transitional Words and Phrases. As drivers need street signs, readers need clear and specific signals to mark their progress in following the process. Use a series of transitional words and phrases to mark stages of a process and steps within each stage, such as

first, second, third
the first step is . . . , next you will . . . , finally do . . .
at the beginning . . . , meanwhile . . . , in the last stage

Give precise and consistent signals; for instance, do not use *second* if you haven't used *first.*

As you write about each major step you should continue providing clear transitional signals within your discussion of each major step. Double check your transitional links between substeps, details, and examples as you revise. Watch for overuse of *first* and *then.* You may be surprised how often these two words creep into your how-to-do-something essay, but how many ''first'' steps can you really have?

Provide Adequate Paragraphing. Your reader needs units of thought, not a long string of facts and information. You know that each paragraph should be about one point, but students sometimes write a page or even two without providing a paragraph break. Usually, you should provide a paragraph break after a half page or so. When your paragraphs look too long, look for a logical place to begin a new paragraph.

POINTS TO REMEMBER ABOUT PROCESS ANALYSIS

Identify your audience's level of knowledge and needs.
Provide a statement that gives an overview of the process.
Make descriptions specific, vivid, and detailed.
List the tools and materials needed.
Define special terms.
Break the process into a few major steps.
Organize minor steps, details, and examples around the major steps.
Anticipate where a reader may have trouble and give special help.
Provide clear and frequent transitional signals.

How To Write a Personal Letter

Garrison Keillor

Best known for his radio show ''Prairie Home Companion'' about a fictitious town in Minnesota, writer and humorist Garrison Keillor has also written several books, including *Lake Woebegone Days,* and articles for *The New Yorker.* The following article was written as an advertisement for the International Paper Company. The advice-giver in this article is the wise narrator of Lake Woebegone.

Thinking Before Reading

Do you like to receive letters? Think about one you received or would like to receive. Is a letter better than those same words spoken? Why or why not? Write a few sentences in your Idea Bank about these thoughts.

Expanding Your Vocabulary from Reading

trudges (2) walks in a heavy-footed way
wahoos (2) humorous term for people, such as nerd or bumpkin
anonymity (4) namelessness, state of being not known
obligatory (6) owed, required
sensuous (8) appealing to the senses, attractive
episode (13) part of a larger series of events or a larger narrative
sibling (13) brother or sister
relic (15) something from a previous period

1 We shy persons need to write a letter now and then, or else we'll dry up and blow away. It's true. And I speak as one who loves to reach for the phone, dial the number, and talk. I say, "Big Bopper here—what's shakin', babes?" The telephone is to shyness what Hawaii is to February, it's a way out of the woods, *and yet:* a letter is better.

2 Such a sweet gift—a piece of handmade writing, in an envelope that is not a bill, sitting in our friend's path when she trudges home from a long day spent among wahoos and savages, a day our words will help repair. They don't need to be immortal, just sincere. She can read them twice and again tomorrow: *You're someone I care about, Corinne, and think of often and every time I do you make me smile.*

3 We need to write, otherwise nobody will know who we are. They will have only a vague impression of us as A Nice Person, because frankly, we don't shine at conversation, we lack the confidence to thrust our faces forward and say, "Hi, I'm Heather Hooten, let me tell you about my week." Mostly we say "Uh-huh" and "Oh really." People smile and look over our shoulder, looking for someone else to talk to.

4 So a shy person sits down and writes a letter. To be known by another person—to meet and talk freely on the page—to be close despite distance. To escape from anonymity and be our own sweet selves and express the music of our souls.

5 Same thing that moves a giant rock star to sing his heart out in front of 123,000 people moves us to take ballpoint in hand and write a few lines to our dear Aunt Eleanor. *We want to be known.* We want her to know that we have fallen in love, that we quit our job, and we're moving to New York, and we want to say a few things that might not get said in casual conversation: *thank you for what you've meant to me, I am very happy right now.*

6 The first step in writing letters is to get over the guilt of *not* writing. You don't "owe" anybody a letter. Letters are a gift. The burning shame you feel when you see unanswered mail makes it harder to pick up a pen and makes for a cheerless letter when you finally do. *I feel bad about not writing, but I've been so busy,* etc. Skip this. Few letters are obligatory, and they are *Thanks for the wonderful gift* and *I am terribly sorry to hear about George's death* and *Yes, you're welcome to stay with us next month,* and not many more than that. Write those promptly if you want to keep your friends. Don't worry about the others, except love letters, of course. When your true love writes *Dear Light of My Life, Joy of My Heart, O Lovely Pulsating Core of My Sensate Life,* some response is called for.

7 Some of the best letters are tossed off in a burst of inspiration, so keep your writing stuff in one place where you can sit down for a few minutes and *Dear Roy, I am in the middle of an essay for International Paper but thought I'd drop you a line. Hi to your sweetie too* dash off a note to a pal. Envelopes, stamps, address book, everything in a drawer so you can write fast when the pen is hot.

8 A blank white 8″ × 11″ sheet can look as big as Montana if the pen's not so hot—try a smaller page and write boldly. Or use a note card with a piece of fine art on the front; if your letter ain't good, at least they get the Matisse. Get a pen that makes a sensuous line, get a comfortable typewriter, a friendly word processor—whichever feels easy to the hand.

9 Sit for a few minutes with the blank sheet in front of you, and meditate on the person you will write to, let your friend come to mind until you can almost see her or him in the room with you. Remember the last time you saw each other and how your friend looked and what you said and what perhaps was unsaid between you, and when your friend becomes real to you, start to write.

10 Write the salutation—*Dear You*—and take a deep breath and plunge in. A simple declarative sentence will do, followed by another and another and another. Tell us what you're doing and tell it like you were talking to us. Don't think about grammar, don't think about lit'ry style, don't try to write dramatically, just give us your news. Where did you go, who did you see, what did they say, what do you think?

11 If you don't know where to begin, start with the present moment: *I'm sitting at the kitchen table on a rainy Saturday morning. Everyone is gone and the house is quiet.* Let your simple description of the present moment lead to something else, let the letter drift gently along.

12 The toughest letter to crank out is one that is meant to impress, as we all know from writing job applications; if it's hard work to slip off a letter to a friend, maybe you're trying too hard to be terrific. A letter is only a report to someone who already likes you for reasons other than your brilliance. Take it easy.

13 Don't worry about form. It's not a term paper. When you come to the end of one episode, just start a new paragraph. You can go from a few lines about the sad state of rock 'n roll to the fight with your mother to your fond memories of Mexico to your cat's urinary tract infection to a few thoughts on personal indebtedness to the kitchen sink and what's in it. The more you write, the easier it gets, and when you have a True True Friend to write to, a *compadre,* a soul sibling, then it's like driving a car down a country road, you just get behind the keyboard and press on the gas.

14 Don't tear up the page and start over when you write a bad line—try to write your way out of it. Make mistakes and plunge on. Let the letter cook along and let yourself be bold. Outrage, confusion, love—whatever is in your mind, let it find a way to the page. Writing is a means of discovery, always, and when you come to the end and write *Yours ever* or *Hugs and Kisses,* you'll know something you didn't when you wrote *Dear Pal.*

15 Probably your friend will put your letter away, and it'll be read again a few years from now—and it will improve with age. And forty years from now, your friend's grandkids will dig it out of the attic and read it, a sweet and precious relic of the ancient Eighties that gives them a sudden clear glimpse

of you and her and the world we old-timers knew. You will then have created an object of art. Your simple lines about where you went, who you saw, what they said, will speak to those children and they will feel in their hearts the humanity of our times.

16 You can't pick up a phone and call the future and tell them about our times. You have to pick up a piece of paper.

Jotting Down Your First Responses

1. What, if any, of Keillor's advice did you find helpful to you?
2. Do you like to write personal letters? Why or why not?
3. What advice about letter writing would you add?

Checking Your Comprehension

1. According to Keillor, what kind of people can benefit most from writing letters?
2. Why do you think Keillor calls a personal letter a gift?
3. Why do shy people need to write?
4. What advice does Keillor give about writing supplies?
5. What should you do once you are sitting with pen in hand before you begin writing?
6. What's one way to begin a letter if you can't think what to say?
7. According to Keillor, what should you do when you make mistakes?

Understanding a Writer's Patterns

1. Who is the intended audience of this article? Why do you think so?
2. What tone does Keillor use to accomplish his purpose?
3. What steps for writing a personal letter does Keillor give?
4. How are the steps organized? Is the organization appropriate? Why or why not?
5. Paragraphs 1 through 5 are the introduction to the process of writing a personal letter. What is the author trying to do in this section of the article? How does he do it?
6. In the introduction Keillor uses several examples. What are two of them? Why does he use them?
7. In paragraph 8 Keillor compares a blank sheet of paper to the state of Montana. Reread that sentence. What is the purpose of the comparison? Does it work for you?
8. Keillor shows he is sensitive to the problems his intended audience may have writing letters. What problems of letter writers does he recognize and give suggestions for?

Making Predictions and Drawing Inferences

1. Reread the first paragraph. What did you expect of this article when you first read that paragraph?
2. Why do you think a letter can become a "relic" of the past? Do you or your family have any such letters?

Making Judgments and Thinking Critically

1. Is the tone of the article appropriate and effective for the author's audience and purpose? Why or why not?
2. This article is one of a series published by the International Paper Company. Do you think it is effective advertising? Why or why not?

Using New Words

1. Add three words from this article to your personal vocabulary list. Make vocabulary cards for them, writing a word on one side of a card and a definition and an original sentence on the other side.
2. In a small group of classmates listen to each other's sentences for the words you chose. Say each word aloud and read the sentence to the group. Help each other become comfortable with using these words.

Responding by Writing

1. Think about something you like to do. It may be related to any area of your life—sports, hobbies, or other "for pleasure" activities. It may be related to home life—installing a television antenna, getting children to bed on time, convincing parents to change a curfew—your social life, your religious life, your life as a commuter, taxpayer, or job seeker. After you have decided on your topic, decide on an audience who needs to know what you have to say. Write a how-to-do-it essay aimed at a specific audience. *Hint:* Choose as a topic an activity that can be accomplished in a short time span.
2. In paragraph 4 Keillor says that we write letters to "escape from anonymity and be our own sweet selves and express the music of our souls." How do you "escape from anonymity" and "express the music" of your soul? Think of an activity in which you affirm your being and express yourself as a unique person. Write an essay about how you do this activity. Write to an audience of this class to encourage others to express their individuality.
3. In paragraphs 14 and 15 Keillor gives advice about writing that is similar to Brenda Ueland's advice in "Be Careless, Reckless! . . ." Do you think their advice to be bold and outrageous when writing is good advice? Write a thesis that includes the gist of this advice and your opin-

ion about it. Then write an essay in which your thesis claims this is good or bad advice.

Use a brief quotation from each essay. Be sure to use the author's name and the title of the article with each quotation. Use quotation marks to punctuate the quotations and the titles of the articles.

Learning to See

Samuel H. Scudder

As a scientist and professor, Samuel H. Scudder studied butterflies for thirty years and published *The Butterflies of the Eastern United States and Canada with Special Reference to New England* in 1888–1889. The following article is about one of his teachers, a famous zoologist and geologist, who taught him an important lesson about science. This lesson is still an important one, for both biologists and writers.

Thinking Before Reading

Think about an important lesson you have learned about life. When and how did you learn it? Who taught you? Write a few sentences in your Idea Bank about this lesson.

Expanding Your Vocabulary from Reading

natural history (1) study of plants and animals
antecedents (1) events and conditions that came before
entomology (8) study of insects
ichthyology (8) study of fishes
infectious (8) contagious, likely to be passed on
aversion (8) strong dislike
interdicted (10) prohibited, not allowed
piqued (16) irritated, resentful
mortified (16) extremely embarrassed

1 It was more than fifteen years ago that I entered the laboratory of Professor Agassiz, and told him I had enrolled my name in the Scientific School as a student of natural history. He asked me a few questions about my object in coming, my antecedents generally, the mode in which I afterwards proposed to use the knowledge I might acquire, and, finally, whether I wished to study any special branch. To the latter I replied that, while I wished to be well grounded in all departments of zoology, I purposed to devote myself specially to insects.

2 “When do you wish to begin?” he asked.

3 “Now,” I replied.

4 This seemed to please him, and with an energetic “Very well!” he reached from the shelf a huge jar of specimens in yellow alcohol.

5 “Take this fish,” he said, “and look at it; we call it a haemulon; by and by I will ask what you have seen.”

6 With that he left me, but in a moment returned with explicit instructions as to the care of the object entrusted to me.

7 “No man is fit to be a naturalist,” said he, “who does not know how to take care of specimens.”

8 I was to keep the fish before me in a tin tray, and occasionally moisten the surface with alcohol from the jar, always taking care to replace the stopper tightly. Those were not the days of ground-glass stoppers and elegantly shaped exhibition jars; all the old students will recall the huge neckless glass bottles with their leaky, wax-besmeared corks, half eaten by insects, and begrimed with cellar dust. Entomology was a cleaner science than ichthyology, but the example of the Professor, who had unhesitatingly plunged to the bottom of the jar to produce the fish, was infectious; and though this alcohol had a “very ancient and fishlike smell,” I really dared not show any aversion within these sacred precincts, and treated the alcohol as though it were pure water. Still I was conscious of a passing feeling of disappointment, for gazing at a fish did not commend itself to an ardent entomologist. My friends at home, too, were annoyed when they discovered that no amount of eau-de-Cologne would drown the perfume which haunted me like a shadow.

9 In ten minutes I had seen all that could be seen in that fish, and started in search of the Professor—who had, however, left the Museum; and when I returned, after lingering over some of the odd animals stored in the upper apartment, my specimen was dry all over. I dashed the fluid over the fish as if to resuscitate the beast from a fainting-fit, and looked with anxiety for a return of the normal sloppy appearance. This little excitement over, nothing was to be done but to return to a steadfast gaze at my mute companion. Half an hour passed—an hour—another hour; the fish began to look loathsome. I turned it over and around; looked it in the face—ghastly, from behind, beneath, above, sideways, at a three-quarters' view—just as ghastly. I was in despair; at an early hour I concluded that lunch was necessary; so, with infinite relief, the fish was carefully placed in the jar, and for an hour I was free.

10 On my return, I learned that Professor Agassiz had been at the Museum, but had gone, and would not return for several hours. My fellow-students were too busy to be disturbed by continued conversation. Slowly I drew forth that hideous fish, and with a feeling of desperation again looked at it. I might not use a magnifying glass; instruments of all kinds were interdicted. My two hands, my two eyes, and the fish; it seemed a most limited field. I pushed my fingers down its throat to feel how sharp the teeth were. I began to count the scales in the different rows, until I was convinced that that was nonsense. At

last a happy thought struck me—I would draw the fish; and now with surprise I began to discover new features in the creature. Just then the Professor returned.

11 "That is right," said he, "a pencil is one of the best eyes. I am glad to notice, too, that you keep your specimen wet, and your bottle corked."

12 With these encouraging words, he added:

13 "Well, what is it like?"

14 He listened attentively to my brief rehearsal of the structure of parts whose names were still unknown to me: the fringed gill-arches and movable operculum; the pores of the head, fleshy lips and lidless eyes; the lateral line, the spinous fins and forked tail; the compressed and arched body. When I had finished, he waited as if expecting more, and then, with an air of disappointment:

15 "You have not looked very carefully; why," he continued more earnestly, "you haven't even seen one of the most conspicuous features of the animal, which is as plainly before your eyes as the fish itself; look again, look again!" and he left me to my misery.

16 I was piqued; I was mortified. Still more of that wretched fish! But now I set myself to my task with a will, and discovered one new thing after another, until I saw how just the Professor's criticism had been. The afternoon passed quickly; and when, toward its close, the Professor inquired:

17 "Do you see it yet?"

18 "No," I replied, "I am certain I do not, but I see how little I saw before."

19 "That is the next best," said he, earnestly, "but I won't hear you now; put away your fish and go home; perhaps you will be ready with a better answer in the morning. I will examine you before you look at the fish."

20 This was disconcerting. Not only must I think of my fish all night, studying, without the object before me, what this unknown but most visible feature might be; but also, without reviewing my discoveries, I must give an exact account of them the next day. I had a bad memory; so I walked home by the Charles River in a distracted state, with my two perplexities.

21 The cordial greeting from the Professor the next morning was reassuring; here was a man who seemed to be quite as anxious as I that I should see for myself what he saw.

22 "Do you perhaps mean," I asked, "that the fish has symmetrical sides with paired organs?"

23 His thoroughly pleased "Of course! Of course!" repaid the wakeful hours of the previous night. After he had discoursed most happily and enthusiastically—as he always did—upon the importance of this point, I ventured to ask what I should do next.

24 "Oh, look at your fish!" he said, and left me again to my own devices. In a little more than an hour he returned, and heard my new catalogue.

25 "That is good, that is good!" he repeated, "but that is not all; go on"; and so for three long days he placed that fish before my eyes, forbidding me

to look at anything else, or to use any artificial aid. "Look, look, look," was his repeated injunction.

26 This was the best entomological lesson I ever had—a lesson whose influence has extended to the details of every subsequent study; a legacy the Professor has left me, as he has left it to many others, of inestimable value, which we could not buy, with which we cannot part.

27 A year afterward, some of us were amusing ourselves with chalking outlandish beasts on the Museum blackboard. We drew prancing starfishes; frogs in mortal combat; hydra-headed worms; stately crawfishes, standing on their tails, bearing aloft umbrellas; and grotesque fishes with gaping mouths and staring eyes. The Professor came in shortly after, and was as amused as any at our experiments. He looked at the fishes.

28 "Haemulons, every one of them," he said; "Mr. ——— drew them."

29 True; and to this day, if I attempt a fish, I can draw nothing but haemulons.

30 The fourth day, a second fish of the same group was placed beside the first, and I was bidden to point out the resemblances and differences between the two; another and another followed, until the entire family lay before me, and a whole legion of jars covered the table and surrounding shelves; the odor had become a pleasant perfume; and even now, the sight of an old, six-inch, worm-eaten cork brings fragrant memories.

31 The whole group of haemulons was thus brought in review; and, whether engaged upon the dissection of the internal organs, the preparation and examination of the bony framework, or the description of the various parts, Agassiz's training in the method of observing facts and their orderly arrangement was ever accompanied by the urgent exhortation not to be content with them.

32 "Facts are stupid things," he would say, "until brought into connection with some general law."

33 At the end of eight months, it was almost with reluctance that I left these friends and turned to insects; but what I had gained by this outside experience has been of greater value than years of later investigation in my favorite groups.

Jotting Down Your First Responses

1. What would you have done if you had been Dr. Agassiz's student in this situation?
2. What do you think of the way Agassiz taught Scudder to observe closely?

Checking Your Comprehension

1. What was the first thing the teacher Agassiz did?
2. How did Scudder feel when given his first assignment, to gaze at a fish?
3. How was he to care for the fish? The specimen bottle? Why?

4. How long did he study the fish before he first began to look for Professor Agassiz?
5. After lunch he continued to study the fish. What tools did he use?
6. What happened when he began to draw the fish?
7. When he reported to Agassiz what he had learned about the fish that day, what was Agassiz's response?
8. After thinking overnight about what he had observed, what did Scudder report about the fish that pleased Agassiz?
9. Why does Scudder say this was the best lesson in his study of insects he ever had?
10. What did the students do one day for fun?
11. On the fourth day what was added to his fish for Scudder to study?
12. How long did this assignment take?
13. In paragraphs 31 through 32 Scudder tells what three lessons Agassiz was teaching him during those months. What are they?

Understanding a Writer's Patterns

1. In this essay Scudder uses narrative and process analysis. Review Points to Remember about Narration on page 115. What elements of a narrative can you identify in this essay? For each element, give the number of a paragraph in which it occurs.
2. In paragraph 9 Scudder refers to time more than once. List the phrases that refer to time. Why does he use several references about time in one paragraph?
3. Look at the introduction. What tense are the verbs? Why?
4. In paragraph 2 the identifying tag ''he asked'' is the same tense as the verbs in the introduction. What tense is the verb *do wish*? Does Scudder follow this pattern of verb tenses in paragraphs 5 through 7? If so, why?
5. Look at the concluding paragraph. Which words interpret and tell the significance of Scudder's experience with the fish?
6. How did Scudder organize his experiences of studying under Agassiz to show how he learned?

Making Predictions and Drawing Inferences

1. Why did Scudder have to keep the fish moistened with alcohol? Why did he have to keep the specimen jar stoppered tightly?
2. Why did Agassiz leave him alone with the fish for such long periods?
3. How was the university in which Scudder was studying like or unlike your college or university?
4. Why do you think magnifying glasses and other instruments were interdicted (prohibited) in Scudder's examination of the fish?

5. What did Agassiz mean when he said "a pencil is one of the best eyes" (paragraph 11)?
6. In the last paragraph what "friends" does Scudder leave? Why does he call them that?

Making Judgments and Thinking Critically

1. What did Agassiz mean when he said "Facts are stupid things until brought into connection with some general law" (paragraph 32)? Do you agree or disagree? Why?
2. How would you summarize Agassiz's teaching method? Could Scudder's education have been speeded up with lecture and textbook assignments? Why or why not?

Using New Words

1. Many words end in the suffix *-logy*. What does this word ending mean? (If you did the vocabulary exercise in Chapter 7 about the suffix *-logist,* you may remember that *-logist* means one who studies a specific field of knowledge.) Make a list of the *-logy* words in this essay and any others that you know.
2. Make vocabulary cards for three words that you want to add to your vocabulary.
3. Define *mute* and *loathsome* from the context in paragraph 9.

Responding by Writing

1. Write about an important lesson you have learned, perhaps the one you wrote about in your Idea Bank before reading. Let your readers (an audience of this class) know why this lesson was important and how you learned it.
2. Make a list of all the things you have done in the past twenty-four hours. Choose one of these activities to teach to someone who doesn't know how to do it. Write a letter to that person, explaining how. Anticipate problems your reader might have by remembering problems you had, and provide special instructions to solve those problems.
3. To become better teachers, teachers often study how students learn. To help your teacher understand you as a learner, write an essay to your teacher about something you learned in school and the way you learned it.
4. Do you think Professor Agassiz was a good teacher? Write an essay supporting your opinion, which will be your thesis. You may add support from your own experiences. Use the title and author's name in your essay.

A Homemade Education

Malcolm X

As a youth, Malcolm X became involved with street gangs and ended up in prison for burglary. During his time in prison he began corresponding with Elijah Muhammad, leader of the Black Muslims, and continued his education. Although he became a militant leader of the Black Revolution, he was preaching the brotherhood of humanity when he was assassinated in 1965. The essay below is an excerpt from *The Autobiography of Malcolm X.*

Thinking Before Reading

Think about a time you decided to learn something, not something you had to learn, but something you wanted to learn—like riding a bicycle or walking in high heels or asking for a date. What motivated you to keep trying until you had mastered the skill? Write in your Idea Bank about what motivated you then.

Expanding Your Vocabulary from Reading

convey (2) to carry from one place to another, communicate
hustler (2) someone who obtains money in questionable ways
articulate (2) able to put one's thoughts in words easily
functional (2) able to do or use something adequately
emulate (4) imitate
riffling (6) thumbing through the pages

1 It was because of my letters that I happened to stumble upon starting to acquire some kind of homemade education.

2 I became increasingly frustrated at not being able to express what I wanted to convey in letters that I wrote, especially those to Mr. Elijah Muhammad. In the street, I had been the most articulate hustler out there—I had commanded attention when I said something. But now, trying to write simple English, I not only wasn't articulate, I wasn't even functional. How would I sound writing in slang, the way I would *say* it, something such as, "Look, daddy, let me pull your coat about a cat, Elijah Muhammad—"

3 Many who today hear me somewhere in person, or on television, or those who read something I've said, will think I went to school far beyond the eighth grade. This impression is due entirely to my prison studies.

4 It had really begun back in Charlestown Prison, when Bimbi first made me feel envy of his stock of knowledge. Bimbi had always taken charge of any conversation he was in, and I had tried to emulate him. But every book I picked up had few sentences which didn't contain anywhere from one to nearly

all of the words that might as well have been in Chinese. When I just skipped those words, of course, I really ended up with little idea of what the book said. So I had come to the Norfolk Prison Colony still going through only book-reading motions. Pretty soon, I would have quit even these motions unless I had received the motivation that I did.

5 I saw that the best thing I could do was get hold of a dictionary—to study and learn some words. I was lucky enough to reason also that I should try to improve my penmanship. It was sad. I couldn't even write in a straight line. It was both ideas together that moved me to request a dictionary along with some tablets and pencils from the Norfolk Prison Colony school.

6 I spent two days just riffling uncertainly through the dictionary's pages. I'd never realized so many words existed! I didn't know *which* words I needed to learn. Finally, just to start some kind of action, I began copying.

7 In my slow, painstaking, ragged handwriting, I copied into my tablet everything printed on that first page, down to the punctuation marks.

8 I believe it took me a day. Then, aloud, I read back, to myself, everything I'd written on the tablet. Over and over, aloud, to myself, I read my own handwriting.

9 I woke up the next morning, thinking about those words—immensely proud to realize that not only had I written so much at one time, but I'd written words that I never knew were in the world. Moreover, with a little effort, I also could remember what many of these words meant. I reviewed the words whose meanings I didn't remember. Funny thing, from the dictionary first page right now, that "aardvark" springs to my mind. The dictionary had a picture of it, a long-tailed, long-eared, burrowing African mammal, which lives off termites caught by sticking out its tongue as an anteater does for ants.

10 I was so fascinated that I went on—I copied the dictionary's next page. And the same experience came when I studied that. With every succeeding page, I also learned of people and places and events from history. Actually the dictionary is like a miniature encyclopedia. Finally the dictionary's A section had filled a whole tablet—and I went on into the B's. That was the way I started copying what eventually became the entire dictionary. It went a lot faster after so much practice helped me to pick up handwriting speed. Between what I wrote in my tablet, and writing letters, during the rest of my time in prison I would guess I wrote a million words.

11 I suppose it was inevitable that as my word-base broadened, I could for the first time pick up a book and read and now begin to understand what the book was saying. Anyone who has read a great deal can imagine the new world that opened. Let me tell you something: from then until I left that prison, in every free moment I had, if I was not reading in the library, I was reading on my bunk. You couldn't have gotten me out of books with a wedge. Between Mr. Muhammad's teachings, my correspondence, my visitors—usually Ella

and Reginald—and my reading of books, months passed without my even thinking about being imprisoned. In fact, up to then, I had never been so truly free in my life.

Jotting Down Your First Responses

1. If you were totally in charge of your education, what would you do? Make a list of activities you would do and a list of books or other resources you would use. How much time would you spend? How often?
2. When Malcolm X tried to read (paragraph 4), most sentences had so many unfamiliar words that he didn't understand what he was reading and began to give up. Have you ever read something you couldn't comprehend? What and when was it? How did you feel? What did you do?

Checking Your Comprehension

1. What situation motivated Malcolm X to educate himself?
2. His limited education showed itself in two ways. What were they?
3. How much formal schooling had Malcolm X had?
4. What did Bimbi have that Malcolm X wanted? Why?
5. What two important decisions did Malcolm X make?
6. Describe his method of study.
7. What were two results from his method of study?

Understanding a Writer's Patterns

1. Why do you think Malcolm X wrote an autobiography (story of his life)? What was his purpose in writing?
2. Who do you think his intended audience was?
3. In paragraph 10, what does he compare a dictionary to? Why?
4. In paragraph 10, what example of information learned from his word study does he give?
5. What phrases does he use to signal one step to another step in his education?
6. What words in paragraph 11 signal the conclusion?
7. The last sentence is not factual information. What kind of concluding sentence is it? How would you describe it?

Making Predictions and Drawing Inferences

1. Why does Malcolm X call his a "homemade education" (paragraph 1)?
2. How did being in prison contribute to his education?
3. Do you think his response to his frustration at not being able to read well and not being able to express his thoughts well is unusual? Why or why not?

4. What did he mean by ''going through only book-reading motions'' (paragraph 4)?
5. Why does he say he would quit ''book-reading motions''? Is this a usual response?
6. What does he mean when he says ''I had never been so truly free in my life'' (paragraph 11)?

Making Judgments and Thinking Critically

1. There are many differences between writing and talking. What are some of them you can think of?
2. How do you think other prisoners and guards might have reacted to Malcolm's dedication to reading and writing? Why?
3. Is it better to study words before you read or after you have read something? Where would you prefer to have the vocabulary help in this book—before or after the reading selection? Why?
4. Many prisons have educational programs. Why don't all prisoners use those opportunities? Would Malcolm X have benefited as much from a prison program as he did from his self-education? Why or why not?

Using New Words

1. In paragraph 2 Malcolm X notes the difference between speech and writing. One difference is the use of slang. Make a list of slang words and phrases you use or hear your friends using during the next twenty-four hours. Or, make a list of slang expressions that another group you know well uses.
2. Make vocabulary cards for two new words from this selection. You might choose ones that sound familiar but that you never use. Just as Malcolm X did in his home education, copy the full dictionary definition, punctuation and all, on the card for each word.

Responding by Writing

1. Since you have registered for this class, we can assume that you, like Malcolm X, want to read and write better. Write an essay about what motivates you to learn to read and write better. Use a quotation from the essay you just read if you can or refer to something Malcolm X did or felt. Use the title of the essay and the author's name in your essay.
2. In paragraph 2 Malcolm X suggests that slang doesn't communicate well in writing. Make a list of slang, if you already haven't, that you and your friends use or that another group you know well uses. Write an essay explaining how to understand slang. Take examples from the list

you made. Write for an audience in this class who wouldn't understand the slang you write about.

3. In "Learning to See" Professor Agassiz left Samuel Scudder alone to educate himself about the fish he was observing. Compare Malcolm X's self-education with Scudder's. How were they alike? What generalization about learning can you make from their experiences? Write an essay comparing the self-education of Scudder and Malcolm X. Let this generalization be your thesis, and write this essay for your college newspaper in a special issue which explores issues and opinions about education.

How To Hunt, Clean and Cook a Pheasant

Robert F. Hanika

Every fall for the last eleven years, Robert Hanika has tried "to outwit wary ducks, geese and pheasants in rural Iowa." Besides hunting, he loves to oil paint wildlife and cook. He works year round at Wet and Wild and goes to college part time. He wrote this essay for a friend who likes to hunt, but who has never hunted pheasant.

Thinking Before Reading

How good are you at giving directions or instructions? Do you tend to explain too much or too little? Do you focus on the content without considering your audience (how much they know or need to know)? Write in your Idea Bank about your skill at giving directions.

Expanding Your Vocabulary from Reading

perseverance (1) continuing of an action or state in spite of difficulties
asset (2) valuable resource, such as a savings account or musical talent
hampered (3) interfered with
assess (7) evaluate a situation to see what actions are needed
wary (8) cautious
flush (8) run from cover, take flight
sienna (10) brownish orange or reddish brown in color
craw (11) pouch for holding food in the throat of a bird
marinate (12) soak in seasoned liquid before cooking
gratification (13) pleasure

1 Cliff, before you can cook a pheasant for dinner, you have to shoot one. I know, it sounds rather easy, and granted sometimes it is. However, that's the

exception, not the rule. Pheasant hunting is actually an extremely complicated adventure. It requires patience, perseverance and a little luck. But, above all, successful pheasant hunting requires a good dog—a dog that understands English.

2 My dog is a mix between a golden retriever and a yellow lab and she is amazing. Her name is Heather. Cliff, she's my pheasant hunting guide, my consultant, and, frankly, my preferred companion. While we are in the field, I simply follow her. She is truly an invaluable asset in the pursuit of one of the most elusive game birds in North America. After five years of chasing pheasants she really knows her business.

3 Last Thanksgiving my little brother shot at a bird and appeared to hit him although he didn't drop. Well, he landed in the middle of a vast standing corn field that we had just tramped through. After a brief conference, we agreed it would be futile to go back and look for the bird, so we continued on our way. About an hour later fate had us plowing through that same field in hot pursuit of several roosters zipping down the corn rows. The weather hampered our efforts considerably. Visibility in the middle of a standing corn field is minimal to begin with, but factor in freezing rain and a gusting north wind, and it's difficult to see at all. Especially, a yellow and gold dog.

4 Cliff, Heather disappeared. Initially, I thought she had ranged a little too far ahead, but a blast on the whistle brought no dog. I was scared. I concluded she was lost and resolved to press ahead, hoping she would be patiently waiting for us, somewhere. Heather eventually found me. In fact, she snuck up behind me with a present in her mouth. I quickly realized that it wasn't for me; it was for my little brother. It was his first pheasant.

5 Preparation is another essential element of successful pheasant hunting. Before you go hunting, be in touch with the weather. The weather plays an important role in determining what the birds will be doing. For example, if there is a cold front, either on its way or leaving, the birds will always spend the day feeding. Then hunt in and around the corn fields. A brisk north wind coupled with snow, sleet or rain always pushes the birds into the pines to seek cover. A clear day usually means you'll do quite a bit of walking so wear a light, comfortable pair of boots.

6 Good boots are instrumental to a pheasant hunter. I've often walked for several miles without seeing so much as a track. After all that walking it's always heartbreaking to kick one up and miss him, so be one with your gun. I prefer a 20-gauge shotgun with a modified choke and I generally shoot #5 lead shot. Always make sure your gun is clean and well oiled. Clothing really depends upon the weather conditions. It is therefore important to own a good selection of hunting clothes. Finally, don't forget a thermos of black coffee. It really doesn't matter if you care for it or not. You just have to have it.

7 Now you are ready to hit the fields. Cliff, you can legally shoot at 8:00 a.m. and it's advisable to be in the general vicinity you wish to hunt by 7:45.

Drink some coffee, assess the situation and at 8:00 get down to business. The first hour should be dedicated to road hunting for two reasons. First, pheasants trickle up the roadsides all morning to pick gravel off the roads, and you can usually pop one or two. Second, it will offer valuable insights to what the birds will be up to later in the day. Make mental notes of where you saw birds, where they flew, and the type of cover they were in.

8 By 10:00 a.m. every pheasant in the county will usually know not only that you're around, but what model of car you're driving. This is where it gets interesting. Cliff, pheasants love to run and hide. They are wary birds after that first scattergun reports the beginning of pheasant season. I've seen them do some fascinating things. They're tricky. They'll sit tight while you walk right by them or they'll run and run until they're out of gun range and then flush wildly. They'll often double back on you and slip out the side. Follow the dog and give your undivided attention to what he or she's doing. Cliff, I've learned that lesson the hard way. On several occasions I've been looking the other way while Heather has been birding and stepped on one. That really upsets her.

9 When finally all that hard work results in a shot, don't miss it. Remember, when shooting, keep both eyes open, pay no attention to the gun barrel, follow through and take your time. Cliff, the flush itself will invariably scare the hell out of you so take a deep breath and make the shot. Once airborne they are very misleading. They look so big, but don't forget their flowing tail feathers are usually at least 20 inches long. A pheasant, without a tail wind, can reach speeds of up to 35 miles per hour within three seconds after lift off. Cliff, believe me, it all happens very fast, so take advantage of it.

10 If you hit the pheasant, the dog will mark where he went down and make the retrieve. Make sure the dog is on him quickly; if the bird is not dead, he'll be off and running. Then it's up to the dog and this is really where a dog pays big dividends. Heather has always excelled when it comes to retrieving a crippled bird. Cliff, I've seen her track a wounded bird for over a mile before finding him. Her tail hits the air and wavers back and forth slowly and her head seems to be part of the cover. Then up her head pops with a scolding rooster in her mouth. She then trots proudly back to me and delivers a mouthful of sienna, orange, green and blue.

11 It's a good idea to field dress the bird on the spot. In doing so there is less of a chance of the meat's being tainted. Cliff, cleaning a pheasant is actually quite simple if done properly. First, clip the wings between the joint. A pair of sharp game shears works well to do this. Second, with your hand grab the skin just below the craw and tear downward exposing the entire breast. Next, grab the breast with one hand and with the other grasp the backbone. Now pull. The breast should come right out leaving you with the best part of the bird.

12 The anticipation of dinner now takes over. Cliff, don't forget to invite a few close friends because this is indeed a treat. The key to cooking pheasant

is simply not to overcook it. There are several ways to prepare the bird. Here is my favorite. Learn this simple phrase: ''Going to cook the pheasant, going to cook the pheasant . . .'' and chant it incessantly throughout the cooking process. It should drive everyone crazy but it is essential to the recipe. Now fillet the breasts off the breast bone leaving you with two boneless fillets. Marinate them in either teriyaki sauce or Italian dressing for four to six hours. Then grill them, Cliff. Four minutes on one side and three on the other. Serve piping hot with crisp vegetables and lots of fresh bread. I enjoy a beer with mine.

13 Stand by for instant gratification. Not only will the food be wonderful but the reaction from your guests will be equally as satisfying. Make sure you take some time to relax, enjoy, and reflect upon what it took to put together a meal that would cost forty dollars in any restaurant. Finally, Cliff, congratulate yourself and scratch your stomach for a little while.

Jotting Down Your First Responses

1. As you read, what activity that you enjoy came to mind? Why do you enjoy it?
2. How do you feel about hunting? If you support hunting for yourself or others, what animals or birds should be protected from hunters? What other restrictions are or should be imposed?
3. Do you have any stereotypes (good or bad) about hunters? What are they?

Checking Your Comprehension

1. Is pheasant hunting easy or complicated, according to Hanika?
2. What does Hanika think is the most important necessity for a pheasant hunter?
3. What must one do before going hunting in order to make other preparations?
4. What four pieces of equipment does Hanika say you need for the hunt?
5. What time of day does the hunt begin?
6. What three tricks of the pheasants does Hanika warn the novice pheasant hunter about?
7. How fast can pheasants fly?
8. In what situation is a dog particularly valuable in a hunt?
9. Why is it important to clean a shot bird immediately?
10. What is the secret to cooking pheasant?

Understanding a Writer's Patterns

1. What sentence in the introductory paragraph is the best overview of the process of hunting, cleaning, and cooking a pheasant? In other words, what is the thesis?

2. How many paragraphs does Hanika devote to discussing a dog as part of the hunt? Why so many paragraphs? Why does he discuss the dog first in his essay?
3. What are two kinds of preparation that Hanika discusses?
4. Could the order of these two kinds of preparation be switched? Why or why not?
5. If you divide the process into three major steps—preparing for the hunt, hunting, and cooking—what minor parts or steps make up each major step? Make a simple outline or use clustering to show the relationship of the major steps and parts.
6. In paragraphs 7 and 8 Hanika describes two phases of the hunt. What time phrase signals the first phase? What time phrase signals the second phase?
7. Hanika offers two reasons for beginning by road hunting. What words signal these two reasons?
8. In paragraph 8 Hanika warns the hunter about a possible problem. What is the problem?
9. What three examples of the problem does he give?
10. What advice does Hanika give about the dog in paragraph 8? What example does he give to support this advice?
11. In paragraph 11 what transitional words mark the steps in cleaning the pheasant?

Making Predictions and Drawing Inferences

1. Why do hunters begin at 8:00 in the morning?
2. Why are pheasants found in cut corn fields?
3. Why does its long tail make it hard to shoot a flying pheasant?
4. What does Hanika mean when he says that the dog has a "mouthful of sienna, orange, green and blue" (paragraph 10)?
5. Do you think Hanika's friend Cliff is a totally inexperienced hunter? Why or why not?

Making Judgments and Thinking Critically

1. What time of year do hunters hunt pheasant?
2. What kinds of weather can pheasant hunters expect?
3. In what kind of place do hunters look for pheasants? Why?
4. Does Hanika sound like an experienced pheasant hunter? Why do you think so?
5. Does Hanika enjoy pheasant hunting? How can you tell?

Using New Words

1. Give antonyms (words with opposite meanings) for the following: *hampered, asset, perseverance, wary.*
2. Add three words from this essay to your set of vocabulary cards. Remember to write the word on one side of the card and a definition and an original sentence on the other side.

Responding by Writing

1. Write a process analysis essay to an audience of one, as Hanika did. Write about something the person wants to do that you know well—taking a photograph, moving to a new house, programming a VCR, hitting in a softball game of men and women, planting a spring garden, raising tropical fish. Choose a physical activity, rather than one that is mostly mental and emotional.
2. Rewrite the essay from question 1 still to an audience of one, but this time to a person who is much younger or older than you or who is very different in some way from the audience of the first essay.
3. Write a process analysis essay about something you know how to do well that is more mental and emotional than physical, such as how to study for a math test, discipline a two-year-old child, ask a stranger to dance, choose a major, appreciate a particular kind of music, get a specific kind of job, be a good listener, be a good bartender. Choose an audience of several people in this class who want the information you have.
4. Whether you are an experienced hunter or a non-hunter, write an essay evaluating Hanika's process analysis. What are the strengths of this essay? What additional information would a hunter need? What other troubleshooting might the writer do for the new hunter?

C H A P T E R

9

DIVISION AND CLASSIFICATION

USING DIVISION AND CLASSIFICATION TO DEVELOP YOUR ESSAY

When you sort clothes into whites and colored items to wash or sift through a stack of magazines to decide which to keep and which to throw away, you are dividing a whole (the dirty clothes or the stack of magazines) into subgroups or categories. In choosing a college, you may divide colleges into several kinds (in state/out of state, private/public, under 5,000 students/5,000 to 10,000/over 10,000) to simplify your decision-making process. Even such an ordinary question as ''What kind of movie do you want to see tonight?'' requires you to think in categories—adventure, romance, comedy.

If you enter a large retail store, you're faced with someone else's classification system. Sometimes the system makes it easy to locate what you're looking for. Sometimes you're puzzled and irritated by a seeming lack of logic. Think about your local video store: current releases, adventure, comedy, horror, foreign, classic, children, travel, concerts. Different video stores create different systems because they have different clienteles, who have different interests. Managers create a classification system to appeal to the interests of their customers so they can rent the greatest possible number of videos. If there are too many categories or the categories overlap, you may have difficulty finding a video you want to rent. Your practical experience with other people's categories demonstrates the importance of creating a logical system of categories when you use division and classification as you write.

When you analyze diverse information to explain a point, you often divide and classify the many pieces of information. *To divide* is to separate items from a large group into small groups of like items. *To classify* is to group similar items or ideas into categories. Division and classification are two sides of the same coin.

Many writing tasks will lead you into using this method of developing essays. For instance, for a biology paper you might be asked to describe pollution in your neighborhood. You might begin by noticing all the instances of pollution that occur in your neighborhood. Instead of just listing all the examples of pollution, you might notice that there are several kinds: litter from fast food restaurants, exhaust from cars, runoff of detergents, oils, and solvents from various car and home maintenance projects. For a sociology course, you might observe the fans of a professional baseball team and write a paper on the kinds of fans that the team has. For a business course in personal finance, you might be asked to keep a list of your expenditures and create categories for a budget. Division and classification is a way of organizing and simplifying diverse behaviors, information, or ideas.

Create Consistent and Exclusive Categories. Any collection of facts, ideas, items, and behaviors can be divided into many different sets of categories. However, to be useful the categories you devise should be consistent and exclusive. *Consistency* means that you decide on one system, or determining principle, for dividing and classifying and stick with it. To classify kinds of desserts, you could use the categories pies, cakes, and cookies, but not pies, cakes, and chocolate, because chocolate is a flavor and the others are not. *Exclusivity* means that categories do not overlap. Each category should be distinct from other categories. To classify kinds of tippers in a restaurant, you could use the categories men and women, but not men, women, and businessmen, because the category businessmen overlaps the category men.

Announce the Pattern of Classification. When using categories to make a point, writers usually announce their thinking and organizing pattern. Words such as *ways, kinds, types, levels, categories,* and *groups* are signals of classification and division. Writers may announce, for example, that there are "three ways people face oppression," "three kinds of discipline," "several levels of friendship," or "two groups of drivers."

ORGANIZING DIVISION AND CLASSIFICATION ESSAYS

Once they choose their categories, writers arrange them in some logical order to make it easier for the reader to follow the development of ideas. Writers may order their categories by number (first, second, third); by size (smallest to largest); or by importance (most to least, or least to most).

Provide Transitions. Good writers follow an announcement of the division and classification pattern with clear transitional words and phrases as they name and discuss each category. Here are some of the transitional words and phrases:

most important, next, least important
one way, another way, still another way
first kind, second kind, third kind
there is, then there is, last there is

Repeat Key Terms. However writers select and order the categories, they help the reader stay on track by using transitional terms and by repeating key words or phrases. Here are sentences from an essay by Martin Luther King, Jr., about the ways of dealing with oppression. Several paragraphs with discussion and examples follow each of the categories in King's essay. The transitional phrases and the repeated key words are in boldface.

Announcement: **Oppressed people** deal with their oppression in three characteristic ways (paragraph 1).
Categories:
One way is acquiescence: **the oppressed** resign themselves to their doom (paragraph 1).
A second way that **oppressed people** sometimes deal with oppression is to resort to physical violence and corroding hatred (paragraph 4).
The third way open to **oppressed people** in their quest for freedom is the way of nonviolent resistance (paragraph 7).

As a reader, remember to notice the announcement of categories, the transitional words and phrases, and the repetition of key words. These writing techniques link each part to the main idea and help you read with comprehension.

POINTS TO REMEMBER ABOUT DIVISION AND CLASSIFICATION

Use categories that are consistent and exclusive.
Decide on a logical order for the categories.
Announce the pattern of classification before you begin discussing any category.
Use transitional words and phrases for each category.
Repeat key words or phrases.

Texas Women: True Grit and All the Rest

Molly Ivins

A journalist known for her close observation of the Texas legislature, national politics, and human nature and for her biting wit, Molly Ivins has written for several newspapers and magazines. The following selection is a chapter from her recent book *Molly Ivins Can't Say That, Can She?,* a collection of her columns.

Thinking Before Reading

If you were going to write a column about types of men or women in your state or region of the country for someone in another part of the country, what are several types of men or women that you would describe? Write a few sentences in your Idea Bank.

Expanding Your Vocabulary from Reading

jargon (1) lingo, special language
deplorable (1) deserving criticism
Clydesdale (2) large horse used for pulling wagons
thoroughbreds (2) sleek racing horses
virulence (3) spitefulness, hostility
pervasive (5) spreading throughout, penetrating
idolatry (5) blind admiration or devotion to
saga (6) long story about heroic deeds
roast (7) gathering at which speakers ridicule someone
misnomer (8) name unsuitably applied
impudence (9) disrespectful behavior, impertinence
contempt (10) scorn, open disgust
animated (12) lively, with energy and movement
rampant (13) spreading everywhere, unrestrained

1 They used to say that Texas was hell on women and horses—I don't know why they stopped. Surely not because much of the citizenry has had its consciousness raised, as they say in the jargon of the women's movement, on the issue of sexism. Just a few months ago one of our state representatives felt moved to compare women and horses—it was the similarity he wanted to emphasize. Of course some Texas legislator can be found to say any fool thing, but this guy's comments met with general agreement from his colleagues. One can always dismiss the entire Legislature as a particularly deplorable set of Texans, but as Sen. Carl Parker observes, if you took all the fools out of the Lege, it wouldn't be a representative body anymore.

2 I should confess that I've always been more of an observer than a participant in Texas Womanhood: the spirit was willing but I was declared ineligible on grounds of size early. You can't be six feet tall and cute, both. I think I was first named captain of the basketball team when I was four and that's what I've been ever since. I spent my girlhood as a Clydesdale among thoroughbreds. I clopped along amongst them cheerfully, admiring their grace, but the strange training rituals they went through left me secretly relieved that no one would ever expect me to step on a racetrack. I think it is quite possible to grow up in Texas as an utter failure in flirting, gentility, cheerleading, sexpottery, and manipulation and still be without any permanent scars. Except one. We'd all rather be blonde.

3 Please understand I'm not whining when I point out that Texas sexism is of an especially rank and noxious variety—this is more a Texas brag. It is my belief that it is virulence of Texas sexism that accounts for the strength of Texas women. It's what we have to overcome that makes us formidable survivors, say I with some complacency.

4 As has been noted elsewhere, there are several strains of Texan culture: They are all rotten for women. There is the Southern belle nonsense of our Confederate heritage, that little-woman-on-a-pedestal, flirtatious, ''you're so cute when you're mad,'' Scarlett O'Hara myth that leads, quite naturally, to the equally pernicious legend of the Iron Magnolia. Then there's the machismo of our Latin heritage, which affects not only our Chicana sisters, but has been integrated into Texas culture quite as thoroughly as barbecue, rodeo, and Tex-Mex food.

5 Next up is the pervasive good-ol'-boyism of the *Redneckus texensis,* that remarkable tribe that has made the pickup truck with the gun rack across the back window and the beer cans flying out the window a synonym for Texans worldwide. Country music is a good place to investigate and find reflected the attitudes of kickers toward women (never ask what a kicker kicks). It's your basic, familiar virgin/whore dichotomy—either your ''Good-Hearted Woman'' or ''Your Cheatin' Heart,'' with the emphasis on the honky-tonk angels. Nor is the jock idolatry that permeates the state helpful to our gender: Football is not a game here, it's a matter of blood and death. Woman's role in the state's national game is limited, significantly, to cheerleading. In this regard, I can say with great confidence that Texas changeth not—the hopelessly intense, heartbreaking longing with which most Texas girls still want to be cheerleader can be observed at every high school, every September.

6 Last but not least in the litany of cultures that help make the lives of Texas women so challenging is the legacy of the frontier—not the frontier that Texas women lived on, but the one John Wayne lived on. Anyone who knows the real history of the frontier knows it is a saga of the strength of women. They worked as hard as men, they fought as hard as men, they suffered as much as men. But in the cowboy movies that most contemporary Texans grew

up on, the big, strong man always protects "the little lady" or "the gals" from whatever peril threatens. Such nonsense. Mary Ann Goodnight was often left alone at the JA Ranch near the Palo Duro Canyon. One day in 1877, a cowboy rode into her camp with three chickens in a sack as a present for her. He naturally expected her to cook and eat the fowl, but Goodnight kept them as pets. She wrote in her diary, "No one can ever know how much company they were." Life for farm and ranch wives didn't improve much over the next 100 years. Ruth White raised nine children on a farm near High, Texas, in the 1920s and thirties. She used to say, "Everything on this farm is either hungry or heavy."

7 All of these strains lead to a form of sexism so deeply ingrained in the culture that it's often difficult to distinguish the disgusting from the outrageous or the offensive from the amusing. One not infrequently sees cars or trucks sporting the bumper sticker HAVE FUN—BEAT THE HELL OUT OF SOMEONE YOU LOVE. Another is: IF YOU LOVE SOMETHING, SET IT FREE. IF IT DOESN'T COME BACK, TRACK IT DOWN AND KILL IT. I once heard a legislator order a lobbyist, "Get me two sweathogs for tonight." At a benefit "roast" for the battered women's shelter in El Paso early in 1985, a couple of the male politicians told rape jokes to amuse the crowd. Most Texas sexism is not intended to be offensive—it's entirely unconscious. A colleague of mine was touring the new death chamber in Huntsville last year with a group of other reporters. Their guide called to warn those inside they were coming through, saying, "I'm coming over with eight reporters and one woman." Stuff like that happens to you four or five times a day for long enough, it will wear you down some.

8 Other forms of the phenomenon are, of course, less delightsome. Women everywhere are victims of violence with depressing regularity. Texas is a more violent place than most of the rest of America, for reasons having to do with guns, machismo, frontier traditions, and the heterogeneous population. While the law theoretically applies to male and female alike, by unspoken convention, a man who offs his wife or girlfriend is seldom charged with murder one: we wind up filed under the misnomer manslaughter.

9 That's the bad news for Texas women—the good news is that all this adversity has certainly made us a bodacious bunch of overcomers. And rather pleasant as a group, I always think, since having a sense of humor about men is not a luxury here; it's a necessity. The feminists often carry on about the importance of role models and how little girls need positive role models. When I was a kid, my choice of Texas role models went from Ma Ferguson to the Kilgore Rangerettes. Of course I wanted to be a Rangerette: Ever seen a picture of Ma? Not that we haven't got real women heroes, of course, just that we were never taught anything about them. You used to have to take Texas history two or three times in order to get a high school diploma in this state: The Yellow Rose of Texas and Belle Starr were the only women in our history

books. Kaye Northcott notes that all the big cities in the state have men's last names—Houston, Austin, Dallas. All women got was some small towns called after their front names: Alice, Electra, Marfa. This is probably because, as Eleanor Brackenridge of San Antonio (1837–1924) so elegantly put it, "Foolish modesty lags behind while brazen impudence goes forth and eats the pudding." Brackenridge did her part to correct the lag by founding the Texas Woman Suffrage Association in 1913.

10 It is astonishing how recently Texas women have achieved equal legal rights. I guess you could say we made steady progress even before we could vote—the state did raise the age of consent for a woman from 7 to 10 in 1890—but it went a little smoother after we got some say in it. Until June 26, 1918, all Texans could vote except "idiots, imbeciles, aliens, the insane and women." The battle over woman's suffrage in Texas was long and fierce. Contempt and ridicule were the favored weapons against women. Women earned the right to vote through years of struggle; the precious victory was not something handed to us by generous men. From that struggle emerged a generation of Texas women whose political skills and leadership abilities have affected Texas politics for decades. Even so, Texas women were not permitted to serve on juries until 1954. As late as 1969, married women did not have full property rights. And until 1972, under Article 1220 of the Texas Penal Code, a man could murder his wife and her lover if he found them "in a compromising position" and get away with it as "justifiable homicide." Women, you understand, did not have equal shooting rights. Although Texas was one of the first states to ratify the Equal Rights Amendment, which has been part of the Texas Constitution since 1972, we continue to work for fairer laws concerning problems such as divorce, rape, child custody, and access to credit.

11 Texas women are just as divided by race, class, age, and educational level as are other varieties of human beings. There's a pat description of "what every Texas woman wants" that varies a bit from city to city, but the formula that Dallas females have been labeled with goes something like this: "Be a Pi Phi at Texas or SMU, marry a man who'll buy you a house in Highland Park, hold the wedding at Highland Park Methodist (flowers by Kendall Bailey), join the Junior League, send the kids to St. Mark's and Hockaday in the winter and Camps Longhorn and Waldemar in the summer, plus cotillion lessons at the Dallas Country Club, have an unlimited charge account at Neiman's as a birthright but buy almost all your clothes at Highland Park Village from Harold's or the Polo Shop, get your hair done at Paul Neinast's or Lou's and drive a Jeep Wagoneer for carpooling and a Mercedes for fun." There is a kicker equivalent of this scenario that starts, "Every Texas girl's dream is a double-wide in a Lubbock trailer park. . . ." But I personally believe it is unwise ever to be funny at the expense of kicker women. I once met a kicker lady who was wearing a blouse of such a vivid pink you could close your eyes

and still see the color; this confection was perked up with some big rhinestone buttons and a lot of ruffles across an impressive bosom. ''My,'' said I, ''where did you get that blouse?'' She gave me a level look and drawled. ''Honey, it come from mah coutouri-ay, Jay Cee Penn-ay.'' And if that ain't class, you *can* kiss my grits.

12 To my partisan eye, it seems that Texas women are more animated and friendly than those from, say, Nebraska. I suspect this comes from early training: Girls in Texas high schools are expected to walk through the halls smiling and saying ''Hi'' to everyone they meet. Being enthusiastic is bred into us, as is a certain amount of obligatory social hypocrisy stemming from the Southern tradition of manners, which does rather tend to emphasize pleasantness more than honesty in social situations. Many Texas women have an odd greeting call—when they haven't seen a good friend for a long time, the first glimpse will provoke the cry, ''Ooooooo—honey, how good to see yew again!'' It sounds sort of like the ''Soooooey, pig'' call.

13 Mostly Texas women are tough in some very fundamental ways. Not unfeminine, nor necessarily unladylike, just tough. It may be possible for a little girl to grow to womanhood in this state entirely sheltered from the rampant sexism all around her—but it's damned difficult. The result is that Texas women tend to know how to cope. We can cope with put-downs and come-ons, with preachers and hustlers, with drunks and cowboys. And when it's all over, if we stick together and work, we'll come out better than the sister who's buried in a grave near Marble Falls under a stone that says, ''Rudolph Richter, 1822–1915, and Wife.''

Jotting Down Your First Responses

1. Did you like Molly Ivins's sarcastic humor? Why or why not?
2. Do you think sexism is a strong part of your culture, either as a male or a female? If so, how has it shaped any of your values, beliefs, or actions?
3. What hardships or unfair situations have you experienced in life? In what way did these shape you?
4. When have you or someone you know used humor to point out a hardship, unfair situation, or problem?
5. What TV programs, books, or movies use humor to point out prejudice, other unfair situations, or problems?

Checking Your Comprehension

1. According to Ivins, why has she always been an observer of Texas womanhood? (paragraph 2)
2. What has caused the strength of Texas women, according to Ivins? (paragraph 3)

3. What four strains of Texas culture does Ivins name as influences on Texas women? (paragraphs 1 to 6)
4. Why does Ivins say that it is hard to tell the difference between amusing and offensive forms of sexism? (paragraph 7)
5. What does Ivins say is the good news for Texas women? (paragraph 9)
6. When did Texas women receive the right to vote? To serve on a jury? To hold property as a married woman? To have "equal shooting rights"? (paragraph 10)
7. Why are Texas women more enthusiastic and friendly than Nebraska women? (paragraph 12)
8. What quality have Texas women developed from coping with sexism? (paragraph 13)

Understanding a Writer's Patterns

1. In paragraph 3, what sentence is the best statement of Ivins's thesis?
2. Who is her primary audience? Who might be a secondary audience? Why do you think so?
3. What is her purpose? How does she accomplish it?
4. Ivins's introduction contains an anecdote and two indirect quotations. What are the two indirect quotations?
5. In what paragraph does Ivins draw from personal experience?
6. In paragraphs 4 through 6, Ivins describes the cultural influences that have led to sexism in Texas. What phrase in the first sentence of paragraph 7 summarizes that discussion and provides a transition to the next part?
7. What are some of the examples of sexism Ivins names in paragraphs 8 and 9?
8. What sentence in paragraph 9 summarizes paragraphs 7 and 8 and provides a transition to the discussion of the strength of Texas women?

Making Predictions and Drawing Inferences

1. What clues in paragraph 1 suggest the humorous approach the writer will take in the article?
2. According to Senator Carl Parker, why wouldn't the Texas legislature be a representative body if you removed all the fools?
3. Why does Ivins establish her position as a feminine misfit in paragraph 2? Does she seem hurt or angry? Why do you think so?
4. What is the tone of Ivins's discussion of women's accomplishments in paragraphs 9 and 10?
5. In paragraph 11 Ivins describes two stereotypes of Texas women. What does she do to attack the stereotypes?

Making Judgments and Thinking Critically

1. Do you think Ivins intends to be outrageous? Why or why not?
2. Does she dislike Texas? Why or why not?
3. Does she dislike men? Why or why not?
4. If you keep Ivins's points and remove the humor, is the essay more or less effective? Why?
5. Is Ivins's discussion of women as "overcomers" with a sense of humor (paragraphs 9 and 10) a strong statement of women's accomplishments? Why or why not?
6. What does Brackenridge mean by "Foolish modesty lags behind while brazen impudence goes forth and eats the pudding" (paragraph 9)?
7. Since stereotypes usually degrade individuals, why does Ivins use two stereotypes in paragraph 11?

Using New Words

1. Choose three words from this selection to add to your set of vocabulary cards. Write each word on one side of the card and a definition and an original sentence on the other side.
2. The prefix *per-* begins many words. Use your dictionary and the sense of the sentences in which the following words occur to figure out the meaning of the prefix *per-: pernicious* (paragraph 4), *pervasive* (paragraph 5), and *permeates* (paragraph 5).
3. Read the sentence in which the word *litany* appears (paragraph 6). From the sentence and your knowledge of the content of the preceding paragraph, what does *litany* mean?
4. Read the sentence in which the word *partisan* appears (paragraph 12). From the sentence and your understanding of Ivins's position as an observer of Texas women, what does *partisan* mean?

Responding by Writing

1. Examine the lyrics of several songs of your favorite kind of popular music or by your favorite musicians. How are women depicted? Write an essay explaining what you have noticed to an audience of this class, many of whom may not be familiar with this music. Name the category of music, the names of the musicians you examined, and the titles of albums or songs. To punctuate correctly, underline the titles of albums and use quotation marks around the titles of songs.
2. Most of us pride ourselves on being keen observers of human nature. What kind of human behavior have you spent the most time observing? You may have watched young children at play, bench warmers on a sports team, people waiting for an airplane or riding a train, the audi-

ence at concerts, fans at a sporting event, customers in a restaurant, shoppers in a mall, dancers in a club, or neighbors in your neighborhood. Write an essay describing several types of people in a situation you are familiar with. Your opinion should be the thesis of this essay. Write to an audience of this class to share your insights.

3. Stand-up comedy routines and skits, such as those in "Saturday Night Live," often use humor to point out the weaknesses and problems of the human condition. Is humor an effective way to deal with problems? Why or why not? Use examples from entertainment and your own experience to explain your point.
4. Ivins writes about sexism in Texas, but her target is broader than just her home state. Evaluate the effectiveness of this essay in making the public aware of sexism as a problem and using humor to deal with it. Write for an audience of a sociology or political science teacher.

Friends, Good Friends—and Such Good Friends

Judith Viorst

Judith Viorst is a poet, journalist, and novelist. She writes for both children and adults. The following essay first appeared in her regular column in *Redbook* in 1977.

Thinking Before Reading

Think of your friends. Are they different ages? Are they from different parts of your life? Do you do different things with different friends? Have you known some of them longer than others? If you were to divide your friends into categories, what would these categories be? Write about these categories of friends in your Idea Bank.

Expanding Your Vocabulary from Reading

charades (2) game in which words or phrases are acted out in pantomime until they are guessed by other players
ardor (2) intense emotion
nonchalant (3) casual, unconcerned
yoga (9) system of exercises to promote control of the mind and body
sibling rivalry (16) competition between persons having parents in common
forge (18) to give shape to
dormant (19) asleep

revived (19) brought back to life
perspective (20) point of view
calibrated (29) adjusted to a standard

1 Women are friends, I once would have said, when they totally love and support and trust each other, and bare to each other the secrets of their souls, and run—no questions asked—to help each other, and tell harsh truths to each other (no, you can't wear that dress unless you lose ten pounds first) when harsh truths must be told.

2 Women are friends, I once would have said, when they share the same affection for Ingmar Bergman, plus train rides, cats, warm rain, charades, Camus, and hate with equal ardor Newark and Brussels sprouts and Lawrence Welk and camping.

3 In other words, I once would have said that a friend is a friend all the way, but now I believe that's a narrow point of view. For the friendships I have and the friendships I see are conducted at many levels of intensity, serve many different functions, meet different needs and range from those as all-the-way as the friendship of the soul sisters mentioned above to that of the most nonchalant and casual playmates.

4 Consider these varieties of friendship:

5 1. Convenience friends. These are women with whom, if our paths weren't crossing all the time, we'd have no particular reason to be friends: a next-door neighbor, a woman in our car pool, the mother of one of our children's closest friends or maybe some mommy with whom we serve juice and cookies each week at the Glenwood Co-op Nursery.

6 Convenience friends are convenient indeed. They'll lend us their cups and silverware for a party. They'll drive our kids to soccer when we're sick. They'll take us to pick up our car when we need a lift to the garage. They'll even take our cats when we go on vacation. As we will for them.

7 But we don't, with convenience friends, ever come too close or tell too much; we maintain our public face and emotional distance. "Which means," says Elaine, "that I'll talk about being overweight but not about being depressed. Which means I'll admit being mad but not blind with rage. Which means that I might say that we're pinched this month but never that I'm worried sick over money."

8 But which doesn't mean that there isn't sufficient value to be found in these friendships of mutual aid, in convenience friends.

9 2. Special-interest friends. These friendships aren't intimate, and they needn't involve kids or silverware or cats. Their value lies in some interest jointly shared. And so we may have an office friend or a yoga friend or a tennis friend or a friend from the Women's Democratic Club.

10 "I've got one woman friend," says Joyce, "who likes, as I do, to take psychology courses. Which makes it nice for me—and nice for her. It's fun

to go with someone you know and it's fun to discuss what you've learned, driving back from the classes.'' And for the most part, she says, that's all they discuss.

11 ''I'd say that what we're doing is *doing* together, not being together,'' Suzanne says of her Tuesday-doubles friends. ''It's mainly a tennis relationship, but we play together well. And I guess we all need to have a couple of playmates.''

12 I agree.

13 My playmate is a shopping friend, a woman of marvelous taste, a woman who knows exactly *where* to buy *what,* and furthermore is a woman who always knows beyond a doubt what one ought to be buying. I don't have the time to keep up with what's new in eyeshadow, hemlines and shoes and whether the smock look is in or finished already. But since (oh, shame!) I care a lot about eyeshadow, hemlines and shoes, and since I don't *want* to wear smocks if the smock look is finished, I'm very glad to have a shopping friend.

14 3. Historical friends. We all have a friend who knew us when . . . maybe way back in Miss Meltzer's second grade, when our family lived in that three-room flat in Brooklyn, when our dad was out of work for seven months, when our brother Allie got in that fight where they had to call the police, when our sister married the endodontist from Yonkers and when, the morning after we lost our virginity, she was the first, the only, friend we told.

15 The years have gone by and we've gone separate ways and we've little in common now, but we're still an intimate part of each other's past. And so whenever we go to Detroit we always go to visit this friend of our girlhood. Who knows how we looked before our teeth were straightened. Who knows how we talked before our voice got un-Brooklyned. Who knows what we ate before we learned about artichokes. And who, by her presence, puts us in touch with an earlier part of ourself, a part of ourself it's important never to lose.

16 ''What this friend means to me and what I mean to her,'' says Grace, ''is having a sister without sibling rivalry. We know the texture of each other's lives. She remembers my grandmother's cabbage soup. I remember the way her uncle played the piano. There's simply no other friend who remembers those things.''

17 4. Crossroads friends. Like historical friends, our crossroads friends are important for *what was*—for the friendship we shared at a crucial, now past, time of life. A time, perhaps, when we roomed in college together; or worked as eager young singles in the Big City together; or went together, as my friend Elizabeth and I did, through pregnancy, birth and that scary first year of new motherhood.

18 Crossroads friends forge powerful links, links strong enough to endure with not much more contact than once-a-year letters at Christmas. And out of

respect for those crossroads years, for those dramas and dreams we once shared, we will always be friends.

19 5. Cross-generational friends. Historical friends and crossroads friends seem to maintain a special kind of intimacy—dormant but always ready to be revived—and though we may rarely meet, whenever we do connect, it's personal and intense. Another kind of intimacy exists in the friendships that form across generations in what one woman calls her daughter-mother and her mother-daughter relationships.

20 Evelyn's friend is her mother's age—"but I share so much more than I ever could with my mother"—a woman she talks to of music, of books and of life. "What I get from her is the benefit of her experience. What she gets—and enjoys—from me is a youthful perspective. It's a pleasure for both of us."

21 I have in my own life a precious friend, a woman of 65 who has lived very hard, who is wise, who listens well; who has been where I am and can help me understand it; and who represents not only an ultimate ideal mother to me but also the person I'd like to be when I grow up.

22 In our daughter role we tend to do more than our share of self-revelation; in our mother role we tend to receive what's revealed. It's another kind of pleasure—playing wise mother to a questing younger person. It's another very lovely kind of friendship.

23 6. Part-of-a-couple friends. Some of the women we call our friends we never see alone—we see them as part of a couple at couples' parties. And though we share interests in many things and respect each other's views, we aren't moved to deepen the relationship. Whatever the reason, a lack of time or—and this is more likely—a lack of chemistry, our friendship remains in the context of a group. But the fact that our feeling on seeing each other is always "I'm *so* glad she's here" and the fact that we spend half the evening talking together says that this too, in its own way, counts as a friendship.

24 (Other part-of-a-couple friends are the friends that came with the marriage, and some of these are friends we could live without. But sometimes, alas, she married our husband's best friend; and sometimes, alas, she *is* our husband's best friend. And so we find ourself dealing with her, somewhat against our will, in a spirit of what I'll call *reluctant* friendship.)

25 7. Men who are friends. I wanted to write just of women friends, but the women I've talked to won't let me—they say I must mention man-woman friendships too. For these friendships can be just as close and as dear as those that we form with women. Listen to Lucy's description of one such friendship:

26 "We've found we have things to talk about that are different from what he talks about with my husband and different from what I talk about with his wife. So sometimes we call on the phone or meet for lunch. There are similar intellectual interests—we always pass on to each other the books that we love—but there's also something tender and caring too."

27 In a couple of crises, Lucy says, ''he offered himself for talking and for helping. And when someone died in his family he wanted me there. The sexual, flirty part of our friendship is very small, but *some*—just enough to make it fun and different.'' She thinks—and I agree—that the sexual part, though small, is always *some,* is always there when a man and a woman are friends.

28 It's only in the past few years that I've made friends with men, in the sense of a friendship that's *mine,* not just part of two couples. And achieving with them the ease and the trust I've found with women friends has value indeed. Under the dryer at home last week, putting on mascara and rouge, I comfortably sat and talked with a fellow named Peter. Peter, I finally decided, could handle the shock of me minus mascara under the dryer. Because we care for each other. Because we're friends.

29 8. There are medium friends, and pretty good friends, and very good friends indeed, and these friendships are defined by their level of intimacy. And what we'll reveal at each of these levels of intimacy is calibrated with care. We might tell a medium friend, for example, that yesterday we had a fight with our husband. And we might tell a pretty good friend that this fight with our husband made us so mad that we slept on the couch. And we might tell a very good friend that the reason we got so mad in that fight that we slept on the couch had something to do with that girl who works in his office. But it's only to our very best friends that we're willing to tell all, to tell what's going on with that girl in his office.

30 The best of friends, I still believe, totally love and support and trust each other, and bare to each other the secrets of their souls, and run—no questions asked—to help each other, and tell harsh truths to each other when they must be told.

31 But we needn't agree about everything (only 12-year-old girl friends agree about *everything*) to tolerate each other's point of view. To accept without judgment. To give and to take without ever keeping score. And to *be* there, as I am for them and as they are for me, to comfort our sorrows, to celebrate our joys.

Jotting Down Your First Responses

1. Which types of friends that Viorst describes do you have?
2. Are there any types in the essay that you don't have? Would you like to have a friend of that type? Why or why not?
3. Do you have any friends that don't fit into Viorst's categories of friends? If so, what would you name the category for those friends?
4. As you read Viorst's definitions of each kind of friend, did you recall anyone you hadn't thought about for a while? Whom did you recall? What kind of friend is he or she?

5. Is it possible to have close friends of the opposite sex? Why or why not?

Checking Your Comprehension

1. What once was Viorst's definition of friendship? (paragraph 1)
2. What does she now believe about types of friends? (paragraph 3)
3. What are convenience friends?
4. What are special-interest friends?
5. What are historical friends?
6. What are crossroads friends?
7. What are cross-generational friends?
8. What are part-of-a-couple friends?
9. Why did she include men who are friends?
10. What is the difference between medium friends, pretty good friends, and very good friends?
11. What don't best friends do?

Understanding a Writer's Patterns

1. What repeated word in paragraphs 1 through 3 tells you that Viorst is going to write about a changed definition of friendship?
2. What words in paragraph 3 indicate a contrasting definition will follow?
3. What is the thesis of this essay (paragraph 3)?
4. Who is the intended audience of this essay? How do you know? Give several pieces of evidence from the essay.
5. What transitional sentence links the thesis sentence to the list of types of friends?
6. What is the primary method of development that Viorst uses to build her new definition of friendship in this essay?
7. Viorst uses many examples. What are examples of special-interest friends?
8. In paragraph 14 what are three examples of "a friend who knew us when . . ."?
9. What are two examples of cross-generational friends?
10. Reread paragraphs 1 and 2. Then read paragraphs 30 and 31. How does Viorst conclude the essay?

Making Predictions and Drawing Inferences

1. After reading paragraph 3 for the first time, what did you expect to find in this essay? Were your expectations fulfilled or not?
2. What kind of research did Viorst do before she wrote this essay?

3. Why did Viorst use division and classification to develop her essay on friendship?

Making Judgments and Thinking Critically

1. Is ''Friends, Good Friends—and Such Good Friends'' an effective title for the essay? Why or why not?
2. Find five direct quotations in the essay, and give the paragraph number of each. Why did Viorst use direct quotations? Are they effective? Why or why not?
3. Why did Viorst use only first names to identify the speakers of direct quotations? What is the general rule for identifying the speaker of direct quotations?
4. Would Viorst change the examples, including the direct quotations, if she were writing for a magazine intended for both men and women readers? Why? In what way?
5. What does Viorst mean by ''we maintain our public face and emotional distance'' (paragraph 7)?
6. Why does Viorst write ''oh, shame!'' in parentheses (paragraph 13)?

Using New Words

1. Make vocabulary cards for three words from this essay that you want to add to your vocabulary. Write a word on one side of a card and a definition and original sentence on the other side.
2. Choose five words from the vocabulary list that precedes this essay. Write one paragraph using all five words.
3. Find the following words and replace them with their opposites: *nonchalant* (paragraph 3), *mutual* (paragraph 8), *rivalry* (paragraph 16), and *forge* (paragraph 18). Notice the changed meaning in the sentence or phrase.
4. The prefix *per-* means ''through''; the root *spec* means ''to look.'' Using the meanings of the prefix and the root, explain what a ''youthful perspective'' is.

Responding by Writing

1. Write an essay to explain a concept that is important to you. Use division and classification to develop your point. Write to people in this class who may have a different perspective than you have on this concept. Possible topics: types of families, hunters, dieters, dates, comedians, politicians, voters, students, or teachers.
2. Write your own essay on the types of friends that a particular group of people have: men, teenagers, retired people, homemakers, Hispanics,

Chinese, or some other group. Interview several people in that group on the various types of friends they have. Write to an audience of this class.

3. Interview several people about the types of friends they have. Write an essay in which you compare their categories of friendship with Viorst's categories. Use the title and author's full name in your essay.
4. Is Viorst's essay on friendship an effective essay? Why or why not? Comment on her methods of development (division and classification and exemplification). Give examples from the essay. Use at least one direct quotation. Be sure to include the title of the essay (in quotation marks) and the full name of the author.

Kinds of Discipline

John Holt

John Holt taught young children for many years. He believed that children are naturally curious and eager to please. He wrote three books about education based on that belief. The following selection is from *Freedom and Beyond.*

Thinking Before Reading

What is the difference between discipline and punishment? How are these terms related to your learning, in school and out? Write a few sentences in your Idea Bank.

Expanding Your Vocabulary from Reading

impartial (1) unprejudiced, fair
indifferent (1) of no importance one way or the other
wheedled (1) persuaded by flattery; coaxed out
contagious (2) transmitted by contact
precautions (3) actions to prevent harm or failure
impotent (3) powerless
vengeful (3) desiring revenge
humiliation (3) disgrace, shame
autocratic (4) domineering
suppleness (4) flexibility
novice (4) beginner
competence (4) adequate ability to perform some task

1 A child, in growing up, may meet and learn from three different kinds of disciplines. The first and most important is what we might call the Discipline of Nature or of Reality. When he is trying to do something real, if he does the wrong thing or doesn't do the right one, he doesn't get the results he wants. If he doesn't pile one block right on top of another, or tries to build on a slanting surface, his tower falls down. If he hits the wrong key, he hears the wrong note. If he doesn't hit the nail squarely on the head, it bends, and he has to pull it out and start with another. If he doesn't measure properly what he is trying to build, it won't open, close, fit, stand up, fly, float, whistle, or do whatever he wants it to do. If he closes his eyes when he swings, he doesn't hit the ball. A child meets this kind of discipline every time he tries to *do* something, which is why it is so important in school to give children more chances to do things, instead of just reading or listening to someone talk (or pretending to). This discipline is a great teacher. The learner never has to wait long for his answer; it usually comes quickly, often instantly. Also it is clear, and very often points toward the needed correction; from what happened he cannot only see that what he did was wrong, but also why, and what he needs to do instead. Finally, and most important, the giver of the answer, call it Nature, is impersonal, impartial, and indifferent. She does not give opinions, or make judgments; she cannot be wheedled, bullied, or fooled; she does not get angry or disappointed; she does not praise or blame; she does not remember past failures or hold grudges; with her one always gets a fresh start, this time is the one that counts.

2 The next discipline we might call the Discipline of Culture, of Society, of What People Really Do. Man is a social, a cultural animal. Children sense around them this culture, this network of agreements, customs, habits, and rules binding the adults together. They want to understand it and be a part of it. They watch very carefully what people around them are doing and want to do the same. They want to do right, unless they become convinced they can't do right. Thus children rarely misbehave seriously in church, but sit as quietly as they can. The example of all those grownups is contagious. Some mysterious ritual is going on, and children, who like rituals, want to be part of it. In the same way, the little children that I see at concerts or operas, though they may fidget a little, or perhaps take a nap now and then, rarely make any disturbance. With all those grownups sitting there, neither moving nor talking, it is the most natural thing in the world to imitate them. Children who live among adults who are habitually courteous to each other, and to them, will soon learn to be courteous. Children who live surrounded by people who speak a certain way will speak that way, however much we may try to tell them that speaking that way is bad or wrong.

3 The third discipline is the one most people mean when they speak of discipline—the Discipline of Superior Force, of sergeant to private, of "you do what I tell you or I'll make you wish you had." There is bound to be some

of this in a child's life. Living as we do surrounded by things that can hurt children, or that children can hurt, we cannot avoid it. We can't afford to let a small child find out from experience the danger of playing in a busy street, or of fooling with the pots on the top of a stove, or of eating up the pills in the medicine cabinet. So, along with other precautions, we say to him, "Don't play in the street, or touch things on the stove, or go into the medicine cabinet, or I'll punish you." Between him and the danger too great for him to imagine we put a lesser danger, but one he can imagine and maybe therefore want to avoid. He can have no idea of what it would be like to be hit by a car, but he can imagine being shouted at, or spanked, or sent to his room. He avoids these substitutes for the greater danger until he can understand it and avoid it for its own sake. But we ought to use this discipline only when it is necessary to protect the life, health, safety, or well-being of people or other living creatures, or to prevent destruction of things that people care about. We ought not to assume too long, as we usually do, that a child cannot understand the real nature of the danger from which we want to protect him. The sooner he avoids the danger, not to escape our punishment, but as a matter of good sense, the better. He can learn that faster than we think. In Mexico, for example, where people drive their cars with a good deal of spirit, I saw many children no older than five or four walking unattended on the streets. They understood about cars, they knew what to do. A child whose life is full of the threat and fear of punishment is locked into babyhood. There is no way for him to grow up, to learn to take responsibility for his life and acts. Most important of all, we should not assume that having to yield to the threat of our superior force is good for the child's character. It is never good for *anyone's* character. To bow to superior force makes us feel impotent and cowardly for not having had the strength or courage to resist. Worse, it makes us resentful and vengeful. We can hardly wait to make someone pay for our humiliation, yield to us as we were once made to yield. No, if we cannot always avoid using the Discipline of Superior Force, we should at least use it as seldom as we can.

4 There are places where all three disciplines overlap. Any very demanding human activity combines in it the disciplines of Superior Force, of Culture, and of Nature. The novice will be told, "Do it this way, never mind asking why, just do it that way, that is the way we always do it." But it probably *is* just the way they always do it, and usually for the very good reason that it is a way that has been found to work. Think, for example, of ballet training. The student in a class is told to do this exercise, or that; to stand so; to do this or that with his head, arms, shoulders, abdomen, hips, legs, feet. He is constantly corrected. There is no argument. But behind these seemingly autocratic demands by the teacher lie many decades of custom and tradition, and behind that, the necessities of dancing itself. You cannot make the moves of classical ballet unless over many years you have acquired, and renewed every day, the needed strength and suppleness in scores of muscles and joints. Nor can you

do the difficult motions, making them look easy, unless you have learned hundreds of easier ones first. Dance teachers may not always agree on all the details of teaching these strengths and skills. But no novice could learn them all by himself. You could not go for a night or two to watch the ballet and then, without any other knowledge at all, teach yourself how to do it. In the same way, you would be unlikely to learn any complicated and difficult human activity without drawing heavily on the experience of those who know it better. But the point is that the authority of these experts or teachers stems from, grows out of their greater competence and experience, the fact that what they do *works,* not the fact that they happen to be the teacher and as such have the power to kick a student out of the class. And the further point is that children are always and everywhere attracted to that competence, and ready and eager to submit themselves to a discipline that grows out of it. We hear constantly that children will never do anything unless compelled to by bribes or threats. But in their private lives, or in extracurricular activities in school, in sports, music, drama, art, running a newspaper, and so on, they often submit themselves willingly and wholeheartedly to very intense disciplines, simply because they want to learn to do a given thing well. Our Little-Napoleon football coaches, of whom we have too many and hear far too much, blind us to the fact that millions of children work hard every year getting better at sports and games without coaches barking and yelling at them.

Jotting Down Your First Responses

1. What example of discipline from your childhood do you recall? What kind of discipline, according to Holt, is it?
2. If you have children or intend to have them, which of these kinds of discipline do you or will you use?
3. Do you have good self-discipline? If not, why not? If so, how did you learn self-discipline?

Checking Your Comprehension

1. According to Holt, how do children benefit from the three kinds of discipline he describes? (paragraph 1)
2. What are Holt's three kinds of discipline? What does he mean by each?
3. Why do children need to *do,* not just read and listen, in order to learn? (paragraph 1)
4. What are three reasons, according to Holt, that the Discipline of Reality is a great teacher?
5. How do children learn to be courteous? (paragraph 2)

6. Which of Holt's disciplines do most people mean when they speak of discipline? (paragraph 3)
7. When is the discipline in question 6 needed? When is it obsolete?
8. What result does too much threat and punishment have on a child?
9. What is the basis of authority for excellent teachers, according to Holt? (paragraph 4)
10. Does Holt think that bribes and threats are necessary for children to learn at home or school? Why or why not?

Understanding a Writer's Patterns

1. What is Holt's topic? What is his thesis?
2. What transitional phrases point out the kinds of discipline, including their combination?
3. Holt lists five examples of the Discipline of Reality. What phrase begins each example?
4. What are three examples of Reality that Holt uses?
5. What examples does Holt give of children learning from the Discipline of Society?
6. What example does Holt give that children can learn about real dangers faster than we think, making our precautions and threats unnecessary? What phrase signals the example for the reader?
7. What example does Holt use to explain a complex activity that uses all three disciplines?

Making Predictions and Drawing Inferences

1. Holt says that Reality is an excellent teacher. What characteristics does he suggest a good teacher should have?
2. What do you think Holt believes about including children in adult activities?
3. What, according to Holt, is the purpose of any discipline?

Making Judgments and Thinking Critically

1. Would you describe Holt as a soft or strict disciplinarian? Why?
2. What place does punishment have in Holt's philosophy?
3. Holt says that children need more chances to learn by *doing,* not just by reading or listening. Does this apply to your own learning—at work, play, home, or school?
4. What example of a complex activity that combines all three disciplines can you give? Explain the part each discipline plays in learning this activity.

Using New Words

1. Choose three words to add to your vocabulary cards. Write a word on one side of a card and a definition and an original sentence on the other side.
2. One of the meanings of the prefix *in-* (and its mutated form *im-*) means "not." What do these words mean: *impersonal* (paragraph 1), *impartial* (paragraph 1), *indifferent* (paragraph 1), and *impotent* (paragraph 3)? Replace these words in their original sentences with synonyms. How do the substitutions change the sound or meaning of the sentences for better or worse?
3. Write three other words beginning with *in-* (*im-*). Does the prefix help you define the word? Does the prefix mean "not" in these words?
4. Holt writes Nature "cannot be *wheedled, bullied,* or *fooled.*" What are synonyms for each of these action verbs?
5. Twenty years ago, when Holt wrote this essay, writers were not sensitive to sexism in language. Today most writers try to avoid using sexist language (referring to both male and female with the pronoun *he*), by using plural nouns and pronouns. Assume that Holt's essay begins "Children . . ." instead of "A child. . . ." Now rewrite sentences 3, 4, and 5. Change the pronouns and the verbs they affect to plural. For example, "When *they are* trying to do something real, if *they do* the wrong thing or *don't* do the right one. . . ."

Responding by Writing

1. Write an essay about the effects of Holt's kinds of disciplines on you, either as a child or as an adult. Give personal examples from home, school, work, or play. Comment on the effects of each of these kinds of discipline on what you learned, how you learned, and how you felt.
2. If you are an artist, a musician, a golfer, a basketball player, a hot rod driver, or accomplished in any other complex activity, you have experienced a combination of Holt's kinds of discipline. Write an essay describing the benefit of each kind of discipline to your expertise. Write to an audience who doesn't know how but wants to perform this activity well.
3. Holt writes that some people believe "that children will never do anything unless compelled to by bribes or threats." Do you agree or disagree? Write an essay stating your opinion and supporting it with examples from your general knowledge, your experience, and from Holt's essay. Think of a person you think needs to hear this: a young parent you know, a teacher, or a grandparent. Write to this person and others like him or her.

   Use at least one quotation. Refer to the essay giving the title in quotation marks and the writer's full name. Remember that you may refer to the writer by his last name after you have used his full name one time.

Twits, Cookies, and Queens

Claudia Reardon

Claudia Reardon was a freshman student at Richland College, a community college, when she wrote the following essay. Now a graduate student, she has returned to teach a course in developmental writing at Richland.

Thinking Before Reading

High school students usually form friendship groups based on particular interests or values. Write a few sentences in your Idea Bank about the high school groups you recall or about friendship groups at the college you are now attending.

Expanding Your Vocabulary from Reading

cliques (1) exclusive group of friends
hypocritical (1) false, phony, two-faced
intimidate (2) make to feel inferior or fearful
humanoid (3) humanlike creature
gawk (3) stare with open mouth
prudes (3) people overconcerned with being or seeming proper or righteous
ionosphere (4) layer of the earth's atmosphere
saunter (4) walk casually and slowly

1 I get the biggest kick out of watching the cliques among high school girls in action. I feel hypocritical when I laugh at them because not long ago I was part of that scene, but it's hard to resist, for they are so ridiculous! There are three main sects in the clique world, and the members can be easily identified by what they wear. ''Tough Cookies'' are the ones who wear leather miniskirts and spiked heels; ''Twits'' wear oversized sweaters, Madonna-style lace in their hair and pink eyeshadow; and ''Fashion Queens'' wear mink coats, Calvin Klein underwear and Gucci watch bands. All three groups are sickening in other ways as well.

2 The Tough Cookies are the girls everyone else in school is afraid of. They slink down the hallways trying to intimidate other girls and turn on the guys. While they strut, they always carry a copy of *Forum* (a porno magazine)

or *Circus* (a hard rock magazine), or deafen themselves by blasting Twisted Sister on their Walkmans. In class they sit on the side of the room with their backs defensively against the wall, trying to stay awake after smoking a couple of joints before school. Ask them who their idols are and they'll reply ''Hulk Hogan, Joan Rivers and Rambo'' or another soft-spoken humanitarian in our society. In general, the Tough Cookies motto is ''Sex, Drugs, and Rock 'n Roll.''

3 Twits are the most annoying of the humanoids. They're the immature, giggly, bubbly type who hide in their rooms while they listen to Dr. Ruth with headphones on. They often become cheerleaders or statisticians for boys' sports just so they can gawk at their muscular bods. They fall in love with someone different at least once a week. Twits are wishy-washy little things; they're easily pressured into smoking or drinking, but they remain prudes by pretending to pass out when guys maneuver them into a bedroom during football parties. They live in a fantasy world filled with Michael J. Fox, Menudo and ''Love Connection.'' Their literary ventures don't go beyond *Teen Beat* and *The National Enquirer* (and they move their lips when they read). Most of the Twits in high schools grow up to become Teri Garr.

4 The ones who read *Vogue* and have extended credit at Bloomingdales are Fashion Queens. These are the girls, excuse me, *Women,* who make the rest of the female population look like Andy Warhols. Most of them are engaged to Sam Malone types (from ''Cheers''), but they always cheat on them. They keep the old guys around because they're football players who drive convertibles, but hang on to the other guys as backups for the prom in case the halfbacks blow them off at the last minute. When they glide down the hallway, they prop their noses into the ionosphere and sway their hourglass figures, sending the freshman boys right into puberty. Without saying a word, they can make other girls burn with jealousy as they saunter by, and because the wenches *know* this, they sway even more. Fashion Queens have an image to keep up. They never drink booze; it makes them puke, which isn't very fashionable. Nor do they smoke pot; it makes them act silly and they might be mistaken for a Twit! Instead they do cocaine, the rich person's drug. They even have their own fourteen-karat gold coke spoon! They listen to rock groups like the Rolling Stones or the Beatles—only widely famous and accepted ''safe'' groups that have no chance of passing with a fad. In general, Fashion Queens are conceited rich bitches who nobody likes except other rich bitches.

5 These main cliques are so different from each other, yet they are all fun to watch in action. It's especially humorous when members of two different groups clash. My favorite conflict is when a Twit and a Fashion Queen are squabbling over a guy. The Twit screams of her undying love (that will last for at least another twenty minutes) and the Fashion Queen with her pseudo-sophisticatedness tells the Twit that he's out of her league.

6 Then there's the nonexistent group of high-schoolers who are stable, mature, level-headed, independent people who can stand alone and still know who they are. Even some of the teachers in high school don't fall into this category! But after all, this *is* high school I'm talking about!

Jotting Down Your First Responses

1. Do you recall students in high school or junior high who fit into any of Reardon's categories? If so, describe the students you recall.
2. What kinds of groups do you recall from earlier schools?
3. Have you ever felt "in" or "out" of a group you wanted to belong to? If so, tell what that was like.
4. What kinds of students were your friends in high school? Did you think of yourselves as a group? What kind of a group was it? Describe your group. Has your view of this group changed since then?

Checking Your Comprehension

1. What are the three cliques Reardon describes?
2. What is the most obvious way to identify the clique a girl belongs to?
3. What is the motto of the Tough Cookies?
4. How do Tough Cookies walk down the halls?
5. Why are the Twits interested in sports?
6. Why do they drink or smoke?
7. How do the Fashion Queens walk?
8. How do Fashion Queens treat guys?
9. According to Reardon, what kind of people don't fit into these categories?

Understanding a Writer's Patterns

1. What is the thesis of the essay?
2. What is Reardon's purpose?
3. What words in the first paragraph show her feelings and attitude about her topic?
4. Reardon describes the clothes of each clique. What are three other points of comparison for each group?
5. What example of each clique's favorite musician or musical group does Reardon use?
6. What titles or names of public figures does the writer use to describe the interests of Twits?
7. With what contrasting idea does Reardon conclude her discussion of high school cliques?

Making Predictions and Drawing Inferences

1. After reading paragraph 1, what attitude did you expect Reardon to have toward her topic? What words from the essay show this attitude? Did you find what you expected? Why or why not?
2. Why do Tough Cookies intimidate other girls?
3. Why do Twits hide in their rooms to listen to Dr. Ruth?
4. Did Reardon belong to one of the cliques she describes in the essay? How do you know?

Making Judgments and Thinking Critically

1. Is Reardon's attitude toward the cliques consistent or uneven? Give evidence from the essay for your answer.
2. How old do you think Reardon was when she wrote this essay? Why do you think so?
3. What is the strength of the essay?

Using New Words

1. Choose two words from this essay that you would like to add to your writing and speaking vocabulary. Make a vocabulary card for each one with the word on one side and a definition and an original sentence on the other side.
2. Choose two classmates to play this vocabulary game. (a) Each player shuffles his or her vocabulary cards. (b) Each player chooses any five cards from another player's cards and holds them. (c) The player with the word beginning with the letter nearest the end of the alphabet begins. To determine who goes first, someone should ask "Who has a word beginning with x, y, or z?" If no one does, "Who has a word beginning with u, v, or w?" Then "r, s, or t" and so forth. (d) Player 1 (the player holding the word beginning with the letter nearest the end of the alphabet) asks the owner of the card (player 2) what the word means. If player 2 answers correctly, player 1 asks him or her to define another word. Player 2's turn continues until he or she misses or defines all five of his or her words. (e) After player 2's turn is completed, he or she begins to question the owner of the cards he or she is holding (either player 1 or player 3). (f) The game continues until the players have defined as many words as they can. The person or persons who define the most words correctly win.
3. Words that end in *-ion* (which means an act or process of) are nouns that have been formed from verbs. Change the following nouns into their verb forms: *humiliation, animation, calibration, competition, intimidation.*

Responding by Writing

1. Write an essay to an audience of this class about the kinds of people you've observed in some activity that you participate in. Perhaps you play or coach a sport in a league. Perhaps you ride public transportation frequently or attend a church or synagogue regularly. Perhaps because you frequently have to wait for someone or something, you spend many hours watching people.

   Once you have identified the kinds of people you want to describe, decide what your attitude is and what tone you will take in expressing it—light, serious, angry, sarcastic, amused, offended. Maintain this same tone throughout the essay.
2. If you are a person who keeps everything, your purse, car, room, desk, or garage may look cluttered and messy to Mr. or Ms Neatnik. Write an essay explaining to Mr. and Ms Neatnik what kinds of things you keep and why. Keep the tone light and humorous, not defensive and angry.
3. Rewrite the essay you wrote about the things you keep. This time the audience is a critical friend, parent, or spouse, and your tone should be angry, sarcastic, and defensive.
4. As either a male or female, do you identify with one of the groups that Reardon described? If so, write her a letter evaluating her description of your group. Are you offended or amused? Is the picture accurate or slanted? What would you add or delete?

CHAPTER

10

COMPARISON AND CONTRAST

USING COMPARISON AND CONTRAST TO DEVELOP YOUR ESSAY

Sometimes the best way to describe or explain or persuade is to show how something is like or unlike something else. To compare is to examine how items, processes, or ideas are alike. *To contrast* is to emphasize how they are different. Comparing and contrasting can be used separately or together to develop an essay.

You may want to use comparison to make readers aware of the similarities of two things, to explain the unfamiliar in terms of the familiar, or to show the superiority of something by comparing it with its competition. For instance, if a friend is undecided about whether to go to your local community college or to a university and you want to convince her to register at the community college, you might compare the two to show her how the college is similar to the university. If a friend wants to buy a dog, you might compare a golden retriever, a breed unfamiliar to your friend, to a labrador retriever, a breed familiar to your friend. Or you might try to convince a coworker that the Oregon Ducks are a superior college team by comparing them with several other college teams.

When you are comparing or contrasting, the items, processes, or ideas must belong to the same class. For instance, if you are doing comparison shopping for a new car, you probably have a class of vehicle in mind. You know you want a van, an economy car, a sports car, or a luxury sedan.

Therefore, you look at several vehicles in the same class. You can compare a Dodge van and a Toyota van on several points. To compare vans, you might consider cost, gas mileage per gallon, horsepower, repair record, and so on. You would want information about both vans on each point of comparison in order to decide which one to buy.

Here is an example of contrast from *Amusing Ourselves to Death* in which the author, Neil Postman, analyzes the effects of television on American culture. He contrasts two views of the future as described in two famous novels written forty years ago.

> . . . alongside Orwell's dark vision, there was another—slightly older, slightly less well known, equally chilling: Aldous Huxley's *Brave New World.* Contrary to common belief even among the educated, Huxley and Orwell did not prophesy the same thing. Orwell warns that we will be overcome by an externally imposed oppression. But in Huxley's vision no Big Brother is required to deprive people of their autonomy, maturity and history. As he saw it, people will come to love their oppression, to adore the technologies that undo their capacities to think.
>
> What Orwell feared were those who would ban books. What Huxley feared was that there would be no reason to ban a book, for there would be no one who wanted to read one. Orwell feared those who would deprive us of information. Huxley feared those who would give us so much that we would be reduced to passivity and egoism. Orwell feared that the truth would be concealed from us. Huxley feared the truth would be drowned in a sea of irrelevance.

Notice that the two things Postman is contrasting are the same kind of thing. Both are views of the future. They are alike in that they are both pessimistic, but they differ as to what the authors feared the future would hold. All comparisons and contrasts must begin with a basic similarity.

Write a Thesis. Comparison and contrast always serve to develop a point—the thesis of the essay or a supporting point. They are not ends in themselves. If a writer does not have a clear thesis for an essay or a clear topic sentence for a supporting point, a comparison or contrast has no purpose. If the writer simply lays out a comparison or contrast with no topic sentence or thesis, a reader is left to wonder, ''So what? What's your point?'' In the example of contrasting views of the future, Postman's thesis in the preface to his book-length essay about the effects of television is that Huxley's view has come true. A comparison or contrast cannot stand alone. When you use comparison or contrast, be sure that you have stated the point that the comparison or contrast is intended to develop.

ORGANIZING POINT-BY-POINT OR SUBJECT-BY-SUBJECT

There are two ways to organize information in comparisons and contrasts—point by point and subject by subject. In *point-by-point* organization a writer discusses a number of ways two things are alike or different. In the excerpt from *Amusing Ourselves to Death,* Postman uses a point-by-point organization. He gives a number of points (about books, information, and truth) and alternates Orwell's and Huxley's view about each point.

Point 1
- a. What Orwell feared were those who would ban books.
- b. What Huxley feared was that there would be no reason to ban a book, for there would be no one who wanted to read one.

Point 2
- a. Orwell feared those who would deprive us of information.
- b. Huxley feared those who would give us so much that we would be reduced to passivity and egoism.

Point 3
- a. Orwell feared that the truth would be concealed from us.
- b. Huxley feared the truth would be drowned in a sea of irrelevance.

Subject-by-subject organization looks at one subject at a time instead of alternating back and forth between subjects. A writer makes all the points about one subject and then all the corresponding points about the other subject. If Postman's contrast were rewritten to be organized subject (Orwell) by subject (Huxley), it might look like this:

> What Orwell feared were those who would ban books. He feared those who would deprive us of information. Orwell also feared that the truth would be concealed from us.
>
> What Huxley feared was that there would be no reason to ban a book, for there would be no one who wanted to read one. He feared those who would give us so much information that we would be reduced to passivity and egoism. Huxley also feared the truth would be drowned in a sea of irrelevance.

The first paragraph contains several of Orwell's fears; the second paragraph contains the corresponding fears of Huxley in the same order.

Choose a Pattern of Organization. The kind and length of a comparison or contrast, as part of an essay or as the basic organizational structure of a whole essay, will help you decide which pattern of organization will work best. In shorter comparison and contrast, subject-by-subject works well. For instance, you might write one paragraph giving all your information about the Dodge van and then one about the Toyota van. In longer comparison and contrast, point-by-point organization works better. For instance, if you had done a full and technical study of the two vans, you might write one or more paragraphs about the power of the two vehicles, then one or more paragraphs about the repair record of both vans, and so on. Once you start an organizational pattern, follow through so you don't lose your reader.

Present similar information in the same order. Since you're going back and forth between subjects or points, the reader can easily become confused. There are several ways to provide coherence. One strategy is to use the same order when you make corresponding points, as in the example above.

Orwell's View	**Huxley's View**
ban *books*	no readers of *books*
deprive people of *information*	give people too much *information*
conceal the *truth*	drown the *truth* in irrelevance

Provide Many Transitional Words and Phrases. Transitions are especially important in comparison and contrast to keep the reader on track. Use transitional words and phrases to signal that you are about to present similarities and differences and to keep readers aware of the order you are using.

To signal that a point is similar or to make additional ones, use such terms as:

also	in the same way
in addition	moreover
similarly	

To signal that a point or detail is different these transitions are helpful:

on the other hand	but
however	although
nevertheless	in contrast
still	contrary to

To keep track of order use such terms as:

first	last
next	finally

Look at Postman's transitions:

> *Contrary to* common belief even among the educated, Huxley and Orwell did not prophesy the same thing. Orwell warns that we will be overcome by an externally imposed oppression. *But* in Huxley's vision no Big Brother is required to deprive people of their autonomy. . . .

Use Parallelism to Show Points of Similarity or Difference. Another strategy to provide clarity, coherence, and emphasis in comparison and contrast is to use parallelism, which is using the same structure for similar ideas. Here are some sentences from Ellen Goodman's essay about friendship in this chapter.

> [O]n the whole, men had buddies, while women had friends. Buddies bonded, but friends loved. Buddies faced adversity together, but friends faced each other. . . . Buddies seemed to "do" things together; friends simply "were" together. . . . Buddies hang tough together; friends hang onto each other. . . . Buddies try to keep the worst from each other; friends confess it.

Notice the similar sentence structure (parallelism). Notice also the use of the transitional word *but,* the use of the semicolon (;) to show the relationships of contrasting ideas, and the point-by-point organization.

POINTS TO REMEMBER ABOUT COMPARISON AND CONTRAST

- Compare and contrast to explain the unfamiliar in terms of the familiar.
- Compare and contrast to show the relative merit of something.
- State the thesis or topic sentence that the comparison or contrast develops.
- Establish points of comparison and give information on those points for all things compared or contrasted.
- Compare or contrast only items, processes, and ideas that belong to the same class.
- Organize information subject by subject or point by point.
- Make corresponding points in the same order.
- Use transitional words and phrases.
- Use parallel structure for corresponding points.

The Tapestry of Friendship

Ellen Goodman

Ellen Goodman writes for *The Washington Post.* Her syndicated column is seen in newspapers throughout the country. Her columns have been collected and published in several books, including *Close to Home* and *Keeping in Touch.*

Thinking Before Reading

What is a friend? What is a buddy? Who of the people you know would you call a friend? Who would you consider a buddy? Write about these two words in your Idea Bank.

Expanding Your Vocabulary from Reading

fragility (2) condition of being easily broken
resiliency (2) ability to recover from change
binge (4) period of uncontrolled self-indulgence, such as an eating or crying binge
celluloid (5) film, more specifically a movie
atavistic (5) characteristic of an earlier stage, like a throwback to an earlier time
palpably (8) capable of being touched or held, physically real
loathsome (10) hateful, disgusting
restraint (15) act of holding back
claustrophobic (16) fearful of being in closed places
intimacy (18) condition of sharing one's deepest nature

1 It was, in many ways, a slight movie. Nothing actually happened. There was no big-budget chase scene, no bloody shoot-out. The story ended without any cosmic conclusions.

2 Yet she found Claudia Weill's film *Girlfriends* gentle and affecting. Slowly, it panned across the tapestry of friendship—showing its fragility, its resiliency, its role as the connecting tissue between the lives of two young women.

3 When it was over, she thought about the movies she'd seen this year—*Julia, The Turning Point* and now *Girlfriends.* It seemed that the peculiar eye, the social lens of the cinema, had drastically shifted its focus. Suddenly the Male Buddy movies had been replaced by the Female Friendship flicks.

4 This wasn't just another binge of trendiness, but a kind of *cinéma vérité.* For once the movies were reflecting a shift, not just from men to women but from one definition of friendship to another.

5 Across millions of miles of celluloid, the ideal of friendship had always been male—a world of sidekicks and "pardners," of Butch Cassidys and Sundance Kids. There had been something almost atavistic about these visions of attachments—as if producers culled their plots from some pop anthropology book on male bonding. Movies portrayed the idea that only men, those direct descendants of hunters and Hemingways, inherited a primal capacity for friendship. In contrast, they portrayed women picking on each other, the way they once picked berries.

6 Well, that duality must have been mortally wounded in some shootout at

the You're OK, I'm OK Corral. Now, on the screen, they were at least aware of the subtle distinction between men and women as buddies and friends.

7 About 150 years ago, Coleridge had written, "A woman's friendship borders more closely on love than man's. Men affect each other in the reflection of noble or friendly acts, whilst women ask fewer proofs and more signs and expressions of attachment."

8 Well, she thought, on the whole, men had buddies, while women had friends. Buddies bonded, but friends loved. Buddies faced adversity together, but friends faced each other. There was something palpably different in the way they spent their time. Buddies seemed to "do" things together; friends simply "were" together.

9 Buddies came linked, like accessories, to one activity or another. People have golf buddies and business buddies, college buddies and club buddies. Men often keep their buddies in these categories, while women keep a special category for friends.

10 A man once told her that men weren't real buddies until they'd been "through the wars" together—corporate or athletic or military. They had to soldier together, he said. Women, on the other hand, didn't count themselves as friends until they'd shared three loathsome confidences.

11 Buddies hang tough together; friends hang onto each other.

12 It probably had something to do with pride. You don't show off to a friend; you show need. Buddies try to keep the worst from each other; friends confess it.

13 A friend of hers once telephoned her lover, just to find out if he were home. She hung up without a hello when he picked up the phone. Later, wretched with embarrassment, the friend moaned, "Can you believe me? A thirty-five-year-old lawyer, making a chicken call?" Together they laughed and made it better.

14 Buddies seek approval. But friends seek acceptance.

15 She knew so many men who had been trained in restraint, afraid of each other's judgment or awkward with each other's affection. She wasn't sure which. Like buddies in the movies, they would die for each other, but never hug each other.

16 She'd reread *Babbitt* recently, that extraordinary catalogue of male grievances. The only relationship that gave meaning to the claustrophobic life of George Babbitt had been with Paul Riesling. But not once in the tragedy of their lives had one been able to say to the other: You make a difference.

17 Even now men shocked her at times with their description of friendship. Does this one have a best friend? "Why, of course, we see each other every February." Does that one call his most intimate pal long distance? "Why, certainly, whenever there's a real reason." Do those two old chums ever have dinner together? "You mean alone? Without our wives?"

18 Yet, things were changing. The ideal of intimacy wasn't this parallel playmate, this teammate, this trenchmate. Not even in Hollywood. In the

double standard of friendship, for once the female version was becoming accepted as the general ideal.

19 After all, a buddy is a fine life-companion. But one's friends, as Santayana once wrote, ''are part of the race with which one can be human.''

Jotting Down Your First Responses

1. What is the difference between buddies and friends, according to Goodman? Do you have buddies? Friends? Who are they?
2. If you agree with Goodman that men's friendships and women's friendships are basically different, does her description of the difference seem accurate to you? If not, how would you describe the difference?
3. If you disagree with Goodman's claim that men's friendships and women's friendships are basically different, why do you disagree? Explain your opinion.

Checking Your Comprehension

1. What three movies about women friends does Goodman name? How are the titles punctuated? How would you punctuate them if you were typing movie titles in an essay you were writing?
2. According to Goodman, what has been the ideal of friendship as portrayed by the movies in the past?
3. What shift in the definition of friendship do more current movies reflect?
4. What word does Goodman use to characterize men's friendships? Women's friendships?
5. What are five points of contrast between these two types of friendships?
6. What does Goodman mean by ''a double standard of friendship'' (paragraph 18)?
7. What does the word *Hollywood* represent and refer to here?
8. Which version of friendship has become the ideal of friendship?

Understanding a Writer's Patterns

1. Why do you think Goodman wrote this essay (her purpose)? Who is her audience?
2. Goodman takes several paragraphs to introduce her subject, hook the reader's interest, and lead up to her thesis. What paragraphs make up the introduction of the essay?
3. What two kinds of hooks does Goodman use in the introduction?
4. What is the thesis of this essay?
5. Does Goodman use a subject-by-subject (men's friendship versus women's friendships) method or a point-by-point method to organize this contrast of men's and women's friendships?

6. In paragraph 8 Goodman uses the pronoun *she*. Who is she and why does the author use this device?
7. In paragraph 8 what transitional word does Goodman use to contrast buddies and friends? How many times does she use this word in the rest of the essay?
8. In paragraph 10 what phrase does Goodman use to show contrast?
9. In paragraphs 11 and 12 what punctuation mark is used to highlight the contrast of other points? Find one other paragraph in which this same device is used to show contrast.
10. Paragraph 13 is a personal example. What does it explain?
11. What is the tone of paragraph 17? Why do you think so?
12. What word in paragraph 18 indicates Goodman is starting the conclusion of her essay?
13. What strategy does she use to conclude?

Making Predictions and Drawing Inferences

1. What does it mean to say that movies reflect life and reality? Some people believe that movies do the opposite of reflecting life. What do these people believe that movies do?
2. In paragraph 18 Goodman says that the "ideal of intimacy wasn't. . . ." What does she imply the ideal of intimacy is?
3. In paragraph 18 Goodman says, "for once the female version was becoming accepted as the general ideal." What does she mean? Why does she say "for once"?

Making Judgments and Thinking Critically

1. How is this essay, which is developed by contrasts, like an essay that is developed by an emphasis on definition?
2. Do you think this is a biased view of the definitions of men's and women's friendships? Why or why not?
3. Do you think movies and television shape reality (for instance, stimulate violence, encourage sexual promiscuity) or reflect reality? Why?

Using New Words

1. Goodman speaks of "loathsome confidences" (paragraph 10). What words could be used instead of "loathsome"? How does the substitution change the meaning?
2. Add three more words to your vocabulary cards.
3. For fun and practice, shuffle your stack of vocabulary cards. Draw five words. Write a paragraph using all five words. Let your imagination loose.

Responding by Writing

1. Write an essay about friendship. You might focus on a special kind of friendship, such as the friendship of children, married couples, men, or teens. You might focus on the different kinds of friends. Write for an audience of this class. As a class project, the essays from the class might be collected into an anthology on friendship. This anthology may be exchanged with another class.
2. Write an essay that answers one of the following questions: (a) Who do you think are better friends—men or women? (b) In the movie *When Harry Met Sally,* Harry argues that men and women can't be friends and Sally disagrees strongly. Do you believe men and women can be good friends?
3. Sometimes we are struck by the change in people we have known well after a life event, such as getting married, enduring a serious illness, living out of the country for a while, or going away to college. Sometimes, after an absence of years we return to a place and are struck by the difference between our memory of it and its reality or by the difference between it then and now. Write an essay comparing two views of a person, place, or possession. Write to an audience of this class. Decide what point you want to make with the contrast, and write a trial thesis to guide you in writing a draft.
4. Writing about friendship, Goodman describes men as "buddies" and females as "friends." Do you agree or disagree with the difference she describes? Write an essay to the teacher in which you answer this question. Your Idea Bank may help you begin.

   Use at least two brief quotations from the essay. Try to incorporate the phrases smoothly into your sentences. For example: Goodman claims that buddies are "linked, like accessories, to one activity."

   Be sure to give the title of the essay (in quotation marks) and the full name of the writer the first time you use it. You may refer thereafter to the writer by last name only.

Private Space

Edward T. Hall

Edward T. Hall is an anthropologist who studies interpersonal phenomena across cultures, especially body language and the space people need to separate themselves from others. His popular books include *The Hidden Dimension* from which this selection is taken.

Thinking Before Reading

If you are talking with a friend and another person approaches the two of you, how close does that person come before you feel that he or she has broken into "your space"? Ask several people of different ages and cultures. Write about the results of your experiment in your Idea Bank.

Expanding Your Vocabulary from Reading

proxemic (1) related to the study of individuals' personal space needs in different cultures
attenuated (1) weakened
intrusion (1) unwelcome entrance
presumptuous (3) extremely forward, taking liberties
P.W.s (7) prisoners of war
Wehrmacht **(7)** the German army
inadvertent (8) unintentional, accidental
rescinded (8) repealed, voided
integrity (9) unity, completeness
epitomize (10) capture the essence of
conspiratorial (11) characteristic of those plotting secretly to create change
hierarchical (12) related to a line of rank or authority
queues (12) lines of people waiting
mores (15) customs
deterrent (15) something that prevents or discourages an action
anathema (15) something that is extremely disliked

1 I shall never forget my first experience with German proxemic patterns, which occurred when I was an undergraduate. My manners, my status, and my ego were attacked and crushed by a German in an instance where thirty years' residence in this country and an excellent command of English had not attenuated German definitions of what constitutes an intrusion. In order to understand the various issues that were at stake, it is necessary to refer back to two basic American patterns that are taken for granted in this country and which Americans therefore tend to treat as universal.

2 First, in the United States there is a commonly accepted, invisible boundary around any two or three people in conversation which separates them from others. Distance alone serves to isolate any such group and to endow it with a protective wall of privacy. Normally, voices are kept low to avoid intruding on others and if voices are heard, people will act as though they had not heard. In this way, privacy is granted whether it is actually present or not. The second pattern is somewhat more subtle and has to do with the exact point at which a person is experienced as actually having crossed a boundary and entered a room. Talking through a screen door while standing outside a house is not

considered by most Americans as being inside the house or room in any sense of the word. If one is standing on the threshold holding the door open and talking to someone inside, it is still defined informally and experienced as being *outside.* If one is in an office building and just ''pokes his head in the door'' of an office he's still outside the office. Just holding on to the doorjamb when one's body is inside the room still means a person has one foot ''on base'' as it were so that he is not quite inside the other fellow's territory. None of these American spatial definitions is valid in northern Germany. In every instance where the American would consider himself *outside* he has already entered the German's territory and by definition would become involved with him. The following experience brought the conflict between these two patterns into focus.

3 It was a warm spring day of the type one finds only in the high, clean, clear air of Colorado, the kind of day that makes you glad you are alive. I was standing on the doorstep of a converted carriage house talking to a young woman who lived in an apartment upstairs. The first floor had been made into an artist's studio. The arrangement, however, was peculiar because the same entrance served both tenants. The occupants of the apartment used a small entryway and walked along one wall of the studio to reach the stairs to the apartment. You might say that they had an ''easement'' through the artist's territory. As I stood talking on the doorstep, I glanced to the left and noticed that some fifty to sixty feet away, inside the studio, the Prussian artist and two of his friends were also in conversation. He was facing so that if he glanced to one side he could just see me. I had noted his presence, but not wanting to appear presumptuous or to interrupt his conversation, I unconsciously applied the American rule and assumed that the two activities—my quiet conversation and his conversation—were not involved with each other. As I was soon to learn, this was a mistake, because in less time than it takes to tell, the artist had detached himself from his friends, crossed the intervening space, pushed my friend aside, and with eyes flashing, started shouting at me. By what right had I entered his studio without greeting him? Who had given me permission?

4 I felt bullied and humiliated, and even after almost thirty years, I can still feel my anger. Later study has given me greater understanding of the German pattern and I have learned that in the German's eyes I really had been intolerably rude. I was already ''inside'' the building and I intruded when I could *see* inside. For the German, there is no such thing as being inside the room without being inside the zone of intrusion, particularly if one looks at the other party, no matter how far away.

5 Recently, I obtained an independent check on how Germans feel about visual intrusion while investigating what people look at when they are in intimate, personal, social, and public situations. In the course of my research, I instructed subjects to photograph separately both a man and a woman in each of the above contexts. One of my assistants, who also happened to be

German, photographed his subjects out of focus at public distance because, as he said, "You are not really supposed to look at other people at public distances *because it's intruding.*" This may explain the informal custom behind the German laws against photographing strangers in public without their permission.

6 Germans sense their own space as an extension of the ego. One sees a clue to this feeling in the term "Lebensraum," which is impossible to translate because it summarizes so much. Hitler used it as an effective psychological lever to move the Germans to conquest.

7 In contrast to the Arab, the German's ego is extraordinarily exposed, and he will go to almost any length to preserve his "private sphere." This was observed during World War II when American soldiers were offered opportunities to observe German prisoners under a variety of circumstances. In one instance in the Midwest, German P.W.s were housed four to a small hut. As soon as materials were available, each prisoner built a partition so that he could have *his own space.* In a less favorable setting in Germany when the *Wehrmacht* was collapsing, it was necessary to use open stockades because German prisoners were arriving faster than they could be accommodated. In this situation each soldier who could find the materials built his own tiny dwelling unit, sometimes no larger than a foxhole. It puzzled the Americans that the Germans did not pool their efforts and their scarce materials to create a larger, more efficient space, particularly in view of the very cold spring nights. Since that time I have observed frequent instances of the use of architectural extensions of this need to screen the ego. German houses with balconies are arranged so that there is visual privacy. Yards tend to be well fenced; but fenced or not, they are sacred.

8 The American view that space should be shared is particularly troublesome to the German. I cannot document the account of the early days of World War II occupation when Berlin was in ruins but the following situation was reported by an observer and it has the nightmarish quality that is often associated with inadvertent cross-cultural blunders. In Berlin at that time the housing shortage was indescribably acute. To provide relief, occupation authorities in the American zone ordered those Berliners who still had kitchens and baths intact to share them with their neighbors. The order finally had to be rescinded when the already overstressed Germans started killing each other over the shared facilities.

9 Public and private buildings in Germany often have double doors for soundproofing, as do many hotel rooms. In addition, the door is taken very seriously by Germans. Those Germans who come to America feel that our doors are flimsy and light. The meanings of the open door and the closed door are quite different in the two countries. In offices, Americans keep doors open; Germans keep doors closed. In Germany, the closed door does not mean that the man behind it wants to be alone or undisturbed, or that he is doing

something he doesn't want someone else to see. It's simply that Germans think that open doors are sloppy and disorderly. To close the door preserves the integrity of the room and provides a protective boundary between people. Otherwise, they get too involved with each other. One of my German subjects commented, "If our family hadn't had doors, we would have had to change our way of life. Without doors we would have had many, many more fights . . . When you can't talk, you retreat behind a door. . . . If there hadn't been doors, I would always have been within reach of my mother."

10 Whenever a German warms up to the subject of American enclosed space, he can be counted on to comment on the noise that is transmitted through walls and doors. To many Germans, our doors epitomize American life. They are thin and cheap; they seldom fit; and they lack the substantial quality of German doors. When they close they don't sound and feel solid. The click of the lock is indistinct, it rattles and indeed it may even be absent.

11 The open-door policy of American business and the closed-door patterns of German business culture cause clashes in the branches and subsidiaries of American firms in Germany. The point seems to be quite simple, yet failure to grasp it has caused considerable friction and misunderstanding between American and German managers overseas. I was once called in to advise a firm that has operations all over the world. One of the first questions asked was, "How do you get the Germans to keep their doors open?" In this company the open doors were making the Germans feel exposed and gave the whole operation an unusually relaxed and unbusinesslike air. Closed doors, on the other hand, gave the Americans the feeling that there was a conspiratorial air about the place and that they were being left out. The point is that whether the door is open or shut, it is not going to mean the same thing in the two countries.

12 The orderliness and hierarchical quality of German culture are communicated in their handling of space. Germans want to know where they stand and object strenuously to people crashing queues or people who "get out of line" or who do not obey signs such as "Keep out," "Authorized personnel only," and the like. Some of the German attitudes toward ourselves are traceable to our informal attitudes toward boundaries and to authority in general.

13 However, German anxiety due to American violations of order is nothing compared to that engendered in Germans by the Poles, who see no harm in a little disorder. To them lines and queues stand for regimentation and blind authority. I once saw a Pole crash a cafeteria line just "to stir up those sheep."

14 Germans get very technical about intrusion distance, as I mentioned earlier. When I once asked my students to describe the distance at which a third party would intrude on two people who were talking, there were no answers from the Americans. Each student knew that he could tell when he was being intruded on but he couldn't define intrusion or tell how he knew when it had occurred. However, a German and an Italian who had worked in

Germany were both members of my class and they answered without any hesitation. Both stated that a third party would intrude on two people if he came within seven feet!

15 Many Americans feel that Germans are overly rigid in their behavior, unbending and formal. Some of this impression is created by differences in the handling of chairs while seated. The American doesn't seem to mind if people hitch their chairs up to adjust the distance to the situation—those that do mind would not think of saying anything, for to comment on the manners of others would be impolite. In Germany, however, it is a violation of the mores to change the position of your chair. An added deterrent for those who don't know better is the weight of most German furniture. Even the great architect Mies van der Rohe, who often rebelled against German tradition in his buildings, made his handsome chairs so heavy that anyone but a strong man would have difficulty in adjusting his seating position. To a German, light furniture is anathema, not only because it seems flimsy but because people move it and thereby destroy the order of things, including intrusions on the "private sphere." In one instance reported to me, a German newspaper editor who had moved to the United States had his visitor's chair bolted to the floor "at the proper distance" because he couldn't tolerate the American habit of adjusting the chair to the situation.

Jotting Down Your First Responses

1. What experiences in your family, neighborhood, or work did this essay about private space remind you of?
2. If someone sits too close to you on a bus or airplane or stands too close to you in an elevator, how do you feel? What do you do?
3. What are the space needs of people in your cultural group or another you have observed?

Checking Your Comprehension

1. When did Hall learn about cultural differences regarding space needs?
2. What did he do that offended the German?
3. According to Hall, what are two basic patterns of space needs in the United States?
4. How do Germans define intrusion in one's space?
5. How did Hall study Germans' sense of intrusion?
6. Acting out of their sense of personal space, what did German prisoners of war do?
7. What problems developed when Germans in Berlin had to share kitchens and bathrooms because of housing shortages?
8. According to Hall, what are German doors like? Why are they so important?

9. How do German and American businesses differ in their attitude toward office doors?
10. According to Hall, how do Germans respond to "Keep Out" signs and the like? What German traits or values does their response to signs reveal?
11. When Hall asked students to describe the distance at which a third party would intrude on two people talking, what differences did he find?
12. Why did the German editor living in the United States bolt to the floor the visitor's chair in his office?

Understanding a Writer's Patterns

1. What is Hall's thesis?
2. Who is his intended audience? How do you know?
3. What was Hall's purpose in writing?
4. Did Hall use a subject-by-subject or a point-by-point method of contrast?
5. Hall interrupts his introductory narrative to explain two American patterns of personal space. In what paragraph does he continue the narrative?
6. Hall "promises" to describe two patterns. What words mark each of these for the reader?
7. In paragraph 5 Hall sets up four categories or kinds of situations for his assistants to use in studying distance in male and female encounters. What are they?
8. In paragraph 7 the first sentence is the topic sentence. How does Hall support and develop this idea?
9. The topic sentence of paragraph 8 is "The American view that space should be shared is particularly troublesome to the German." How does Hall support and develop this idea?
10. What aspect of culture is discussed in paragraphs 9, 10, and 11? Why is it important?
11. In paragraph 15 Hall contrasts American and German use of chairs. What word marks or indicates the contrast when he turns from discussing American use to German use?

Making Predictions and Drawing Inferences

1. After reading the first sentence, what do you expect to follow?
2. What does Hall mean when he says that Hitler used the Germans' sense "of their own space as an extension of the ego" as an "effective psychological lever to move the Germans to conquest" (paragraph 6)?
3. When and why is the matter of open or closed office doors an issue in business?

4. Why does proxemics (the study of individuals' needs for personal space in different cultures) have increasing importance in today's world?

Making Judgments and Thinking Critically

1. Hall begins with a personal experience narrative, interrupts it with a description of two American patterns of proxemics, and then completes the narrative. Would it be more effective to omit the personal reference in paragraph 1 and begin the narrative after the description of American patterns? Why or why not?
2. Hall moves from the narrative in paragraphs 1, 3, and 4 to another example in paragraph 5. What is the pattern or logic of this movement?

Using New Words

1. Give antonyms (opposites) of the following words: *inadvertent, hierarchical, deterrent, anathema, flimsy.*
2. Choose three words you want to add to your vocabulary. Make vocabulary cards for these words and add them to your collection of new words.
3. What does *acute* (paragraph 8) mean?
4. Hall writes of the "integrity of the room" (paragraph 9), but what does it mean for a person to have integrity?

Responding by Writing

1. Write an essay in which you compare your needs for space with those of someone with very different needs, perhaps someone in your family or at work. Write to an audience of this class.
2. Write an essay about a difference in attitude or behavior you have noticed in two groups. You might take as your subjects men and women, an older generation and a younger one, one race and another, or one religious group and another. The difference you have noticed might be respect for the elderly, value placed on education, use of alcohol, respect for authority, watching televised sports, forming study groups, value placed on leisure time, attitude toward work, and so forth. If you can, interview several people from the two groups about this difference to check out your observation, just as Hall did, and to gather examples to use in your essay.
3. Each region of the United States has a distinct culture. Sometimes cities and neighborhoods have their own cultures, too. Write an essay to describe the culture of the most important place you've lived. Write to students in this class who have never lived there.
4. In some parts of the United States yards are open and unfenced; in other

parts privacy fences separate each yard from the others. Sometimes differences in the needs for personal space are revealed in the way people stand in line or drive in traffic. If you have lived in more than one community or region, you may have noticed differences in the space needs of people. Write an essay about those differences and what those differences say about people's values. Write to an audience of this class.

Other Cultures, Other Times

Ann McGee-Cooper

Ann McGee-Cooper has taught students of all ages and businesspeople in several industries how to tap their own creativity to increase learning and productivity. Her books include *Time Management for Unmanageable People* and *You Don't Have To Go Home From Work Exhausted.*

Thinking Before Reading

Do you like to plan how much time you spend on specific activities or do you prefer to be spontaneous and let things take as much time as you feel like? Write a few sentences in your Idea Bank about how you feel about scheduling your time.

Expanding Your Vocabulary from Reading

cultures (1) behavior patterns, beliefs, and institutions of groups of people
brevity (2) shortness
affront (2) insult
perceiving (3) becoming aware of, understanding
absolute (4) unrelated to and independent of anything else
resolve (6) find a solution to
intangibles (6) things that cannot be perceived by the senses or precisely identified, such as love or trust
illusion (11) erroneous perception of reality

1 In other cultures and in our own past, time had a different meaning. In Socrates' day, a speech wasn't considered worth hearing if it didn't last for a few hours. In ancient Greek culture, when invited to spend an evening with friends, one arrived at what seemed like the right time and left when the visit seemed complete.

2 When Abraham Lincoln delivered his now-famous Gettysburg Address, most of the listeners thought he had disgraced himself. The custom was that

a speaker should honor his listeners with long speeches. The Gettysburg Address took only a few minutes to deliver, and its brevity was an affront to those present. Lincoln, on the other hand, was not concerned. He said what he had to say, and sat down.

3 There are many different ways to view and evaluate time. In our current culture, we are locked into a very narrow view of what effective time management is. We think that pressing the very highest number of things into the smallest number of minutes is the most efficient, but, in fact, we may be lessening the quality of our work, narrowing our span of vision, increasing our tension and worry, and cutting off the possibility of creativity and satisfaction in work by this narrow view. It may, in fact, significantly increase our effectiveness if we can broaden our awareness of the different ways of perceiving time.

4 Two opposite ways of viewing time are monochronic and polychronic. Monochronic time refers to linear time—time measured by the clock and typically decided in advance. When you function in monochronic time, you reward and appreciate promptness, speed, brevity, and punctuality. Shorter and faster are seen as better. On the other hand, polychronic time refers to time relative to many complex factors, typically decided intuitively in the moment as events play out. It is a more complex system of time in that time is not absolute, but relative and flexible. When you function in polychronic time, you reward and appreciate flexibility, intuition, dedication, inspiration, imagination, and many other factors. Trust, bonding, pleasure, and quality of life influence our decisions.

5 You can apply monochronic skills and thinking to tasks that are predictable. For example, you probably can predict fairly accurately how long it takes you to get dressed for work, or boil an egg, or word process six pages.

6 In contrast, how long does it require to fall in love, gain the trust of a new client, solve a computer problem, create a new product or service, resolve a bitter argument, or gain the total support of your team? These are far more complex polychronic issues, and typically not predictable in advance. Notice that most deal with people, feelings, and intangibles. In fact, if you stay too focused on the clock, you can actually slow down or sabotage your goal. The implied message—"Time and speed are more important than people, trust, consensus, and win-win"—can heavily or permanently discount your motives and the relationship. This issue has become a major barrier in American/Pacific Rim business relationships. We honor others by speed, getting to the point, and pushing for quick closure. They honor others by listening, developing long-term relationships, and keeping the dialogue open. This is a classic mismatch of monochronic versus polychronic processing.

7 Some professions require their employees to work primarily in monochronic time. Airline employees, assembly-line workers, cab and bus drivers,

and cashiers all are governed by the clock. In these fields, faster is better, watching the clock and staying punctual are essential.

8 Other professions are less bound to monochronic time and require instead a sensitivity to polychronic time. Although there are time requirements, schedules, appointment times, and deadlines, teaching, counseling, sales, and the arts require scheduling the task to fit the time. The more you deal directly with people, the more polychronic you must become. Many managers make the mistake of never shifting time perception. They continue to push for speed alone and consequently lose the trust and support of their team. Sometimes slowing down and listening to other people's ideas, problems, and concerns will give them a greater advantage in the long term.

9 In our society, women and mothers who are homemakers especially are polychronic by necessity. Just try to get a family of three small children dressed and in the car by a certain time. The baby throws up or wets his diaper just as you are ready to leave. The dog knocks over the goldfish bowl and you are frantically rescuing fish, not to mention the cut on your finger from picking up the broken glass. Your day is planned, and then the washing machine overflows on the new kitchen carpet. This kind of lifestyle encourages polychronic thinking about time. You must stay very flexible around your time expectations just to keep your sanity. Keeping strictly to a pre-planned clock schedule is simply impossible.

10 Business, on the other hand, has traditionally forced both men and women into monochronic time by necessity. Being punctual is a top priority. If you arrive late to a sales call or client meeting, you might as well forget it. Meeting appointments and deadlines is an essential quality to earning respect and credibility among your peers. When you think about it, much of the business world runs on a monochronic schedule.

11 The train runs every seven minutes; the stock exchange opens and closes at a certain time; the office is closed for lunch from 12:00 to 1:00. Of course there are many factors that aren't so reliable, but the outside structure gives the illusion of predictability and that illusion slips into our assumptions about life in general. We act as if we believe that all of life can be predicted in advance and kept on a schedule. Sometimes we even try to take our monochronic focus home. The response to this can best be understood by the reply of a fourteen-year-old to his executive parent, "I'm not just another agenda item on your list of to-do's for you to check off."

12 The more you work with and are responsible for small children and people in general, the less monochronic thinking will work for you. The more you work with things which can be controlled and predicted, the more you can successfully use monochronic time and may become blinded to the need to expand your thinking about time.

13 So why does all of this matter? If you judge and evaluate yourself in

terms of strictly monochronic time, yet your responsibilities require polychronic skills, you will be forever frustrated unless you learn the fine art of blending both approaches into a far more successful whole. If you judge yourself and others simply on the basis of whether a specific schedule was kept, you may find you are overlooking essential elements in the process.

Jotting Down Your First Responses

1. Does the concept that time is a cultural perception surprise you? Does it seem like a valid concept? Why or why not?
2. Is your sense of time basically monochronic or polychronic? Give some examples. Explain where and how you learned this perception of time.
3. Does the concept of monochronic and polychronic time explain any frustrations or conflicts in your life? If so, what are they?

Checking Your Comprehension

1. What two famous men from the past does McGee-Cooper use as examples of different views of time?
2. In ages past how long were good speeches? Why?
3. According to our current culture, what is good time management? What view of time does this reflect?
4. According to McGee-Cooper, what qualities does a monochronic time view value?
5. What qualities does a polychronic time view value?
6. What kinds of activities are monochronic? What are two examples that McGee-Cooper gives?
7. What kinds of activities are polychronic? Give two of McGee-Cooper's examples.
8. What is a major barrier in American–Pacific Rim (Chinese, Japanese, Korean) business relationships?
9. What are some professions that work primarily on monochronic time?
10. What are some professions that need a polychronic sense of time?

Understanding a Writer's Patterns

1. What is the thesis of this essay?
2. What is McGee-Cooper's purpose?
3. Describe the intended audience of the essay.
4. Paragraphs 1 and 2 are the introduction. How does McGee-Cooper hook the reader's interest and introduce the subject?
5. After the introduction and the thesis McGee-Cooper provides a rationale for her essay. Which sentences in paragraph 3 explain the need and therefore the importance of what she has to say in this essay?

6. McGee-Cooper develops the thesis by defining two important terms, giving many examples, and using contrasts. She uses all three of these methods in paragraph 4. Which sentences are definition?
7. Which phrases in paragraph 4 indicate she is giving examples?
8. Which phrases in paragraph 4 indicate she is using contrast?
9. Which words in paragraphs 7 and 8 indicate that McGee-Cooper is contrasting professions that rely on monochronic and polychronic views of time?
10. Which phrases in paragraphs 9 and 10 indicate contrasting time views of two other groups?
11. What strategy does McGee-Cooper use to create closure to this essay?

Making Predictions and Drawing Inferences

1. Which view of time does McGee-Cooper value as superior? Why do you think so? Give evidence from the essay.
2. Why did people in Abraham Lincoln's time (the mid-1800's) value long speeches?
3. What happens when a person with a monochronic sense of time has a job dealing with people, such as sales, teaching, or business management?
4. Why do highly industrialized nations have a monochronic sense of time?

Making Judgments and Thinking Critically

1. Is answering questions after the reading selections in this book a monochronic or a polychronic activity? Explain.
2. Is writing an essay a monochronic or a polychronic activity? Explain.
3. Do you think a monochronic or polychronic view of time is better? Why do you think so?

Using New Words

1. Choose three words you want to add to your writing and speaking vocabulary. Make vocabulary cards for these words. Write the word on one side of the card and a definition and an original sentence on the other side.
2. Find and list the nouns in paragraph 3 that have these common noun endings: *-ment, -ty, -ion,* and *-ness.*
3. Change the nouns that you found in question 2 into their verb forms.
4. Using the meanings of the prefixes and root forms below, define the following words: *monotheism* and *polytheism, monogamy* and *polygamy, monochrome* and *polychrome.*

Prefixes		Roots	
mono-	one	*-theism*	belief in existence of a god or gods
poly-	many	*-gamy*	marriage or mate
		-chrome	color

5. Since you know the root *chrono* means time, what do *chronometer* and *chronology* mean? (Clues: What does one use a meter for? a log?)

Responding by Writing

1. Are you often late? Do you procrastinate? Overschedule yourself? Stay up late? Underestimate how long assignments will take? If you have problems with time, examine them. Can any of them be explained with the concepts of monochronic and polychronic time? If so, write an essay in which you explain your time problems and use these concepts to help you understand them and solve them. Write to an audience of your teacher.
2. There are often differences between the way things used to be and the way they are now or between the way things are and the way they should be. The following list may help you recall a change you've observed or would like to observe: courtesy to other drivers, the safety of young children in the neighborhood, the behavior of fans at sporting events, attitudes toward authority of all kinds, respect for the elderly, computer literacy, interest in recycling, saving money, using credit, substance abuse. Decide what point you wish to make about this observed or desired contrast and who your intended audience is. Then write an essay.
3. McGee-Cooper wrote "Other Cultures, Other Times" to use in her work as a business consultant. Do you think this essay would be an effective way to help managers and executives understand cultural differences that affect employee relations? Why or why not? Considering the audience and purpose, write an essay in which you evaluate this reading selection.

Carbon Copy

Rosa Mathe

Rosa Mathe is a student at Texas Women's University in Denton, Texas. A wife and mother of two daughters ages 23 and 17, she returned to college after years of raising children, moving frequently because of her husband's career, and doing volunteer service. This essay won second prize in the 1991 Literary Festival at Richland College.

Thinking Before Reading

Think about a time you felt "different" and didn't "fit in"—in school, with your peers, at work, in a new neighborhood. Did you make changes to conform? Why or why not? How did you feel at the time? Write about this situation in your Idea Bank.

Expanding Your Vocabulary from Reading

tortilla (1) flat, round bread of cornmeal or wheat flour
ridiculed (1) made fun of
ethnic (1) relating to a racial, religious, cultural or national group
assimilate (1) make similar in appearance and behavior
tamales (2) rolls made of cornmeal and a spicy meat filling wrapped in a corn husk and steamed
barrio (3) Spanish-speaking neighborhood, usually isolated from the main-stream culture; a ghetto
parochial (3) supported by a parish, church-supported
conformity (10) behavior that is similar to current styles, customs, or rules

1 It was a sub-zero day, and Mom packed me a lunch so I would only have to make the trip back home once. The morning went by quickly and soon Sister Huberta was telling us to clear our desks because it was lunchtime. As I began to eat, I realized the other children were staring at me. Soon Sister Huberta came to see what the fuss was all about. As soon as she saw my sandwich, made with a tortilla, her eyes filled with disgust. She then announced loudly to the class, "That is not food." I never told my parents or anyone about what happened in school that day. I was too ashamed. Never again would I knowingly allow myself to be ridiculed again. That day I learned to hide my ethnic difference and to assimilate into the accepted white culture.

2 America is the melting pot of the world, so I melted. Even though I loved Mexican food, I refused to admit it. When asked how I could eat greasy Mexican food, I lied and said I hated it. Then I would tell them how much I hated tamales. It was true. I was proud of it because this made me more like everyone else.

3 My mother made two decisions that would entrench me forever in a white, middle class environment. She decided we would not live in the "barrio" with the rest of the Spanish-speaking community and that we would attend a private parochial school. Few minorities could afford a parochial school tuition when I was growing up, so all my friends were white. From them I learned to dress, act and speak in order to be accepted.

4 The first visible change I made was in my style of dress. Spanish people

are simple people. They derive enjoyment from simple pleasures, like color. They do not believe that red and green should be worn only during the Christmas season. They wear them together, year-round, along with all the other colors of the rainbow. I gave this up and learned to dress with class and no flash.

5 Next, I had to eliminate my laid-back attitude. Much has been said about the Hispanics' low-key lifestyle. They really enjoy life, and if they move too fast, they will miss it. Their strong Catholic faith encourages them to take care of today and leave tomorrow in God's hands. I quickly learned that the Anglos are futuristic. Today's deeds are only of value if they will benefit you tomorrow. They also believe God helps those who help themselves. This mentality promotes busy hands, busy minds and leaves little time to enjoy life. Enjoyment is structured into their busy schedules; it is called a vacation.

6 Then I had to relearn how to make friends. Common amongst Hispanics is the joy of visiting and dropping in unannounced. My friends taught me that coming over to visit unannounced was a display of bad manners. I learned to accept the principle that relationships were built on longevity rather than spontaneity.

7 The most difficult trait I had to overcome was to stop using hand gestures when I spoke. Hispanics, traditionally, are emotional and the idea of expressing themselves verbally, without hand gestures, is inconceivable. To me it is like watching a celebrated maestro create a masterpiece. He would not be able to conduct his song without the emotional use of his hands. The white, European culture is reserved and they see this cultural difference as a public display of emotion and in poor taste. I gave up using my hands to express my emotion and lost a cultural gift.

8 Speaking English without an accent was easier to learn because at the age of six, I stopped speaking Spanish so I could become like everyone else. Spanish people continue to speak their mother language and the pronunciation of their English words is usually uttered with a heavy accent. Though many whites have taken a Spanish class, they forget how difficult it is to let go of their English dialect and how unnatural their attempts to speak a foreign language sound. I learned to speak English so well that when I spoke Spanish, I sounded like my white friends—unnatural. Eventually I began to look, act, and speak just like my friends. The only time I looked different was after summer vacation, when I would be golden brown. Each new school year would find me praying for my summer tan to quickly fade.

9 I came one step closer to becoming assimilated when fate, disguised as a Spanish teacher, stepped in and changed the spelling of my last name. My maiden name was Delao, but my sister's Spanish teacher convinced her that our name should be written "DeLao." Written this way made my name appear to be that of Italian origin, like DeMark, or DeLouise. I was then able to hide my ethnic difference and many people assumed I was of Italian descent.

10 My quest to sever ethnic ties was further enhanced by the Sisters of Saint Dominic, who were strict disciplinarians and excellent educators. The command at our school was to obey authority and to conform. Our uniforms made us look the same. The sisters made us act the same. Conformity is just what I wanted to learn. I also needed a safe haven where I could hide from my ethnicity and work on eliminating it. The sisters produced prototypes and I became their best model.

11 However, ethnic ties cannot be severed completely. In fifth grade we were given a family tree assignment. My grandmother was part Apache and, in order to impress my classmates, I told them that grandma had been an Indian princess. This strategy worked, and that day I learned that it was good to be the same, and even better to be above average.

12 I learned to excel in academics, sports and leadership. I was not just liked, I was popular. I was not just good in sports, I won trophies. I was not just good in school, I was excellent. My classmates liked me, their parents liked me, and the sisters liked me. For only the small price of my ethnic identity, I had become a perfect carbon copy.

Jotting Down Your First Responses

1. Compare the situation and your reaction to it that you wrote about before reading this selection with Mathe's situation and her reaction. How were they similar or different?
2. Do you think Mathe was smart to change so she could fit in? Why or why not?
3. What insights did you have about your own or another culture as you read Mathe's essay?

Checking Your Comprehension

1. What did Mathe bring to school for lunch?
2. What did the teacher and children do that embarrassed her?
3. What decision did Mathe make after the lunch incident?
4. What decisions did her mother make that changed Mathe's life forever?
5. What are three changes Mathe made to conform?
6. What are two ways her school shaped her conformity?
7. What results did her conformity have on her school life? On her sense of self?

Understanding a Writer's Patterns

1. What is the thesis of the essay?
2. Describe the intended audience of Mathe's essay.
3. Why did Mathe select the lunch incident to introduce the essay?

4. What other specific incidents does Mathe use as examples in her essay?
5. In paragraph 3 Mathe announces three ways she intended to change in order to be accepted—dress, behavior, and speech. In which paragraphs does she write about each?
6. Three sentences in the conclusion begin with a negative "I was not" and end with a contrasting positive "I was." Reread these sentences leaving out the "I was not" portion of each sentence. Is something lost or gained by omitting the negatives? What effect does the contrast of negative and positive have?
7. These three sentences follow a pattern: "I was not . . . , I was . . ." This pattern is an instance of parallelism. What is the effect of this parallelism on you, the reader?

Making Predictions and Drawing Inferences

1. Read the first paragraph again. Did you predict accurately what would follow when you read the essay? Why or why not?
2. Did Mathe usually eat lunch at school? How do you know?
3. What do her mother's decisions reveal about the mother's values and hopes for Mathe?
4. How does Mathe feel about all the acts of conformity now? How do you know?
5. Do you think Mathe's conforming actions were acts of strength or weakness? Why?
6. How does Mathe feel about her Catholic education? How do you know?

Making Judgments and Thinking Critically

1. What is a carbon copy, literally? Figuratively? Is "Carbon Copy" an effective title for Mathe's essay? Why or why not?
2. From reading the essay, how would you describe Mathe's attitude about the changes she made to conform? If she could live her life over, do you think she would undo those changes? Why or why not?

Using New Words

1. Choose three words from the essay to add to your set of vocabulary cards. Choose words whose sounds you like. Practice saying them aloud so you'll be comfortable when you want to use them in conversation.
2. What are three words from other cultures or languages that are frequently used by English speakers? Ask someone from another culture if you don't know any such words or phrases.
3. Give antonyms (words with opposite meanings) for the following words: *ridicule, assimilate, conform.*

Responding by Writing

1. Growing up, moving to a new part of the country or to a new country, going to college, or starting a new career can create pressure to change one's dress, eating habits, manners, activities, speech, and relationships. Some changes are visible and some are invisible. Write an essay to an audience of this class about a situation in which you either conformed or resisted conforming. Be sure you make clear the contrast between before and after or between reality and the desired change.

   You may use the writing you did before reading or after reading to get started. Decide what your feeling or attitude is about the changes you made or didn't make. Use a consistent tone throughout your essay. Use at least three examples to support your thesis.
2. Observe a group from a culture other than your own. If possible, talk with one of the group about his or her culture. Then write an essay to inform your classmates about that culture. Use examples to explain your observations.
3. If you are bicultural (belonging to two cultures or ethnic groups), write an essay using comparison or contrast to explain some point (thesis) you wish to make about those cultures. Your audience should be those who are *not* of one of the cultures you are writing about. For instance, Mathe writes about her Hispanic culture to a non-Hispanic audience.
4. Mathe wrote, "America is the melting pot of the world, so I melted." Is "melting" good for individuals and for the United States? Write an essay explaining why you think it is good or bad for individuals from other cultures to "melt" in this country. Use examples to support your opinion. Include the name of the writer and title of the essay in your discussion.

CHAPTER

11

DEFINITION

USING DEFINITION TO DEVELOP YOUR ESSAY

Because words have many subtle meanings in addition to several dictionary definitions, you will often need to define words important to your essay. You need to define technical terms and any other terms your audience might not know. For instance, if you are writing an essay about rock climbing, you would define *belaying rope* and *piton*. You also need to define familiar words used in a particular sense. If you are writing about family values, you should state what you mean by the term *family values* because your audience is likely to interpret it differently.

Definitions can be different lengths—a word, a phrase, a sentence, a paragraph, or a whole essay. The length depends on your purpose and audience. Sometimes just a synonym is an adequate definition. For instance, the synonym *subcultures* defines *worlds* in the following sentence: ''Some hobbies or jobs create their own worlds, or subcultures, such as bikers . . .'' Other times you will need to give a formal definition which includes the general class (what kind of thing it is) and special characteristics of the word you are defining. Use a noun to define a noun, use a verb to define a verb, and so forth.

Word	General Class	Characteristics
gate	structure in an airport terminal	for controlling passengers entering and exiting planes
cholesterol	substance in the blood	that can block arteries and contribute to heart attacks

Develop Extended Definitions. You may write extended definitions for abstract or controversial terms, such as friendship, commitment, or child abuse. You may need extended definitions for complex technical or scientific terms, such as immune system, windshear, or theory of relativity. To develop an extended definition, you may

Give characteristics of the term
Tell what the word doesn't mean
Narrate an experience that explains the word
Cite an example of it
Compare or contrast the word with similar or dissimilar terms
Give various types or kinds of the word

At the end of Chapter 4 you read "The Watcher at the Gates," an essay by Gail Godwin about the inner critic that causes writers to procrastinate, fear failure, or reject what they have written. In that essay Godwin defines the watcher with a quotation and many examples, some from her own experience and some from other writers. Briefly look at that essay to see how Godwin defines "a watcher at the gates."

In an article about reading (referred to in Chapter 4), the author Frank Smith discusses two views of learning—the official view and the informal view. Here is his definition of the informal view of learning. See if this definition fits the way you learn.

1 But there is an alternative view of learning that is at least 2,000 years old and, as far as I can discover, is well known in every culture in the world. It is a commonplace view for everyone outside education—and even for most educators when they are off duty. I shall call it the *informal view.* This view is that learning is continuous, spontaneous, and effortless, requiring no particular attention, conscious motivation, or specific reinforcement; learning occurs in all kinds of situations and is not subject to forgetting. In this view, learning is social rather than solitary. It can be summarized in seven familiar words: *we learn from the company we keep.*

Smith begins his definition by giving characteristics and by showing what learning is not.

He continues by giving an example from common experience.

2 That we learn from the company we keep is common everyday wisdom. Every parent knows that children learn to talk exactly like their friends. They also learn to dress and behave and perceive the world in exactly the same way their friends do.

Further in the extended definition of the informal view of learning, Smith uses the metaphor (a kind of comparison) of joining a club to explain the social aspect of learning.

> 3 I have characterized this coming to be like the company we keep as "joining the club." Children learn to talk by their membership in the "spoken language clubs" made up of the people they will come to talk like; first family, then friends. And children learn to read and write if they join the "literacy club," literally identifying themselves with people who read and write.

Still further in the article, Smith uses a powerful example of learning that illustrates the informal view.

> 4 Tremendous but unsuspected amounts of learning are accomplished in this way. . . . Four-year-olds learn about 20 new words a day. By the time they enter school, they know around 10,000 words. They don't all know the same 10,000 words, of course, but they know most of the 10,000 words that their friends know. They don't know all the words that their teachers know, but they may know words that their teachers don't know.
>
> 5 By the time they leave school, they know at least 50,000 words and perhaps a great many more (depending, not surprisingly, on how much reading they do).

Because the reader must understand what the two views of learning are in order to follow Smith's point in his essay about learning to read, Smith spent a third of his essay defining the two concepts. When you explain something about which there is controversy or that is complex, remember to define important terms fully.

Provide Transitions. Besides using transitional words and phrases, writers also use pronouns and repetition of key words and phrases to keep the reader from getting lost. In our first excerpt from Smith's article, Smith uses the word *view* five times. Reread the paragraph and circle the word *view.* Notice that in the last two repetitions Smith also uses the pronoun *this*—"*This view* that learning is continuous . . ." and "In *this view,* learning is social. . . ."

Smith uses repetition throughout to create coherence and provide transitions. Circle and draw a line connecting "we learn from the company we keep" in excerpt 1 and excerpt 2 and "the company we keep" in excerpt 3.

Circle and connect the word *club* or *clubs* in excerpt 3 and then the phrases "By the time they . . . school" in excerpts 4 and 5. Notice that the variation of "enter school" and "leave school" in the repeated phrases provides an instance of parallelism that gives emphasis to the amazing number of words each of us knows.

POINTS TO REMEMBER ABOUT DEFINITION

Define technical words your reader might not know.
Define any terms that are important to your essay that your reader might not know.
Define familiar words that are important to your essay because they may have other meanings to readers.
Define a term by giving both its general class and special characteristics.

For an extended definition, use a combination of ways to define a word:
Give characteristics of a term.
Tell what it is not.
Narrate an experience to explain it.
Cite an example of it.
Provide comparisons or contrasts to it.
Give various types or kinds of it.

The Rewards of Living a Solitary Life

May Sarton

May Sarton is a poet and author who lives alone in Maine. Her many books include *A Reckoning* and *Journal of Solitude*. The following essay first appeared in the *New York Times* in 1974.

Thinking Before Reading

Do you like to be alone? Why or why not? How much time do you spend alone? Would you like to spend more or less time alone? What do you do when you're alone? Have you ever lived alone? Write in your Idea Bank about being alone.

Expanding Your Vocabulary from Reading

gregarious (1) sociable, liking to be with people
bliss (1) profound happiness
inevitably (2) unavoidably, inescapably

diffused (2) spread out, made less brilliant
solitude (3) state of being alone
abiding (4) remaining in a place or state
acutely (5) sharply
human intercourse (5) interaction with people, conversation
surf (9) ocean waves that break on shore, the splash and sound of the breaking waves
converse (9) exchange thoughts and opinions

1 The other day an acquaintance of mine, a gregarious and charming man, told me he had found himself unexpectedly alone in New York for an hour or two between appointments. He went to the Whitney [an art museum in New York City] and spent the "empty" time looking at things in solitary bliss. For him it proved to be a shock nearly as great as falling in love to discover that he could enjoy himself so much alone.

2 What had he been afraid of, I asked myself? That, suddenly alone, he would discover that he bored himself, or that there was, quite simply, no self there to meet? But having taken the plunge, he is now on the brink of adventure; he is about to be launched into his own inner space, space as immense, unexplored and sometimes frightening as outer space to the astronaut. His every perception will come to him with a new freshness and, for a time, seem startlingly original. For anyone who can see things for himself with a naked eye becomes, for a moment or two, something of a genius. With another human being present vision becomes double vision, inevitably. We are busy wondering, what does my companion see or think of this, and what do I think of it? The original impact gets lost, or diffused.

3 "Music I heard with you was more than music." Exactly. And therefore music *itself* can only be heard alone. Solitude is the salt of personhood. It brings out the authentic flavor of every experience.

4 "Alone one is never lonely: the spirit adventures, walking/In a quiet garden, in a cooled house, abiding single there."

5 Loneliness is most acutely felt with other people, for with others, even with a lover sometimes, we suffer from our differences of taste, temperament, mood. Human intercourse often demands that we soften the edge of perception, or withdraw at the very instant of personal truth for fear of hurting, or of being inappropriately present, which is to say naked, in a social situation. Alone we can afford to be wholly whatever we are, and to feel whatever we feel absolutely. That is a great luxury!

6 For me the most interesting thing about a solitary life, and mine has been that for the last twenty years, is that it becomes increasingly rewarding. When I can wake up and watch the sun rise over the ocean, as I do most days, and know that I have an entire day ahead, uninterrupted, in which to write a few

pages, take a walk with my dog, lie down in the afternoon for a long think (why does one think better in a horizontal position?), read and listen to music, I am flooded with happiness.

7 I am lonely when I am overtired, when I have worked too long without a break, when for the time being I feel empty and need filling up. And I am lonely sometimes when I come back home after a lecture trip, when I have seen a lot of people and talked a lot, and am full to the brim with experience that needs to be sorted out.

8 Then for a little while the house feels huge and empty, and I wonder where my self is hiding. It has to be recaptured slowly by watering the plants, perhaps, and looking again at each one as though it were a person, by feeding the two cats, by cooking a meal.

9 It takes a while, as I watch the surf blowing up in fountains at the end of the field, but the moment comes when the world falls away, and the self emerges again from the deep unconscious, bringing back all I have recently experienced to be explored and slowly understood, when I can converse again with my hidden powers, and so grow, and so be renewed, till death do us part.

Jotting Down Your First Responses

1. Does Sarton make you think about being alone in a new way? If so, how? If not, why not?
2. Do you ever "kill" time? What do you do with "empty" time, such as when you are waiting for someone? How do you feel?
3. When do you typically feel lonely? How do you "cure" loneliness?
4. Is there anything you disagree with Sarton about? If so, what?

Checking Your Comprehension

1. What is a solitary life?
2. How did Sarton's friend feel about his hour alone in the museum?
3. Why was her friend afraid to spend time alone, according to Sarton?
4. What new adventure was her friend beginning?
5. How long has Sarton lived alone? (paragraph 6)
6. When, according to Sarton, is loneliness most often felt? (paragraph 5) Why?
7. What are the rewards of a solitary life?
8. What are some situations that cause Sarton to lose her sense of self and to feel lonely? (paragraph 7)
9. How does she recapture her self?
10. What happens to her loneliness as a result?

Understanding a Writer's Patterns

1. What strategy does Sarton use to introduce the subject and hook the reader?
2. In paragraph 2, Sarton shifts from using the pronoun *he* referring to her friend to *we, my,* and *I.* Why?
3. Although we are clear about her subject from the beginning of the essay, Sarton's thesis doesn't appear until paragraph 6. What is the thesis?
4. Sarton has used several ways to define solitude. Find an anecdote, a use of contrast, and several examples (tell what they are examples of).
5. Sarton uses similes (comparisons using *like* or *as*) or metaphors to make her meaning clear and to heighten her writing. What two things are being compared in the last sentence of paragraph 1?
6. There are two metaphors in the sentence beginning ''But having taken the plunge . . .'' (paragraph 2). What are they? Explain the comparisons in both.
7. What does the quotation in paragraph 3 explain or develop?
8. What does the quotation in paragraph 4 explain or develop?
9. What is the attitude of Sarton's intended audience toward solitude?
10. What is Sarton's purpose in this essay, which defines a solitary life?

Making Predictions and Drawing Inferences

1. What plunge (paragraph 2) has Sarton's friend taken?
2. What is one's ''own inner space'' (paragraph 2)?
3. Why is music heard with someone ''more than music'' (paragraph 3)?
4. What does Sarton mean when she writes that her ''self is hiding'' (paragraph 8)?
5. What does ''the world falls away'' (paragraph 9) mean?

Making Judgments and Thinking Critically

1. In paragraph 2 Sarton uses the metaphor of space exploration to explain the nature of her friend's experience of learning to be alone. Is it an effective metaphor? Why or why not?
2. Why does Sarton wait until paragraph 6 to state her thesis?
3. Is the placement of the thesis effective? Why or why not?
4. What is Sarton's definition of loneliness?

Using New Words

1. Make vocabulary cards for three words from this selection that you would like to add to your writing and speaking vocabulary. Write the

word on one side of a card and a definition and an original sentence on the other side.

2. The words *acutely* (paragraph 5) and *inevitably* (paragraph 2) are adverbs. Reminder: Adverbs modify verbs, adjectives, or other adverbs. Notice the adverb ending *-ly*. Change each of these adverbs into its adjective form and write a phrase or sentence to show its use.

Adverb	**Adjective**	**Example**
cheerfully	cheerful	a cheerful nurse
acutely		
inevitably		

3. The words *abiding* (paragraph 4) and *diffused* (paragraph 2) are used as adjectives. Reminder: Adjectives modify nouns and pronouns. Change each of these adjectives into its adverb form and write a phrase or sentence to show its use.

Adjective	**Adverb**	**Example**
blissful	blissfully	He was blissfully happy.
abiding		
diffused		

Responding by Writing

1. If you agree with Sarton about the value of solitude, imagine an ideal day alone. Choose the place, season of the year, weather, activities, music, food—anything that would "fill you up." Consider your thoughts and feelings as they might change through the day. Write an essay about this day of solitude and its effect on you. Perhaps your teacher will collect these essays for a class anthology about solitude, so write for an audience of this class—both those who cherish and those who avoid solitude.
2. If you disagree with Sarton about the value of solitude, write an essay in which you compare your view with hers. Write to an audience of this class. Be sure to describe your view and define any terms that readers might define differently. Even though you can assume your classmates have read Sarton's essay, be sure to state your understanding of her view clearly. Use the title of the essay and the author's full name.
3. Using Sarton's essay as a model, write an essay about the rewards of something you enjoy or value that many others don't seem to understand. Your audience is those who don't share your opinion or interest.
4. "Solitude is the salt of personhood. It brings out the authentic flavor of every experience" (paragraph 3). Write an essay in which you agree or

disagree with this quotation. Explain the quotation. Remember to refer to the title and author of the essay from which the quotation comes.

Permanent Record

Bob Greene

Bob Greene writes for the *Chicago Tribune.* His columns appear in over 150 newspapers throughout the country and have been collected and published in several books. The following essay is from *Cheeseburgers: The Best of Bob Greene.*

Thinking Before Reading

Do you think that people as a whole are less moral than they were twenty or thirty years ago? What makes you think so? If you think there is increased immorality, what do you think are the causes? Write your opinions in your Idea Bank.

Expanding Your Vocabulary from Reading

unethical (5) contrary to principles of just and fair action
nagging (5) insistent, complaining
cringe (8) shrink back in fear
scorning (9) treating with dislike and contempt
candor (11) openness, frankness
deduced (12) figured out from the situation or evidence
inscribe (13) write so as to make a lasting record
purge (13) cleanse, purify
naive (14) unsophisticated, simple
jauntily (15) in a light-hearted and lively manner

1 There are thousands of theories about what's gone wrong with the world, but I think it comes down to one simple thing: The death of the Permanent Record.

2 You remember the Permanent Record. When you were in elementary school, junior high school, and high school, you were constantly being told that if you screwed up, news of that screw-up would be sent down to the principal's office, and would be placed in your Permanent Record.

3 Nothing more needed to be said. No one had ever seen a Permanent Record; that didn't matter. We knew they were there. We all imagined a steel filing cabinet, crammed full of Permanent Records—one for each kid in the

school. I think we always assumed that when we graduated our Permanent Record was sent on to college with us, and then when we got out of college our Permanent Record was sent to our employer—probably with a duplicate copy sent to the U.S. Government.

4 I don't know if students are still threatened with the promise of unpleasant things included in their Permanent Record, but I doubt it. I have a terrible feeling that mine was the last generation to know what a Permanent Record was—and that not only has it disappeared from the schools of the land, but it has disappeared as a concept in society as a whole.

5 There once was a time when people really stopped before they did something they knew was deceitful, immoral, or unethical—no matter how much fun it might sound. They didn't stop because they were such holy folks. They stopped because—no matter how old they were—they had a nagging fear that if they did it, it would end up on their Permanent Record.

6 At some point in the last few decades, I'm afraid, people wised up to something that amazed them: There is no Permanent Record. There probably never was.

7 They discovered that regardless of how badly you fouled up your life or the lives of others, there was nothing permanent about it on your record. You would always be forgiven, no matter what; no matter what you did, other people would shrug it off.

8 So pretty soon men and women—instead of fearing the Permanent Record—started laughing at the idea of the Permanent Record. The kinds of things that they used to be ashamed of—the kinds of things that they used to secretly cringe at when they thought about them—now became "interesting" aspects of their personalities.

9 If those "interesting" aspects were weird enough—if they were the kinds of things that would have really jazzed up the Permanent Record—the people sometimes wrote books confessing those things, and the books became bestsellers. And the people found out that other people—far from scorning them—would line up in the bookstores to get their autographs on the inside covers of the books.

10 The people started going on talk shows to discuss the things that, in decades past, would have been included in their Permanent Records. The talk-show hosts would say, "Thank you for being so honest with us; I'm sure the people in our audience can understand how much guts it must take for you to tell us these things." The Permanent Records were being opened up for the whole world to see—and the sky did not fall in.

11 If celebrities had dips in their careers, all they had to do to guarantee a new injection of fame was to admit the worst things about themselves—the Permanent Record things—and the celebrity magazines would print those things, and the celebrities would be applauded for their candor and courage. And they would become even bigger celebrities.

12 As Americans began to realize that there was no Permanent Record, and probably never had been, they deduced for themselves that any kind of behavior was permissible. After all, it wasn't as if anyone was keeping track; all you would have to do—just like the men and women with best-sellers and on the talk shows and in the celebrity magazines—was to say, "That was a real crazy period in my life." All would be forgiven; all would be erased from the Permanent Record, which, of course, was no longer permanent.

13 And that is where we are today. Without really thinking about it, we have accepted the notion that no one is, indeed, keeping track. No one is even *allowed* to keep track. I doubt that you can scare a school kid today by telling him the principal is going to inscribe something on his Permanent Record; the kid would probably file a suit under the Freedom of Information Act, and gain possession of his Permanent Record by recess. Either that, or the kid would call up his Permanent Record on his computer terminal, and purge any information he didn't want to be there.

14 As for us adults—it has been so long since we have believed in the Permanent Record that the very mention of it today probably brings a nostalgic smile to our faces. We feel naive for ever having believed that a Permanent Record was really down there in the principal's office, anyway.

15 And who really knows if our smiles may freeze on some distant day—the day it is our turn to check out of this earthly world, and we are confronted with a heavenly presence greeting us at the gates of our new eternal home—a heavenly presence sitting there casually leafing through a dusty, battered volume of our Permanent Record as we come jauntily into view.

Jotting Down Your First Responses

1. Did you have a permanent record in school? If so, did you ever consider it a threat in any way?
2. What other kinds of collective records are kept on individuals and who keeps them?
3. Do you agree or disagree with Greene that permanent records of some kind instill moral behavior in people? Explain.
4. Do you always do what is truthful, moral, and ethical? To what degree or in what ways does the fear of discovery affect your behavior? Examples of behavior that might be affected are obeying posted speed limits, cheating on tests, returning extra change given to you when you pay a bill, being sexually faithful to your mate, lying to avoid blame or anger from someone, paying income taxes, and making questionable insurance claims.

Checking Your Comprehension

1. What, according to Greene, is the answer to the question "What's gone wrong with the world?"

2. What kinds of things were kept on the permanent record, according to Greene?
3. In the past what kept people from immoral behavior?
4. What has been the effect of the discovery that there is no permanent record of our behavior?
5. What are best-selling books and talk show interviews often about?
6. What effect do celebrities' confessions usually have on their careers?
7. According to Greene, what was the result when Americans deduced that there were no permanent records?
8. Where does Greene say we may see our permanent records after all?

Understanding a Writer's Patterns

1. What strategy does Greene use to introduce his essay?
2. Who is Greene's intended audience?
3. What is Greene's purpose? What does he want to accomplish?
4. Greene used the time pattern to organize this essay: past, present, future. What paragraphs deal with the past? The present? The future?
5. What is the main idea of the paragraphs about the past?
6. What is the main idea of the paragraphs about the present?
7. What is the main idea of the paragraph about the future?
8. What is the tone of this essay (Formal, informal, preachy, critical, humorous, ironic, solemn, and so forth)? Use more than one word to describe Greene's tone. What led you to decide this is his tone?

Making Predictions and Drawing Inferences

1. Reread the introductory paragraph. What did you accurately predict about the essay when you first read the introduction?
2. What did you predict that didn't follow in the essay?
3. What in the introduction seems clearer now that you have read the essay?
4. What is the school record a symbol of in Greene's essay?
5. Why does Greene think that kids today can't be scared by a permanent record? (paragraph 13)
6. What allusion (reference to a well-known literary, biblical, or mythical work) does Greene make in the conclusion?

Making Judgments and Thinking Critically

1. Does Greene exaggerate the power of the threat of a permanent record? Why or why not?
2. Greene repeats the words "Permanent Record" in almost every paragraph. Why? Is this an effective use of repetition? Why or why not?
3. Why is the public so fascinated with the deceitful, immoral, and unethical behavior of celebrities?

4. What part does humor play in this essay? Is it effective in terms of the writer's thesis, audience, and purpose?

Using New Words

1. Choose three words from this essay to expand your vocabulary. Make vocabulary cards and add them to your set.
2. Read aloud several times all the words in your set of vocabulary cards. Practice until you can say each word easily.
3. Use the vocabulary list at the beginning of this essay and your knowledge about changing the forms of words to explain the italic words in the following questions.

    What is an *inscription* on an award trophy?
    What is his *naivete* about his odds in winning the lottery?
    What is a *jaunty* angle of her hat?
    What is a *candid* reply to a question?

4. What are the prefixes of *immoral* and *unethical*? What do they mean?

Responding by Writing

1. Write an essay in which you define morality and explain what it means to you to an audience of your peers. Decide if your purpose is to make them aware of the issue of morality, to encourage them to examine their own morality, or to anger them about the immoral behavior of someone else. Define morality by giving examples, telling what it isn't, using contrast, using an anecdote, or any combination of other ways to develop an essay.
2. Define any abstract term about which you feel strongly: honesty, responsibility, commitment, leadership, shame, humor, violence, loyalty, individualism, competition, cooperation. Write an essay as an article for your college newspaper in order to increase awareness about this important concept.
3. Everyone has morals, but we have different moral codes which we follow imperfectly. Where do your beliefs about good and bad, acceptable and unacceptable, valuable and worthless come from? What part does fear play in your ''good'' behavior? Write an essay about your sense of morality for Bob Greene to read.
4. Write an essay in which you agree or disagree with Greene's opinion that the disappearance of the Permanent Record (or what it symbolizes) has been one of the causes for increased immorality. You may agree or disagree that morality has declined. You may agree or disagree that lack of public accountability is one of the causes. Use the title and the author's full name in your essay.

Americanization Is Tough on "Macho"

Rose del Castillo Guilbault

Rose del Castillo Guilbault works as director of editorial and public affairs for KGO-TV, the ABC affiliate in San Francisco. For two years she wrote a column called "Hispanic USA" for the weekly magazine of the *San Francisco Chronicle*. The following selection appeared in that column.

Thinking Before Reading

When you think of the ideal man, what do you think of? Make a list in your Idea Bank of qualities or characteristics you think an adult male should have.

Expanding Your Vocabulary from Reading

connotations (2) implied meanings beyond the literal ones, usually suggesting an attitude or feeling
disdain (4) low regard, scorn
chauvinist (6) person with excessive attachment and devotion to a group to which he or she belongs
ambiguities (10) uncertainties; words, states, or events that can be interpreted several ways
stoically (10) with quiet acceptance, without showing feeling or pain
menial (11) lowly, appropriate for a servant
indulgent (11) yielding to desires or whims, pampering
refute (12) prove something false
Chicanas (16) female Hispanics
prototype (16) model, typical example

1 What is *macho*? That depends which side of the border you come from.

2 Although it's not unusual for words and expressions to lose their subtlety in translation, the negative connotations of *macho* in this country are troublesome to Hispanics.

3 Take the newspaper descriptions of alleged mass murderer Ramon Salcido. That an insensitive, insanely jealous, hard-drinking, violent Latin male is referred to as *macho* makes Hispanics cringe.

4 *"Es muy macho,"* the women in my family nod approvingly, describing a man they respect. But in the United States, when women say, "He's so macho," it's with disdain.

5 The Hispanic *macho* is manly, responsible, hardworking, a man in charge, a patriarch. A man who expresses strength through silence. What the Yiddish language would call a *mensch*.

6 The American *macho* is a chauvinist, a brute, uncouth, selfish, loud, abrasive, capable of inflicting pain, and sexually promiscuous.

7 Quintessential *macho* models in this country are Sylvester Stallone, Arnold Schwarzenegger and Charles Bronson. In their movies, they exude toughness, independence, masculinity. But a closer look reveals their machismo is really violence masquerading as courage, sullenness disguised as silence and irresponsibility camouflaged as independence.

8 If the Hispanic ideal of *macho* were translated to American screen roles, they might be Jimmy Stewart, Sean Connery and Laurence Olivier.

9 In Spanish, *macho* ennobles Latin males. In English, it devalues them. This pattern seems consistent with the conflicts ethnic minority males experience in this country. Typically the cultural traits other societies value don't translate as desirable characteristics in America.

10 I watched my own father struggle with these cultural ambiguities. He worked on a farm for twenty years. He laid down miles of irrigation pipe, carefully plowed long, neat rows in fields, hacked away at recalcitrant weeds and drove tractors through whirlpools of dust. He stoically worked twenty-hour days during harvest season, accepting the long hours as part of agricultural work. When the boss complained or upbraided him for minor mistakes, he kept quiet, even when it was obvious the boss had erred.

11 He handled the most menial tasks with pride. At home he was a good provider, helped out my mother's family in Mexico without complaint, and was indulgent with me. Arguments between my mother and him generally had to do with money, or with his stubborn reluctance to share his troubles. He tried to work them out in his own silence. He didn't want to trouble my mother—a course that backfired, because the imagined is always worse than the reality.

12 Americans regarded my father as decidedly un-*macho.* His character was interpreted as nonassertive, his loyalty non-ambition, and his quietness ignorance. I once overheard the boss's son blame him for plowing crooked rows in a field. My father merely smiled at the lie, knowing the boy had done it, but didn't refute it, confident his good work was well known. But the boss instead ridiculed him for being ''stupid'' and letting a kid get away with a lie. Seeing my embarrassment, my father dismissed the incident, saying ''They're the dumb ones. Imagine, me fighting with a kid.''

13 I tried not to look at him with American eyes because sometimes the reflection hurt.

14 Listening to my aunts' clucks of approval, my vision focused on the qualities America overlooked. ''He's such a hard worker. So serious, so responsible.'' My aunts would secretly compliment my mother. The unspoken comparison was that he was not like some of their husbands, who drank and womanized. My uncles represented the darker side of *macho.*

15 In a patriarchal society, few challenge their roles. If men drink, it's because it's the manly thing to do. If they gamble, it's because it's how men

relax. And if they fool around, well, it's because a man simply can't hold back so much man! My aunts didn't exactly meekly sit back, but they put up with these transgressions because Mexican society dictated this was their lot in life.

16 In the United States, I believe it was the feminist movement of the early '70s that changed *macho*'s meaning. Perhaps my generation of Latin women was in part responsible. I recall Chicanas complaining about the chauvinistic nature of Latin men and the notion they wanted their women barefoot, pregnant and in the kitchen. The generalization that Latin men embodied chauvinistic traits led to this interesting twist of semantics. Suddenly a word that represented something positive in one culture became a negative prototype in another.

17 The problem with the use of *macho* today is that it's become an accepted stereotype of the Latin male. And like all stereotypes, it distorts truth.

18 The impact of language in our society is undeniable. And the misuse of *macho* hints at a deeper misunderstanding that extends beyond mere word definitions.

Jotting Down Your First Responses

1. Were the characteristics of an ideal man that you wrote in your Idea Bank more like the Hispanic *macho* or the American macho?
2. What other names for people or groups of people did you think about as you read this essay?
3. Did you have trouble thinking of Rose del Castillo Guilbault's father as she described him as *macho*? If so, does your response support the writer's ideas?

Checking Your Comprehension

1. According to Guilbault, what do Hispanic women mean by *macho*?
2. What do U.S. women mean by *macho*?
3. Who are some models of the American concept of *macho*?
4. Who are some models of the Hispanic concept of *macho*?
5. How does Guilbault describe her father? Does she consider him *macho*?
6. How did Americans see Guilbault's father?
7. What behaviors are typical of men in a patriarchal society?
8. According to Guilbault what change did the Spanish word *macho* undergo in the early 1970s?

Understanding a Writer's Patterns

1. Who is Guilbault's intended audience and what is her purpose? Look for a clue in paragraph 2.
2. In paragraph 3 Guilbault gives an example. What is it an example of?
3. One of the ways Guilbault defines *macho* is to use contrast. Find two examples of contrast in the essay.

4. Guilbault also uses many examples to develop points she wishes to make in her extended definition of *macho.* What point do the examples in paragraph 7 develop?
5. What point do the examples in paragraph 8 develop?
6. In paragraphs 10 through 12 Guilbault uses her father as an example. What point does she develop with this example?
7. In paragraph 10 Guilbault uses a general-to-specific pattern two times to develop the topic sentence. Underline the topic sentence. What two general statements support this topic sentence? What specific details explain each general statement?
8. Guilbault concludes with some comments about the significance of the changed meaning of *macho.* Why does she say this changed definition is important? Is this a successful conclusion for the essay? Why or why not?

Making Predictions and Drawing Inferences

1. Why does Guilbault say that the "negative connotations of *macho* . . . are troublesome to Hispanics" (paragraph 2)?
2. Why does she sometimes look at her father with "American eyes" (paragraph 13)? What does the phrase mean?
3. What do you think a patriarchal society is? Do you know any families, groups, or nations you would describe as basically patriarchal? If so, what are they?
4. What are some advantages of a patriarchal society? Disadvantages?
5. Guilbault claims that the "impact of language in our society is undeniable" (paragraph 18). What is the impact of the misuse of the word *macho*?

Making Judgments and Thinking Critically

1. According to Guilbault, *macho* is misused in the United States. Why does its misuse create a problem?
2. Do you agree that language can have an effect on people's attitudes and actions? Why or why not?
3. What words have been misused or have caused problems in your experience?

Using New Words

1. Choose three words from this selection that you want to add to your working vocabulary and make cards for them.
2. Look through your set of vocabulary cards and select five words. Write a paragraph using all these words. Be creative and have fun with these sentences. Read your paragraph aloud to someone.

3. What do you think *quintessential* and *exude* (paragraph 7) mean? Use the sense of the sentence in which the word appears to figure out its meaning. You may also back up several sentences to provide yourself with additional context clues. Use the dictionary to check your definition. Say the words aloud several times until you can say them easily.

Responding by Writing

1. Write an essay defining a word or phrase about which you feel strongly and which probably has different meanings to different people. Here's a list of terms to start you thinking: family values, patriotism, peace, American dream, sports fan, biker, stud, chick, conservative, liberal, fair play, prejudice, commitment. Use a variety of ways to define—examples, comparison, contrast, telling what it is not. Let your intended reader, perhaps someone who uses this word or phrase vaguely or differently from you, understand the importance of this word to you.
2. Write an essay in which you define what you mean by "a real man" or "a real woman." What qualities of appearance, personality, character, and behavior does this person have? Whom do you know that is this ideal?
3. Write an essay about a specific kind of relationship: mother/adult daughter, parent/child, husband/wife, life partners, close dating relationship, grandparent/grandchild, men friends, women friends, and so forth. Whatever kind of relationship you choose, define a good relationship of that particular kind. Write to an audience of people in the kind of relationship you are defining.
4. Write an essay in which you agree or disagree with Guilbault that macho has a negative meaning. Be sure to use the title of the essay (in quotation marks) and the writer's name in your essay.

The Liberated Woman

Mies Frank

Mies Frank, born in Holland, is married and has two children, one in college and one in high school. She returned to school to gain knowledge and increase her English vocabulary. She wrote the following essay to an audience of women who, like her, have chosen to stay home with their children but who feel criticized by society as "an inferior breed."

Thinking Before Reading

What is your definition of a liberated woman or a liberated man? What are the values and priorities of such a person? Write several sentences in your Idea Bank.

Expanding Your Vocabulary from Reading

conjures (1) calls up as if by a magic spell
chic (1) stylish
corridors (1) halls
attaché cases (1) briefcases to carry business papers
involuntary (2) not performed willingly, forced
coincides (2) corresponds or agrees with
transformation (3) change of appearance
compiled (3) collected together
abode (8) home, dwelling place
gloating (8) showing smug or triumphant pleasure

1 The name alone conjures up visions of women attired in chic, conservatively styled suits hurrying along plush, carpeted corridors on their way to important conferences. Faces radiate confidence, reflect expensive make-up and the latest in hairstyles. Eelskin attaché cases complete the total package. On the surface these women appear to have it all: college degrees, corner offices and promising careers. Society in general labels them "liberated in the USA." But are they really?

2 The Random House College Dictionary defines this word as "to set free from involuntary servitude." A broad interpretation could translate into no more cooking, no more cleaning. This definition coincides quite nicely with a remark a friend of mine made some months ago. During a lengthy telephone conversation, we argued and debated which one of us represents a truly liberated woman. Naturally, she voted for herself. Her main criterion was financial independence from her husband. Mine, freedom of choice. I form part of a special category of women to whom this option applies: the almost disappearing species of housewives. I very strongly feel that, within the framework of my responsibilities, I enjoy total freedom. Moreover, I am accountable only to myself. My friend is not.

3 As a homemaker I enjoy the privilege and the opportunity to schedule my days exactly as I wish. Over the years I have perfected a highly efficient program of cleaning, shopping and laundering. Monday is scrubday. Believe me, this is really necessary. The entire family has the chance (and uses it) to clutter, litter and soil the house over the weekend. But in the morning, a transformation starts taking place. And by the end of the afternoon I have the intense satisfaction of wandering from room to room to enjoy the fruits of my

labor. Wednesdays mean errands. Cookbooks are consulted, menus compiled, shopping lists prepared. I am still amazed at the amount of time that is involved to just run to the grocery store or drop by the cleaners. Laundry and ironing take place on Fridays. No more griping and complaining that there is nothing to wear for the weekend. Planning major household chores every other day of the week leaves me ample time to pursue a college degree, various hobbies and club activities. Not all women are this free (read liberated), though.

4 ''Having it all really means doing it all'' is the conclusion of working women who have been interviewed by the *Dallas Morning News* recently. The majority of them complain that after a full day at the office, another schedule awaits them at home. Apparently only a small percentage of husbands share in the housework. The bulk of the hulk collapses in front of the TV and stretches out until dinner. Their excuses include ''two left hands,'' ''chores are for women'' or ''my Mom did not teach me to pick up after myself.'' So much for the ''liberated'' woman.

5 My alarm clock is set for 7 a.m. After fixing breakfast and lunch for the family, I make time for myself. Ann Landers and Abigail Van Buren share in a leisurely consumption of toasted English muffins and steaming hot coffee (two of each). No early hours for me to rush in the shower and hurry dressing. No early hours for me to locate missing socks and correct homework problems. No early hours for me to face a husband dropping wet towels on the floor and leaving beard stubbles in the sink. Yes, I feel truly free!

6 When planning menus on Wednesdays, I take plenty of time to select recipes which provide nutritious and well-balanced meals for the family. Consideration is given to the various fruits and vegetables in season. My careful planning has enabled my children to sample quite a variety of different foods throughout the years. Regular trips to the nearest fast-food restaurant are an exception, rather than the norm, as they would be for the liberated household.

7 The few childhood diseases of my children presented minor problems. No need to juggle schedules or alternate staying at home. Regular visits to the pediatrician were followed by periodic dental appointments. When headaches, colds and flus showed up, so did I, armed with pills and powders. No need to impose on neighbors and friends or use precious vacation time. Daycare centers with their associated germs, contagious infections or inadequate care never formed part of my children's upbringing. Instead, a nurturing and encouraging environment was provided at home.

8 I consider myself very fortunate that I had options when the children came along. Not every mother is in this position. A deliberate decision was made at the time that I would quit my job. From then on, my career consisted of taking care of the family and the house. Promotions and a corner office disappeared from the picture, as did financial independence. Conferences were canceled. Casual clothing replaced suits, open sandals substituted for high heels. The result of all these changes is that now my house sparkles, my yard

has flowers and the front porch is swept. My children come home to me, unaccompanied by a latchkey. Let me tell you that it gives me a great deal of satisfaction and pride when I can show my "liberated" friend my cozy, clean and comfortable abode. She may have an eelskin attaché case, but she was deprived from comforting her baby when the first tooth broke through and from gloating when the first step was taken. I waited and knitted while my children took piano lessons or practiced soccer after school. My rich friend had to work. Another housewife had to take her children to their various activities. Being at home may have its dull and boring moments; so does every other job. But I enjoy the freedom to organize my day my way. I am my own boss. And that is what I call truly liberated.

Jotting Down Your First Responses

1. Do you agree or disagree with Frank's definition of a "liberated woman"? Explain.
2. Do you agree that women who work have less freedom and more responsibility than women who stay at home with their children? Explain.
3. What questions would you like to ask Mies Frank?

Checking Your Comprehension

1. What is society's definition of a liberated woman?
2. What is a dictionary definition of the word *liberate*?
3. What is Frank's friend's definition of a liberated woman?
4. What is Frank's definition?
5. What limits Frank's freedom?
6. What is Frank's system for doing major household chores and having time to go to college and have hobbies?
7. What written source does Frank use to support her claim of freedom?
8. Why, according to that written source, does a working woman have less freedom than Frank does?
9. What is Frank's morning schedule?
10. How has Frank's family's nutrition profited from her freedom?
11. How did the health of Frank's children profit by her decision to stay home?
12. What is Frank's present career?

Understanding a Writer's Patterns

1. What strategy does Frank use in the introduction of the essay? (See page 38.)
2. What personal contrast does Frank use to help define a liberated woman?
3. What is the writer's thesis?

4. Paragraphs 3 through 6 develop one major supporting point for Frank's thesis. What is this major supporting point?
5. Paragraphs 7 and 8 develop another major supporting point for Frank's thesis. What is it?
6. What are some of the ways to develop an essay that Frank used to define liberated women?

Making Predictions and Drawing Inferences

1. What are Frank's responsibilities? Do these limit her freedom?
2. What are her friend's responsibilities? Do you think she has children? Why or why not?
3. Does the friend have more or less freedom than Frank, according to Frank's definition? According to the friend's definition?
4. What does Frank suggest the friend loses as a parent?

Making Judgments and Thinking Critically

1. Is the audience of the essay an appropriate one? (See the headnote about the writer.) Why or why not?
2. Since Frank has not been freed from cooking and cleaning (paragraph 2), why does she claim to be liberated?
3. Where else might paragraph 6 be placed in the essay? Would this improve the organization of the essay? Why or why not?
4. In five or ten years, after her children graduate from college, will Frank need to redefine her idea of a liberated woman? Why or why not?

Using New Words

1. Choose three words from this selection that you would like to add to your writing and speaking vocabulary. Make cards for each, writing the word on one side of a card and a definition and an original sentence on the other side.
2. If Frank had written "The name usually means career women attired in chic . . ." instead of "The name alone conjures up visions of women attired in chic . . ." (paragraph 1) something would have been lost. What does the phrase "conjures up visions" add to the paragraph's meaning?
3. Give antonyms (opposites) for the following words: *chic, involuntary, coincides, gloat.*

Responding by Writing

1. Write an essay in which you define a liberated man or a liberated woman. Consider if this definition applies to young, middle aged, or older people. Write to an audience of the opposite sex.

2. Compare your definition of a liberated man with the American or the Hispanic *macho* in "Americanization Is Tough on 'Macho.'" Write an essay in which you quote from that essay; be sure to refer to its author and title. Choose an audience who needs to hear what you have to say. Describe that audience before you write the essay.
3. Frank's essay grew out of a disagreement she and a friend had over how they would define a liberated woman. Choose a word or phrase about which you and others disagree strongly. Write an essay defining this phrase for those who disagree with you in order to make a clearer case for your definition than you have been able to make by talking.
4. Write a letter to Mies Frank in which you agree or disagree with her definition of liberated women. Use the title of her essay and at least one quotation from it. You may paraphrase or summarize her points, ask questions, politely point out weaknesses, or comment on the strengths of her essay.

CHAPTER

12

CAUSE AND EFFECT

USING CAUSE AND EFFECT TO DEVELOP YOUR ESSAY

In a cause and effect essay, you consider the causes and effects (results or outcomes) of an event, situation, or condition, such as the Los Angeles riots, the cost of gasoline, or your increasing indebtedness. A causal analysis may focus on just the causes, on just the effects, or on both. The question *why?* seeks to find causes. The questions *what happened then?* and *what if . . . ?* seek to find effects. Causes occur *before* an event, situation, or condition; effects occur *after* an event, situation, or condition.

Daily life offers you many opportunities to analyze cause and effect. Why do you have stomach cramps? Why won't your car start? Why are you and your mate arguing so much lately? Why are the Cubs or Dodgers losing? Why are the fleas so bad this year? Determining the cause or causes of a situation sometimes allows you to decide what action to take. For instance, if you decide your car won't start because of a starter that's been acting up, not because the car is out of gas or needs a new battery, you know you need to have the starter replaced.

News broadcasts, newspapers, and magazines are full of cause and effect analysis of local, national, and international situations. These are usually labeled ''analysis'' or ''opinion'' because they are interpretive pieces, not just reports. Why is the recession so long and economic recovery so slow? What are the causes of rising crime rates in Dallas? What are the results of the savings and loan abuses and failures of the 1980s?

Causal analysis and process analysis (which you studied in Chapter 8) are quite different. When you emphasize *how to* do something, you are doing process analysis. When you emphasize *why* something happened or *what happened or might happen* because of an earlier event or situation, you are doing causal analysis. The motivation behind the "why?" is to find out and understand causes, sometimes in order to predict, shape, or control the effects. For instance, AIDS research seeks to find the causes of the devastating disease in order to control the effects, that is, to reduce the number of cases and find a cure.

You may use causal analysis as the basic method of developing an entire essay, that is, as the basic pattern of organization for the essay. Or, you may use discussion of cause and effect to develop a major supporting point.

USING THE STEPS OF PROBLEM SOLVING

Many of the events, situations, or conditions that people analyze are problems. Although people often ask "why?" in order to whine or blame or satisfy, a mild curiosity, a real "why?" indicates the recognition of a problem and the desire to solve it. Therefore, the steps of problem solving can help you think systematically and write clearly about causes and effects. Here are the steps:

Define and describe the problem.
List contributing factors or causes.
List possible solutions.
Evaluate each proposed solution.
Select the most effective, possible, affordable solution.
Make plans to enact the selected solution.

Often a cause and effect essay will deal with only one step of problem solving. For instance, a writer in your local newspaper might address voters, emphasizing the many positive effects that will result from the passage of a city bond to build a convention center, such as increased sales taxes from more tourist spending, more hotel and restaurant business, and more jobs. Your vote, and the votes of your neighbors will cause the bond to pass.

Another example of focusing on one step is from John Holt's "Kinds of Discipline" (Chapter 9), an essay which serves as a model for both division and classification and cause and effect as methods of development. Holt set up three categories of discipline (division and classification). At one point in the essay, he discusses the effects (causal analysis) of threat and force, the third kind of discipline.

> But we ought to use this discipline only when it is necessary to protect the life, health, safety, or well-being of people or other living creatures, or to prevent destruction of things that people care about. We ought not to assume too long, as we usually do, that a child cannot understand the real nature of the danger from which we want to protect him. The sooner

> he avoids the danger, not to escape our punishment, but as a matter of good sense, the better. He can learn that faster than we think. In Mexico, for example, where people drive their cars with a good deal of spirit, I saw many children no older than five or four walking unattended on the streets. They understood about cars, they know what to do. A child whose life is full of the threat and fear of punishment is locked into babyhood. There is no way for him to grow up, to learn to take responsibility for his life and acts. Most important of all, we should not assume that having to yield to the threat of our superior force is good for the child's character. It is never good for *anyone's* character. To bow to superior force makes us feel impotent and cowardly for not having had the strength or courage to resist. Worse, it makes us resentful and vengeful. We can hardly wait to make someone pay for our humiliation, yield to us as we were once made to yield. No, if we cannot always avoid using the Discipline of Superior Force, we should at least use it as seldom as we can.

After discussing the positive effect that the discipline of threat or force may have—protecting people from physical harm—Holt discusses the negative effects of this kind of discipline used unnecessarily. It prevents the child from "learning to take responsibility for his life and acts." He then describes the effect of discipline of force on all of us, not just children. It "makes us feel impotent and cowardly" and makes us "resentful and vengeful."

Notice that Holt describes the importance of protecting children until they can understand and avoid danger on their own. A problem occurs in our country when people continue to use this kind of discipline when children no longer need it. He gives an example of young children in Mexico walking safely where there was heavy traffic. After the example he describes the effect of the discipline of force on all of us, not just children.

AVOIDING PROBLEMS IN LOGICAL THINKING

There are several common pitfalls in cause and effect essays, all of them based on faulty reasoning. Recognizing problems in logical thinking can make you a more discerning reader and a better writer. Three general types of faulty reasoning are jumping to hasty conclusions, assuming a causal relationship where it does not exist, and oversimplifying.

Don't Jump to Hasty Conclusions. If your cat refuses to eat his dinner, do you jump to the conclusion that he doesn't like dry food? He could be ill, he could have eaten something when he was at the neighbor's, or he could object to a change of food brand. One jumps to a hasty conclusion when one considers only the first cause or effect that comes to mind or the most obvious one.

When you are writing about causes or effects, ask yourself ''What else could have caused this?'' or ''What are other results or effects?'' Ask readers of your draft if they can think of other causes or effects. Use the answers to revise.

Don't Assume a Causal Relationship. If you wear your T-shirt backwards one day and win the lottery, do you then believe that it's lucky to wear your shirt backwards? People sometimes assume that because one event occurred before a second event, the first caused the second. Superstitions are born just this way.

Events are not necessarily related by cause. Events may be associated with each other, that is they may often occur at or near the same time, without one causing the other. For instance, drug use is often associated with rock and roll, but the music doesn't cause drug use. A woman in a miniskirt may be raped, but her clothing has not caused the rape.

When you write about causes and effects, think carefully about causal relationships. Look at sentences with words such as ''because,'' ''the reason is,'' ''the effects are.'' Is one thing really ''caused by'' another? Is there a clear causal relationship or does another kind of relationship exist? Would another connecting word be more precise? Test anything you state as a cause or effect.

Don't Oversimplify. People sometimes say they long for the good old days when right was right, wrong was wrong, and there were simple answers to all of life's questions. Whether or not the old days were ever that simple, most situations and events are complex. There is rarely a single cause or a single solution to a complex problem. Politicians of one party tend to blame all the country's economic woes on the President and his political party. The President's political party blames the woes on members of the other party in Congress. Both parties promise that the single act of electing their Presidential candidate will solve the problem. Such fuzzy thinking oversimplifies the definition of the problem, its multiple causes, and the multiple solutions needed. Beware of oversimplifying when you write about causes and effects. There are often multiple causes. Some causes are apparent and immediate; other causes may be more obscure. Often there is a causal chain, in which the effect of one event becomes the cause of another, like standing dominoes in a long line and tapping the front one to make the rest topple one after another.

ORGANIZING CAUSE AND EFFECT ESSAYS

There are three parts of a cause and effect analysis: the event, situation, problem, or condition; the causes; and the effects. Although in reality there's a natural time sequence from causes to situation to effects, you may vary the order of the three parts and your emphasis on them.

In "Kinds of Discipline," Holt discusses three kinds of discipline. He begins the discussion of the first discipline, the Discipline of Reality, with a list of effects. Notice the "if this, then that" pattern that signals effects.

> When he is trying to do something real, if he does the wrong thing or doesn't do the right one, he doesn't get the result he wants. If he doesn't pile one block right on top of another, or tries to build on a slanting surface, his tower falls down. If he hits the wrong key, he hears the wrong note. If he doesn't hit the nail squarely on the head, it bends, and he has to pull it out and start with another. . . .

After listing many possible effects, Holt defines the discipline of reality. Holt has moved from effects to the situation (here, the definition of discipline).

However, in discussing the discipline of threat and force, Holt begins with the situation—a clear definition and description of this kind of discipline: "The third discipline is the one most people mean when they speak of discipline—the Discipline of Superior Force, of sergeant to private, of 'you do what I tell you or I'll make you wish you had.' " Holt's explanation continues for several sentences before he begins to describe the effects of too much of this kind of discipline (see the excerpt on pages 276–277). Thus you see within a single essay two variations of cause and effect organization.

REMINDER

Define, describe, and explain the situation clearly so that your readers will understand the importance of the causes or effects you discuss.

Besides varying the order of the parts, you may also vary the amount of discussion of each part. For instance, Linda Ellerbee's essay "When Television Ate My Best Friend" (later in this chapter) is a humorous and poignant account of the effect of television on a childhood friendship. The cause is the purchase of a family's first television set; the situation is the change in the friendship. Most of the essay describes the effects of television.

Provide Transitions. If you are clear in your own mind about the situation, its causes, and its effects, you can provide clear transitions for your readers to indicate the causal relationships.

Words that indicate causes include

cause	because	if

Words that indicate effects are

results	so
outcomes	thus
effects	then

Notice the number of parallel sentences in the Holt passage that use "If . . . , then . . ." transitions. These are all examples of the Discipline of Reality which show cause and effect.

POINTS TO REMEMBER ABOUT CAUSE AND EFFECT

Use the problem-solving sequence to think through possible causes, effects, or both.
Clarify and describe three parts:
- Situation, event, or condition
- Causes
- Effects

Recognize faulty reasoning and avoid the pitfalls of
- Jumping to hasty conclusions
- Assuming a causal relationship
- Oversimplifying

Organize analysis by presenting its three parts—situation, causes, effects—in an order and with emphasis appropriate to your subject and purpose.
Use transitional words and phrases to show the relationship of causes, a situation, and its effects.

Do You Know Who Your Friends Are?

Larry Letich

Larry Letich is currently working to create a new magazine about men's issues and progressive politics for a broad audience. The following article appeared in *The Utne Reader*.

Thinking Before Reading

Do you think mainstream American culture encourages or discourages men from being close friends? At what ages? How? Why? Write a few sentences in your Idea Bank.

Expanding Your Vocabulary from Reading

lamented (2) expressed sorrow, mourned aloud
homophobia (3) fear of homosexuality or homosexuals
precludes (3) causes the exclusion of, makes impossible

impulse (5) sudden urge, forceful motivation
sniggered (5) ridiculed
denigration (6) act of belittling or making to seem less valuable
golden parachutes (7) large salaries and benefit packages that protect top executives when they lose their jobs
faux pas (7) mistake, social blunder; from the French words meaning "false step"
passion (8) intense emotion
laudable (9) praiseworthy, admirable
campaign (11) planned activities to achieve a goal

1 "You gotta have frieeends," sang Bette Midler. But most men past the age of 30 don't have friends—not really. They have colleagues and work buddies, golf partners and maybe a "couple" friend or two, where the bond is really between the wives. If they say they *do* have a best friend, often it turns out to be an old friend whom they see or speak to once every few years.

2 Sadly, for most men in our culture, male friendship is a part of their distant past. One man spoke for many at a recent men's conference in Montclair, N.J., when he lamented, "I haven't made a new friend in 25 years."

3 Why is this so? All sorts of theories are thrown around, from "homophobia" to the absurd idea that men are biologically geared to competitiveness, which precludes friendship. But the major reason for the shortage of true friendship among men in America is that our culture discourages it.

4 Male friendship is idealized in the abstract (think of *Butch Cassidy and the Sundance Kid* and numerous other "buddy movies"), but if a man manages to have any true emotional attachment to another man, a lot of subtle pressures are placed on him to eliminate it. The most obvious time this happens is when a man gets married (especially if he's still in his 20s). Think of the impression that comes to mind from a thousand movies and TV shows about the guy who "leaves his wife" for the evening to "go out with the guys." Invariably, the other guys are shown as both immature *and* lower-class, losers who'll never amount to anything in life. The message is clear—no self-respecting middle-class man hangs out regularly with his friends.

5 In fact, friendship between men is rarely spoken of at all. Instead, we hear about something called male bonding, as if all possible non-sexual connection between men is rooted in some crude, instinctual impulse. More often than not, male friendship, reduced to male bonding, is sniggered at as something terribly juvenile and possibly dangerous.

6 This denigration of male friendship fits well into Reagan- and Thatcher-style capitalism. The decline in blue-collar jobs and the great white-collar work speed-up of the 1980s made no man's job safe. And money—not the richness of a man's relationship with family, friends, and community—became even more so the universally accepted value of a man's worth.

7 In this system, men (at least those men without golden parachutes) are put in the position of constantly, and often ruthlessly, competing with all other men for the limited number of positions higher up the ladder—or even to hold onto their jobs at all. Men are encouraged not to trust one another, and are frankly told never to band together. (For example, in most places it is a serious faux pas, and often a dismissable offense, simply to tell a fellow worker what you make for a living; supposedly it is "bad for morale.") Naturally, this keeps men—and women, too—constantly knocking themselves out for the next promotion rather than demanding real changes, like cutting the CEO's million-dollar salary down to size.

8 Given the kind of sterile, high-pressure work environments men are expected to devote themselves to, it's not surprising that the ideal American man is supposed to feel little or no passion about anything. As Robert Bly has pointed out, the most damaged part of the psyche in modern man is the "lover," meaning not just the ability to make love, but the ability to love life, to feel, to be either tender or passionate. But passion—and with it the capacity for intimacy—is absolutely essential for friendship.

9 It's also not surprising that our society's ideal man is not supposed to have any emotional needs. Since few men can actually live up to that ideal, it's considered acceptable, even laudable, for him to channel all his emotional needs in one direction—his wife and children. A man who has any other important emotional bonds (that are not based on duty, such as an ailing parent) is in danger of being called neglectful or irresponsible, or weak, because forging emotional bonds with others takes time—time that is supposed to be spent "getting ahead."

10 Small wonder that the only friendships allowed are those that serve a "business" purpose or those that can be fit effortlessly into one's leisure time. Maintaining one's lawn is more important than maintaining one's friendships. In keeping with this, there are no rituals and no respect given a man's friendships. When was the last time you heard a grown man talk proudly about his best friend?

11 Despite all these obstacles, it *is* possible to develop a real male friendship—the kind men remember from their childhood, high school, college, or military days—after the age of 30. My best friend today, with whom I share a deep and abiding bond, is a man I met five years ago when I was 30. But to forge real male friendships requires a willingness to *recognize* that you're going against the grain, and the *courage* to do so. And it requires the sort of conscious, deliberate campaign worthy of a guerrilla leader.

Jotting Down Your First Responses

1. Do you basically agree or disagree with Letich? Why?
2. Are there any parts of the essay that you disagree with or feel uncomfortable about? If so, what are they?

3. How long has your best friend been your best friend? How did you become friends?

Checking Your Comprehension

1. According to Letich, what kinds of friends do men have?
2. What are three theories that explain why men don't have true friends?
3. How are men's friendships usually portrayed in movies?
4. What happens to men's friendships when they marry?
5. What term is talked about instead of male friendship?
6. Why does job insecurity discourage male friendship?
7. What effect does a "sterile, high-pressure work environment" have on men?
8. What quality is essential for true friendship?
9. According to Letich, in what relationships does our culture allow men to have important emotional bonds?
10. What, according to the writer, is needed to create true male friendships?

Understanding a Writer's Patterns

1. What is the thesis of the essay? (paragraph 3)
2. What do you think Letich wanted to accomplish with this essay?
3. Who is the intended audience? Give evidence from the essay.
4. What common strategy does Letich use to introduce the essay?
5. Is the essay mainly about the causes or the effects of the lack of men's friendships?
6. What sentence in paragraph 3 indicates that Letich will analyze the causes or effects of the lack of men's friendships?
7. What words indicate that Letich is giving an example of marriage (paragraph 4) as a pressure to eliminate male friendships?
8. What words at the beginning of paragraphs 6 and 7 link the paragraphs with the previous one? Explain the link.
9. What chain of causes and effects does Letich present?
10. What common strategy does Letich use to conclude the essay?

Making Predictions and Drawing Inferences

1. Why does Letich ignore women's friendships?
2. In the essay Letich tells what friendship is not. How do you think he would define "true friendship"?
3. How, according to Robert Bly (paragraph 8), is the American male damaged?

Making Judgments and Thinking Critically

1. Does Letich make a good case for his view of male friendships? What strengths and weaknesses do you see in the essay?
2. Are male friendships allowed and encouraged for children and teenagers in this culture? Give evidence for your opinion.
3. Why is male friendship considered dangerous? (paragraph 5)
4. Why is passion essential for friendship? (paragraph 8)

Using New Words

1. Choose three words from this essay to add to your vocabulary. Make cards with a word on one side and a definition and an original sentence on the other side.
2. Substitute *renamed* for *reduced* in paragraph 5. How is the meaning changed by the substitution?
3. Substitute *laughed at* for *sniggered* in paragraph 5. How is the meaning changed by the substitution?
4. Substitute *make* for *forge* in paragraph 11. How is the meaning changed by the substitution?

Responding by Writing

1. Write an essay about the effect of contemporary American culture on women's friendships. Write for an audience of this class.
2. If you are from another country or from a minority culture in the United States, write an essay about the effect of your culture on male or female friendships. Write for an audience of this class, especially those from cultures other than yours.
3. Write an essay analyzing the causes and effects of a problem that people your age often face. Of course, you must choose a problem that you have some insight into. Describe the problem and tell why it is a problem or how big a problem it is. Discuss the causes and effects. Remember that you don't have to discusss both. Write for an audience of your age group. Decide what you want the readers to do as a result of reading your essay.
4. Do you agree with Letich that money, not relationships, is the "accepted value of a man's worth" in our culture? If not, what do you think is most valued about men? Think about the most admired men in your community, in the news, and in sports and entertainment. Why are they admired?

   Write an essay about these most admired qualities in men in our culture. Choose and describe an audience who needs to hear what you have to say. Describe this audience's age group and its attitudes about male friendship.

Use evidence from both "Americanization Is Tough on 'Macho' " (pages 265–267) and Letich's essay. Use two brief quotations. State the titles of the essays and the authors' full names the first time you refer to them.

Loss of Intimacy

Richard Rodriguez

Richard Rodriguez grew up in Sacramento, California, in the 1950s and received his doctorate in English literature from the University of California at Berkeley. The selection below was taken from his autobiography, *Hunger of Memory.*

Thinking Before Reading

All of us have felt loss when a treasured relationship changes. Perhaps a good buddy at work was promoted to being your boss or your best friend went away to college and you stayed home to work. Write a few sentences in your Idea Bank describing what caused the change and your feelings about the changed relationship.

Expanding Your Vocabulary from Reading

intrinsically (1) essentially, inherently
incongruity (2) lack of harmony or compatibility
tact (4) diplomacy, ability to act and speak in a way to avoid giving offense
complied (4) acted as requested
accentuated (4) emphasized
***ahora* (4)** Spanish word meaning "now"
overanglicizing (5) exaggerating the English language sounds
inevitable (5) unable to be avoided or prevented
profound (5) deep, far-reaching
obliged (6) required or caused to
assurance (6) absence of self-doubt or uncertainty
bemused (7) in deep thought, somewhat confused
***hijito* (11)** Spanish word for "my boy"
convent (11) a religious community, especially of nuns

1 Because I wrongly imagined that English was intrinsically a public language and Spanish an intrinsically private one, I easily noted the difference between classroom language and the language of home. At school, words were directed to a general audience of listeners. ("Boys and girls.") Words were

meaningfully ordered. And the point was not self-expression alone but to make oneself understood by many others. The teacher quizzed: "Boys and girls, why do we use that word in this sentence? Could we think of a better word to use there? Would the sentence change its meaning if the words were differently arranged? And wasn't there a better way of saying much the same thing?" (I couldn't say. I wouldn't try to say.)

2 Three months. Five. Half a year passed. Unsmiling, ever watchful, my teachers noted my silence. They began to connect my behavior with the difficult progress my older sister and brother were making. Until one Saturday morning three nuns arrived at the house to talk to our parents. Stiffly, they sat on the blue living room sofa. From the doorway of another room, spying the visitors, I noted the incongruity—the clash of two worlds, the faces and voices of school intruding upon the familiar setting of home. I overheard one voice gently wondering, "Do your children speak only Spanish at home, Mrs. Rodriguez?" While another voice added, "That Richard especially seems so timid and shy."

3 *That Rich-heard!*

4 With great tact the visitors continued, "Is it possible for you and your husband to encourage your children to practice their English when they are home?" Of course, my parents complied. What would they not do for their children's well-being? And how could they have questioned the Church's authority which those women represented? In an instant, they agreed to give up the language (the sounds) that had revealed and accentuated our family's closeness. The moment after the visitors left, the change was observed. "*Ahora,* speak to us *en inglés,*" my father and mother united to tell us.

5 At first, it seemed a kind of game. After dinner each night, the family gathered to practice "our" English. (It was still then *inglés,* a language foreign to us, so we felt drawn as strangers to it.) Laughing, we would try to define words we could not pronounce. We played with strange English sounds, often overanglicizing our pronunciations. And we filled the smiling gaps of our sentences with familiar Spanish sounds. But that was cheating, somebody shouted. Everyone laughed. In school, meanwhile, like my brother and sister, I was required to attend a daily tutoring session. I needed a full year of special attention. I also needed my teachers to keep my attention from straying in class by calling out, *Rich-heard*—their English voices slowly prying loose my ties to my other name, its three notes, *Ri-car-do.* Most of all I needed to hear my mother and father speak to me in a moment of seriousness in broken—suddenly heartbreaking—English. The scene was inevitable: One Saturday morning I entered the kitchen where my parents were talking in Spanish. I did not realize that they were talking in Spanish however until, at the moment they saw me, I heard their voices change to speak English. Those *gringo* sounds they uttered startled me. Pushed me away. In that moment of trivial misunderstanding and profound insight, I felt my throat twisted by unsounded grief. I turned quickly and left the room. But I had no place to escape to with

Spanish. (The spell was broken.) My brother and sister were speaking English in another part of the house.

6 Again and again in the days following, increasingly angry, I was obliged to hear my mother and father: ''Speak to us *en inglés. (Speak.)* Only then did I determine to learn classroom English. Weeks after, it happened: One day in school I raised my hand to volunteer an answer. I spoke out in a loud voice. And I did not think it remarkable when the entire class understood. That day, I moved very far from the disadvantaged child I had been only days earlier. The belief, the calming assurance that I belonged in public, had at last taken hold.

7 Shortly after, I stopped hearing the high and loud sounds of *los gringos.* A more and more confident speaker of English, I didn't trouble to listen to *how* strangers sounded, speaking to me. And there simply were too many English-speaking people in my day for me to hear American accents anymore. Conversations quickened. Listening to persons who sounded eccentrically pitched voices, I usually noted their sounds for an initial few seconds before I concentrated on *what* they were saying. Conversations became content-full. Transparent. Hearing someone's *tone* of voice—angry or questioning or sarcastic or happy or sad—I didn't distinguish it from the words it expressed. Sound and word were thus tightly wedded. At the end of a day, I was often bemused, always relieved to realize how ''silent,'' though crowded with words, my day in public had been. (This public silence measured and quickened the change in my life.)

8 At last, seven years old, I came to believe what had been technically true since my birth: I was an American citizen.

9 But the special feeling of closeness at home was diminished by then. Gone was the desperate, urgent, intense feeling of being at home; rare was the experience of feeling myself individualized by family intimates. We remained a loving family, but one greatly changed. No longer so close; no longer bound tight by the pleasing and troubling knowledge of our public separateness. Neither my older brother nor sister rushed home after school anymore. Nor did I. When I arrived home there would often be neighborhood kids in the house. Or the house would be empty of sounds.

10 The silence at home, however, was finally more than a literal silence. Fewer words passed between parent and child, but more profound was the silence that resulted from my inattention to sounds. At about the time I no longer bothered to listen with care to the sounds of English in public, I grew careless about listening to the sounds family members made when they spoke. Most of the time I heard someone speaking at home and didn't distinguish his sounds from the words people uttered in public. I didn't even pay much attention to my parents' accented and ungrammatical speech. At least not at home. Only when I was with them in public would I grow alert to their accents. Though, even then, their sounds caused me less and less concern. For I was increasingly confident of my own public identity.

11 I would have been happier about my public success had I not sometimes recalled what it had been like earlier, when my family had conveyed its intimacy through a set of conveniently private sounds. Sometimes in public, hearing a stranger, I'd hark back to my past. A Mexican farmworker approached me downtown to ask directions to somewhere "¿*Hijito* . . .?" he said. And his voice summoned deep longing. Another time, standing beside my mother in the visiting room of a Carmelite convent, before the dense screen which rendered the nuns shadowy figures, I heard several Spanish-speaking nuns—their busy, singsong overlapping voices—assure us that yes, yes, we were remembered, all our family was remembered in their prayers. (Their voices echoed faraway family sounds.) Another day, a dark-faced old woman—her hand light on my shoulder—steadied herself against me as she boarded a bus. She murmured something I couldn't quite comprehend. Her Spanish voice came near, like the face of a never-before-seen relative in the instant before I was kissed. Her voice, like so many of the Spanish voices I'd hear in public, recalled the golden age of my youth. Hearing Spanish then, I continued to be a careful, if sad, listener to sounds. Hearing a Spanish-speaking family walking behind me, I turned to look. I smiled for an instant, before my glance found the Hispanic-looking faces of strangers in the crowd going by.

Jotting Down Your First Responses

1. When have you been an outsider in a group? In school, social, or work situations? Were you silent? Why? How did you feel?
2. If you grew up with two languages, what language did you prefer and why?
3. When you hear a conversation in another language, what do you do? Do you listen to the sounds, try to understand, or tune out? How do you feel? Curious, annoyed, envious? Explain.

Checking Your Comprehension

1. What three differences did Rodriguez notice about classroom language and the language of home?
2. How long was Rodriguez in school before the nuns came to visit his parents?
3. What did the nuns ask Rodriguez's parents to do?
4. What three things (paragraph 5) caused Rodriguez to want to learn English?
5. What incident at home made Rodriguez decide to learn classroom English? (paragraph 5)
6. What surprised Rodriguez when he finally spoke in class?
7. As Rodriguez began to speak English, what shifted in his listening? (paragraph 7)
8. What sense of identity resulted from his speaking English?

9. What loss resulted from his speaking English?
10. How did Rodriguez feel when he heard his parents speak English in public?
11. What situations recalled the family intimacy of Rodriguez's past for him?

Understanding a Writer's Patterns

1. Is the loss of family intimacy the cause, the situation, or the effect in this essay? Explain.
2. What paragraphs tell the story of how Rodriguez became an English speaker?
3. What paragraphs tell the effects of becoming an English speaker?
4. What transitional word signals the discussion of the effects? Why did Rodriguez use a signal word that shows contrast?
5. Although there are three brief incidents in paragraph 11, what other three incidents are expanded into anecdotes in the essay?
6. How does Rodriguez bring a sense of closure in the concluding paragraph?
7. Paragraph 2 begins with three short sentences. Paragraph 3 is a short sentence. Why does Rodriguez use these short sentences?
8. Why does Rodriguez use the Spanish *ahora* (paragraph 4), *en inglés* (paragraph 4), *los gringos* (paragraph 7), and *hijito* (paragraph 11)?
9. Why does Rodriguez write *Rich-heard* in paragraphs 3 and 5 and *Ri-car-do* in paragraph 5?
10. Which one of the senses dominates the description of Rodriguez's past?

Making Predictions and Drawing Inferences

1. What kind of school did Rodriguez attend?
2. What kind of students were Rodriguez's brother and sister?
3. What connections did the nuns make between Rodriguez's silence and his brother's and sister's progress?
4. What does Rodriguez mean when he says "their English voices slowly prying loose my ties to my other name, its three notes, *Ri-car-do* (paragraph 5)?
5. Why was it "suddenly heartbreaking" (paragraph 5) to hear his parents speaking English?
6. What does Rodriguez mean when he says that he finally felt that he "belonged in public" (paragraph 6)?

Making Judgments and Thinking Critically

1. Does Rodriguez successfully re-create the child's view and feelings of home and school? Why or why not?

2. Is Rodriguez's early response in the classroom typical or unusual? What other kind of responses might he have had?
3. What other reasons are children (or adults) silent in classrooms? How do you know?
4. Was his parents' decision to speak English in their home an easy or difficult decision? Why do you think so?
5. Is this an emotional essay? Explain.
6. Supporters of bilingual education believe that children should be taught in their native languages and learn English as they progress in school. Opponents of bilingual education, including Rodriguez, believe that non-English–speaking children should be taught in English and given extra help. If you are a bilingual person or have experience that gives you special insight into this controversy, are you for or against bilingual education? Why?

Using New Words

1. Choose three words from this essay to add to your writing and speaking vocabulary. Make vocabulary cards for them.
2. Review all your vocabulary words, include their spelling, to prepare for a team competition.

   Preparation: (a) Students form teams of five (or six) and sit together. (b) Each student shuffles his or her set of vocabulary cards, word side up, and places the shuffled set in front of him or her. (c) A member of an opposing team draws any five cards from each set and places them in front of the owner of the cards. The owners of the cards put their unused cards away. (d) A scorekeeper keeps score on the board, giving each team 5 points for each correct definition and 5 points for each correct spelling.

   The play: Round 1: The teacher moves from team to team, asking one student from each team one vocabulary word from his or her stack of five. Round 2: The teacher begins with another team and moves through the teams again, asking another student on each team one card from his or her stack of cards. Rounds 3, 4, and 5: The teacher repeats the questioning until all students have had a turn. (If some teams have six students, the teacher makes a sixth round, asking one student from each team of five a sixth word.)

   Scoring: The scorekeeper totals the team scores and declares the first-, second-, and third-place teams.
3. The prefix *in-* can mean ''in'' or ''on''; it can also mean ''not.''What is the meaning of *in-* in *intrinsically, incongruity,* and *inevitable*?

4. What are the five nouns in the vocabulary list from the reading selection?
5. Give antonyms for the following words: *tact, profound, complied.*

Responding by Writing

1. Write an essay about a decision you have made that led to a dramatic change in your attitude or behavior in some way. Write about the causes and effects, as Rodriguez did. Write for an audience of those in this class who also choose to write about this topic. Your responses to Thinking Before Reading and Jotting Down Your First Responses may help you begin.
2. If you have ever tried to learn a foreign language, write an essay describing this experience. Include information about the process, your progress speaking the language, and your feelings. Give specific examples. Write to those in your class who have never tried to learn another language so they can understand more about Rodriguez's experience.
3. If you have ever been an outsider in some situation—in a foreign country, a new neighborhood, at work—write an essay in which you describe this experience. Rodriguez emphasized his family's intimacy and isolation. Decide what you want to emphasize and write a thesis. Include only incidents and details that support your thesis. Write for your school newspaper, which is running a series on building community in your college.
4. Both Rodriguez and Rosa Mathe in ''Carbon Copy'' (Chapter 10) make a strong case for the connection between language and sense of identity. Since you are in this class to learn academic thinking, reading, writing, and vocabulary, one might make a case that you, too, may be changing your identity and relationships. Will your new language skills change you? In what ways? Write an essay in which you answer these questions to an audience of your teacher. Refer to Rodriguez and Mathe and the titles of their essays. Use at least one quotation from one of these essays.

When Television Ate My Best Friend

Linda Ellerbee

Linda Ellerbee, NBC news correspondent and writer, has been a disc jockey, newscaster, program director, and co-anchor of a daily news magazine. The following essay is from her book *Move On: Adventures in the Real World.*

Thinking Before Reading

What games or activities do you recall from your childhood? What adventures did you enact or imagine? Write a few sentences about your childhood games in your Idea Bank.

Expanding Your Vocabulary from Reading

worldclass (1) one of the best in the world
pumping (10) moving arms, legs, and body repeatedly in such a way as to cause a swing to move
irresistible (11) impossible to resist, having an overwhelming appeal
meander (14) wandering path
lollygag (14) to waste time
sashayed (15) walked with a sassy spirit, walked as though making a sliding dance step
bewitched (24) fascinated, as if under a magic spell
flickering (24) fluttering

1 I was eight years old when I lost my best friend. My *very first* very best friend. Lucy hardly ever whined, even when we kids played cowboys and she had to be Dale Evans. Nor did she cry, even when we played dodge ball and some big kid threw the ball so hard you could read *Spalding* backward on her legs. Lucy was worldclass.

2 Much of our time together was spent in my back yard on the perfect swing set: high, wide, built solid and grounded for life. But one June day long ago, something went wrong. I was swinging as high as I could, and still higher. The next time the swing started to come back down, I didn't. I just kept going up. And up.

3 Then I began to fall.

4 "Know what? Know what?" Lucy was yelling at me.

5 No, I didn't know *what.* All I knew was that my left arm hurt.

6 "Know what? For a minute there, you flew. You seemed to catch the wind and . . . soar! Right up until you must have done something wrong, because you fell."

7 Wearing a cast on my broken arm gave me time to work out the scientifics with Lucy. Our Theory was that if you swing just high enough and straight enough, and you jump out of the swing at just the right moment and in just the right position—*you just might fly.*

8 July was spent waiting for my arm to heal. We ran our hands across the wooden seat, feeling for the odd splinter that could ruin your perfect takeoff. We pulled on the chains, testing for weak links.

9 Finally came the day in August when my cast was off, and Lucy and I were ready. Today we would fly.

10 Early that morning, we began taking turns—one pushing, one pumping. All day we pushed and pumped, higher and higher, ever so close. It was almost dark when Lucy's mother hollered for her to come home right this minute and see what her daddy had brought them.

11 This was strictly against the rules. Nobody had to go home in August until it was altogether dark. Besides, Lucy's daddy wasn't a man to be struck with irresistible impulses like stopping at the horse store and thinking, *Golly, my little girl loves ponies! I better get her one!*

12 So we kept on swinging, and Lucy pretended not to hear her mother—until she dropped *Lucee* to *Lucille Louise.* Halfway through the fourth *Lucille Louise,* Lucy slowly raised her head as though straining to hear some woman calling from the next county.

13 "Were you calling me, Mother? Okay, okay, I'm coming. Yes, ma'am. *Right now.*"

14 Lucy and I walked together to the end of my driveway. Once in her front yard, she slowed to something between a meander and a lollygag, choosing a path that took her straight through the sprinklers. Twice.

15 When at last Lucy sashayed to her front door, she turned back to me and, with a grin, gave me the thumbs-up sign used by pilots everywhere. *Awright.* So we'd fly tomorrow instead. We'd waited all summer. We could wait one more day. On her way in the house, she slammed the screen door.

16 *Bang!*

17 In my memory, I've listened to that screen door shut behind my best friend a thousand times. It was the last time I played with her.

18 I knocked on the door every day, but her mother always answered saying Lucy was busy and couldn't come out to play. I tried calling, but her mother always answered saying Lucy was busy and couldn't come to the phone. Lucy was busy? Too busy to play? Too busy to fly? She had to be dead. Nothing else made sense. What, short of death, could separate such best friends? We were going to fly. Her thumb had said so. I cried and cried.

19 I might never have known the truth of the matter, if some weeks later I hadn't overheard my mother say to my father how maybe I would calm down about Lucy if we got a television too.

20 A what? What on earth was a *television?* The word was new to me, but I was clever enough to figure out that Lucy's daddy had brought home a television that night. At last I knew what had happened to Lucy. The television ate her.

21 It must have been a terrible thing to see. Now my parents were thinking of getting one. I was scared. They didn't understand what television could do.

22 "Television eats people," I announced to my parents.

23 "Oh, Linda Jane," they said, laughing. "Television doesn't eat people. You'll love television just like Lucy. She's inside her house watching it right this minute."

24 Indeed, Lucy was totally bewitched by the flickering black and white shapes. Every afternoon following school, she'd sit in her living room and watch whatever there was to watch. Saturday mornings, she'd look at cartoons.

25 Autumn came. Around Thanksgiving, I played an ear of corn in the school pageant. Long division ruined most of December. After a while, I forgot about flying. But I did not forget about Lucy.

26 Christmas arrived, and Santa Claus brought us a television. "See?" my parents said. "Television doesn't eat people." Maybe not. But television changes people. It changed my family forever.

27 We stopped eating dinner at the dining-room table after my mother found out about TV trays. Dinner was served in time for one program and finished in time for another. During the meal we used to talk to one another. Now television talked to us. If you absolutely had to say something, you waited until the commercial, which is, I suspect, where I learned to speak in 30-second bursts.

28 Before television, I would lie in bed at night, listening to my parents in their room saying things I couldn't comprehend. Their voices alone rocked me to sleep. Now Daddy went to bed right after the weather, and Mama stayed up to see Jack Paar. I went to sleep listening to voices in my memory.

29 Daddy stopped buying Perry Mason books. Perry was on television now, and that was so much easier for him. But it had been Daddy and Perry who'd taught me how fine it can be to read something you like.

30 Mama and Daddy stopped going to movies. Most movies would one day show up on TV, he said.

31 After a while, Daddy and I didn't play baseball anymore. We didn't go to ball games either, but we watched more baseball than ever. That's how Daddy perfected The Art of Dozing to Baseball. He would sit in his big chair, turn on the game and fall asleep within minutes. At least he appeared to be asleep. His eyes were shut, and he snored. But if you shook him, he'd open his eyes and tell you what the score was, who was up and what the pitcher ought to throw next.

32 It seemed everybody liked to watch television more than I did. I had no interest in sitting still when I could be climbing trees or riding a bike or practicing my takeoffs just in case one day Lucy woke up and remembered we had a Theory. Maybe the TV hadn't actually eaten her, but once her parents pointed her in the direction of that box, she never looked back.

33 Lucy had no other interests when she would go home and turn on "My Friend Flicka." Maybe it was because that was as close as she would get to having her own pony. Maybe if her parents had allowed her a real world to stretch out in, she wouldn't have been satisfied with a 19-inch world.

34 All I know is I never had another first best friend. I never learned to fly either. What's more, I was right all along: television really does eat people.

Jotting Down Your First Responses

1. What childhood schemes—to run away, to make money, to build a fort—did you recall as you read Ellerbee's essay?
2. Did you enjoy the essay? If not, why not? If so, what about the content did you enjoy? What did you enjoy about the writing itself?
3. If you (or your children) had a best friend in childhood, who was it and what was that friendship like?

Checking Your Comprehension

1. How old was the narrator when the events took place?
2. Who was her best friend?
3. What was their favorite pastime?
4. How did an accident occur?
5. What was their theory? Their goal?
6. What event stopped the test of their theory and changed their relationship?
7. How did Lucy change suddenly?
8. When Ellerbee heard that her family might purchase a television, what was her reaction?
9. What were five effects of television on Ellerbee's family?

Understanding a Writer's Patterns

1. What point of view does the second sentence reveal that the opening narrative will be told from—an adult's or a child's? How do you know?
2. What paragraphs make up the opening narrative?
3. How does Ellerbee let the reader know the time span of the narrative?
4. What gesture does Lucy make before her entry into her house? Why is it a dramatic and appropriate gesture?
5. What kinetic and auditory (the senses of movement and sound) details does Ellerbee use to dramatize the sudden end of the girls' relationship? How does the writer emphasize these details?
6. How did time pass for the writer once summer ended and how does she create this feeling? (paragraphs 26, 27)
7. What sentence in paragraph 26 is the thesis of the essay?
8. Without transitional words, how does Ellerbee signal each new effect that she lists?
9. What repetitions does the writer use in the conclusion (paragraphs 32 through 34) to create closure?

Making Predictions and Drawing Inferences

1. Why is *Spalding* printed backward (paragraph 1)? Is this a literal or exaggerated incident?
2. What is a scientific theory? Why is ''Theory'' (paragraph 7) capitalized?
3. What does ''rules'' mean in paragraph 11?
4. What does the slammed screen door symbolize?
5. How did her thumb ''say'' (paragraph 18) they were going to fly?
6. Why are some words in italics in paragraphs 11 through 16?
7. What is ''My Friend Flicka'' (paragraph 33)? What is it about?

Making Judgments and Thinking Critically

1. A paragraph in a sociology or history textbook might explain more briefly than this essay the effects of television on people's lives. Which type of explaining do you like better? Which do you learn more from? Why?
2. What parts of the essay are written from a child's point of view? What parts are written from an adult's point of view?
3. Why does the writer use two points of view? Is the dual point of view a successful strategy?
4. Why does the child Ellerbee think that television has eaten Lucy?

Using New Words

1. Add three words to your set of vocabulary cards. Make the cards as you have been doing.
2. What synonyms does Ellerbee use for Lucy's walk in paragraphs 14 and 15? What is gained by using these synonyms?
3. The prefix *tele-* means ''distant, far off.'' Explain the words *telecommunication, telecast, telegram, telescope, telepathy, telephone,* and *telephoto.*
4. Form a new word by adding a different prefix to the root of each word in question 3, for example, *metacommunication,* and give the meaning for each.

Responding by Writing

1. Write an essay about a technological invention created during your lifetime that has changed life for you. Write to an audience of this class. As Ellerbee's essay made clear her sense of loss, your essay should make clear the effect of this invention on your life and your feelings about this change. Use narration and description in your essay.

2. All agree that television has had a profound effect on all aspects of life. Some effects have been positive; some have been negative. Do you think the main impact of television has been positive or negative? Write an essay about your opinion to an audience of this class. Use examples in several areas of life; use some examples of its effects on you.
3. "Maybe if her parents had allowed her a real world to stretch out in, she wouldn't have been satisfied with a 19-inch world," writes Ellerbee. Do you agree or disagree that television limits people? If so, whom does it limit? Under what conditions? How does it limit them?

   Write an essay explaining your point of view to classmates. Use the quotation in the essay. State the name of the writer and the title of the essay. Explain the quotation as fully as you can. Your teacher may compile class essays into an anthology as a study about the effects of television.
4. Write an essay to an audience of your teacher about the different ways to develop an essay that Ellerbee used. You have studied using examples, narration, process analysis, division and classification, comparison and contrast, definition, and cause and effect. Which of these did she use and why? Use quotations, the writer's name, and the title of the essay.

My Public Address

Chrissy Poelman

A champion artistic roller skater and honor student in high school, Chrissy Poelman is now majoring in developmental psychology because she wants to help abused children. She wrote the following essay to students younger than she who also struggle with the fear of speaking in public.

Thinking Before Reading

How do you feel when you have to make a speech, ask a question, or make an announcement before a class or other group? Write a few sentences in your Idea Bank about your feelings about speaking in public or about writing for college classes.

Expanding Your Vocabulary from Reading

strutted (1) swaggered, showed off
flickered (1) fluttered
psyched up (5) mentally prepared
sanctuary (7) refuge; safe, protected place

petrified (7) paralyzed with fear
rehearsing (10) repeating for practice
distractions (10) things that divert one's attention
receptive (13) willing to receive or accept

1 She stood before the class in her favorite outfit. A nice white lace-trimmed blouse was neatly tucked into a short black skirt tastefully decorated with red and yellow tulips. She wore white socks with a lace ruffle to balance the lace on the blouse. Her feet proudly strutted a pair of black patent leather shoes. Her brown hair was waist length and the shorter bangs fell just above her eyebrows. She had dressed for the coming occasion, yet fear still flickered in her dark brown six-year-old eyes.

2 Her knees weakened, her hands were shaking, her stomach was in knots, and she could not remember anything. She thought she was going to cry.

3 This was my first experience with public speaking. Actually, I just had to say a three-line poem in front of my first grade class. I will never forget that day. I was a nervous wreck.

4 Eight years later that same little girl with the frightened eyes stood before her freshman English class.

5 That year of high school we were required to do a research paper, free to choose our own topic, free to approach our topic in any manner we saw fit. Who could ask for a better assignment? The only catch was reading our final copy to the class. How could Mrs. Hodges put us through such torture? I had psyched myself up for two weeks. I was going to deliver a nerve-free, flawless presentation. Who was I fooling?

6 The day came and once again, the same weak knees, the same shaky hands. I just knew I was going to be sick.

7 It was my turn, and I felt the frightened little six-year-old inside of me rising from the sanctuary of her desk and tip-toe to the front of the room. As I turned around, my breathing became unsteady and my eyes grew larger as they washed over thirty classmates, all looking intently at me, all waiting for me to begin speaking. I felt like disappearing. Maybe the wall would swallow me up. I could only pray for a firedrill. Better yet, maybe Mrs. Hodges would see how petrified I was and not make me go through with this. No such luck.

8 I began the presentation with a forced smile. The first few sentences went smoothly, but then I began talking more swiftly and more softly. My classmates in the back repeatedly asked me to slow down or speak up. I felt like an idiot, and by the time I finished, I had a knot in my throat and something in my eye. That ten-minute presentation must have lasted ten hours. Something had to change!

9 I could not stand it anymore! I was not shy. My friends probably thought I did not know how to be quiet. My presentations were always good and prepared, and yet speaking in front of people was a living nightmare. Some-

where inside of me that shy little girl snapped and decided to take control of her situation.

10 I began rehearsing presentations the night before, walking through all possible distractions and mistakes until I had a clever way to deal with everything. Nothing would make me "lose my cool" again. The morning before a presentation I would run through it in front of a mirror to make sure I was portraying confidence and making eye contact with the audience. I also began to change my thinking. Instead of telling myself, "Nobody wants to hear this," I began thinking to myself, "I am the person they asked to speak, so of course they want to hear me."

11 By this time my public speaking was no longer limited to classroom presentations. I was now giving lectures on the style and technique of competitive roller figure skating. If it had not been for that frightened girl within me attempting to solve her problem with public speaking, I would have missed out on several wonderful opportunities to share my knowledge with others.

12 After only a short period of time the butterflies had completely vanished, my hands no longer shook uncontrollably, my breathing even became more natural, and I was able to remember my lectures. I no longer find myself desperately searching for a "witty" remark weeks in advance, but find it very easy to come up with one "on the spot." In contrast to how quiet my voice used to be when asked to speak, I now find it very easy to project my voice clearly without the aid of a microphone and often prefer not to use one.

13 Through determination and extensive practice, a terrified first grader learned to conquer a fear she thought would plague her the rest of her life. My presentations and lectures are one hundred percent more effective now that I am confident with my speaking abilities. The key to interacting with any audience is to maintain a relaxed frame of mind. The more relaxed and confident a speaker becomes, the more relaxed and receptive the audience will become. If a speaker is not comfortable with the audience, the audience will not feel comfortable with the speaker.

Jotting Down Your First Responses

1. Did Poelman's fear seem real to you?
2. Was her solution convincing?
3. What fear or other problem of yours did you recall as you read this essay?
4. What, if anything, would you like to ask Poelman to clarify or tell more about?

Checking Your Comprehension

1. What was Poelman's first experience with public speaking? When was it?

2. What was her second experience with public speaking? When was it?
3. When did Poelman decide to do something about her problem?
4. What are four things Poelman did to overcome her fear of public speaking?
5. What speeches did Poelman frequently make?
6. What are six effects of her solutions to the problem?
7. What effect does a speaker's confidence have on audiences?

Understanding a Writer's Patterns

1. What strategy does Poelman use in the introduction?
2. How does Poelman establish the seriousness of the problem for the reader?
3. How does Poelman show her mental state?
4. How does the "frightened little six-year-old inside" work in the essay? Why does Poelman use that image repeatedly in paragraphs 4, 7, 9, 11, and 13?
5. In the concluding paragraph the first three sentences are in the first person—her experience. What shift takes place in the last three sentences?

Making Predictions and Drawing Inferences

1. From reading this essay, what can you tell about Poelman's character? What kind of person is she?
2. Did Poelman forget her poem?
3. How can a ten-minute presentation take ten hours? Is this literal or figurative language?

Making Judgments and Thinking Critically

1. Identify the problem, solutions, and effects in this cause and effect essay from the following: (a) confident feelings and behavior in public speaking situations, (b) fearful responses in public speaking situations, (c) intense preparations to speak.
2. Break the essay into the three parts: problem, solutions, effects. Which paragraphs are in each part?
3. Which part is most developed? Why?
4. There are several one-sentence paragraphs in this essay. Which paragraphs could be combined to improve paragraphing?

Using New Words

1. Add three words to your set of vocabulary cards. Write each word on one side of a card and a definition and an original sentence on the other side.

2. Replace *sanctuary* (paragraph 7) with *safety* and *they washed over* (paragraph 7) with *I looked at.* How do these substitutions change the passage?
3. Practice with the commonly confused words *loose* and *lose.* These words rhyme with *loose*: moose, caboose, goose, noose. Say the words aloud, exaggerating the *oo* sound. Now write *lose* has lost an *o*; sing *lose* has lost an *o*. Silly actions and laughter can help you learn these words.

Responding by Writing

1. Write an essay to an audience of this class about a problem, such as Poelman's fear of public speaking, and your solutions to it. Describe the problem fully so that a reader is convinced of the weight of the problem. The emphasis may be on the causes and nature of the problem or the solutions and effects. Here are other examples to help remind you of problems you have solved.

   Fears: of getting hit in contact sports, of asking for dates, of going to the dentist, of taking tests
   Money: keeping a budget, overusing credit cards, money squabbles with a mate, saving money
   Habits: procrastinating, being late, substance abuse
   Work: handling a difficult boss or coworker, summer or after-school jobs, finding a new career
   Family: settling fights between kids, dinnertime uproar, sharing household chores, neatness versus sloppiness, keeping romance alive, discipline for different ages
   College: teacher or student apathy, freedom of speech, registration, required advisement before registration or another policy
   Local problems: voter apathy among students, community and police relations, violence in the schools, self-interest versus community concern

2. Causal analysis doesn't apply only to problems and bad situations. One can also analyze the causes and effects of good situations, events, or conditions in order to give credit to those who are responsible or to repeat the successful experience. Write an essay in which you analyze the causes and effects of a good situation, event, or condition. Choose and describe an audience who needs to hear what you have to say.
3. Write an essay in which you compare and contrast "How To Relax in a Crowd" (pages 160–163) and "My Public Address" for an audience of your teacher. Both essays are about the fear of public speaking and the solutions of the writers. Here are some points you might compare and

contrast: the writers' purposes, their audiences, their use of personal experience, their use of dialogue, their types of development (using description, examples, process analysis, division and classification, comparison and contrast, definition, and cause and effect analysis).

Use quotations from both essays. Include the titles of the essays in quotation marks and the full names of the writers. After the first reference to the name, you may use the last name only.

CHAPTER 13

ARGUMENTATION

RECOGNIZING ARGUMENTATION IN DAILY LIFE

When you take a position about an issue and try to convince an audience to agree with you or, at least, to understand your position and your reasoning, you are making an argument. Argumentation is not arguing in the sense of fighting. Although it usually arises out of opinions you hold strongly, it does not seek to make others angry or feel bad. An argument is not a rant in which you dump all your feelings on other people or overwhelm them with your anger. It is not propaganda, like advertising, which seeks to influence through exploiting common needs and emotions, such as popularity, sex appeal, or fear. So argument, as a technical term, does not mean intimidating, browbeating, or manipulating others with the power of emotions. Argumentation seeks to influence the opinion or action of others through logic and evidence, not emotions and power.

In all human relationships and public institutions, including those of business, religion, and education, people will always differ about what to value most, what rules to abide by, and what actions to take. Differences are natural and inevitable. Because violence or withdrawal is the only alternative to using words to create agreement, argumentation is an important kind of communication. In order to have community, we must seek agreement, not by overpowering each other emotionally or physically, politically or economically, not by turning our backs on the problem, but by persuading each other with words. Even children can be taught to use their words, not their fists or their sticks. Perhaps to address the problem of violence in our country, we adults need to learn to use words to settle our differences and find common ground.

(In this paragraph I have just made an argument for the importance of argumentation.)

Besides occurring in relationships and institutions, argumentation often appears in the media. Editorials and columns called "Viewpoints" or "My View" or "Here I Stand" are argumentation. Some television and radio pieces, especially those accompanied by the disclaimer that the opinions of the speaker are not necessarily those of the station, are argumentation. Even comedy, such as the satiric skits on *Saturday Night Live,* is argumentation. Satire has an implied thesis that something should or should not be.

WRITING AN ARGUMENTATIVE ESSAY

You have probably already written some argumentative essays during this course, and you will notice that some of the examples in this lesson are drawn from other chapters in this book. So argument is not entirely new to you. The main difference between argumentative essays and other essays is purpose. The purpose of many essays is *to inform or to entertain* an audience or *to express* the writer's feelings and experience. However, the primary purpose of the argumentative essay is *to convince* the audience of the thesis. Because the purpose in argumentation is to convince the audience to believe or do something that they are not now believing or doing, the writer must pay more attention to the needs, concerns, and values of the audience than in essays to express, entertain, or inform.

Test Your Argumentative Thesis. A strong argument has a single, clear thesis, although sometimes it is implied. If your audience isn't sure what position you are taking on an issue, you can't influence them to your point of view. The words *should, must,* and *ought* often indicate an opinion or belief. When you write an argumentative essay, the main point you want to make is an opinion or claim (you believe and claim that something is true).

Although most of us have opinions about everything—about music, movies, which highway to take, what doctor to use—most of these opinions will not work as thesis statements for argumentation because they are generalities, statements of facts, or they are personal preferences. Here are some tests your thesis for an argumentative essay should pass:

1. The thesis is worth taking a stand about. It's not trivial or obvious.
   No There are many movies about friendships.
2. It requires evidence and support because some people disagree with it.
   No Friendship is important.
3. It is not just personal preference.
   No You'll love the movie *Thelma and Louise,* which is about the friendship of two women.

4. It is not a fact, not something that can be verified in a record book.
   No Movies about men's friendships earn more money than movies about women's friendships.
5. It is specific enough that you can make a good case for it. (Statements with words such as *always* and *never* are too broad to support.)
   No Women always have close friendships, but men seldom do.

Here is the argumentative thesis of Ellen Goodman's "The Tapestry of Friendship" which passes all the tests:

> **Yes** Movies about friendships reflect a shift of the definition of friendship from buddies to intimates.

Focus on the Concerns and Knowledge of an Appropriate Audience.

The audience of an argumentative essay is readers who disagree with you or who haven't formed an opinion about the subject yet. There's no point arguing a position with those who already agree with you, although you may be more comfortable talking about controversial subjects with like-minded people. Since your purpose is to sway the opinion of others, or at least to convince them that you have a reasonable position, you must know your audience well.

For instance, as the manager of a store, you try to convince employees, who are about your age, that they can and should help cut down on shoplifting. If you can tie reduced losses to increased wages, you'll get some changes. They'll be more likely to follow store policies about the number of items in the dressing rooms and to watch shoppers with bags or big coats. If you tell them how you confronted a suspected shoplifter and what you said, your example will give weight to your argument. It's important to tailor your argument to a specific audience.

If you know your audience well, you should be able to anticipate their objections to your claim (thesis) and evidence. In the example about shoplifting, a teenage employee might say to the manager, "I can't say anything to that shopper. She looks like my mom." Or, "I know those guys from school. They'll think I'm a nerd." Or, "They're just little kids." You have to anticipate these objections and solve the problems they represent. If your evidence and logic do not address your audience's concerns, they may say "Yes, I agree, but I can't . . ." and nothing will change. In addressing the audience's objections, you don't have to give equal time to an opposing side of an argument. The argumentative essay is not a debate in which you present opposing sides of an issue and let the audience decide what they believe. You have decided what you believe (your thesis) and are seeking to convince the audience of that viewpoint.

To focus on your audience, make an audience profile before you write an argument. Answer the following questions in writing. The profile of the store manager's audience is given (in italics) as an example.

Thesis: Employees should help reduce shoplifting.

What common ground (shared values, beliefs, and interests) do we have in relation to this issue?

Shoplifting reduces store profits. Increased profits are tied to increased wages. Shoplifting is wrong. This is a good store with good products.

What beliefs or concerns does the audience have about this issue?

Shoplifting isn't a big deal. It doesn't concern me. It's not my store. Preventing shoplifting and confronting shoplifters aren't my job. I'm in sales.

What objections or disagreements with the thesis or my beliefs and concerns about this issue will the audience have?

I'm not responsible for customer actions. I can't confront friends or adults like my parents. I don't know what to say.

As you develop your argument, you must decide what kind of evidence and support will have weight with the specific audience. Remember that you are not manipulating them by making them feel guilty, fearful, obliged, angry, or fired up emotionally. You are appealing to their reason with logic and the weight of evidence. As a writer, you must decide what evidence supports your thesis, what evidence will be effective with your intended audience, and how much evidence is needed to convince the audience.

Tailor Evidence to the Argumentative Thesis. Although argumentation provides support for an opinion or belief, that support is evidence, not proof. You cannot *prove* very much in this world. Two renters claim a landlord owes them their deposit. The landlord denies it. The renters and the landlord offer evidence (logical statements and reasons) and supporting information, witnesses, and records to support their evidence. Both sides are convinced of the truth of their positions, and there is probably truth on both sides. However, the jury must decide which side has the most convincing evidence and support for their position.

In an argumentative essay your reader is both the opposing side and the jury. You must give enough evidence and support to convince a reader of your argumentative thesis. Evidence includes statements and reasons arranged in a logical sequence that supports the argumentative thesis. For instance, in "The Tapestry of Friendship" Goodman develops her argument with this evidence:

Recent movies about friendship have been about female friendships.

Earlier movies about friendship were about male friendships.

Men are buddies; they do things together.

Women are friends; they love each other.

Therefore, recent movies about friendship show a change in the definition of friendship.

This evidence is clearly connected to and supports the thesis: Movies about friendships reflect a shift of the definition of friendship from buddies to intimates. However, each statement presented as evidence needs development.

Develop Evidence With Adequate and Appropriate Support. Goodman develops the evidence in her argument through examples, definition by contrasts of male and female friendship behaviors, and personal experience. Here are examples of her support.

Examples of movies about female friendship: Julia, The Turning Point, Girlfriends

Definition by contrasts: Men share activities; women share confidences.

Personal experience: A friend once telephoned her lover, just to find out if he were home. She hung up without a hello when he picked up the phone . . .

Because students tend to underexplain the evidence they present in an argument, study the following examples of ways to develop the reasons or supporting statements (evidence) of your argument.

Definition of important terms:

"When you take a position about an issue and try to convince an audience to agree with you or, at least, to understand your position and your reasoning, you are making an argument. Argumentation i not . . ." (paragraph 1 in this chapter)

Verifiable facts:

"Thirty-six years ago, on a bus in Montgomery, Ala., Rosa Parks refused to give up her seat to a white man, defying a Southern tradition of decades." (" 'I Wanted To Be Treated Like a Human Being' ")

Examples, including personal experience:

"Recently I was invited to lecture on anxiety to several hundred mental-health professionals in Boston. My talk was scheduled to follow those of a number of prominent psychiatrists. When my turn came, I was especially nervous because the speaker before me had been particularly impressive and charming." ("How To Relax in a Crowd")

Recognized authority on the subject:

"While affiliated with Penn State University, psychologist Michael J. Mahoney and gymnastics coach Marshall Avener investigated the impact of anxiety on gymnasts at the 1976 U.S. Olympic Team trials." ("How To Relax in a Crowd")

Quotations, especially from an authority:

Frank Smith, author of fifteen books on language and learning, describes learning as "continuous, spontaneous, and effortless, requiring no particular attention, conscious motivation, or specific reinforcements.''

Statistics:

``A 1984 National Institute of Mental Health (NIMH) survey estimated that two to four million Americans are handicapped by social phobias in their personal and professional lives.'' (``How To Relax in a Crowd'')

The examples above are only models of the kinds of support you might use to support evidence. However, they are not support as presented here because there's nothing for them to support. In argument isolated, free-floating facts and information are not support. These things may be support if they are logically and clearly connected to a piece of evidence.

In addition to these kinds of support for the evidence in an argument, you may use any one or several of the methods for developing an essay that you have studied in this book. For instance, in ``How To Relax in a Crowd'' David Burns argues (by exemplification and process analysis) that people who have a fear of speaking in public can develop confidence in stressful situations. In ``The Rewards of Living a Solitary Life'' May Sarton argues (by definition) that a solitary life is rewarding. In ``Do You Know Who Your Friends Are?'' Larry Letich argues (by cause and effect) that our culture discourages men's friendships. In ``Other Cultures, Other Times'' Ann McGee-Cooper argues (by comparison and contrast) that our culture is locked into a narrow view of time that creates problems.

REMINDER

An argumentative essay must have an argumentative thesis (a claim or position about a subject).

The argumentative thesis must be supported by evidence (reasons or supporting statements arranged in a logical way).

Evidence must have adequate and appropriate support, such as definition of important terms; verifiable facts; examples, including personal experience; quotations from recognized authorities on the subject; and statistics.

ORGANIZING AN ARGUMENTATIVE ESSAY

The placement of the thesis is particularly important in argument. Usually the thesis is near the beginning of the essay because readers become impatient if the main point is not clear early in the essay. If they quit reading in irritation or for lack of interest, you can't convince them of your thesis. Sometimes, however, the thesis is in the conclusion of the argument for dramatic impact.

The writer may create tension in the essay and lead up to the thesis. Like attorneys arguing a courtroom case, most writers of complex arguments state their thesis in the introduction and again in the conclusion for emphasis. In short arguments this repetition is not necessary. The most important issue about the thesis is that it is clearly stated so the audience knows what it is that you want them to agree with or do.

If you find that the main method of developing your argumentative essay is definition, process analysis, comparison and contrast, or causal analysis, you can apply what you learned about organizing when you studied those kinds of development.

Provide Clear and Obvious Connections. Since an effective argument must communicate sound reasoning, both organization and connections are particularly important. Some writers can outline a clear and complete argument before they begin writing, but others actually think by writing. No matter which kind of writer you are, you should make sure your argument is logically organized.

To check the organization of an argument, make an outline of your draft. Concentrate on how each paragraph relates to the thesis. Is there a clearly stated relationship? Is the order logical and does it meet the needs of the audience? At this point you may uncover a problem. The evidence may not fit the thesis, or an important piece of evidence needed to build a logical case may be missing, or the connections between sentences or the elements of the argument may be weak or missing.

The connections of the evidence to the argumentative thesis and the relationship of each piece of evidence to others should be logical and obvious. Also the connection of the supporting information to the evidence must be logical and obvious. As in other clear writing, sentences and parts of the essay should be coherent. Here are some of the transitions and strategies for coherence you have studied:

Transitional words that show organization by time, space, or importance: *first, next, after, before, meanwhile, immediately, finally*
Clear signals for examples: *an instance, one time, for example*
Repetitions of key word and phrases
Careful pronoun use so that pronouns refer clearly to the nouns or pronouns they are substitutes for
Parallelism to show ideas or information of similar importance

Students tend to think the audience can grasp the importance and connection of the evidence to the thesis or of support to evidence just because they can. If you discover missing connections in your draft, revise to include connections, and transitions that will make your argument coherent.

POINTS TO REMEMBER ABOUT ARGUMENTATION

Write a thesis that is a clear statement of an opinion or claim that needs evidence.
Address a disbelieving audience, not one that already agrees with you.
Focus on the beliefs, values, and interests of a specific audience to develop your argument.
Tailor the evidence to the thesis and a specific audience.
Provide obvious connections of the evidence to the thesis.
Provide adequate and appropriate support for each piece of evidence with clear connections to the evidence.
Use transition words, clear pronoun reference, repetition, and parallelism to create coherence.

The Case for Offensive Humor

David Segal

David Segal's work has appeared in *The New Republic, The Washington Post, The Wall Street Journal* and *The Utne Reader.* He formerly was speechwriter for Israel's ambassador to the United States and presently is an editor of *The Washington Monthly.* He is, however, happiest when singing and playing rhythm guitar for The Bremmers, a D.C.-based rock and blues band.

Thinking Before Reading

What kinds of humor make you laugh? What kinds of humor offend you? Write a few sentences in your Idea Bank.

Expanding Your Vocabulary from Reading

minyan (1) the number of adult Jews—ten—required in order to conduct a communal ceremony
gratuitous (1) unearned, unnecessary
***mazel-tov* (1)** word from Hebrew meaning congratulations
constituency (2) supporters, people served by an institution
pundits (2) learned persons
lament (2) express grief for, mourn
risqué (3) off-color, suggestive
tics (4) repeated behaviors

disarming (4) overcoming the suspicion of
stymie (4) block, stand in the way of
anti-Semitism (4) prejudice against Jews
vigilance (4) watchfulness
lampoon (5) a satiric piece that ridicules
foils (5) thwarts, prevents from being successful
disdain (5) a feeling of contempt or scorn
perpetrate (5) bring about, commit (as a crime)
euphemisms (5) acceptable substitutions for offensive words
bereft (7) deprived of, lacking something wanted or needed
lucrative (8) profitable

1 It was inevitable that the chill of sensitivity now felt in public discourse and academic life would eventually come to comedy. But politically correct humor has arrived more swiftly—and completely—than even ardent activists could have hoped. Take two films written and directed by David and Jerry Zucker and Jim Abrahams. *Airplane,* released in 1980, has a slew of gay bits, two black men speaking indecipherable jive over subtitles, close to a minyan of Jewish jokes, drug gags, references to bestiality, nun jokes, five obscenities, and one gratuitous front shot of a naked woman. In *Naked Gun 2 1/2*, released in 1991, there were no obscenities, no frontal nudity, just two ethnic slurs, three tentative gay jokes, and one muttered "mazel-tov."

2 It's been a long slide downhill. Like the federal budget deficit, off-color humor touches everyone but has no constituency, and neither politicians nor pundits will be clamoring for its return anytime soon. But there are good reasons to lament its passing. Let me count the ways.

3 • *Risqué humor defuses tensions.* Lenny Bruce used to do a stand-up routine in which he'd gesture to each ethnic minority in the room and call them the most offensive names in the book: "I got a nigger here, two spics there . . ." When his audience was ready to assault him, he'd reveal his point: that epithets get at least part of their sting precisely by being placed off-limits. By spreading the abuse about, you take the sting out of it.

4 • *Risqué humor educates.* The experience of American Jews in this country may be the best example of how this works. For decades the capacity of Jewish comedians to poke fun at the peculiar tics of their people helped make Jewish otherness, a quality that aroused suspicion and hatred in bygone eras, something disarming. It's a safe bet that the films of Mel Brooks and Woody Allen did more to stymie anti-Semitism in the past 20 years than all the wide-eyed vigilance and arm-waving of the Anti-Defamation League. Gays have used humor the same way. You'd be hard-pressed to watch *La Cage Aux Folles,* a musical about a troupe of mincing gay entertainers, and have your homophobia strengthened.

5 • *Risqué humor disarms.* A classic—and rare—modern example is *In Living Color,* which showcases merciless skits about black culture. (The reason it survives the p.c. police is that it's largely written and acted by blacks.) Witness the show's *Star Trek* spoof, "The Wrath of Farrakhan," a vicious lampoon of the black Muslim leader; or a sketch making fun of West Indians' habits of hard work. One regular skit centers on "Handi Man," a caped, spastic superhero who foils villains with his dwarf sidekick. To believe this hardens prejudice against people with disabilities is to believe that people are fundamentally barbaric; and assuming the handicapped are too tender a subject for humor is more patronizing than outright disdain. Indeed, there may be no better way to perpetrate a myth of disabled otherness than coming up with euphemisms like "the differently abled" and making irreverent utterances off-limits.

6 • *Risqué humor undermines prejudices.* A black comic said he got so mad when a grocery clerk snickered about his purchase of frozen fried chicken that "I just grabbed my watermelon and tap-danced on out of there." The joke both played with stereotypes and ridiculed them: Sometimes the best offense is offense. Allowing ethnic humor means that blacks are allowed to make fun of whites (Eddie Murphy), gays are allowed to make fun of straights (Harvey Fierstein), and women are allowed to make fun of men (Roseanne Barr). In today's more ethnically and sexually diverse media, little of this opportunity for humor is being realized.

7 • *Risqué humor is funny.* Ethnic humor's final defense is that it makes people laugh. In a free society, this is an irrepressible—and admirable—activity, and one I suspect we did more of some years back. Ask yourself: Were you laughing harder a decade ago? In 1967 Mel Brooks won a best screenplay Academy Award for *The Producers,* which was full of Jewish, gay, and Nazi jokes and is now a confirmed classic. Brooks' 1991 offering was *Life Stinks,* which was bereft of anything off-color and was rightly panned by the critics.

8 As we've pushed the risqué off stage, we've brought violent slapstick back on as a means of keeping the audience's attention. Last year's *Home Alone,* the story of a little boy who fends off two burglars from his house by, among other things, dropping a hot iron on their heads, became the most lucrative comedy of movie history. The violence in it was far more explicit than anything the Three Stooges ever came up with. Compare this with *Animal House,* which used to be the top-grossing comedy; it was filled with sexist—and hilarious—moments, but few violent ones.

9 In a multicultural society like ours, humor is not a threat, it's a critical support. It keeps us sane, and it's a useful safety valve. If we can't be cruel about each other in jest, we might end up being cruel to each other in deadly seriousness. The politically correct war against insensitive humor might end up generating the very social and racial tension it is trying to defuse.

Jotting Down Your First Responses

1. Have any of the kinds of offensive humor Segal writes about ever offended you? What kinds did he leave out?
2. What movies, videos, songs, jokes, or other forms of entertainment that you have seen or heard have offended you? What entertainers?
3. Does violent slapstick or risqué humor have more potential for harm? For good? Explain.
4. Does Segal make a good case for offensive humor? Explain.
5. What does it mean to have a good sense of humor?

Checking Your Comprehension

1. According to Segal, in what three areas has the idea of political correctness (sensitivity to the feelings of specific groups) become important?
2. In the introduction what two films does Segal contrast in terms of sensitivity to the feelings of specific groups? What are the dates of those films?
3. What does Segal compare off-color humor with in paragraph 2? How are the two things alike?
4. What has happened to off-color humor?
5. Why does Segal regret the loss of offensive humor?
6. How does offensive humor diffuse tension?
7. In what way does offensive humor educate?
8. How does it disarm, rather than harden, viewers and listeners?
9. How does it undermine prejudice?
10. What kind of comedy has replaced risqué humor?

Understanding a Writer's Patterns

1. In the introduction what example of contrasts does Segal use as evidence that comedy has changed?
2. What is the thesis of the essay? (paragraph 2)
3. Who is Segal's intended audience? What is their probable attitude toward offensive humor?
4. What kind of evidence does Segal use to develop the thesis? How many supporting points are there?
5. What are four ways Segal helps the reader notice each of these pieces of evidence? (Use the Table of Contents of this book to review the ways to develop an essay.)
6. What forms of comedy does Segal use as examples of his five supporting points?
7. What group of words in paragraph 8 provides a transition from Segal's discussion of the value of offensive humor to his comment about its replacement with comedy of violence?

8. What contrast does Segal use in paragraph 8 to support his claim that comedy has gone from offensive to violent?
9. What opposing beliefs does Segal use to conclude his essay?
10. How does Segal overcome (explain away) the belief that is the opposite of his?

Making Predictions and Drawing Inferences

1. When you first read ''But there are good reasons to lament its passing. Let me count the ways'' (paragraph 2), did you predict Segal's method of development in this essay? When did you first recognize his pattern of development? What words in the quotation signal the pattern of development for you?
2. Is offensive humor in comedy thoughtful or thoughtless humor? Explain.
3. Is Segal sensitive to particular types of prejudice? If so, which? Why do you think so?
4. Do you think Segal is concerned about all prejudice or just particular types? Explain.
5. Does Segal think the shift from offensive to violent humor is a good or bad shift? Explain.

Making Judgments and Thinking Critically

1. Do you agree with Segal that ''By spreading the abuse about, you take the sting out'' (paragraph 3)? Why or why not?
2. Do you agree with Segal that comedy does more to educate people about prejudice (paragraph 4) than organizations that educate about prejudice?
3. How can a joke both use stereotyping and ridicule the prejudice of that stereotype (paragraph 6)?
4. Do you think the shift from offensive to violent humor is good or bad? Why?
5. Does Segal make a good case for offensive humor? Does he convince you? Why or why not?
6. If there a difference between a prejudicial joke told to friends and such jokes in comedy? Explain.

Using New Words

1. Choose three words from this essay you would like to add to your writing and speaking vocabulary. Make vocabulary cards for them. Write the word on one side of the card and a definition and an original sentence on the other side.

2. Give antonyms for *stymie, foil, disdain, lament,* and *vigilance.*
3. Substitute "without" for "bereft" in the last sentence of paragraph 7. What meaning is lost in the substitution?

Responding by Writing

1. Write an essay in which you make a case for something you believe is important or worthwhile that others believe is unimportant or of no value. Examples: the value of a defensive driving course, a case against organized sports for children in elementary school, the benefits of a meatless diet, the importance of recycling or other individual action for the environment, the need to report suspected child abuse. Write to an audience who does not agree with you.
2. Do you think prejudice about age, race, religion, or sex is a problem of your friends, your college, your religious group, or your community? If so, what might be some solutions? Write an argumentative essay in which you describe the problem, the degree to which it is a problem, and some solutions. Your audience is those who are not aware of the problem or who disagree that prejudice is a problem.
3. If you have been the subject of prejudice, write an essay in which you describe the prejudice and its effects on you. Use a specific incident (narration and description) as an example. Write to an audience of those who are unaware of or insensitive to this kind of prejudice and its effects.
4. Write an essay to your teacher in which you evaluate Segal's essay. Whether you agree or disagree with his thesis, decide if Segal has made a strong case for his belief. Did he change your mind in any way or make you think about prejudice or about comedy? Use at least one quotation from the essay. Include the title of the essay in quotation marks and the writer's full name the first time you use it.

A Hard Lesson in Smoking's Danger

Jean Warren

Jean Warren is a retired English teacher and a regular contributor to the *Big Spring (Texas) Herald.*

Thinking Before Reading

Life teaches us many lessons. Some of us have to learn some of them the hard way. What is one lesson you learned "the hard way"? How did you learn? Write about this lesson in your Idea Bank.

Expanding Your Vocabulary from Reading

shrugged aside (5) minimized the importance of
chronic (5) prolonged, constant
emphysema (8) condition of the lungs that results in labored breathing and susceptibility to infections
monumental (10) impressively large
respiratory (11) of or pertaining to breathing
sustained (12) supported, nourished
Herculean (13) tremendously difficult; resembling Hercules, the mythical Greek hero known for his strength
ominously (15) in a threatening way, with foreboding of evil
anguish (16) intense distress or pain
indulge (17) yield to desires or whims

1 Oregon is the first state to include smoking as a contributory factor on death certificates. A recent analysis revealed that almost a quarter of the deaths in that state in 1989 were smoking-related.

2 Smokers, weary of ding-donging on the evils of their addiction, may brush this report aside as one more scare tactic. I hope not. At least they have the opportunity to understand the dangers of smoking.

3 My husband grew up in an era when smoking was the norm, when all movie heroes smoked and thoughtfully lit cigarettes for their lovely leading ladies. Remember? Tough Humphrey Bogart with a cigarette hanging from his lips, and Bette Davis puffing away ever so elegantly.

4 When Paul and I were married, I never thought that smoking might be harmful to him, and I enjoyed the companionable glow of his cigarette in the dark. He always had to have that last cigarette before going to sleep, and he reached for a cigarette first thing when he awoke in the morning.

5 The years went by. Paul shrugged aside my concern about his chronic cough, but suddenly it seemed that our camping trips to the mountains of New Mexico were not much fun for him. ''Too hard to breathe there,'' he said.

6 He thought about quitting smoking. He changed to filter cigarettes, then to smoking with a filter. Finally he managed to quit.

7 And it was better for a while. He didn't cough as much, but 35 years of smoking could not be canceled out.

8 When he took early retirement from his position with the federal government, his final papers said ''disability,'' and the doctor's diagnosis was emphysema. I knew nothing of the disease then, but I learned. Oh! how I learned.

9 It was all very gradual.

10 Walking became a planned activity with rest periods to get outside to the

car—then it turned into a monumental effort—and finally he could manage trips from the bedroom to the living room only on his motorized scooter.

11 The amount of oxygen he used was gradually increased until the oxygen machine ran 24 hours a day. There were visits by a kindly respiratory therapist and medicine, medicine, medicine.

12 Through the years, Paul was sustained by his faith and his love for his family; he kept his interest in politics and world events. Much as I admire his courage, my heart breaks when I think of all he missed those last five years.

13 The fishing trips he should have been able to enjoy in retirement, but could not. His daughter's graduation from college and her wedding. She walked down the aisle alone because ''if Daddy can't give me away, no one else will.'' The last year of his life it was a Herculean effort to go outdoors, even to sit on the porch and watch a beautiful Texas moonrise.

14 In the last month of his life, he grew steadily weaker. One morning as I was giving him his bath, he inquired a couple times if the mail had come. When I saw the postman pass by, I asked Paul if he wanted me to get the mail and let him rest a little before finishing his bath. He said yes.

15 When I returned to the house, it was ominously quiet. For a moment I did not realize that it was the sound of the oxygen machine I did not hear. Paul had turned it off and then taken a revolver and put an end to his suffering.

16 The anguish of regrets cannot change the past.

17 I can only tell others what I have learned firsthand—that to indulge in smoking is to gamble with your life, and the odds are against you.

Jotting Down Your First Responses

1. In this essay who learned ''a hard lesson''? Why do you think so?
2. Do you have a habit that is potentially bad for your health? Do you know someone with such a habit? Explain.
3. What was Paul's retirement like? How do you picture your retirement?
4. Is this essay a scare tactic? Why or why not?

Checking Your Comprehension

1. How many Oregon deaths were related to smoking in 1989?
2. What influenced Warren's and her husband's attitude toward smoking?
3. Before he retired, what changes did Paul make to cope with the problems smoking was causing?
4. How long did Paul smoke?
5. How did emphysema affect Paul's daily activities?
6. How was his illness treated?
7. What activities was Paul unable to do in retirement?
8. What feelings does Warren have about the past?

Understanding a Writer's Patterns

1. Who is the intended audience of the essay? Give evidence from the essay.
2. Use the title to help locate the thesis. What is the argumentative thesis? How is it an opinion, or claim, that something is true?
3. What strategy does Warren use to introduce the subject of her essay?
4. How does Warren develop the thesis? (Recall the kinds of development you have studied in this course.)
5. What strategy does she use to conclude the essay?
6. Paragraphs 9 and 16 are each a single brief sentence. What is the effect of those brief paragraphs?
7. What are five phrases that show the time sequence of the narrative?
8. What words in paragraph 14 indicated an anecdote?
9. How does Warren use the general-to-specific pattern in paragraph 3?

Making Predictions and Drawing Inferences

1. What suggests Warren knew smoking was harming her husband long before he became ill?
2. What suggests Paul knew that smoking was harmful?
3. How old was Paul when he retired?
4. Why did Paul retire?
5. Why does Warren describe her husband as courageous?
6. How do you know about Paul's frail condition in the last month of his life?
7. On the morning of his death, why was he interested in the mail delivery?
8. How did Paul's smoking, illness, and death affect Warren's life?

Making Judgments and Thinking Critically

1. Why does Warren use the Oregon example in paragraph 1?
2. Is the statistic (a research-based number) in paragraph 1 an effective strategy? Would more statistics strengthen the introduction? Why or why not?
3. What is Warren's tone? Is it forceful, preachy, bossy, angry, self-pitying, demanding, blaming, whining, complaining, ranting, reasonable, emotional? Give evidence from the essay.

Using New Words

1. Select three words from the essay to add to your working vocabulary. Make vocabulary cards for them and add the cards to your set.

2. Substitute "to smoke" for "to indulge in smoking" (paragraph 17). What change in meaning occurs?
3. Choose any ten verbs from your set of vocabulary cards. Write a brief story using all these words in the present tense; read the story. Then change all the verbs to past tense; reread the story.

Responding by Writing

1. Write an essay about a habit (good or bad) to an audience whom you want to encourage to acquire or break the habit. Describe your purpose and audience clearly. Write an argumentative thesis and test it before you write, knowing you may revise the thesis as you write drafts. Possible topics include exercising, reading, visiting your grandmother weekly, studying before you watch television or go out, keeping a budget, meditating.
2. Write an essay about a lesson you have learned "the hard way." Write to an audience who could benefit from your experience. Decide on a trial argumentative thesis before you write.
3. Does noise (loud music, phone calls to sell you services, continuous talk during a movie, boisterous talk in a restaurant) intrude on your space? If you feel your space is frequently intruded upon by some kind of noise or other annoyance, write an essay describing these intrusions and what changes you'd like to see. Write this essay as an opinion piece for your college newspaper. Your specific audience, besides the student readers of the newspaper, is those who intrude on your space.

   Use support (information, examples, quotations) from at least two of the essays by May Sarton (pages 256–257), Edward T. Hall (pages 234–238), Ann McGee-Cooper (pages 241–244), or Rosa Mathe (pages 247–249). Give credit to the source of the evidence you use by including the writer's name and the title of the essay.

Rewriting History

Ellen Goodman

Ellen Goodman writes a column that is syndicated in newspapers throughout the country. Her columns have been collected and published in several books. The following essay, first published in August 1982, is from *Keeping in Touch.*

Thinking Before Reading

History books (not just textbooks) are revised to add information about events that occurred after the books were written. Why else are books about history revised? Why are there many books written about each historical event and person? Write in your Idea Bank.

Expanding Your Vocabulary from Reading

catalyst (2) an action that sparks a later event
biographies (2) written accounts of a person's life
ambiguity (9) uncertainty; word, state, or event that can have multiple interpretations
muted (10) softened, muffled
justification (12) act of proving an action is just, right, reasonable, or legal
grotesque (13) distorted from the natural to a point of ugliness or absurdity
Holocaust (13) the destruction of six million Jews by the Nazis in World War II
hoax (13) deceptive act, fraud, trick
instill (14) implant by gradual, persistent actions
expunge (14) erase, strike out, eliminate
reparations (16) things done to make amends for a wrong or damage

1 It isn't often that a school textbook triggers an international incident. It would never have happened if the subject were math or Spanish. Facts are facts: One plus one equals two; "yes" equals "sí."

2 But the catalyst for this event was history, and history isn't as cool as math and doesn't translate as easily as a foreign language. Beyond the data and datelines, its facts are often as complex as a billion biographies, as objective as memory, as important as truth, and as hot as politics.

3 So the news that the Japanese are literally rewriting history was enough to prompt bomb threats in Korea and official protests in China.

4 It appears that the Japanese Education Ministry ordered changes in the new books for the fall term: changes in emphasis, changes in wording, changes in the way they tell their youngsters about World War II.

5 As of this fall, the Japanese will have no longer launched "invasions" in China, Southeast Asia, and the Pacific. They will have "advanced." In the rape of Nanking, they will have no longer "killed and assaulted" 200,000 Chinese willfully but rather "in the midst of the confusion. . . ."

6 To understand the impulse of the Japanese Education Ministry, just imagine the difficulty of teaching young children about the brutality, the aggression, the wrong committed by the country they are also expected to love.

7 To understand the effect of these rewritings on Asians (an estimated eighteen million of whom died in World War II), just imagine how we would

respond if the Japanese began to teach their children that on December 7, 1941, the Imperial Air Force "advanced" on Pearl Harbor.

8 The entire incident is in many ways a textbook case. It's a textbook case on the complicated role that history plays in our lives, our understanding of our world, country, families. It's a textbook case on the manipulation of history in the service of politics.

9 What happened in Japan is not all that unusual. In some way or other, every culture—every country—struggles with its past. To this day there are even heated arguments in this country about whether our early history should be taught as national heroics, led by profiles in courage, or with a more earthy ambiguity.

10 The more uneasy we are about that past, the more tarnished it seems to us, the more trouble we have telling it to our children. The Japanese have subtly muted their own blame. The official Egyptian guide who led a group of friends to the Pyramids three years ago described how they were built by "volunteer labor." For generations we have had extraordinary difficulty teaching children about the realities of slavery or the myths of cowboys and Indians.

11 As for our present history, I don't envy those publishers who will update the books to include Vietnam. The war is still being fought. The battle that raged over a monument in Washington was not about architecture, but about the place of the Vietnam War in American history.

12 The teaching of the past can be an explanation, a judgment, a justification. History can tell sides or take sides. In Argentina and Great Britain, a conflict that grew in part from two sets of history books will be written (I guarantee it) in two separate versions as well as languages. It happens all the time.

13 But the national autobiography of aggression and guilt is subject to the most peculiar revisions. Germany doesn't rest any more easily on its recent past than Japan. It took until 1962 for German schools to teach children about the death camps. Today there are new "historians" who assault those dead with grotesque rewrites of Nazi reality, calling the Holocaust a hoax.

14 It is as hard for nations, as it is for parents, to talk about their wrongs. They want respect from the young, and want to instill self-respect in the young. But we can't teach false pride. When we expunge guilt, pretend that it didn't happen, we are tainted by it, committing the ultimate assault on the victims.

15 Our friendship with our old enemy is due in measure to the way the Japanese acknowledged their aggression as well as their defeat. They told us they were wrong. They told their children they were wrong.

16 There is a statute of limitations to national guilt. On the whole, few blame the Japan of 1982 for the Japan of 1941. The next generation does not inherit the sins of its parents or grandparents. But it must know those sins. These are the only lasting reparations.

Jotting Down Your First Responses

1. Are there various versions of your family's history? If so, what accounts for the differences?
2. Would an Iraqi history of the Gulf War differ from a U.S. history of the war? If so, what kinds of differences might you expect to find? What accounts for the differences?
3. Where, when, and how have you learned U.S. history? World history?

Checking Your Comprehension

1. What situation caused an international uproar?
2. What kind of changes were ordered?
3. Why was the change ordered?
4. What are two examples of the change?
5. What other countries face the problem of how to tell their past?
6. How did the Egyptian tour guide soften a piece of Egypt's history? Why?
7. What are three approaches to teaching history? (paragraph 12)
8. Why, according to Goodman, is it hard for parents and nations to talk about their mistakes?
9. What happens, according to Goodman, if we don't tell our mistakes in our personal and national histories?
10. What acts of Japan helped change the Japanese from enemies to friends of the United States after World War II?

Understanding a Writer's Patterns

1. Does the title indicate Goodman's opinion about the topic? What does it tell?
2. What are the six comparisons Goodman uses in the introduction (paragraphs 1–2) to describe "history"?
3. What is the argumentative thesis of this essay? (Because it is an implied thesis, you will have to write a thesis. See paragraphs 14 and 16.)
4. Who is the audience?
5. Which block of paragraphs is about the Japanese textbook incident?
6. Which paragraph states the point of telling about the Japanese textbook incident?
7. Which block of paragraphs generalizes from Japan to other countries, explaining and giving examples?
8. What other countries does Goodman cite as examples of those rewriting their histories?
9. What does Goodman compare nations with? Why?
10. What strategy does Goodman use in the conclusion? (paragraphs 14–16)

Making Predictions and Drawing Inferences

1. Does Goodman think history is an objective account (without bias) of the past?
2. What does Goodman mean when she says that history is "as objective as memory"?
3. What nations would take the most offense to another nation's softening the accounts of its acts of aggression?
4. What does Goodman mean by the "myths" of cowboys and Indians? (paragraph 10)
5. Besides Vietnam, what other parts of U.S. history have presented or now present a problem to U.S. historians?
6. Why did it take twenty-five years for Germans to teach their children about the death camps for Jews in World War II?

Making Judgments and Thinking Critically

1. What makes Goodman's essay easy to read and understand?
2. What makes the essay difficult to read and understand?
3. In general, has history as you've been taught it in school been an explanation, a judgment, or a justification?
4. In what conditions and to what age groups should history be taught as explanation, judgment, or justification?

Using New Words

1. Choose three words from the reading selection that you want to add to your writing and speaking vocabulary. Make vocabulary cards for them by writing the word on one side of a card and a definition and an original sentence on the other side.
2. Review all your vocabulary cards by saying the words aloud into a tape recorder. Play the tape and read the words as you listen to them.
3. Choose five nouns from your set of vocabuary cards. (Some nouns endings are *-ity, -ion, -ace, -ence,* and *-ance.*) Write a paragraph with these nouns.
4. The root *graph* means something written or an instrument for making records. Use the root to define these words: *biography, autobiography, autograph, paragraph, stenographer, telegraph, graphite.*

Responding by Writing

1. "History can tell sides or take sides" (paragraph 12). Do you believe it does both? Write an essay in which you interpret this quotation from Goodman's essay and take a position on her statement. Write to an audience of this class. Use at least one quotation from Goodman's essay;

give credit to the author by stating the title of the essay and her full name the first time you use it.

2. Family members (or close friends) often have different memories about the same event. Ask a family member or friend to help you with an experiment. Choose an incident that you both were a part of, either as spectators or as participants, but that you disagree about. (If this was an emotional situation, avoid replaying any blame, anger, or guilt. Leave the old feelings in the past.) Each of you should write an account of the incident. Then read the two accounts. What are the similarities and differences? Can you explain why the similarities and differences occurred?

   Write an essay to an audience of your teacher in which you compare and contrast the two accounts and give the reasons for the differences between them. Draw some connections to other kinds of history; make some connections with "Rewriting History" if you can.
3. Write an editorial for your college newspaper about a college or local issue you feel strongly about—lack of child care on campus, need for recycling soft drink cans and paper, need for more accessible financial aid information, some aspect of student behavior, college policy, etc. Choose an issue that people in your college community can do something about. Write a trial argumentative thesis and describe your audience and purpose before you write a draft.
4. Should history be required for a college degree? Why or why not? Write an essay in which you argue for or against requiring history for a specific degree or major. Make clear how many courses, what kinds of courses, for which majors or degrees history should be required. Give your reasons. Give examples from your experience and reading. Write as a student to an audience of the curriculum committee of your college which is revising degree requirements.

Making Amends with Mom

Shayna K. Smith

Shayna K. Smith works and goes to college part-time. She wrote the following essay after reading several books and articles about a problem she had. Her audience is young adult women who have troubled relationships with their mothers. Her purpose is to convince them of the benefits of a loving relationship between mother and daughter.

Postscript. Smith and her mother mended their relationship before her mother died suddenly a year after the essay was written.

Thinking Before Reading

Even in the closest families troubled relationships or areas of trouble in relationships are common. Write briefly about a problem in a relationship with a parent, brother, sister, or other close relative. How was the problem solved or how could it be solved?

Expanding Your Vocabulary from Reading

transition (1) process of changing from one state to another
tolerate (1) put up with, endure
ironically (2) with contrast between appearance and reality
vitally (2) essentially
status quo (3) existing condition
petty (5) small-minded, mean-spirited
bickering (5) quarreling over unimportant matters

1 As girls make the transition into womanhood, all mother and daughter pairs experience a great amount of conflict and emotional turmoil in their relationship with each other. Some are able to tolerate each other when this change takes place, but unfortunately, many mother and daughter teams cannot withstand this conflict that arrives when the roles are shifted. As the daughter matures and begins establishing her sense of self and independence, the rocky road of transition begins to unfold. In order for the relationship to survive and withstand these pressures, the people involved must be willing to work very hard at the relationship. This is far from easy. I know, because I have experienced this struggle first-hand with my own mother. I have found that when daughters make amends with their mothers, many advantages and rewards follow. These advantages are more crucially important and necessary than one might think. In "Mother and Daughter Bond," Maggie Scarf and Susan Merrell claim that opposition is a way of staying stuck in the relationship (207).* In order to move forward and achieve harmony, daughters must take the first step and attempt to be friendly with their mothers.

2 Some daughters do not believe this theory. In "Mothers: Tired of Taking The Rap," it is stated that some daughters decide to take an angry stance toward their mothers, that is, although a normal aspect of psychological separation, it is not always the best road to take. Some women I know have used geographical distance, including rare visits and infrequent telephone calls, to persuade themselves that their mother is now someone unimportant and irrelevant to their lives. Psychologists claim that these daughters, ironically, are actually hiding the painful truth from themselves that they are the most over-

* The number in parentheses indicates the page number.

involved and unseparated of all. I went for approximately one year without speaking to my mother because of our difficulties. I went into this isolation thinking that if I did not associate with her I would get her off my mind and live a conflict-free life. Actually, my mother ended up always on my mind. I continually felt like something vitally important was missing in my life. I firmly believe that women who are brave enough to face the issue and attempt to make things work are the ones who benefit.

3 First of all, the relationship works for the daughter's own benefit. Being on bad terms with one's mother is hurting the daughter the most. If no communication is taking place, the relationship is neither improving or worsening—it is staying wedged in the status quo and will not get any better. This is precisely what happened in my relationship with my mother. We wound up wasting a precious year of our lives by staying stuck in opposition. I found one major benefit of a pleasant relationship with one's mother is that both the mother and daughter will be happy and free of major conflicts in their lives. No one needs conflict in their lives because life is too stressful and complicated.

4 Secondly, the daughter must take into consideration that her relationship with her mother will be the role model relationship for her own daughter, once she decides to have children. Furthermore, the adult daughter must realize that her mother will be the grandmother to her children. Grandmothers play an enormous role in a little girl's world. When I was a child, my mother was always on bad terms with my grandmother. I always missed interaction with my grandmother. All my friends would always be doing something with their grandmothers, having little pet names for them like ''Mimi'' for example. Their grandmothers always showered them with attention and presents. Obviously, this was not my situation and I felt left out. Children have a keen sense of being aware of when adults are at fault with one another. Being as young as I was, I could always tell that something was not quite right between my mom and my grandma. This made me sad. A positive and loving relationship must be established in order for the chidren to learn from it and model themselves and their future relationships after it in a healthy and productive way. Since neither my mother nor I had this healthy example, we started out at a disadvantage.

5 Furthermore, a daughter who is in disagreement with her mother must also consider her mother's feelings. This is probably the hardest aspect of this issue to contend with because it takes a great deal of maturity. Again, I am speaking entirely from experience. Time passes very quickly once adulthood is reached. The later years of an adult's life should be spent in peace, not involved in competition and fighting, or even worse, loneliness. My mother was diagnosed with chronic diabetes and has been hospitalized in intensive care several times within the last few years. This illness was actually a blessing because it made me realize that my mother will not be around forever. I felt panicked and lonely when first learning of my mother's disease. I told myself

that the childish and petty state of bickering that we were involved in was not worth our precious time. Also, once the children grow up and leave home, mothers always have an enormously painful adjustment period. In fact, some mothers never recover from this and suffer incredible feelings of abandonment, especially if the husband is not present in their lives. In my opinion, no matter how difficult it is to keep the peace in a mother-daughter relationship, I feel it is cruel to abandon one's mother leaving her lonely and sad.

6 Another reason for daughters to get along with their mothers is simply because happiness spreads. Victoria Secunda, author of *When You and Your Mother Can't Be Friends: Resolving the Most Complicated Relationship of Your Life,* explains that the daughter's relationship with her mother affects all other important relationships in her life (268). The relationship the daughter has with her intimate partner feeds back on the type of bond she had with her parents. I had always had trouble with my boyfriends when I was fighting with my parents. As a result of inner frustration, I unconsciously took anger out on the people who were close to me. If the daughter is happy and content with her own life, these feelings flow into all other aspects of her life. This goes both ways. If the daughter is emotionally distressed, her other close relationships will suffer because of this conflict. If she is in a love relationship and has a great deal of inner turmoil, she is frequently disappointed, resentful and feels abandoned because of the unresolved pain she has toward her mother. Again, I learned this the hard way.

7 Many women stumble into roadblocks when making amends with their mothers. These obstacles include pride, stubbornness, and large egos. I had a tremendous amount of trouble with these personality hindrances. Either party does not want to admit they are wrong. Some women think that the relationship is too much trouble and that they do not have enough time to work on improving the union. They do not understand that the relationship they have with their mother is the core to all their other personal relations. Even though many difficulties might stand in the way, it is certainly in the best interest of both parties to make amends with each other. I now have an improved union with my mother and feel very happy and harmonious inside. The time I have with my mother means the world to me.

Jotting Down Your First Responses

1. Is Shayna Smith writing this argument from an informed position? Explain.
2. Does Smith make a good case for the importance of mending broken mother-daughter relationships? Explain.
3. What reasons or other evidence could you add to this argument? What reasons or other evidence against this argument could you make?
4. Could one make a similar argument for the importance of father-son relationships? Explain.

Checking Your Comprehension

1. When do many mothers and daughters experience conflict?
2. What changes cause the conflict, according to Smith?
3. How does Smith know about the difficulties of the conflict and the rewards of mending the relationship?
4. According to Smith, who must take the first step in mending the relationship?
5. What do some psychologists think it means when daughters ignore their mothers for a long period of time?
6. What effect does solving the mother-daughter conflict have on other relationships?
7. According to Smith, how do mothers learn to have good relationships with their daughters?
8. What event made Smith aware of the need to make amends because of passing time?
9. What stumbling blocks prevent some women from making amends with their mothers?

Understanding a Writer's Patterns

1. What is Smith's thesis?
2. What two kinds of sources provide Smith with evidence?
3. Why is Smith's personal experience appropriate evidence for the intended audience?
4. What paragraph addresses the reasons readers might have for disagreeing with Smith?
5. What transitional words in paragraphs 3 through 6 signal each of Smith's supporting points?
6. Where does Smith address the feelings of the mother?
7. In the conclusion, why does Smith acknowledge the difficulty of taking action to mend a troubled mother-daughter relationship before repeating the thesis?
8. Why is the title in paragraph 2 in quotation marks and the title in paragraph 6 in italics?

Making Predictions and Drawing Inferences

1. How old do you think Smith was when she wrote this essay? Why?
2. About how long did making amends with her mother take?
3. What did you expect the essay to be about when you read the introductory paragraph? How did you expect the essay to be developed? Which of your expectations were met? Which were not met? What surprises were there?

Making Judgments and Thinking Critically

1. If you agree with Smith's thesis in part, but disagree on some point, what is that opposing point?
2. Why did Smith write only about the advantages of a mended mother-daughter relationship to daughters, not to mothers? Why does she ask only daughters to take action?
3. Do you agree that it takes courage "to face the issue and attempt to make things work" (paragraph 2)? Why or why not?
4. What would strengthen Smith's argument for her audience?
5. Is this an emotional subject? What part does emotion play in this argumentative essay?

Using New Words

1. Choose three words that you would like to add to your working vocabulary. Make vocabulary cards for these words.
2. The metaphor "rocky road of transition" (paragraph 1) compares the period of maturing from childhood to womanhood to a rocky road. Is this an appropriate comparison? Why or why not? Why is the metaphor more effective than the words "difficult transition" would have been?
3. Replace the strong action verbs *wedged* (paragraph 3) and *stumble* (paragraph 7) with weak verbs. Rewrite the phrases in which the strong action verbs appear to make your substitutions fit. What is lost with the substitutions?
4. Review your set of vocabulary cards. Select ten words that seem most useful or most interesting to you. Practice spelling them. Ask a partner to dictate the words to you and to check your spelling; do the same for your partner. To make this a team sport, add your score for correct answers to your partner's score or to those of a small group, and compare with other class pairs or groups.

Responding by Writing

1. Locate and read a magazine or newspaper article about a problem or issue you face or have faced. If you have an opinion about some aspect of this problem or issue, write down your opinion as a trial thesis. Remember that *must, should,* and *ought* often signal an opinion. If this trial thesis passes the tests for an argumentative thesis (see pages 304–305), decide on an audience who needs to hear or would benefit from what you have to say. Describe the audience.

   Write an argumentative article about your thesis to your intended audience. Argue your point; don't lapse into giving advice. Include a quotation from the article you read, the title of the article in quotation marks, and the full name of the author. You may refer to the writer by his or her last name after you have cited the full name one time.

In college, when you write about what you read, you will often be required to prepare a separate Works Cited page as Shayna Smith did (page 396). To make a Works Cited page for your argumentative article, follow the pattern she used for a magazine article. Refer to the handbook your college uses for more information and examples about reference pages. However, here is the basic information you'll need. Follow the punctuation and spacing carefully.

a. Entitle the page Works Cited, using a capital letter to begin each word with no quotation marks or underlining.
b. Begin the first line of each entry at the left margin, and use the full line. Indent the second and all following lines five spaces.
c. Write the author's name—last name, comma, first name, period, double space.
d. Write the title of the article in quotation marks. Capitalize each major word in the title. Place a period after the title inside the quotation marks. Double space.
e. Write the publication information of the magazine or newspaper. Capitalize the name of the publication and underline it. Write the date, colon, page numbers, and period. For the date abbreviate the name of the month and use no internal commas or extra spaces.

2. Write an argumentative essay about a book, movie, or television series you think is particularly worthwhile and well done. Write to an audience who hasn't read the book or seen the movie or series and doesn't want to. Before you write a draft, write a profile of your intended audience and a trial thesis, using the tests for an argumentative thesis in the introduction of this chapter.
3. Write a letter to a close friend or relative about something you want him or her to do, believe, or value. This issue should be important to you; it may be a sensitive subject, something you can write about more easily than talk about. Write the trial thesis and a profile of the intended audience before you write a draft. You may or may not choose to send this letter.
4. Write an essay to your teacher in which you evaluate Smith's argument. Use common sense and what you have learned about argument in this chapter. Although you may discuss strengths and weaknesses, you should have a clear argumentative thesis about her essay. Reread your answers to some of the questions after the essay for some ideas. Write a trial thesis as a starting point for your draft.

PART 3

A Writer's Handbook

A QUICK GUIDE TO A WRITER'S HANDBOOK

Your instructor may use the following symbols on your drafts to indicate words or sentences that need to be corrected. To use the guide, read the explanation of the symbol for each error and then turn to the page and reference section in the handbook to find ways to edit your sentences.

To review methods you can use to revise your sentence style, see Sentence Variety and Style, pages 361–365. To review the elements of a complete sentence, see Understanding the Sentence, pages 334–335.

adj, adv	Change the form of the comparative or the superlative. Pages 373–374, 10–15
cap	Capitalize the letter. Pages 379–380, 8–13; page 335, 4
cl	Substitute fresh language for the cliché. Page 371, 7
frag	Revise the sentence fragment. Pages 335–338, 5a–d
dm	Revise the dangling modifier. Page 340, 7c
mm	Revise the misplaced modifier. Page 339, 7a–b
^ p	Change the punctuation. Pages 383–391 For a quick guide to punctuation, see pages 380–383
pl	Change the plural form of the noun. Pages 359–360, 1–5
poss	Change the possessive form of the noun. Pages 360–361, 6–10
pron	Change the form of the pronoun. Pages 353–355, 1–2 Be consistent in your use of pronouns. Page 358, 8
pron ref	Make sure the pronoun refers to a specific noun. Pages 355–356, 3
pron agr	Change the pronoun or the antecedent noun so they agree in person and number. Pages 356–358, 4–7
r-o	Revise the run-on sentence. Pages 338–339, 6a–d
sp	Spell the word correctly. Pages 377–378, 1–4 Spell the number correctly. Pages 378–379, 5–7

(Continued)

S-V agr	Change the subject or the verb so they agree in person and number. Pages 343–347, 3–11
vb	Change the tense or form of the verb. Pages 347–352, 12–20
	For a list of irregular verb forms, see pages 351–352, 20
	Be consistent in your use of verb tenses. Page 349, 17
WW	Change the word to a more appropriate one. Pages 369–370
	For a list of commonly confused words, see pages 374–377
W	Revise the sentence to avoid wordiness. Pages 372–373, 9
//	Revise the faulty parallelism. Pages 340–342, 8

Once you have finished revising, editing, and proofreading your paragraph or essay, refer to Paper Format, pages 391–393, to put your work into final form.

When you have a problem with or want to review grammar, punctuation, or usage, use this brief table of contents or turn to the full table of contents in the front of the book.

A Brief Table of Contents for the Handbook

SENTENCE STRUCTURE

Understanding the Sentence

1. **A sentence must express a complete thought.** There must be a sense of completeness even though the sentence is related in meaning to the sentences before and after it.

Then he saw the eagles across the distance.
They were golden eagles, a male and female, in their mating flight.

2. **A sentence must contain a subject.** The subject is the person, thing, or idea that the sentence is about or that is doing the action of the sentence. The subject may be a noun (a word that names a person, place, thing, or idea) or a pronoun (a substitute for a noun).

The *boy* watched their silent flight in the bright morning. (noun)
The *span* of her broad wings was greater than a man's height. (noun)
She flew with a flourishing motion. (pronoun)

3. **A sentence must contain a main verb.** The main verb of a sentence can be an action verb—a verb that expresses the action the subject is performing. Or it can be a linking verb—a verb that expresses the relationship between the subject and another word (or words) that identifies or describes the subject. To find the main verb of a sentence, ask yourself "What word tells what the subject did or experienced?"

The eagles *swooped* and *hovered.* (action)
They *leaned* on the air as they *flew.* (action)
She *was* deceptively fast. (linking)
Her pivots and wheels *were* wide and full-blown. (linking)

The main verb of a sentence can consist of more than one word.

A rattlesnake *was hanging* from her feet.
It *had floated* down slowly when the male sailed up.

4. **A sentence must begin with a capital letter and end with a mark of final punctuation (period, exclamation point, or question mark).**

She climbed high and let the snake go. (period)
Did her mate see the snake fall? (question mark)
He hit the snake in the head! (exclamation point)

Identifying and Correcting Fragments

5. **Avoid sentence fragments,** or word groups that are punctuated as if they were sentences but that are not complete.

Picking tomatoes, my summer chore since I was eight. (fragment)
When I started throwing tomatoes at my brother. (fragment)

Also chunked crab apples that had fallen on the ground. (fragment)
Especially the soft, juicy ones on the ground. (fragment)
Making a target the size of a barn. (fragment)

5a. Check to be sure your sentences have subjects. Correct a *missing-subject fragment* either by adding a subject or by attaching the fragment to the sentence that precedes or follows it.

Also chunked crab apples that had fallen on the ground. (The word group has no subject.)
I also chunked crab apples that had fallen on the ground. (A subject has been added to the fragment.)

Making a target the size of a barn. (The word group has no subject or verb.)
Making a target the size of a barn, my sister was bending over. (The fragment has been added to a sentence.)

5b. Check to be sure your sentences have verbs. Correct a *missing-verb fragment* either by adding a verb or by attaching the fragment to the sentence that precedes or follows it. When you add a verb to a fragment, you may have to add a few words to complete the thought or change the structure of the sentence slightly.

My sister was a girl with big hips. *A target the size of a barn.* (The second word group has no verb.)
My sister was a girl with big hips, *a target the size of a barn.* (The fragment has been attached to the sentence preceding it.)

My brother and I threw tomatoes at each other. *Especially the soft, juicy ones on the ground.* (The second word group has no verb.)
My brother and I threw tomatoes at each other, *especially the soft, juicy ones on the ground.* (The fragment has been attached to the sentence preceding it.)
My brother and I threw tomatoes at each other.The soft, juicy ones *on the ground made the best splat.* (A verb and some other words have been added to the fragment to complete the thought.)

5c. Check your sentences for *-ing, -ed,* or *-en* fragments. Correct this type of fragment either by adding a helping verb (*is, are, was, were, will be, has, have, had, will have, has been, have been, had been, will have been*) or by attaching the fragment to a sentence to which it is logically related.

> I *aiming* at my sister when my mother called from the kitchen window. *Taken* back by her calling me. I had to decide quickly between obedience and pleasure. (The word *aiming* cannot function as a verb without a helping verb. The second word group has no subject and the verb form *taken* cannot function as a verb without a helping verb.)
>
> I *was* aiming at my sister when my mother called me from the kitchen window. *Taken back by her calling me,* I had to decide quickly between obedience and pleasure. (A verb has been added to the first fragment. The second fragment has been attached to the sentence following it.)

5d. Check your sentences for dependent-word fragments. A *dependent-word fragment* is a clause or a phrase that is set off like a sentence. It does not express a complete thought and therefore cannot stand alone; the clause or phrase ''depends on'' another word group to complete its meaning. Correct a dependent-word fragment either by omitting the word that introduces it (a subordinator) or by attaching the fragment to a sentence to which it is logically related. Some dependent words are *after, although, because, before, if, since, though, unless, until, when, wherever, while, who, which,* and *that.*

> *When my mother called.* I had to decide quickly between obedience and pleasure. I decided. The rotten tomato hitting the target made a memorable sound. My sister came after me fast. *After a whoop and a yell.* (The first fragment is a dependent clause; the second is a prepositional phrase.)
>
> *When my mother called,* I had to decide quickly between obedience and pleasure. I decided. The rotten tomato hitting the target made a memorable sound. My sister came after me fast *after a whoop and a yell.* (The fragments have been corrected by attaching them to sentences.)

HOW TO CORRECT FRAGMENTS: A REVIEW

Check to be sure each of your sentences has a subject and a verb. Read each sentence one at a time to see if the sentence sounds like a complete idea. If you find a fragment, decide what kind of fragment it is. Then correct the fragment in one of these ways:

Add a subject.
Add a verb.
Add a helping verb.
Omit a subordinator, preposition, pronoun, or other word that introduces a dependent clause or phrase.
Attach the fragment to a sentence to which it is logically related.

Identifying and Correcting Run-ons

6. Avoid run-ons. A run-on sentence is the incorrect combination and punctuation of two sentences as though they are one sentence.

> We didn't exactly get along she was spreading rumors about me. (no punctuation)
>
> We didn't exactly get along, she was spreading rumors about me. (comma alone cannot separate sentences)

Run-ons often occur because students don't want to stop a reader with a period when sentences are connected in meaning. However, placing sentences one after another in a paragraph shows this connection. Also, using coordinators, subordinators, or semicolons shows connections between sentences.

To find run-ons in your writing, check especially long sentences and sentences with commas. Test the word group before the comma: Does it express a complete thought? Does it have a subject? Does it have a verb? Apply the same test to the word group after the comma. (Know the basic comma rules so you can ignore commas you used properly.) There are four ways to correct run-ons.

6a. Separate the two sentences with a period and a capital letter.

> We didn't exactly get along. She was spreading rumors about me.

6b. Insert a comma and a coordinator after the first sentence. Coordinators are *and, but, yet, for, or, nor,* and *so.*

> We didn't exactly get along, *and* she was spreading rumors about me.

6c. Insert a dependent word (also called a subordinator). Some common subordinators are *when, since, after,* and *because.* See pages 366–367 for a longer list of subordinators.

We didn't exactly get along *because* she was spreading rumors about me.

6d. Separate the two sentences with a semicolon (;).

We didn't exactly get along; she was spreading rumors about me.

Identifying and Correcting Dangling and Misplaced Modifiers

7. Avoid dangling and misplaced modifiers. A modifier is a word or group of words that describes a noun or pronoun or that gives further information about the action of the sentence.

7a. Misplaced modifiers are descriptive words that are not next to the words they are describing. The placement of modifiers affects the meaning of the sentence.

I began my presentation with a forced smile *in class.* (Does "in class" describe the writer's smile or the presentation?)
I began my presentation *in class* with a forced smile.

My classmates in the back asked me to slow down or speak up *repeatedly.* (Does *repeatedly* describe her actions—slowing down and speaking up—or the class action—asking?)
My classmates in the back *repeatedly* asked me to slow down or speak up. (The adverb *repeatedly* may go before the verb "asked" or after "asked me.")

7b. The modifiers *almost, only, even,* and *hardly* should be placed immediately before the words they modify.

Only I asked for pie, not for pie and ice cream. (I was the only one who asked for pie alone.)
I asked *only* for pie, not for pie and ice cream. (The only thing I asked for was pie.)

Chris *almost* knew everyone at his high school reunion. (Chris knew everyone so slightly that he couldn't remember anyone's name.)
Chris knew *almost* everyone at his high school reunion.

7c. Dangling modifiers are modifiers that describe words that are missing from the sentences altogether.

Talking more swiftly and more softly, my classmates asked me to slow down and speak up. (Who is talking—my classmates or me?)

Because I was talking more swiftly and softly, my classmates asked me to slow down and speak up. (Add a subject and verb to make the dangling modifier a dependent word group.)

Rehearsing my presentations the night before, my speeches became polished. (Were my speeches rehearsing?)

Rehearsing my presentation the night before, I became polished. (Rewrite the sentence so that the subject of the sentence is the actor of the dangling modifier.)

Instead of telling myself "Nobody wants to hear this," my thoughts were "I am the person they asked to speak." (Were "my thoughts" telling?)

Instead of telling myself "Nobody wants to hear this," I began thinking to myself "I am the person they asked to speak." (Rewrite the sentence so that the subject is the actor of the dangling modifier.)

HOW TO CORRECT MISPLACED AND DANGLING MODIFIERS: A REVIEW

Make sure that every modifier has a noun or pronoun (person, place, thing, or idea) or verb that it is describing.

Make sure that the descriptive word or phrase is next to the word it is modifying.

Check the modifiers *almost, only, even,* and *hardly.* These should be placed immediately before the word that they are describing.

Identifying and Correcting Faulty Parallelism

8. Avoid faulty parallelism. Parallelism is the expression of similar and related ideas in the same grammatical form. Parallelism helps a reader see the relationship of similar ideas or the writer's emphasis of a point.

8a. Errors in parallelism often occur in a series of nouns, adjectives, verbs, or *-ing* verb forms.

Problem in a noun series. Jake wanted to buy *a tape, a pair* of shoes, and *eat a hamburger.* (Jake wanted to buy three things, but the third item has the verb ''eat'' in it.)

Jake wanted to buy *a tape, a pair* of shoes, and *a hamburger.*

Problem in an adjective series. She is frequently *disappointed, resentful,* and *feels abandoned* because of the unresolved pain she has toward her mother. (She has three feelings, but the third item in the series has the verb ''feels.'')

She frequently feels *disappointed, resentful,* and *abandoned. . . .* (Now three adjectives follow the verb ''feels.'')

She frequently *is disappointed, is resentful,* and *feels abandoned. . . .* (Now each item in the series has a verb and an adjective.)

Problem in a verb series. Men friends *talk* about work, *watch* sports on television, and *playing* golf together. (Men do three things: talk, watch, and play; but the third verb in the series is an *-ing* form ''playing.'')

Men friends *talk* about work, *watch* sports on television, and *play* golf together.

Problem in an *-ing* series. Men like *talking* about work, *watching* sports on television, and *to play* golf together. (''To play'' is not parallel with ''talking'' and ''watching.'')

Men like *talking* about work, *watching* sports on television, and *playing* golf together.

8b. Errors in parallelism also occur frequently after paired conjunctions (both . . . and, either . . . or, neither . . . nor, not only . . . but also).

Television watching *not only teaches* children many new things *but it also keeps* them from healthy physical activity. (The verb ''teaches'' follows ''not only,'' but the pronoun ''it'' interrupts ''but also.'')

Television watching *not only teaches* children many new things *but also keeps* them from healthy physical activity. (Now a verb follows each part of the paired conjunction.)

Sentences and clauses can also be parallel for emphasis of a point.

> On the whole, men had buddies, while women had friends. Buddies bonded, but friends loved. Buddies faced adversity together, but friends faced each other. . . . Buddies seemed to ''do'' things together; friends simply ''were'' together. (All the sentences have the same form. A short sentence about buddies is contrasted with a parallel sentence about friends.)

HOW TO CORRECT FAULTY PARALLELISM: A REVIEW

Within sentences, check every pair or series to see that you have been consistent in using nouns, verbs, adjectives, phrases, and clauses. Within a paragraph or an essay, check sentences that express related ideas to see that they are expressed in parallel form and word order.

SUBJECTS AND VERBS

Subjects

1. **The subject of a sentence is the person, thing, place, or idea that the sentence is about.** A subject can be a noun, such as ''employee,'' ''Arizona,'' and ''budget,'' or a pronoun, a word that stands for or takes the place of a noun, such as ''she,'' ''it,'' and ''they.'' (For more information on pronouns, see Pronouns, pages 353–359.) The subject has both **person** and **number.**

> The *computer lab* is available to all students at the college.

1a. **Person refers to the writer's relation to the subject of his or her sentence.** First person subjects are *I* and *we.*

> *I* require a typed draft of your essay, so *we* will meet in the computer lab on Tuesday. (first person)

The second person subject is *you.*

> Muhammad, since *you* are a lab employee and a class member, will you answer questions about using the computer to type a draft? The rest of *you* in the class may ask either Muhammad or me for help. (second person)

The third person subjects are *he, she, it,* and *they.* If the subject of the sentence can be replaced by the words *he, she, it,* or *they,* then it is a third person subject.

> Many *people* have computer phobia. Before *a person* begins to use a computer, *he* or *she* often is nervous. People's *worries* seem to dissolve as *they* start using a computer. (third person)

1b. Number indicates whether the subject is singular (one person or thing) or plural (more than one). Singular subjects include *I, you, he, she, it,* and one thing (such as ''a tomato''). Plural subjects include *we, you, they,* and several things (such as ''three problems'').

> The *student* likes to type her essay on the computer. (singular)
> The *students* like to type their essays on the computer. (plural)

Most plurals are formed by adding an *-s* or *-es* ending. (For more information on plurals, see pages 359–360.)

> The computer *screen* turned blue when the *student* pressed the ''on'' *switch.* (singular)
> The computer *screens* turned blue when the *students* pressed the ''on'' *switches.* (plural)

Other plurals are formed by a change in spelling—a change in vowels, a change in consonants, or the addition of an irregular ending.

> A *woman* brought her *child* to class. (singular)
> Several *women* brought their *children* to class. (plural)

Verbs

2. The verb of a sentence states what the subject is doing or experiencing. The time of the action or condition expressed by the verb is called its **tense.** (For a review of verb tenses, see Verb Tenses, pages 347–349.)

Subject-Verb Agreement

3. In Academic Written English (also called Standard American English), the main verb of every sentence must agree with its

subject. Grammatical agreement means that the form of the verb matches the person and the number of the subject of the sentence.

3a. In the present tense a third person singular subject (*he, she, it,* or any noun that these words replace) needs an *-s* ending on its verb.

The President *likes* to jog.
He *tries* to exercise every day.

3b. In the present tense the verbs *be, do,* and *have* change their spelling to indicate different types of subjects.

Be	**Do**	**Have**
I am	I do	I have
you are	you do	you have
he, she, or it is	he, she, or it does	he, she, or it has
we are	we do	we have
you are	you do	you have
they are	they do	they have

The President *does* make over 10,000 appointments.
The Senate *is* responsible for confirming many of the President's appointments.
It *has* confirmed the President's cabinet nominations.

3c. In the past tense the verb *be* changes its spelling to indicate different types of subjects.

Past Tense of *Be*

I was
you were
he, she, or it was

we were
you were
they were

Yesterday, a new President *was* inaugurated for a four-year term.
I *was* proud of our nation's ability to transfer power from one President to another in a peaceful way.

For more information on irregular verbs, see Regular and Irregular Verbs, pages 350–352.

4. **A compound subject usually needs a plural form of the verb.** A compound subject is made up of two or more nouns or pronouns that are joined by *and.*

    The House of Representatives and the Senate together *are* the legislature.
    The President, the House, and the Senate work together to pass laws and govern our nation.
    He and the legislature also *create* a national budget.
    The President, the Congress, and the federal courts compose our national government.

5. **When two or more nouns or pronouns are joined by *or, nor, either . . . or,* or *neither . . . nor,* the verb form usually agrees with the noun that is closest to the verb.**

    Neither the President nor the two *houses govern* alone.
    Neither the two houses nor the *President governs* alone.
    The President or his *aide records* their meetings.

6. **Words that come between a subject and its verb do not affect the number of the subject.**

    The *senator* from Colorado *wants* to talk with the President.
    The *senators* from Colorado *want* to talk with the President.

    Some words between a subject and a verb sound as if they are making the subject plural, for example, *in addition to, as well as, including,* and *together with.* These expressions do *not* make the subject plural.

    The *President,* together with the senators from Colorado, *supports* the bill for water conservation.

7. **A verb agrees with its subject, whether the verb comes after the subject or before it.**

    At the end of the hall *is* the President's *Oval Office.*
    At the end of the hall *are* several office *doors.*

    7a. **When a sentence begins with the "dummy" subjects *there* or *here,* the actual subject follows the verb and determines its form.**

        There *is basic agreement* about the need to protect the environment.
        There *are many differences* about what to protect.

7b. The dummy subject *it* always requires a singular verb, even if the subject that follows it is plural.

It *is* the *differences* that get most of our attention.

8. When the subject is a singular, indefinite pronoun, it requires a singular verb for agreement. Here are some indefinite pronouns that are always singular:

another	everybody	nothing
anybody	everyone	one
anyone	everything	somebody
anything	neither	someone
each	no one	something
either	nobody	

Everybody is represented by two senators and a representative.
Each represents one district of his or her state.

8a. Five indefinite pronouns may take either a singular or a plural verb, depending on their meaning in a particular sentence. They are *all, any, most, some,* and *none* (*not any*).

Some of the proposed bills *addresses* air pollution. (''Some'' means a part of several bills.)
Some of the proposed bills *address* air pollution. (''Some'' means several bills.)
Most of the air pollution *is* caused by automobile exhaust. (Part of a quantity that can't be counted is singular.)
Most of the automobiles *are* inspected for exhaust controls. (Part of a quantity that can be counted is plural.)

9. When the subject is a collective noun, it may take either a singular or plural verb depending on its meaning in a particular sentence. If you are writing about the group as a single unit, use a singular verb. If you are writing about the individual members of a group, use a plural verb. Some examples of collective nouns are *team, committee, family, class, audience,* and *group.*

The Senate *committee has* been studying air pollution.
The Senate *committee have* been studying air pollution in their own states.

10. Subjects that state a quantity or amount (of time, money, height, length, width, space, or weight) usually function like singular subjects and need singular verbs. However, they can function like plural subjects when they refer to individual items.

Ten days is the time it takes for a bill passed by both houses to become law without the President's signature.
Two-thirds of the Senate are present today in the session.

11. Subjects that are plural in form but singular in meaning require a singular verb for agreement. Some examples are *politics, news,* the names of some school subjects (*mathematics*), the names of some diseases (*measles*), and the names of some publications.

The *news is* about the influence of special interest groups on members of the legislature.
Politics is the art of compromise to reach agreement.
Economics is a partner of politics.
The New York Times is a good source of news about politics and economics.

Verb Tenses

Verb **tense** tells when the action or the condition in the sentence happens—in the past, in the present, or in the future.

The roofers *nail* each shingle in place. (present)
They *nailed* each shingle in place. (past)
They *will nail* the shingles in place on Monday. (future)

12. The present tense describes what is happening or exists now, what happens regularly, or what is generally true.

The roofers *hammer* steadily. They *begin* every day at 7:00 A.M.
The foreman *checks* the progress of the crew often.
The asphalt in the shingles *is* a mineral compound.

For most English verbs, the present tense is the form of the verb that follows the word *to* in the form called the *infinitive,* as in *to hammer* or *to finish.* (See Subject-Verb Agreement, pages 343–344, for the use of the *-s* ending in the formation of the present tense.)

12a. The *-ing* (or progressive) form of the present tense is usually used to indicate that the action or condition expressed by the verb is occurring at the moment and is continuing. To form a progressive tense, use the helping verb *be* (am, are, is, was, were, and the *-ing* form of a verb).

The roofers *hammer* steadily. (''Hammer'' indicates that they do this action on a regular basis.)
The roofers *are hammering* steadily now. (''Are hammering'' indicates that they are doing this action at the

moment the writer is writing and that the action is continuing.)

13. **The future tense expresses an action or condition that is yet to happen.** To form the future tense, use the helping verb *will* or *shall* in front of the present tense form.

    The roofers *will stop* for lunch at 11:30.

14. **The past tense indicates that an action has been completed or that a condition has ended.** To form the simple past tense of most English verbs, add *-ed* or *-d* to the end of the present tense form. (Add *-d* if the verb already ends in an *e*.)

    The manager *checked* their work.
    The owner *liked* the work of the roofers.

15. **The present perfect tense indicates that an action or condition began in the past and is still occurring.** To form the present perfect tense, use the helping verb *have* or *has* with the past tense form of the main verb.

    The owner *has watched* the roofers each morning since they began work. The roofers *have waved* politely to the old man each day.

    The present perfect tense is also used to indicate that an action or condition occurred some time in the indefinite past and is related to the present.

    The roofer *has replaced* many roofs, but he still is nervous about heights. Most roofers *have grown* comfortable about working high above ground level.

15a. **To refer to an action or a condition that has been occurring over a period of time and that is still occurring, combine the present perfect form of the verb *be* (*has been* or *have been*) and the *-ing* form of the main verb.**

    That roofer *has been roofing* houses for five years.

16. **The past perfect verb tense indicates that an action or condition occurred in the past before another past action or condition (mentioned or implied in the sentence) and that it was completed at some point in the past.** To form the past perfect tense of most English verbs, use the helping verb *had* with the past tense form of the main verb.

The supervisor *had worked* as a roofer for five years before he was promoted to supervisor. He *had worked* as a carpenter before he began work for this roofing company.

VERB TENSE: A REVIEW

Present tense: The roofers *pound* three nails into each shingle. The best roofer *pounds* with exact hammer blows.
Future tense: He *will pound* a hundred nails without missing.
Past tense: He *pounded* a hundred nails without missing.
Perfect tenses: He *has pounded* all the nails that he had in his apron. He *has been pounding* the nails all day. He *had pounded* all the nails before the supervisor returned with more.

REMINDER

When you write past, present perfect, and past perfect verbs and past participle adjectives, make sure you add the *-d* or *-ed* ending.

He *dropped* one plate, but she *has dropped* something each time she loaded the dishwasher. The *dropped* plate did not break.

Verb Tense Consistency

17. Do not switch verb tenses in the middle of a sentence or a paragraph unless you are writing about events that take place at different times.

Necessary switch in verb tenses. Our big dog *is* under the bed because she *thinks* that I *will bathe* her next. (The dog is now thinking under the bed, but the bath is still to occur, so the tense change is appropriate.)

Confusing switch in verb tenses. Our dogs *love* to swim in Joe's Creek, which *ran* behind our house. They *will get* a bath about once a week in the summer when we *have had* time. (Does the creek still run behind the house? When are the baths—in past, present, or future summers?)

Revised in the present tense to make the time clear. Our dogs *love* to swim in Joe's Creek, which *runs* behind our house. They *get* a bath about once a week in the summer when we *have* time.

Revised in the past tense to make the time clear. Our dogs *loved* to swim in Joe's Creek, which *ran* behind our house. They *got* a bath about once a week in the summer when we *had* time.

18. Generally, when you are writing about an essay or other printed literature, use the present tense.

> In *The Joy Luck Club* Amy Tan *writes* about growing up in a Chinese family in the United States. Her books *inform* American audiences about Chinese culture.

Regular and Irregular Verbs

19. A verb is called regular if its past tense form and its past participle form are both produced by adding *-d* or *-ed* to the infinitive form. *Past participle* is the technical name for the verb form that you use with the helping verbs "has," "have," and "had" to create the perfect tenses. The past tense form and the past participle form of most English verbs are the same. (Each verb has three principal parts: present tense, past tense, and past participle, for example, *work, worked, worked.*)

> Seamus Heaney, the poet visiting the college, *recited* thirteen poems, which he *had memorized.* He *surprised* students with his perfect memory and sense of humor. Only a few students *have attended* a poetry reading before.

20. A verb is called irregular if its past tense or past participle form is not created by adding *-d* or *-ed* to the present tense (or infinitive) form. Instead, these forms are produced by changing the spelling of the present tense form. The verb *be* is the most commonly used irregular verb. It can be more confusing than the other irregular verbs because even its present tense is irregular.

Forms of the Verb *Be*

Present Tense	Past Tense	Present Perfect Tense (*have* + past participle)
I am	I was	I have been
you are	you were	you have been
he, she, or it is	she was	he has been
we are	we were	we have been
you are	you were	you have been
they are	they were	they have been

On page 351 is a list of the principal parts of common irregular verbs, grouped according to their spelling patterns.

COMMON IRREGULAR VERBS

Present	Past Tense	Past Participle
	Begin, Began, Begun Pattern	
begin	began	begun
drink	drank	drunk
ring	rang	rung
sing	sang	sung
sink	sank	sunk
spring	sprang	sprung
swim	swam	swum
	Break, Broke, Broken Pattern	
break	broke	broken
choose	chose	chosen
freeze	froze	frozen
steal	stole	stolen
speak	spoke	spoken
	Blow, Blew, Blown Pattern	
blow	blew	blown
draw	drew	drawn
fly	flew	flown
know	knew	known
throw	threw	thrown
	Drive, Drove, Driven Pattern	
drive	drove	driven
ride	rode	ridden
rise	rose	risen
strive	strove	striven
write	wrote	written
	Bleed, Bled, Bled Pattern	
bleed	bled	bled
creep	crept	crept
feed	fed	fed
feel	felt	felt
lead	led	led
leave	left	left
mean	meant	meant
weep	wept	wept

(Continued)

Present	Past Tense	Past Participle
	Bring, Brought, Brought Pattern	
bring	brought	brought
buy	bought	bought
catch	caught	caught
fight	fought	fought
teach	taught	taught
think	thought	thought
	Verbs Without a Pattern	
am, are, is	was, were	been
do	did	done
eat	ate	eaten
find	found	found
forget	forgot	forgotten
go	went	gone
run	ran	run
see	saw	seen
take	took	taken
tear	tore	torn

REMINDER

- **Do *not* use the *-d* or *-ed* ending on the following types of verbs.**
- irregular verbs that form the past tense and the past participle by changing the spelling of the infinitive: They *forgot* the speaker's name. (Not *forgotted*)
- the infinitive form of a verb: Angel hoped *to start* her own business. (Not *to started*)
- a verb that follows the helping verb *do:* Gabriel *did work* two jobs last semester. (Not *did worked*)
- a verb that follows the helping verbs *can, could, should, would, may,* or *might:* Juan could study at work. (Not *could studied*)

Past Participle Adjectives

21. An adjective (word that describes nouns) may be created from the past and present participles of a verb.

The *surprised* students wanted to read more of his poems. (The adjective *surprised* is the past participle of the verb *to surprise.*)

The *dripping* faucet made a *surprising* mess under the sink. (The adjectives *dripping* and *surprising* are present participles of *drip* and *surprise.*)

PRONOUNS

A **pronoun** is a word that stands for or takes the place of an antecedent noun (a noun that was mentioned previously in a sentence or a paragraph). Pronouns make a paragraph coherent by linking ideas within sentences together. (See pages 356–358.) Here is an example.

> According to David Segal, offensive humor plays a valuable role in a multicultural society like ours. *It* releases tension. For instance, comedian Lenny Bruce used to insult the audience. *He* made racial and ethnic jokes about everyone in the audience. *They* laughed at *themselves* and each other. Spreading the abuse about took the sting out of *it.*

Pronoun Form

1. **The correct form of a pronoun, or its case, is determined by how the pronoun functions in the sentence.** There are three pronoun cases.

   1a. Pronouns in the **subjective case** are used as the subject of sentences or after linking verbs (*am, are, is, was, were, has been, have been, had been*).

   > *We* had to show the winning ticket.
   > Carlos, *who* had never won anything before, whooped with joy.
   > The winners were Carlos and *I.*

   1b. Pronouns in the **objective case** are used as the object of action verbs and prepositions.

   > The committee chose *him* to run security for the Olympics.
   > The one *whom* they selected had been a successful police chief. (*Whom* is the object of *selected.*)
   > He gave *himself* a month to accomplish two goals.
   > The committee gave the prize to Carlos and *me.*

   1c. Pronouns in the **possessive case** are used to describe a noun or to take the place of a possessive pronoun and the noun it describes.

Chief Rathburn made *his* choice of jobs. The decision was *his.*

The city manager, *whose* refusal to give him a five-year contract allowed him to accept the new job offer, regretted losing the police chief.

2. There are several kinds of pronouns: personal, relative, and reflexive. Many of them have several forms.

2a. A **personal pronoun** refers to an individual or individuals. There are different forms to express different number, case, person, and gender.

Forms of Personal Pronouns

	Subjective	Objective	Possessive
First Person			
Singular	I	me	mine, my
Plural	we	us	ours, our
Second Person			
Singular and plural	you	you	yours, your
Third Person			
Singular	he	him	his
	she	her	hers, her
	it	it	its
Plural	they	them	theirs, their

PUNCTUATION POINTER

There is no apostrophe in the third person singular possessive pronoun *its.* An apostrophe does occur in the completely different word *it's,* which is a contraction of *it is.*

It's a status symbol to have a beeper, but *its* irritating sound annoys even *its* owners.

2b. A **relative pronoun** connects a dependent clause to the pronoun's antecedent.

The beeper, *which* used to be owned only by professionals, has become a status symbol with teenagers.

Forms of Relative Pronouns

	Subjective	Objective	Possessive
Human	who	whom	whose
Nonhuman	that	that	
	which	which	whose

2c. A **reflexive pronoun** refers to the subject of the clause.

He bought a beeper for *himself.* They gave the beeper to me. (Not "to myself.")

Forms of Reflexive Pronouns

	Singular	Plural
First person	myself	ourselves
Second person	yourself	yourselves
Third person	himself	themselves
	herself	
	itself	

REMINDER

Don't use *theirselves* in Academic Written English. Use *themselves.*

2d. **Indefinite pronouns** are used to refer to antecedents that are not specifically named persons or things. They include the singular indefinite pronouns listed on page 346 and others such as *few, many, several,* and *some.*

2e. A **demonstrative pronoun** is used to refer to and point out or identify specific nouns: *this, that, these, those, such.* A demonstrative pronoun can be used by itself or with a noun.

He wanted *this* cup and *those* plates.
Did you see *that*?

2f. An **interrogative pronoun** is used to introduce a question: *who, which, what, whoever, whichever, whatever.*

What do you mean? *Who* brought the popcorn?

Pronoun Reference

3. Every pronoun should refer clearly to an antecedent noun stated earlier in the same sentence or in a preceding sentence. An unclear pronoun reference confuses readers. If a pronoun doesn't have an obvious antecedent or if there is a chance that a reader might be unsure about a pronoun's antecedent, replace the pronoun with its antecedent noun, even if this means repeating the noun a few times.

When *you* register for classes, *they* make *you* fill out a dozen different forms, and I hated *it.* (Who is ''they''? Who is ''you''—the person registering or the person spoken to? What is ''it''—registering or filling out the forms?)

When *people* register for classes, *the college* makes *new students* fill out a dozen different forms, and I hated *filling out the forms.*

3a. A subject pronoun cannot be used to refer to a possessive noun. Using the noun instead makes the reference clear.

In *Brenda Ueland's* book about writing, *she* says that ''everybody is talented, original, and has something important to say.'' (*She* refers to the possessive noun *Brenda Ueland's.*)

In *her* book about writing, *Brenda Ueland* says that ''everybody is talented, original, and has something important to say.''

Pronoun-Antecedent Agreement

4. Pronouns must agree with the nouns they refer to or replace. Every pronoun should match its antecedent noun in two ways. It should express the same **person** (first, second, or third) and the same **number** (singular or plural).

An income tax form comes in the mail in January, but *it* doesn't have to be filed until April 15. The taxpayer must collect *his or her* W-2 form and other statements of earnings, taxes, and interest. *These* usually arrive in the mail during January and February. People expecting a tax refund usually file *their* tax forms early, but people paying taxes often wait until the deadline. (*It* is singular to agree with *form. His or her* is singular to agree with *taxpayer. These* is plural to agree with *statements. Their* is plural to agree with *people.*)

Pronoun-Antecedent Agreement

	Singular	**Plural**
First person	Judy Lambert = I, me, mine	my family = we, us, our, ours

	Singular	Plural
Second person	audience = you, you, your, yours	audience = you, you, your, yours
Third person	man = he, him, his	men = they, them, their, theirs
	woman = she, her, hers	women = they, them, their, theirs
	cat = it, its	cats = they, them, their, theirs

4a. When the antecedent noun is a word such as *person* or *individual* (or a word meaning a person, such as *taxpayer, student,* or *plumber*), the pronoun forms that agree with it in number are *he or she, his or her, him or her.* If you don't want to use these forms, then change the antecedent noun to a plural, and use *they, them,* or *their* to refer back to it.

Each wage earner must file *his or her* income tax form.
All wage earners must file *their* income tax forms.

5. When the antecedent is a singular indefinite pronoun, use a singular pronoun. In speech most people carelessly use plural forms of a pronoun to refer back to a singular indefinite pronoun, but Academic Written English requires writers to use a singular pronoun.

Everyone with a tax refund files *their* forms early. (incorrect pronoun)
Everyone with a tax refund files *his or her* form early.

Singular Indefinite Pronouns

another	everybody	nothing
anybody	everyone	one
anyone	everything	somebody
anything	neither	someone
each	no one	something
either	nobody	

5a. If you want to avoid using *his or her,* change both the singular antecedent and the pronoun that refers to it to the plural form.

Everyone with a tax refund files *his or her* form early.
All *people* with tax refunds file *their* forms early.

5b. Five indefinite pronouns may be referred to with singular

or plural pronouns, depending on their meaning in a particular sentence. They are *all, any, most, some,* and *none* (*not any*).

> *All* of us fill out *our* own tax forms early. *Some* will receive *their* refunds quickly. (plural)
> *All* of this tax will be returned to the state of *its* payer.
> *Some* of the dog tax benefits *its* payers. (singular)

6. **A collective noun (*family, group, committee, team*) may take either a plural or a singular pronoun, depending on its meaning in a particular sentence.** When the noun refers to the group as a single unit, use a singular pronoun to refer to it. When the noun refers to the individual members of the group, use a plural pronoun to refer to them.

> The baseball team will play two of *its* games away this semester. (Singular because the sentence refers to the team as a unit.)
> The baseball team tried on *their* new green and purple uniforms. (Plural because the sentence refers to team members acting individually.)

7. **When two or more antecedent nouns are joined by *or, nor, either . . . or,* or *neither . . . nor,* the pronoun should agree with the noun that is closest to it.**

> Neither Coach Neal nor the players gave *their* opinions.
> Neither the players nor Coach Neal gave *his* opinion.

Pronoun Consistency

8. **Do not shift the person (first, second, third) or number (singular or plural) of pronouns unnecessarily.**

> Many people want to reduce the fat and cholesterol in *their* diets, but some fat is necessary for *your* health. *One* can eliminate fried foods, eat more chicken and fish, and eat smaller portions of meat, about the size of *your* palm. (The pronouns shift from third person plural *their* to second person *your* to third person singular *one* to second person *your.* The second person pronouns may be considered either singular or plural.)

> Many people want to reduce the fat and cholesterol in *their* diets, but some fat is necessary for *their* health. *They* can eliminate fried foods, eat more chicken and fish, and eat smaller portions of meat, about the size of *their* palm. (The pronouns are all third person plural.)

You may want to reduce the fat and cholesterol in *your* diet, but some fat is necessary for *your* health. *You* can eliminate fried foods, eat more chicken and fish, and eat smaller portions of meat, about the size of your palm. (The pronouns are all second person.)

REMINDER

When you edit a paragraph or essay, check to make sure you use pronouns consistently. Check your writing for shifts from a third-person pronoun (*he*, *she*, *it* or *they*) to the second-person pronoun (*you*) and/or to the first-person pronoun (*I*).

PLURALS AND POSSESSIVES

Edit your writing to make sure that you have included the correct endings on nouns to indicate number and possession.

Plural Nouns

1. **To form the plural of most nouns, add *-s* to the end of the noun.**

wedding	weddings	guest	guests
muffin	muffins	Riley	Rileys

2. **To form the plural of a noun that ends in *-s, -x, -z, -ch,* or *-sh,* add *-es.***

bus	buses	dish	dishes
batch	batches	sex	sexes
mess	messes	buzz	buzzes

3. **To form the plural of a noun that ends in *-y* preceded by a consonant, change the *y* to *i* and add *-es* (except for a proper name that ends in *y*).**

candy	candies	country	countries
opportunity	opportunities	balcony	balconies
quality	qualities	bully	bullies

4. **To form the plural of a number, letter, or symbol, add an apostrophe and *-s* (*-'s*). If you write out the word for the number, letter, or symbol, add only the *-s* to form the plural.**

x	x's	ABC	ABC's
		DJ	DJ's
3	3's	SAT	SAT's
three	threes		

5. **To form the plurals of compound nouns, add an *-s* ending to the main word.**

brother-in-law	brothers-in-law
baby-sitter	baby-sitters
editor-in-chief	editors-in-chief

THE *-s* ENDING ON NOUNS AND VERBS: A REVIEW

- When a plural noun, which usually ends in *-s,* is the subject of a sentence, it requires the plural form of the verb, which usually does *not* end in *-s.*

  Restaurants (plural) *respond* to the public's interest in healthful eating.

- When a singular noun, which usually does *not* end in *-s,* is the subject of a sentence, it requires the singular form of the verb, which usually does end in *-s.*

  Regular *exercise* (singular) *creates* (singular) more energy.

Possessive Nouns

6. **To form the possessive of most nouns (to indicate that a noun "possesses" another noun), add an apostrophe and *-s* (*-'s*) to the noun.**

cake	the cake's icing	the icing of the cake
groom	the groom's ring	the ring of the groom
bride	the bride's bouquet	the bouquet of the bride

To test whether a noun ending in *-s* is functioning as a possessive and should therefore correctly end in *-'s,* change the noun to an "of" phrase.

todays news = the news *of today* = *today's* news.

7. **To form the possessive of singular nouns that end in *-s,* add an apostrophe and *-s* (*-'s*) to the end of the noun.**

bus	the bus's fumes
Jones	Mr. Jones's party
boss	boss's office

8. **To form the possessive of plural nouns that end in *-s,* add an apostrophe only.**

buses	several buses' fumes

bullies	several bullies' fear
countries	several countries' borders
Joneses	several of the Joneses' cars

9. **To form the possessive of compound nouns, add the -*'s* ending to the last word.**

brother-in-law	my brother-in-law's computer
baby-sitter	the baby-sitter's phone number
editor-in-chief	the editor-in chief's policy

10. ***Never* add an apostrophe or an apostrophe and -*s* to a possessive pronoun.**

hers (Not *her's*)
theirs (Not *their's*)

> **REMINDER**
> The word *it's* is not a possessive pronoun nor does it indicate possession. It is a contraction of *it is* and the apostrophe stands for the omitted letter.

SENTENCE VARIETY AND STYLE

An effective sentence style and variety in sentence patterns make writing clear and interesting to read. As you are revising, you can use several methods to make your sentences more lively, varied, and precise.

Adding Descriptive Words and Phrases

1. **Use details that let readers see, hear, smell, taste, and feel the things and actions you are describing.**

Original: We watched some mountain goats.
With added details: After studying the glacier, we spent some time watching the mountain goats on the rocky crags of the peaks.

Original: We could see only specks.
With added details: We could see only white specks moving around.
With more added details: With the human eye we could only faintly make them out—white specks moving around.

Original: A lady had a pair of field glasses.
With added details: One lady, the wife of the big man, had a pair of field glasses, and she let us look through them.

2. Add prepositional phrases to tell where, when, how, or why the action in the sentence occurs. A prepositional phrase is a group of words that begins with a preposition and ends with the object of the preposition.

After studying the glacier, we spent some time watching the mountain goats *on the rocky crags of the peaks. With the human eye* we could only faintly make them out—white specks moving around. One lady, the wife *of the big man,* had a pair *of field glasses,* and she let us look *through them.*

After I had looked through them *for a long time,* she asked, "Did you see the goats?"

"Yes," I said, just being polite.

But I didn't see the goats. I didn't see anything. All I saw was the blurred, watery surface *of the lens.* I have never been able to see any more than that *through field glasses.*

Common Prepositions

about	by	onto
above	during	outside
across	except	over
after	for	through
among	from	to
around	in	toward
at	inside	under
before	into	until
behind	near	up
below	of	with
beneath	off	within
beside	on	without
between		

Original: She had broken her arm.
When: She had broken her arm *in July.*
How: She had broken her arm *in July in an accident.*
Where: She had broken her arm *in July in an accident on the swing in her backyard.*

2a. Shift prepositional phrases to different places in sentences to emphasize meaning and to vary sentence patterns.

Original: He drove to Phoenix on a motorcycle in May.
Shift: *In May* he drove to Phoenix on a motorcycle. (Emphasizes *when*)
Shift: *On a motorcycle* he drove to Phoenix in May. (Emphasizes *how*)

Shift: *To Phoenix* he drove on a motorcycle in May. (Emphasizes *where*)

3. **Use verb phrases (phrases beginning with *-ing, -ed, -en* verb forms) to combine two sentences with the same subject.** (For information about avoiding fragments when using *-ing, -ed,* and *-en* verb forms, see page 337.)

   Original: The zipper was invented by Whitcomb L. Judson in 1892. The zipper was named for the galoshes with slide fasteners made by the B. F. Goodrich Company.

   With a verb phrase: *Invented by Whitcomb L. Judson in 1892,* the zipper was named for the galoshes with slide fasteners made by the B. F. Goodrich Company.

   With a verb phrase: The zipper, *invented by Whitcomb L. Judson in 1892,* was named for the galoshes with slide fasteners made by the B. F. Goodrich Company.

   With a verb phrase: *Named for the galoshes with slide fasteners made by B. F. Goodrich Company,* the zipper was invented by Whitcomb L. Judson in 1892.

4. **Add appositives.** An appositive is a word or phrase that renames or defines the noun it follows.

   Original: Albert Einstein is the famous scientist. He developed the theory of relativity and the quantum theory of light. He was also a talented violinist who liked to play beautiful music. His favorite was the music of Mozart.

   With appositives: Albert Einstein, *the famous scientist,* developed the theory of relativity and the quantum theory of light. A talented violinist, he also liked to play beautiful music, *especially the music of Mozart.*

Varying Sentence Beginnings

5. **Vary the beginnings of your sentences.** Begin some sentences with descriptive phrases, other sentences with verb phrases, and still others with prepositional phrases.

   By the time I got to high school I had mastered English. *During my sophomore year* I became aware of a Vietnamese girl in my math class who reminded me of myself seven years ago. *Mispronouncing her name everyday after roll call,* the boys in our class substituted every letter in the alphabet for the ''n'' in ''Namm.'' *Terrified and confused by their rude questions,* she just sat still and ignored them. *Silent* she remained to them and to me when I tried to communicate with her on numerous occasions. *Finally,* in broken English, she said to me, "Thank you. You are much kind."

6. **Revise sentences that begin with the dummy subjects *there* and *it.*** To make these sentences stronger, start them with the "real" subject.

   Original: There are two opposite ways of viewing time. They are monochronic and polychronic.
   Revised: Two opposite ways of viewing time are monochronic and polychronic.

   Original: It is important to be prompt, speedy, brief, and punctual in monochronic time.
   Revised: Monochronic time values promptness, speed, brevity, and punctuality.

   Original: It is important to be flexible, intuitive, dedicated, and imaginative in polychronic time.
   Revised: Polychronic time values flexibility, intuition, dedication, and imagination.

   Note: Some English sentences require a dummy subject. For example, to describe the weather English speakers say, "It is raining" or "It's sunny."

7. **Repeat a sentence pattern or sentence opener for special effect.**

   I was not just liked, I was popular. *I was not just* good in sports, I won trophies. *I was not just* good in school, I was excellent. Everyone liked me. For only the small price of my ethnic identity, I had become a perfect carbon copy.

   The most important kind of discipline a child can learn from is the Discipline of Reality. *If he does the wrong thing . . . ,* he doesn't get the result he wants. *If he doesn't pile one block right on top of another . . . ,* his tower falls down. *If he hits the wrong key,* he hears the wrong note. *If he doesn't hit the nail squarely on the head,* it bends. . . . *If he closes his eyes when he swings,* he doesn't hit the ball.

SENTENCE STYLE AND VARIETY: A REVIEW

Expand sentences to clarify exact meanings by adding sensory details, prepositional phrases, verb phrases (*-ing, -ed, -en* verbs), and appositives.

(Continued)

Vary sentences by shifting the placement of prepositional phrases, adding appositives, and eliminating dummy subjects.
Begin some sentences with descriptive phrases, some with verb phrases, and others with prepositional phrases.
Repeat a sentence pattern or sentence opener for special effect.

Combining Sentences

Combining short simple sentences into longer ones enables you to express the relationships among your ideas more precisely, and it also makes your sentences clearer and more interesting to read.

8. **Combine sentences using prepositional phrases, verb phrases, and appositive phrases (as described on pages 362–363).**

   Original: Gloria learned through her experiences. She was a foreigner in an American school. She became a stronger individual.

   Combined with prepositional phrases: Gloria learned through her experiences *as a foreigner in an American school.* She became a stronger individual.

   Combined with an -ed *verb phrase:* *Having learned from her experiences as a foreigner in an American school,* Gloria became a stronger individual.

   Combined with an -ing *verb phrase:* *Learning from her experiences as a foreigner in an American school,* Gloria became a stronger individual.

   Combined with an -en *verb phrase:* *Shaken by her experience as a foreigner in an American school,* Gloria became a stronger individual.

   Combined with an appositive phrase: Gloria, *a foreigner in an American school,* became a stronger individual through her experiences.

9. **Combine sentences using coordination.** Combine two or more complete sentences that are equally important by using a comma and a coordinator (also called a *coordinating conjunction*). The coordinator does more than link sentences. It adds meaning because it expresses a relationship between the two sentences it joins. Therefore, choose the coordinator that expresses your meaning precisely. Don't overuse *and* to join sentences. English has only seven coordinators:

Coordinators

and	for
but	so
or	yet
nor	

Original: I am fortunate that I had options when the children came along. Not every mother is in this position.

Combined with for: I am fortunate that I had options when the children came along, *for* not every mother is in this position. (*For* indicates that the second clause provides reasons for the information in the first clause.)

Combined with and: My husband and I decided that I would quit my job, *and* from then on my career was taking care of the family and the house. (*And* indicates that the second clause provides similar or additional information.)

Combined with but: Promotions and a corner office disappeared from the picture, *but* my children came home to me, unaccompanied by a latchkey. (*But* and *yet* indicate that the second clause provides contrasting or different information.)

Combined with or: I knitted while my children took piano lessons, *or* I read while they played soccer. (*Or* indicates that the second clause provides an alternative to or a consequence of the information in the first clause.)

Combined with nor: My working friend could not comfort her baby when the first tooth broke through, *nor* could she keep her house sparkling and flowers growing in her yard. (*Nor* indicates that the second clause continues a negative statement begun in the first clause.)

Combined with so: I enjoy the freedom to organize my day my way, *so* I am truly a liberated woman. (*So* indicates that the information in the second clause is caused by the information in the first clause.)

10. Combine sentences using subordination. Combine two or more complete sentences that are *not* equally important by using a *subordinator* (also called a *subordinating conjunction*). Subordinate the idea that is less important by placing the subordinator at the beginning of the less important sentence.

Some Common Subordinators

after	if	unless
although	in order that	until

as	rather than	when
as if	since	where
because	so that	whether
before	than	while
even though	that	why
how	though	

Original: Sunday evenings were my Granny's favorite time. We sang lots of hymns.

Combined with because: Sunday evenings were my Granny's favorite time *because* we sang lots of hymns. Or, *Because* we sang lots of hymns, Sunday evenings were Granny's favorite time. (*Because* introduces the less important idea.)

Original: Together we would sing "Blest Be the Tie That Binds." Ribbons of color from the windows danced across the hymnal.

Combined with while: Together we would sing "Blest Be the Tie That Binds" *while* ribbons of color from the windows danced across the hymnal. Or, *While* ribbons of color from the windows danced across the hymnal, together we would sing "Blest Be the Tie That Binds." (*While* introduces the less important sentence.)

PUNCTUATION POINTER

When a sentence begins with a subordinate clause, put a comma after the clause. When a sentence begins with an independent clause (the clause that is more important, or not subordinated) do not separate the clauses with a comma.

Because successful athletes broke their task into a series of small steps, they were able to control their fear. (Use a comma *after* a subordinate clause at the beginning of a sentence.)

Successful athletes were able to control their fear *because* they broke their task into a series of small steps. (Do not use a comma *before* the subordinate clause when it follows the independent clause.)

11. **Combine sentences using relative pronouns.** To combine two sentences that have the same word (usually a noun), replace the repeated word with a relative pronoun. Combining sentences with relative pronouns links the ideas together more closely and reveals the rela-

tionships between them. It also eliminates short, choppy sentences and words that are repeated unnecessarily.

Relative Pronouns

who	whatever
whom	whoever
whose	whomever
which	
that	

Original: Albert Einstein was a scientist. Albert Einstein developed the Theory of Relativity. This theory states that everything in the universe is moving and that all motion is connected.

Revised: Albert Einstein was a scientist *who* developed the Theory of Relativity, *which* states that everything in the universe is moving and that all motion is connected.

PUNCTUATION POINTER

Do not use commas before and after a relative clause that is essential for the reader to identify the word the clause is describing.

But every book I picked up had many sentences *that* contained anywhere from one to nearly all of the words that might as well have been in Chinese. (The *that* clause is necessary to identify the "sentences" being talked about.)

I would have quit even these book reading motions unless I had received the motivation *that* I did. (The *that* clause describes "motivation.")

I reviewed the words *whose* meanings I didn't remember. (The *whose* clause is necessary to identify the "words" being talked about.)

Anyone *who* has read a great deal can imagine the new world *that* opened. (The *who* clause describes "anyone." The *that* clause describes "world.")

PUNCTUATION POINTER

Insert a comma before and after a relative clause that adds information that is not essential for identifying the word the clause is describing. If the nonessential clause ends the sentence, the second comma isn't needed.

Malcolm X wanted to write letters to Elijah Muhammad, *whose* teachings motivated Malcolm X to profound change. (The *whose* clause adds information about Elijah Muhammad that isn't essential for understanding the main clause.)

Elijah Muhammad, *who* was a Muslim leader in the U.S., changed Malcolm X's life through his teachings. (The *who* clause adds information about Elijah Muhammad that isn't essential for understanding the main clause.)

COMBINING SENTENCES: A REVIEW

Combine short, simple sentences into longer ones by using prepositional phrases, verb phrases, and appositive phrases.

Combine sentences using coordination to show an equal relationship among the ideas in the sentences.

Combine sentences using subordination to show that one idea is more important than another.

Combine sentences using relative clauses to eliminate the unnecessary repetition of words.

EFFECTIVE WORD CHOICES

Choosing your words carefully is part of being a good writer. Effective word choice improves clarity and tone. It shows a keen sense of the needs of an audience and the requirements of a situation.

Denotations and Connotations

1. **Make sure the words you use have the connotations you intend.** Many words have several layers of meaning. The denotation of a word is its objective, literal definition. The connotation of a word is an implied or associated meaning, often suggesting a feeling or attitude. Two words can have the same denotation, but quite different connotations.

   The customer *asked* the waiter about every item on the bill.
   The customer *interrogated* the waiter about every item on the bill.

   The words *asked* and *interrogated* have the same denotation; they both mean "to question." But *asked* has a neutral connotation of seeking information, while *interrogated* has a negative connotation of accusing the waiter of error.

2. **Be careful when using "loaded words"—words intended to provoke strong feelings.** Using loaded words will bias or slant your writing. The italicized loaded words below not only describe the roommate, but also convey the critical feelings the writer has about the roommate. The neutral words are descriptive words without such negative connotations.

   Loaded words: My roommate is a *fat* senior who *binges* on *junk food* constantly. He's a sociable person who is *gabby* and *overcommitted.* He *can't keep schedules,* so he's often late or supposed to be in two places at the same time. He's entirely *unorganized* about life.

   Neutral words: My roommate is a *stocky* senior who *snacks* constantly. He's a sociable person who is *talkative* and *busy.* He's *relaxed* about schedules, so he's often late or supposed to be in two places at the same time. He's entirely *flexible* about life.

Levels of Usage

Choosing the right word or expression depends on the situation in which you are using the word. The choices appropriate in different situations are called levels of usage. Levels of usage vary from the most formal (for written reports and college essays) to the most informal (for notes to yourself or your family). Use the dictionary to identify the usage level when you need to check if a word is appropriate for your situation.

3. **More formal writing generally does not use contractions, uses the third person rather than the first or second person, and uses abstract as well as concrete words.**

   According to George A. Miller, a psychologist, the average person can hold only three to seven pieces of information in short-term memory. The short-term memory holds this information for only about twenty seconds unless the mind can connect it to something already known in the long-term memory.

4. **Less formal writing generally uses contractions, often uses the first person ("I" or "we"), and uses concrete rather than abstract language. This writing sounds more conversational than formal writing, as though it might have been written in a person's Idea Bank or in a letter to a friend.**

I've discovered why *I* forget people's names and *can't* remember everything *I* study for tests. The psychologist George A. Miller says *we* have short-term and long-term memories. *We* can hold only three to seven pieces of information in short-term memory. *We* can remember this information for only about twenty seconds if *we can't* connect it to something *we* already know in our long-term memories.

5. **Slang is very informal and is almost always inappropriate for academic writing.** It is often the ''in'' language of an age or interest group. Before he educated himself, Malcolm X could only speak in slang (''Look, daddy, let me pull your coat about a cat . . .''). Although slang is colorful and energetic, most slang words and expressions go out of style quickly and communicate meaning only to a limited audience.

Vague Words and Expressions

6. **Avoid vague words and expressions.** Words that are clear to you might not be clear to your readers if you use words that are general, indefinite, and imprecise. Find specific and precise words to replace such tired, all-purpose words as these:

great, terrific, incredible, wonderful
good, nice, okay, all right, interesting
terrible, awful, bad, strange
a lot, lots, many, plenty, very
thing, aspect, factor, stuff

Clichés

7. **Avoid clichés.** Clichés are phrases that have been used so much that they have lost their meaning. Substitute more original and more precise language for clichés in your writing. Here are some examples of clichés.

acid test
at a loss for words
blood is thicker than water
first and foremost
get down to brass tacks
goes without saying
green with envy
many and varied
nipped in the bud
remedy the situation
sadder but wiser
sit up and take notice
spirited debate
stubborn as a mule
the worse for wear
too funny for words
view with alarm

Sexist Language

8. **Avoid sexist language.** Many people are offended by the use of masculine nouns and pronouns to refer to people of both genders and the use of words that make a distinction between work done by men and by women.

8a. Use *he or she, his or her,* and *him or her* to refer to indefinite pronouns and indefinite, nongender-specific nouns.

Anyone with a sense of humor can laugh at *his or her* own peculiarities.

The *scientist* must be scrupulous about *his or her* research.

8b. To avoid the *his or her* construction, use plural nouns and pronouns instead of singular ones and omit unnecessary pronouns.

People with a sense of humor can laugh at *their* own peculiarities.

A person who values laughter must continue to find humor in life. (Instead of "in *his or her* life")

8c. If a title is necessary, use *Ms.* in writing to or about a woman unless she has a professional title (Dr., Prof.) or has requested that you use *Mrs.* or *Miss.*

Ms. Garcia was the first woman in her family to earn a college degree.

8d. Avoid gender words that exclude women and the use of *woman* as a descriptive word with an occupation.

Sexist Term	Nonsexist Term
mankind	humanity
working man	worker
salesman	salesperson
woman doctor	doctor
waitress	server

Wordiness

9. **Wordiness is the use of several words when one or a few will do.** Unnecessary words can make sentences confusing or boring. Eliminate the following words and phrases as you revise your writing.

Wordy Phrases and Possible Replacements

Wordy Phrase	Replacement
"At" Phrases	
at the present time	currently
at this point in time	now
at a later date	later
"That" Phrases	
regardless of the fact that	although
in view of the fact that	since
in light of the fact that	because
aware of the fact that	know
in spite of the fact that	despite
for the reason that	because
it is important that	should
in the event that	if
on the condition that	if
"Of" Phrases	
on the subject of	about
pertaining to the subject of	about
in lieu of	instead

Comparatives and Superlatives

Modifiers—adjectives and adverbs—describe people, places, things, ideas, and actions. Most English adjectives and adverbs have different forms to express comparison. When you compare *two* people or things, use the comparative form. When you compare *three or more* people or things, use the superlative form.

10. With a modifier that is one syllable, add the ending *-er* to compare two things and add the ending *-est* to compare three or more things.

	Comparative	Superlative
loud	louder	loudest
near	nearer	nearest
light	lighter	lightest

11. With an adjective that is two syllables, add the ending *-er* to compare two things and add the ending *-est* to compare three or more things.

	Comparative	Superlative
happy	happier	happiest
cloudy	cloudier	cloudiest
heavy	heavier	heaviest

12. With an adjective of more than two syllables, use "more" and "most."

	Comparative	Superlative
beautiful	more beautiful	most beautiful

13. With an adverb that is two or more syllables, use the word *more* with the modifier to compare two things and the word *most* to compare three or more things.

	Comparative	Superlative
quickly	more quickly	most quickly
boldly	more boldly	most boldly
spitefully	more spitefully	most spitefully

14. Avoid the double comparative and superlative. Do not use *more* with a word ending in *-er* or *most* with a word ending in *-est.*

The volume was *more louder* than I could stand.
The bridesmaids' dresses were the *most lightest* shade of pink.

15. Some modifiers have irregular comparative and superlative forms. Here is a list of them.

	Comparative	Superlative
bad	worse	worst
badly	worse	worst
good	better	best
little	less	least
many	more	most
much	more	most
well	better	best

Commonly Confused Words

English has several sets of words that writers frequently confuse because the words resemble each other. When you edit your revisions, find and correct such misuses. Here are some commonly confused words and their meanings.

accept to receive. Marty can *accept* feedback on a draft without defensiveness.

except excluding or leaving out. Everyone in our group *except* Chris has given Marty feedback.

advise verb; to recommend or suggest. Vera *advised* her friend to lease a car instead of buying one.
advice noun; a recommendation or suggestion. A friend's *advice* often has more weight than a parent's.

affect to influence or change. The feedback of the group will *affect* how Marty revises the draft.
effect verb; to cause or bring about. Specific feedback can *effect* good revisions.
effect noun; the result or consequence. The *effect* of specific feedback on a draft is often an improved draft.

all ready set or prepared. Our group is *all ready* to revise our drafts.
already previously or by this time. Terry has *already* revised his draft.

among in the midst of several. She planted the tulips *among* the pansies.
between in the midst of two. He planted the rose bush *between* the driveway and the house.

amount refers to masses of things that cannot be counted. The *amount* of steak on his plate could feed the whole team.
number refers to things that can be counted. Carey guessed the *number* of jelly beans in the jar.

beside by the side of. The remote control is *beside* the television.
besides in addition to. They bought video and compact disc players *besides* a television.

fewer refers to things that can be counted. She had *fewer* CD's than her sister.
less refers to things that cannot be counted or to degree. Her sister has *less* interest in music than she has.

good adjective; describes nouns and pronouns. He gave a *good* speech.
well adverb; describes verbs. He spoke *well* in front of the class.

its possessive pronoun; belonging to it. Our red oak doesn't shed all *its* leaves until March.
it's contraction of *it is. It's* almost time for the trees to bud.

lie to rest or recline. Today the newspaper *lies* (present tense) on the kitchen table. Yesterday the newspaper *lay* (past tense) on the living room floor.
lay to put or place. Please *lay* (present tense) the newspaper on the chair. A neighbor *laid* (past tense) our papers on the porch while we were away.

like preposition; similar to. Cookie dough, *like* candy, is sweet.
as subordinate conjunction; I eat the cookie dough *as* I bake cookies. Do *as* I say, not *as* I do.

lose verb; to misplace. If you *lose* (present tense) your student ID card, you must pay to have it replaced. I *lost* (past tense) mine last semester.
loose adjective; unattached. *Loose* pages often become lost.

moral adjective; good or having good values. Tony is a *moral* person.
moral noun; a lesson. The *moral* of the story is to dream big and work hard.
morale spirit or mental condition. The family's *morale* was raised by the surprise party.

passed verb; past tense form of *to pass,* to go by, to move. The bus *passed* the corner as she ran toward it.
past noun; a previous time or the history of a person or thing. Her *past* was marked by many near misses.
past preposition; by or farther on than. This time the bus rolled *past* the corner just as she approached.

principal adjective; the most important. Ancient differences were the *principal* causes of the civil war.
principal noun; a person in authority or a sum of money. Students met with the *principal* about the senior gift to the school. The new sound system for the auditorium was possible because of the *principal* (money made from many car washes) and the interest earned.
principle a law, fact, or rule of conduct. The *principle* of extreme loyalty to an ethnic group or religion makes some groups hostile to others.

quiet adjective; silent or still. The audience was *quiet* as the speaker continued.
quiet noun; silence. We enjoyed the *quiet* after all that noise.
quite rather, very, or exactly. The speech was *quite* entertaining.

real adjective; genuine or actual. Their complaint was *real.*
really adverb; actually or truly. They complained *really* long before they were taken *really* seriously.

sit to rest. The books *sit* (present tense) on the bench where you left them. They *sat* (past tense) there all weekend.
set to place. You always *set* (present tense) the books on the bench. You *set* (past tense) the books there after class.

than conjunction; used to compare people or things. The phone rang louder *than* the television blared.
then adverb; at that time. When the phone rang, *then* she turned the television down.

their possessive pronoun; belonging to them. Shoppers should watch *their* packages as they try on clothes.
there adverb; in that place. You can put your packages *there* for safekeeping.
they're contraction of *they are. They're* safe under this counter.

your possessive pronoun; belonging to you. Would you print this file on *your* printer?

you're contraction of *you are.* While *you're* printing that file, would you also print this one?

SPELLING AND CAPITALIZATION

Spelling Words

To improve your spelling, edit your writing carefully. Use a dictionary to look up any word you are unsure of, and keep a list in your Idea Bank of words you frequently misspell. If you are using a word processor, remember to use the spelling checker but don't count on it to find correctly spelled words that are used incorrectly (such as *set* for *sit, an* for *and, broke* for *broken*).

The five causes of spelling errors listed below can help you recognize words you frequently misspell, and the following three spelling rules can help you spell many words correctly.

1. Use these five causes of spelling errors to recognize your spelling problems.

- *Addition.* You add a letter, usually because you pronounce the word with this letter:

  hund*e*reds (hundreds) athe*l*etes (athletes)

- *Deletion.* You leave out a letter, usually because you don't pronounce it:

  Fe*bu*ary (February) temper*me*ntal (temperamental)

- *Transposition.* You transpose (switch) a letter with the letter next to it:

  jew*le*ry (jewelry) rec*ie*pt (receipt)

- *Substitution.* You substitute a letter that has a similar sound:

  absen*s*e (absence) excell*a*nt (excellent)

- *Homonym.* You confuse a word with another word that sounds like it. (See Commonly Confused Words on pages 374–377.)

  principle/principal sight/cite/site

Almost every spelling rule has so many exceptions that it is useless to memorize it. However, here are three rules that are worth memorizing.

2. To add a suffix to a word, double the final consonant if it meets these three conditions: (a) if the word ends in a single consonant, (b) if the suffix begins with a vowel, (c) if the word consists of only one syllable or is accented on the final syllable.

Doubled	Not Doubled
fit, fitted	bigot, bigoted
hop, hopping	hope, hoping
bar, barred	bare, bared
refer, referral	appear, appearance
forbid, forbidden	mistake, mistaken
propel, propeller	design, designer
begin, beginning	benefit, benefiting

2a. The **exception** to this rule is any word that ends in an *x*.

tax, taxed	relax, relaxed

3. **To add a suffix to a word that ends in a silent *e* (an *e* that is not pronounced), drop the *e* if the suffix begins with a vowel, but keep the *e* if the suffix begins with a consonant.**

care, caring	care, careful
rare, rarity	rare, rarely

3a. Some exceptions to this rule are:

true, truly	mile, mileage
argue, argument	agree, agreeable
change, changeable	notice, noticeable

4. **To add a suffix to a word that ends in a *y*, change the *y* to *i*. If the suffix begins with *i*, keep the final *y*.**

marry, marriage	marry, marrying
fry, fried	fly, flying

4a. The **exceptions** to this rule are:

day + ly = daily	lay + ed = laid
pay + ed = paid	say + ed = said

Spelling Numbers

5. **When you begin a sentence with a number, always spell out the number.**

   One hundred eleven callers had questions for the guest on the radio program.

6. **When you use a number within a sentence, spell it out if it can be written as one or two words.** The two-word numbers from *twenty-one* through *ninety-nine* require a hyphen when they are spelled out.

Only *twenty-three* of the callers spoke with the radio guest.

7. **When you use more than one number within a sentence, if any of the numbers are more than two words, use numerals for all of the numbers.**

Of the *111* callers, only *23* asked the talk show guest questions.

Capitalization

Here are the most important capitalization rules in Academic Written English.

8. **Capitalize the names of days, months, and holidays.** Do not capitalize the seasons of the year (fall, spring, summer, and winter).

Wednesday May Memorial Day

9. **Capitalize the names of specific people, institutions, religions, and places, including the names of cities, states, regions of a country, and countries and their languages.**

The famous poet from Ireland, Seamus Heaney, spoke at Richland College in Dallas, Texas, in Fannin Building. Living half of each year in the East while he teaches at Harvard University, he rarely travels to the Southwest. He spoke about the roots of the Catholic and Protestant conflict.

9a. **Do not capitalize directions.**

Turn east at the stop light.

10. **Capitalize the first word of every sentence and of every sentence within a quotation.**

A voice from the speaker at the drive-through window said, "*H*ow may I help you?"

10a. **Do not capitalize quoted words that are not a complete sentence.**

A voice from the speaker asked if I wanted "*c*ream, sugar, or dessert."

11. **Capitalize people's titles (and their abbreviations).**

*M*r. Heaney was introduced by *P*rofessor *J*erry *M*c*E*lveen.

11a. **Do not capitalize titles used without names or institutions or organizations without names.**

Heaney had been invited to our college for five years.
Heaney had been invited to Richland College for five years.

The president greeted the distinguished guest.
The distinguished guest was greeted by President Mittelstet.

12. Capitalize the names of specific courses.

Zoltan, who is *R*ussian, is registered for sixteen hours. He is taking *S*panish, history, a computer course, political science, and *E*nglish. In *H*istory 101 and *P*olitical *S*cience 201 he will study *A*merican history and government.

If the writer had left out the course numbers, then the course names "history" and "political science" would *not* be capitalized. Note that Spanish and English are capitalized as languages, not as the names of courses.

13. Capitalize the first word, the major words, and the first word after a colon in a title. Do not capitalize articles (*a, an, the*), coordinating conjunctions (*and, or, for*), and prepositions under five letters long (*of, by, on*) within titles.

Beauty and the Beast (movie title)
"*T*he *L*ast *L*aughs: *T*he *B*est and *W*orst of 1992" (essay title)
No Jacket Required (album title)
"*A*nother *D*ay in *P*aradise" (song title)
Sports Illustrated (magazine title)

A GUIDE TO PUNCTUATION

Period (.)

1. Use a period to end a sentence that makes a statement or is a command. Page 383, 1a.
2. Use a period after most abbreviations. Page 388, 6a.

Question Mark (?)

1. Use a question mark to end a sentence that asks a direct question. Page 383, 1b.
2. Do not use a question mark with an indirect question. Page 383, 1c and page 388, 5e
3. When a quotation is a question, put the question mark inside the final quotation mark. Page 384, 1d

Exclamation Point (!)

1. Use an exclamation point to end a sentence that expresses strong emotion, surprise, or emphasis. Page 384, 1e

Semicolon (;)

1. Use a semicolon to join two sentences when the idea in the second sentence is a continuation of the one in the first. Page 384, 2a
2. Use a semicolon to join two sentences when the second sentence begins with a transitional word or phrase, such as *then, however,* and *therefore.* Page 384, 2b
3. Do not use a semicolon when you join two sentences with a coordinator such as *and, but,* and *or.* Page 384, 2c
4. Use a semicolon to separate items in a series when any of the items includes a comma. Page 385, 3b

Colon (:)

1. Use a colon to connect a sentence with another sentence if the second sentence contains an illustration of the first. Page 385, 2d
2. Use a colon after a statement that clearly indicates a list, particularly after expressions such as "the following" or "are as follows." Page 391, 6m
3. Use a colon after the opening in a formal letter. Page 391, 6n

Comma (,)

1. Use a comma and a coordinator (*and, but, or, nor, for, so,* and *yet*) to link two related sentences. Page 385, 2e
2. Use commas to separate items in a series (three or more words, phrases, or sentences). If one of the items includes a comma, use a semicolon to separate the items. Page 385, 3a, 3b
3. Use a comma to separate an introductory phrase from the main sentence. Page 386, 4a
4. Use commas before and after descriptive words, phrases, or clauses that interrupt the flow of a sentence *if* they are not necessary for identifying the word being modified. Page 386, 4b
5. Use a comma to separate a phrase equivalent to "she said" from a direct quotation. Page 387, 5

(Continued)

6. Use a comma to separate items in dates and addresses. Page 388, 6b
7. Use a comma before and after a title or an abbreviation following a person's name. Page 389, 6c
8. Use a comma after the salutation of a friendly letter and after the closing. Page 389, 6d
9. Do not separate a subject and its verb with a comma. Page 389, 6e
10. Do not use a comma before a coordinator (usually *and*) when the coordinator is joining two subjects or two verbs in a sentence. Page 389, 6f

Quotation Marks ("...")

1. Use quotation marks before and after a direct quotation—the actual words that someone spoke or wrote. Pages 387–388, 5
2. Use quotation marks before and after the titles of stories, poems, songs, magazine and newspaper articles, and chapters in books. Pages 390–391, 6l
3. Do not use quotation marks to set off an indirect quotation—a quotation that summarizes what was spoken (and is often preceded by the word "that"). Page 388, 5e

Dash (—)

1. Use dashes before and after information that interrupts a sentence if you want to emphasize the information. Page 387, 4e

Parentheses ( )

1. Use parentheses before and after information that interrupts a sentence if you want to deemphasize the information. Page 387, 4e

Apostrophe (')

1. Use an apostrophe to indicate the omitted letter or letters in a contraction. Page 389, 6g
2. Use an apostrophe *s* (-'*s*) to form the possessive of nouns. Add an apostrophe only to form the possessive of plural nouns that end in *s*. Page 390, 6h
   - 2a. Add an apostrophe and -*s* to form the possessive of nouns not ending in -*s*.
   - 2b. Add an apostrophe *only* to form the possessive of plural nouns that end in -*s*.
   - 2c. Add an apostrophe and -*s* to singular nouns that end in -*s*.

3. Do not add an apostrophe to a possessive pronoun. Page 390, 6i
4. Use an apostrophe to form the plurals of numbers, letters, and symbols. Page 359, 4

Underlining (XXXX)

1. Underline the titles of books, plays, television programs, and albums. Page 390, 6k

PUNCTUATION

Punctuation signals the relation among your ideas and between the parts of your sentences. It also tells the readers where you want them to stop, to pause, or to notice your emphasis. Punctuation serves six basic functions in writing: (1) to end sentences, (2) to combine sentences, (3) to separate items in a series, (4) to identify and separate modifiers from the rest of the sentence, (5) to separate quoted material from the rest of the sentence, (6) to mark and form several constructions.

1. Punctuation marks are used to end sentences. The period, the question mark, and the exclamation point are used at the ends of sentences.

> According to Alan Durning, we have become a consumer society. He says that we have become "long on things and short on time." Do we really need all the things we have and want? Has consumerism brought happiness? No, instead it has brought us spiritual and environmental poverty!

1a. Use a period to end a sentence that makes a statement or is a command.

> We want improved products, new styles, the latest technology, and a great variety of goods and services.
> Think about the marketplace today.

1b. Use a question mark to end a sentence that asks a direct question.

> Did you know that twenty percent of the world's people earn sixty-four percent of the world's income?

1c. Do not use a question mark with an indirect question. Use

a period instead. An indirect question reports a question but does not ask it directly.

> Mr. Durning's question is if we can learn to measure our wealth in hours instead of dollars. (Indirect question)
> Can we learn to measure our wealth in hours instead of dollars? (Direct question)

1d. When a quotation is a question, put the question mark inside the final quotation mark. When the quoted material is not a question, but the rest of the sentence is a question, put the question mark outside the quotation mark.

> The article asks, "Will our desire for new things destroy the environment?" (Quotation is a question.)
> Did the writer say, "Human desires will destroy the environment unless we shift from material to nonmaterial goals"? (Sentence that is a question contains a quotation that is not a question.)

1e. Use an exclamation point to end a sentence that expresses strong emotion, surprise, or emphasis.

> We must become less materialistic to save the environment!

2. Punctuation marks combine sentences. You can combine sentences with a semicolon, a colon, or a comma with a coordinator. (See pages 365–366 for more information on coordination.)

2a. Use a semicolon to join two sentences when the idea in the second sentence is a continuation of the one in the first. A semicolon links the ideas more closely than a period. Remember that you cannot join two sentences with a comma.

> Consumerism strengthens our economy. A strong economy means more jobs.
> Consumerism strengthens our economy*; a* strong economy means more jobs.

2b. Use a semicolon to join two sentences when the second sentence begins with a transitional word or phrase (also known as a conjunctive adverb). (See page 339, 6d for a list of transitions.)

> Our appetite for new cars, the latest style of jeans, and a new brand of hairspray keeps growing*; therefore,* our economy keeps growing.

2c. Do not use a coordinator if you are using a semicolon.

Our economy is structured to consume or decline, *but* there is an alternative.

2d. Use a colon to connect a sentence with another sentence if the second sentence contains an illustration of the first sentence. Note that the sentence following a colon begins with a capital letter.

Alvin Toffler pointed out that we have become a throw-away society: We buy disposable diapers, paper plates, and plastic forks.

2e. Use a comma and a coordinator to link two related sentences.

Rachel is studying pollution in our city, *and* Kevin is investigating indoor pollution, especially secondhand smoke.

3. **Punctuation marks separate three or more items in a series.** The items in a series can be words, phrases, or independent clauses. The items can be separated by commas and semicolons.

3a. Use a comma after each item in a series, including the item before the conjunction (*and, or*) before the last item (unless your instructor tells you that this last comma is not necessary).

Pollution has affected our *air, soil,* and *water.* (Words in a series)

Fancy wrapping on gifts, colorful labels and containers on detergents, and *styrofoam containers for fast food* add to pollution problems. (Phrases in a series)

We can wrap gifts in the Sunday comics, we can buy products in plain containers, and *we can ask for paper instead of styrofoam for our hamburgers.* (Independent clauses in a series)

3b. Use a semicolon to separate the items in a series when any of the items includes a comma.

My recycling center accepts *newspapers with the slick pages removed; flattened corrugated boxes; clear and brown glass, but not green;* and *plastic milk bottles.*

4. **Punctuation marks separate modifiers and other information that interrupts the sentence from the rest of the sentence.** Mod-

ifiers include adjectives, adverbs, prepositional phrases, appositive phrases, and participial phrases (phrases that begin with *-ing, -ed,* and *-en* verb forms). Interrupting modifiers and other information can be set off by commas, dashes, and parentheses. Use two commas (one before and one after) to set off a phrase in the middle of a sentence.

4a. Use a comma to separate an introductory phrase from the main sentence.

Transitional expression: *As a result,* companies are responding to consumer interest by producing biodegradable packaging for their products.
Prepositional phrase: *With very little effort,* concerned people can change their buying habits.
Appositive phrase: *A good source of information,* the booklet *50 Simple Things You Can Do to Save the Earth* makes practical suggestions for concerned people.
Participial phrase: Changing our life-styles individually, we can make a difference collectively.

4b. Use a comma before *and* after descriptive words, phrases, or clauses that interrupt a sentence if these are not necessary for identifying the word being described. Such a word, phrase, or clause is called "nonessential."

Some students, *reluctant to attend the library orientation,* find the forty-five minute session worthwhile. Students are delighted to learn about MASE, *the database that indexes magazine articles,* because it will search for articles on their subjects and print out summaries of articles. (The pair of commas in both these sentences indicates that the information they enclose could be left out without confusing readers.)

4c. Do not use commas to set off modifiers that are essential to the meaning of the sentence.

The librarians *teaching the orientation session* surprise students with their helpful attitude. Information *learned in the session* helps launch students in their research.

4d. Do not use commas before and after a phrase or relative clause that is necessary for identifying the word that the phrase or clause is describing. Such a phrase or clause is called "essential," and it is *not* set off by commas.

The librarians *who teach the orientation sessions* recommend that students begin by reading background information in specialized encyclopedias. Students *who know about general encyclopedias* often aren't aware that there are also specialized encyclopedias on almost every subject. Books *that cannot be checked out of the library* are called reference books; books *that can be checked out* are called circulating books.

4e. Use dashes or parentheses to enclose information that interrupts a sentence. Use dashes when you want to emphasize the information and parentheses to deemphasize it.

Dashes: The sources librarians recommend as the best place to start a research project—*specialized encyclopedias about your topic*—are ones students seldom know about.

Parentheses: The librarians also suggest having a research plan *(described briefly in the library handbook)* so you can search more efficiently when you are in the library.

5. Punctuation marks separate quoted material from the rest of the sentence. Use a pair of quotation marks to set off the exact words that someone has spoken or written. A comma usually separates a phrase equivalent to "she said" from the quotation.

Francis Bacon said, "Knowledge is power."
"Knowledge is power," said Francis Bacon.

5a. Put commas and periods *inside* the closing quotation mark.

David Segal argues in "The Case for Offensive Humor" that "in a multicultural society ethnic and racial comedy serves as a critical support and safety valve."

5b. Put colons and semicolons *outside* the quotation mark.

Segal argues that "racial humor undermines prejudice"; he claims that it is educational and tension-relieving.

Segal asserts that such comedy "diffuses tensions": Lenny Bruce insulted everyone in the audience to spread abuse around and take the sting out.

5c. Put question marks and exclamation points *inside* the closing quotation mark when they are part of the quoted material.

Believing that the body's healing mechanics are affected by the mind, Dr. Siegel writes that "a sense of humor is an enormous asset." "Can laughter help seriously ill people get well?" He wondered, "Yes!" he discovered from his work with cancer patients and many other doctors.

5d. Put question marks and exclamation points *outside* the closing quotation mark when they are part of the larger sentence in which the quotation is being enclosed.

Bernie S. Siegel, a surgeon who works with cancer patients, believes, "The truth is: love heals. Miracles happen to exceptional patients every day." Is it enough for a patient to have hope and "trust in the healer"? No, the doctor must have "certain essentials—compassion, acceptance, availability, a willingness to provide information"!

5e. Do not use quotation marks to set off an indirect quotation, or a paraphrase of what someone said or wrote. Often the word *that* comes before an indirect quotation.

Margaret said that she feels better now. (Indirect quotation preceded by *that*)
Margaret said, "I feel better now." (Direct quotation—the exact words that Margaret spoke)

6. Other conventions of Academic Written English require punctuation marks.

6a. Use a period after many types of abbreviations. Periods are generally not used with acronyms, groups designated by initials, compass points, and many technical units.

Mrs.	St.	pp.	NATO	NE
Lt.	Rd.	A.M.	AMA	SSW
Sen.	Ave.	Ph.D.	CBS	BTU

6b. Use a comma to separate items in dates and addresses.

On September 23, 1987, in Texas alone, volunteers collected from beaches 31,773 plastic bags, 30,295 plastic bottles, 15,631 plastic six-pack rings, 28,540 plastic lids, and 1,914 disposable diapers. For more information write Center for Marine Conservation, 1725 DeSales St. NW, Washington, D.C. 20036.

REMINDER

Use a comma after the last item in a date or address.

On September 23, 1987, in Texas alone . . .
Write Center for Marine Conservation, 1725 DeSales St. NW, Washington, D.C. 20036, for more information.

6c. Use a comma before and after a title or an abbreviation following a person's name.

Bernie S. Siegel, *M.D.,* wrote about the lessons he learned from working with patients.

6d. Use a comma after the salutation and after the closing (the words before the signature) of a friendly letter.

Dear Paxton,

Your postcard arrived from Guatemala and cheered my blue Monday. I'm glad you're having fun and appreciate your thinking of me. I'll call you next week to hear about your adventures.

With fond regards,

6e. Do not place a comma so that it separates a subject and its verb. An appositive or other phrase enclosed within two commas may be placed between a subject and its verb.

Writing a postcard to a friend, is hard for most people on vacation. (Incorrect comma)

6f. Do not use a comma before a coordinator when the coordinator is joining two subjects or two verbs in a sentence.

The *postcards* that he wrote quickly the last evening of their vacation, *and* the *gifts* that he bought that last day were appreciated by his friends. (Incorrect comma. The coordinator *and* joins the subjects *postcards* and *gifts.*)

He *bought* gifts for several friends in the morning, *and wrote* postcards to other friends in the evening. (Incorrect comma. The coordinator *and* joins the verbs *bought* and *wrote.*)

6g. Use an apostrophe to indicate the omitted letter or letters in a contraction.

If *you're* (you are) sleepy, take a nap. When *I'm* (I am) overtired, I *can't* (cannot) study effectively.

6h. Use an apostrophe to indicate possession in nouns. (See pages 360–361 for more complete information on possessives.) **Add an apostrophe and *-s* to form the possessive of nouns not ending in *-s*.**

The essay**'s** title was funny, but misleading.
The girl**'s** essay was read aloud to the class.
The wasp**'s** stings caused both eyes to swell shut. (one wasp)
The children**'s** eyes followed the action on the screen. (a plural noun not ending in *-s*)

Add an apostrophe *only* to form the possessive of plural nouns that end in *-s*.

The essay**s'** titles were funny, but misleading.
The girl**s'** essays were read aloud in class.
The wasp**s'** stings caused the child to have trouble breathing. (several wasps)
The bus**es'** fumes made the waiting commuters ill. (several buses)
The Jons**es'** party was a big success.

Add an apostrophe and *-s* to singular nouns that end in *s*.

The bus**'s** fumes made the waiting commuters ill. (one bus)
When I heard Dr. Jones**'s** nickname was "Bones Jones," I laughed.
He turned on headquarter**s's** heat before they arrived for the meeting.

6i. Do not add an apostrophe to a possessive pronoun.

She followed the stream to **its** source.
The decision was **theirs** to make.

6j. Use an apostrophe to form the plural of numbers, letters, or symbols.

There are four i's in Mississippi.

6k. Underline (or italicize) the titles of books, plays, television programs, and albums.

Amy Tan wrote about her experience as a Chinese girl growing up in the United States in *The Joy Luck Club.* (Book title)

6l. Use quotation marks to set off the titles of stories, poems, magazine and newspaper articles, and chapters in books.

In "The Case for Offensive Humor" David Segal makes an interesting argument about the value of ethnic and racial comedy. (Magazine article)

6m. Use a colon after a statement that clearly indicates a list, or an enumeration is to follow.

Students are concerned about three environmental issues: garbage disposal, clean air, and the ozone layer.
Students participate in the following activities: recycling, community action groups, and educational programs.

6n. Use a colon after the opening in a formal letter.

Dear Dr. Crawford:
I am investigating pollution in our city for a project in my English class because I am worried about the future of our world. . . .

6o. Use a colon between the hour and minute in writing time.

10:25 A.M. 3:10

PREPARING A FINAL DRAFT

When you finish proofreading and editing your revisions, you need to prepare the final copy according to academic manuscript format. Here are general guidelines for the format of college writing assignments.

Typed or Computer-Printed Papers

- Use $8\frac{1}{2}$- by 11-inch unruled, white, standard typing paper. Do not use onionskin or erasable paper (both smudge). Do not use printer paper thinner than 20-weight (it tears easily).
- Leave $1\frac{1}{4}$-inch margins on all four sides of each page. If a word processor program has preset margins of 1 inch, most instructors will accept them.
- Type or print on only one side of each page.
- Use only a fresh black typewriter or printer ribbon.
- Double-space each line.
- Leave two spaces after a period; leave one space after all other punctuation marks.
- Indent the first line of every paragraph five spaces.
- Proofread the final copy whether it is typed or computer-printed.
- If you need to make a few simple insertions or corrections, write them in by hand carefully and neatly. (Check with your instructor to see what kind of handwritten corrections will be accepted.)

Handwritten Papers

- Use $8\frac{1}{2}$- by 11-inch ruled, white paper.
- Leave 1-inch margins on all four sides of each page.
- Write on only one side of the page.
- Use dark blue or black ink (*not* pencil).
- Ask your instructor whether to write on every line or to leave alternate lines blank.
- Make sure that capital letters are clearly distinct from lower-case letters.
- Indent the first line of every paragraph about half an inch.
- Write all punctuation marks firmly and clearly.
- Proofread the final copy.
- If you need to make a few simple insertions or corrections, write them carefully and neatly. (Check with your instructor to see what kind of handwritten corrections will be accepted.)

Word-Processing Tips

- Check to see that your disk is formatted correctly.
- If you use a word processor, be sure to set the margin on left justification or the computer will add some spaces between words to maintain the set line length.
- Save your work often; don't wait until the end of a work session or the end of an essay.
- Create a backup file for each assignment at the end of your first work session; save the work of each new session on the backup file.
- Proofread your writing on the monitor and use your spell checker (and grammar checker, if you have one) before you print the final copy of an assignment.

Corrections

- Use correction paper or correction fluid to white out small errors.
- If your instructor permits it, add missing letters, words, or punctuation marks with a caret (∧).
- If there are several misspelled words and other mistakes, insertions, or deletions, retype or reprint the entire page.

First Page

- Ask your instructor if he or she has a preferred format for the first page. Where should you put your name, course name, section number, and the date? Is there to be a cover page? (See sample cover page on page 394.)

- Center the title of the assignment on the first line of the first page, even if you have a cover page. Do not underline the title, and do not put quotation marks around it.
- Capitalize the first word and the major words in the title.
- If the assignment is double-spaced, do not add an extra space between the title and the first line of the text. If the assignment is single-spaced, double space between the title and the first line.

Numbering Pages

- Number all pages except the cover page and the first page. Although you should not put a number on the first page, think of it as page 1, so the second page should be numbered page 2.
- Use numerals (2, 3, 4, etc.) to number the pages. Do *not* write "page" or "p." before the number.
- Write or type the number in the upper right-hand corner or the center on the top of each page.
- When your assignment is followed by a Works Cited page, continue numbering the pages.

Making Amends with Mom

by
Shayna Smith

English 102, Section 014
Professor Judith Lambert
May 5, 1992

Making Amends with Mom

As girls make the transition into womanhood, all mother and daughter pairs experience a great amount of conflict and emotional turmoil in their relationship with each other. Some are able to tolerate each other when this change takes place, but unfortunately, many mother and daughter teams cannot withstand this conflict that arrives when the roles are shifted. As the daughter matures and begins establishing her sense of self and independence, the rocky road of transition begins to unfold. In order for the relationship to survive and withstand these pressures, the people involved must be willing to work very hard at the relationship. This is far from easy. I know, because I have experienced this struggle first hand with my own mother. I have found that when daughters make amends

6

Works Cited

"Mothers: Tired of Taking the Rap." Editorial. *New York Times,* 10 June 1990, fiche 52, grid 18A.

Scarf, Maggie, and Susan Merrell. "Mother and Daughter Bond." *Self,* May 1990: 260+. Rpt. in *Family.* Vol. 4. Social Issues Resources Series. Boca Raton: SIRS, 1991. Article 55.

Secunda, Victoria. *When You and Your Mother Can't Be Friends: Resolving the Most Complicated Relationship of Your Life.* New York: Delacorte, 1990.

APPENDIX
Progress Logs

I. Writing-Editing Log

II. Teacher Conference Log

Use these logs to keep track of your writing progress and problems.

WRITING-EDITING LOG

Each time your instructor returns a piece of your writing—in your writing course *and* in every other course—make notes about the piece in this log. You will be able to chart your progress and identify areas that need further improvement.

Date ______________ Course ______________________________

Title of Paper ______________________________________

Strengths:

Problems and Errors:

If you need more Writing-Editing Logs pages, make copies of this page.

Date ________________ Course ____

Title of Paper ____

Strengths:

Problems and Errors:

TEACHER CONFERENCE LOG

Each time you have a conference with your writing teacher, summarize his or her comments in the space below. Use these notes to help you remember your teacher's comments and suggestions for future papers.

Date of Conference ____________________

Material Discussed ____________________

Teacher's Comments, Suggestions, and Assignments:

If you need more Conference Log pages, make copies of this page.

Date of Conference ______________________________

Material Discussed ______________________________

Teacher's Comments, Suggestions, and Assignments:

Dear Reader:

Please let us know your opinion of this textbook and of its strengths and weaknesses. When you finish the book, please write me a letter about what you liked and disliked about it. (Send the letter to me at the address below.) If you don't have the time to write me a letter, please fill out the form that follows and return it to the address below.

Judith R. Lambert
c/o Skills Editor, College Division
HarperCollins College Publishers
10 East 53rd Street
New York, NY 10022-5299

Please be honest and be very specific so that we can make the next edition of the book better. If you include your name and address, we will write you a letter back.

If you are writing a letter to us, please use a separate piece of paper. If you are filling out the following form, please do so in the spaces provided below.

1. How does this textbook compare to other writing texts or English texts that you have used? ______________________________

____

____

____

____

2. Which chapters were most helpful to you? Why? ______________________________

____

____

____

____

3. Which chapters were least helpful? Why?

4. What materials or exercises in this book did you *dis*like? Why?

5. What materials, exercises, readings, or writing tasks would you like to see in the next edition of this textbook?

CREDITS

TEXT CREDITS

Chapter 2

Alison Robertson, "Every Penny Counts." Used by permission.

Chapter 4

"The Watcher at the Gates" by Gail Godwin, *The New York Times,* January 9, 1977. Copyright © 1977 by The New York Times Company. Reprinted by permission.

Chapter 5

"The Flight of Eagles" from HOUSE MADE OF DAWN by N. Scott Momaday. Copyright © 1966, 1967, 1968 by N. Scott Momaday. Reprinted by permission of HarperCollins Publishers.

"Be Careless, Reckless! Be a Lion! Be a Pirate! When You Write," copyright © 1987 by the Estate of Brenda Ueland. Reprinted from IF YOU WANT TO WRITE with permission of Graywolf Press, Saint Paul, Minnesota.

"Love, Brenda" by George Sheehan in RUNNER'S WORLD, December 1990. Copyright © 1990 by Rodale Press, Inc. All rights reserved. Reprinted by permission.

Lynn H. Kleifgen, "First Methodist Church." Used by permission.

Chapter 6

"I Wanted to Be Treated Like a Human Being" by Marie Ragghianti. First appeared in PARADE. Reprinted by permission of the author and the author's agents, Scott Meredith Literary Agency, Inc., 845 Third Avenue, New York, New York 10022.

"Momma, the Dentist, and Me" from I KNOW WHY THE CAGED BIRD SINGS by Maya Angelou. Copyright © 1969 by Maya Angelou. Reprinted by permission of Random House, Inc.

"I Just Wanna Be Average." Reprinted with permission of The Free Press, a division of Macmillan, Inc. From LIVES ON THE BOUNDARY: THE STRUGGLES AND ACHIEVEMENTS OF AMERICA'S UNDERPREPARED by Mike Rose. Copyright © by Mike Rose.

Gloria Cruz, "One More Foreigner, One More Stranger." Used by permission.

Chapter 7

From Chapter 30, pp. 231–2, METAPHORS WE LIVE BY by George Lakoff and Mark Johnson. Copyright © 1980 by The University of Chicago. All rights reserved. Reprinted by permission.

"My Friend, Albert Einstein" by Banesh Hoffmann. Reprinted with permission from the January 1968 Reader's Digest. Copyright © 1967 by The Reader's Digest Assn., Inc.

"Notions and Nations of Sweat" from A NATURAL HISTORY OF THE SENSES by Diane Ackerman. Copyright © 1990 by Diane Ackerman. Reprinted by permission of Random House, Inc.

"How to Relax in a Crowd" from INTIMATE CONNECTIONS and THE FEELING GOOD HANDBOOK by David D. Burns, M.D. Copyright © 1985, 1989 by David D. Burns. Reprinted with permission from the January 1991 READER'S DIGEST and by permission of William Morrow & Company, Inc.

Amy M. Jones, "Don't Press Your Luck." Used by permission.

Chapter 8

"How to Write a Personal Letter" by Garrison Keillor from International Paper's POWER OF THE PRINTED WORD series. Reprinted by permission of International Paper.

Samuel H. Scudder, "Learning to See," 1874.

"A Homemade Education" from THE AUTOBIOGRAPHY OF MALCOLM X by Malcolm X with Alex Haley. Copyright © 1964 by Alex Haley and Malcolm X. Copyright © 1965 by Alex Haley and Betty Shabazz. Reprinted by permission of Random House, Inc.

Robert F. Hanika, "How to Hunt, Clean, and Cook a Pheasant." Used by permission.

Chapter 9

Martin Luther King, Jr., STRIDE TOWARD FREEDOM. New York: Harper and Row, Publishers, Inc. 1958.

"Texas Women, True Grit and All the Rest" from MOLLY IVINS CAN'T SAY THAT CAN SHE? by Molly Ivins. Copyright © 1991 by Molly Ivins. Reprinted by permission of Random House, Inc.

"Friends, Good Friends—And Such Good Friends" by Judith Viorst. Reprinted by permission.

"Kinds of Discipline" from "On Discipline" in FREEDOM AND BEYOND by John Holt. Copyright © 1972 by John Holt. Reprinted by permission.

Claudia C. Reardon, "Twits, Cookies, and Queens." Used by permission.

Chapter 10

Excerpt from AMUSING OURSELVES TO DEATH by Neil Postman. Copyright © 1985 by Neil Postman. Used by permission of Viking Penguin, a division of Penguin Books USA Inc.

"The Tapestry of Friendship" by Ellen Goodman. Copyright © 1979. The Boston Globe Newspaper Company. Reprinted with permission.

"Private Space" from THE HIDDEN DIMENSION by Edward T. Hall. Copyright © by Edward T. Hall. Used by permission of Doubleday, a division of Bantam Doubleday Dell Publishing Group, Inc.

"Other Cultures, Other Times" by Ann McGee-Cooper. From UNDERSTANDING CULTURAL DIFFERENCES by Edward T. Hall and Mildred Reed Hall. Reprinted with permission of Edward T. Hall Associates.

Rosa Mathe, "Carbon Copy." Used by permission.

Chapter 11

Excerpts from LEARNING TO READ: THE NEVER ENDING DEBATE by

Chapter 12

Chapter 13

INDEX

INSTRUCTOR'S MANUAL
TO ACCOMPANY

THE ADVANCING WRITER

BOOK 3

Reading and Writing Essays

Judith R. Lambert
Richland College

Harvey S. Wiener, Series Editor
Adelphi University

HarperCollinsCollegePublishers

CONTENTS

READING AND WRITING ESSAYS IN THE ADVANCING WRITER SERIES

UNDERLYING PRINCIPLES

As Book 3 of *The Advancing Writer* series, this book shares a foundation of similar principles. Students are inexperienced writers who can think and communicate well in other contexts. Respect for students, their experiences, views, and writing is essential in order for students to learn. Because of the differences in the rhetorical worlds of students and the academy, students need to be taught the conventions of written discourse important for success in college. Teaching must draw into the classroom students' knowledge and skills in the world and build on them.

Writing in itself is a worthwhile activity for self-expression, learning, and communication. Therefore classroom practice includes much writing for the self as audience and elicits students' opinions and reactions, seeking to teach by asking for clarification or support.

Personal experience is a legitimate source for writing and can be a bridge to academic writing. Student writing can reveal aspects of the human condition just as Maya Angelou's powerful autobiographical selection does. Writing can legitimize personal experience, put one's experience into a broader perspective by seeking to communicate it to readers, and draw the world into the classroom, humanizing and making education more relevant and thereby motivating students. As familiar material, personal experience can also be good practice ground for developing synthesis and evaluation and linking written sources (often perceived as otherworldly by students) with personal views and experiences, using the conventions of academic discourse.

Students need practice at all levels of instruction. Although clear presentation of concepts and processes and lucid models are needed, students need *to do* in order to learn. Knowing how to hit a golf ball is not the same as being able to drive that ball off the tee and down the fairway. Students must perform tasks in part and in whole, practicing without penalty for errors or failure to achieve the ideal.

Varied sources engage student interest and stimulate their writing. The content of the professional and student essays and excerpts used within the teaching material was selected to inform and to evoke. Some provide human interest, some describe cultural differences, some address student skills.

Process leads to product and includes grammar instruction within the context of students' writing. Research reveals that there is no transfer of isolated learning of grammar and mechanics to students' writing. Therefore, such instruction should occur in the process of writing to communicate when students discover readers can't understand them or are distracted by their errors. Grammar instruction is appropriately subordinated to matters of content, audience, and purpose and integrated into the writing process as part of revising and editing.

Collaboration improves writing and motivates students. Since students are predominately social creatures and learn by doing, and since they are learning to communicate in writing, collaboration is a natural and effective methodology. Collaboration mimics most learning situations outside the classroom. In collaboration, students learn that talking is a part of the writing process at every stage from discovery through editing. Peer readers become living surrogates for their intended audiences, and their audience responses confront and support them. Collaboration brings the element of social interaction to otherwise lonely tasks, and students learn with and from each other.

Regular assessment of various kinds promotes growth. Self assessment, peer assessment, and teacher assessment provide a chain of continuous links alternating goal-setting and progress checks. Students need to be informed about their skills as writers and users of language.

OVERVIEW OF *READING AND WRITING ESSAYS*

This text is a process-oriented composition textbook that integrates reading and writing. Part One teaches the writing and reading processes. Student samples show discovery strategies, drafts, revisions, and final drafts. Individual and small group activities allow students to practice with the writing process, and "Exploring Further" at the end of each chapter takes students through the writing process of producing an essay.

Part Two provides readings and ample apparatus for each selection to choose from. Each chapter contains three professional selections and a student paper. Readings have been selected with an eye for the cultural diversity that makes up our classrooms and for content relevant to beginning students' success in college. Although this section has a modal organization to allow for specific writing lessons, writing assignments stress content, audience, and purpose over form. For example, the fourth prompt after the student essay in the narration chapter calls for synthesis instead of narration, linking several readings. Collaboration and the reading and writing processes should be continued, but are not specified in this section. Pre- and post-reading writing prompts allow students to use writing for themselves as audience to express personal opinions and experiences that the readings call to mind. A vocabulary list and exercises emphasize student choice and playful but consistent work on vocabulary. Questions for comprehension, rhetorical analysis, and critical thinking precede the writing prompts which include audience and purpose and draw both on students' experiences and the readings. The personal writing students do before and after reading and the analytical or evaluative writing they do responding to rhetorical and critical thinking questions may contain beginning places for their essays.

Part 3 is a handbook. Because the books in the series have been created together, the same topics are covered in the same order and terminology is the same. Keyed to errors and correction symbols, the handbook is designed for students to use for editing or for study. Two "Quick Guides" and a list of major headings in the handbook allow for easy reference when editing or for studying a section. Each section contains the rules, several examples (often sentences taken from readings), and brief instruction about correcting the problem. Ancillary materials for both rhetoric and grammar provide exercises for practice and transparencies for instruction.

LINKS BETWEEN BOOKS 2 AND 3

Students who have used *Paragraphs and Essays* will find familiar ground in *Reading and Writing Essays,* which can help them tap the processes and information they learned in the previous course and build on them as they break new ground—the essay. Since the series is designed to be recursive, students will find familiar assignments challenging because of higher expectations in thinking, form, and expression. Here are some of the features that link Books 2 and 3:

- Emphasis on writing as a process
- Use of collaboration for reading and writing
- Emphasis on writing for different audiences and purposes
- Subordination of traditional modes as ways to develop ideas
- Grammar instruction integrated with students' writing process
- Five qualities (focus, development, unity, coherence, and correctness) used to define good writing and to aid in revising

Idea Bank, a place for expressive writing to respond personally, reflect, and record ideas to write about later
Similar terminology and marking symbols for errors

THE CLASSROOM AS A READING AND WRITING COMMUNITY

For students to succeed in college they must become part of a community of readers and writers, no small feat for the nonreading majority of students who make up our classes. We must help them approach and produce increasingly difficult texts with increasing comfort, appreciation, and skill. *Reading and Writing Essays* is intended to help you orchestrate a learning environment in which students have much experience reading, writing, and talking about essays—those in this book and their own.

We are so accustomed to reading a variety of texts in our daily and professional lives that we sometimes are not aware of the paucity of regular contact our students have with reading and writing on a daily basis. Do they read movie reviews, compare their analysis of the movie with the reviewer's or yours? Do they read a book purely for enjoyment and discuss it with a friend? You might do some informal classroom research to find out who reads a newspaper or magazine and with what regularity, who subscribes to a publication of any kind, who considers him or herself good or weak readers and writers, who has a job that requires writing beyond filling in forms of some kind, who keeps a journal, how much and what kind of writing each student has done in the past year.

Even a short questionnaire can reveal the experience level of a class and their attitudes about reading and writing. Such research should be shared with the class and be part of the community building that I think is important in a writing class. To be a community, a group must have shared goals and focus, mutual trust, and enjoyment. Talking about this classroom research begins to establish the commonality essential for community building. The readings and the discussions about them also become part of the common experience as the semester progresses, and as students share their opinions about the readings and associated personal experiences, these too become part of the common experience which binds students together as a community.

Why build community? Here's my stream-of-consciousness in support of its importance. Learning is basically a social activity; we learn by interacting with others. Students are primarily social creatures, more experienced interacting with people than with texts. Reading and writing are social acts of communication. To engage in the social acts of communication, students need much practice, but they often avoid writing because they are afraid of ridicule and failure in its myriad forms. Because student writers are social beings, they need each other. Because they are afraid, they need support from each other. Because they need much practice reading, writing, and talking about texts, they need each other. They learn by interacting with each other about the readings and their writing. To interact freely, students need to be in community.

How to build community? Students must feel like they belong, that what they say and write matters and that it will be treated with respect. They must also feel safe to express their reactions, opinions, answers, and experiences, much less share their writing. When one is skilled, a task is easy; when the task is new, one is clumsy and error prone, and the task is difficult. Reading and writing is natural and easy for us, but it is not for students.

Although we are teachers, not counselors, we must nonetheless be concerned about students' feelings in the classroom because feelings either alienate or connect students to the endeavors so dear to our hearts, that is reading and writing. Feelings either enable or block learning; they either motivate or discourage persistence; they either create energy or extinguish it.

I continue to be surprised in my classroom research at the feelings students experience about themselves and the acts of reading and writing. My greatest interest and concern is for their intellectual growth; theirs is for their feelings of frustration, being overwhelmed, being criticized, and associated fears of ridicule, failure, being wrong, or incapable. Only the courageous can risk the errors and effort required in forging into the unfamiliar dark woods of reading and writing for college.

In the face of new and difficult tasks and attending negative feelings, students need to know that others are struggling and have the same feelings, that they are supported by classmates and the teacher, that falling short of the mark is natural in new endeavors, that there's no shame or penalty for missing the mark, and that more practice or another draft allows them to improve. Drafting, teacher comments on a draft about strengths and suggestions for improving or similar comments in student-teacher conferences, and collaboration provide ways to support students and promote growth in reading and writing.

Another ingredient of community is enjoyment, just plain old laughter and fun. Humor and pedagogical games and the social interaction that goes with them helps lessen tension and frustration, change pace in the classroom, and create a healthy environment for learning. Games, like those described in the vocabulary section on page IM-17, and the social interaction of collaboration can turn many anxiety- or boredom-producing tasks into cooperative and pleasant learning experiences.

COLLABORATION

The *rationale* for building a community in the classroom supports the methodology of collaboration. I would add the following reasons to those above. Collaboration is a natural part of the writing process outside the classroom. I run even important memos to the English faculty by a colleague before ''publishing'' them, and certainly in larger efforts, such as articles and books, I rely on the responses and suggestions of supportive, and sometimes antagonistic, colleagues and reviewers to develop a piece of writing. Surely this is an integral part of the writing process for most of us in the academy and other workplaces, but students don't know that. They often think it's cheating or not worthwhile or too time-consuming. Therefore, they must be taught to explore the potential of collaborating at various times in the writing process in order to learn to collaborate and develop a piece of writing.

Collaboration also promotes learning in the class by releasing the energy of students rather than turning it off and creating passive learners (an oxymoron if I've ever heard one). So it energizes and motivates students. Finally, collaboration on a piece of writing is a process they can adapt and use for writing in other college courses and in the workplace.

There are many *opportunities for collaboration* in a course using this book. I have already written about collaborating on drafts in Chapter 1 and more fully in Chapter 3. But collaborating can also be quite useful in the discovery phase of writing (''What's a writing possibility for you in response to this assignment? Say a few words to a neighbor.''). It can help students focus after they have received feedback from several people on a draft (''What's the most important thing you can do to take this draft to the next level? Tell your group.''). It can help students check specific aspects of a draft (''To check the organization of your essay, ask a member of your writing group to make an outline from the draft.''). It can also help students edit their drafts after revising (''Mark any sentences or punctuation or spelling that seems incorrect. Let the writer of the essay make corrections if they are needed.'').

In addition to working on drafts, collaboration can be used to answer questions in the apparatus or to check these answers. Since one of my goals for a writing class is to engage students in talking with each other about what they read, I assign a reading and the questions in ''Jotting Down Your First Responses'' before asking students to clarify their understanding of or to analyze a selection. I used to try to get students to delay their reactions until they had understood and analyzed an essay or story. Their opinions popped out anyway. Students were animated and energized as they talked about their reactions, but they became self-conscious and much less talkative when I insisted they work on matters of comprehension and analysis. So I've learned to honor their initial reactions and associations and then move them into a comprehension check and analysis. Students can share the answer to a specific question in ''Jotting Down'' with their small group; then they can work together to answer the comprehension questions. If they read a second essay in a chapter, they might answer the comprehension questions as part of their homework and compare their answers in small groups. Such comparison helps move students away from the mentality of getting the right answer to clarifying the content of the essay.

OPPORTUNITIES FOR COLLABORATION

- Finding a topic to write about
- Deciding on audience and purpose
- Looking at introductions or conclusions
- Responding to a draft to practice giving feedback
- Checking for development
- Checking for organization
- Giving feedback on a draft to aid in revising
- Editing for correctness
- Sharing their reactions to the readings
- Answering questions after the readings
- Practicing with vocabulary words

Although Part 2 does not give instructions for group activities as Part 1 does, I hope that you will continue to mix solitary and collaborative activities as you select from the questions supplied. Only the vocabulary section suggests group activities, but it's easy to turn any of the questions into group tasks answering questions or comparing responses.

A warning: In my persistence in creating an active and interactive learning environment, I discovered that too many small group activities destroy community in the classroom. Therefore it is important to find the right blend of small group and large group activities. One strategy is to have small groups report to the whole class. After answering comprehension questions together, the reporters for each group can ask questions that were left unanswered or whose answers were disputed in the group. Or, small groups can report to the class after answering questions calling for inference-making or evaluation. The class discussions that follow such small group work become the shared conversation necessary for community.

If you have not used groups before, these *guidelines* may help. Groups seem to function best with three to five members, depending on the task. Groups with a set membership seem to work best because students have to develop trust before they will share their opinions and ideas, either orally or in writing. I prefer to let students group themselves and try out the groups a time or two. I may adjust the groups according to my observation or their comments any time during the semester, but basically group membership is permanent with adjustments as needed for task or group problems.

To make group work productive, you must have clear goals about what learning you want to occur and then structure the task accordingly. You should describe the task very specifically, in no more than three or four steps, and set a specific time limit. I find that I have to simplify most tasks I initially design because they are too complex and require too much class time. Students need more time than we would to do the tasks. Sometimes you have to pare down the task because you can allot only a limited amount of class time. Be sure to make the outcome of the group work and the amount of time specific. Write the group task on the board or on a transparency. Assign and clarify group roles. Some tasks require a timekeeper if all group members are reading drafts or a recorder and a reporter if the small group will report to the whole group.

GUIDELINES FOR COLLABORATION

- Have specific learning goals
- Design a task with few steps
- Set time limits
- Give group task orally and in writing
- Assign group roles as needed: observer, recorder, reporter, timekeeper

Successful group work requires considerable skill to design and manage, and it also requires teaching students to be good group members, take group work seriously, and expect to learn or receive help with a draft. I find a little coaching along the way helps. I talk about the timidity most people feel in reading aloud, not knowing all the words, in sharing their opinions in class, and letting others read their writing. (Chapter 3 gives much of my coaching to students.) I talk about the gift of listening, and of being a good listener. (See Brenda Ueland's wonderful article about listening as a gift and its effect on the creativity of the speaker.) I comment on the principle of reciprocity in all relationships and the need to be supportive of each other as we take risks by sharing our talk and our writing. In spite of my lectures about the value of collaboration, many students report at the end of a course that they didn't like reading and commenting on each other's drafts at first but that they gradually got better at giving and receiving feedback on drafts. As they improved these skills, they began to trust the process more and finally they often found their peers' feedback on a draft more helpful than mine.

An exercise such as the faculty did in a Writing Across the Curriculum workshop led by Maxine Hairston may well be worth class time to demonstrate the value of collaboration. Individuals listed all the parts of photosynthesis (or the male reproductive system, etc.). Then they worked in small groups to pool their individual knowledge. The composite list of each group was inevitably longer than any individual's list. It was immediately clear that several heads were more productive than one, that collaboration is a legitimate and enjoyable way to learn. In part, learning to use collaboration effectively is a matter of weaning students (and sometimes teachers) from the teacher-dominated classroom, a valuable lesson for students who are learning to be self-directed and to work with others.

Something about *problem students*. The unprepared, mordantly silent, or dominating student can become a group problem. You can monitor group functioning by simply observing, asking group members to give their group a grade and tell why in a brief letter to you, or by asking students to evaluate themselves as group members. You might put something like this on a transparency and ask students to write their names on a sheet of paper, number 1–5, and rate themselves as group members on a scale of 1 (low) to 5 (high) for each item.

SELF-EVALUATION AS A GROUP MEMBER

1. I have the assigned draft or exercises completed for work in group.
2. I am clear about what we are to accomplish.
3. I listen attentively to each person.
4. I give useable feedback or thoughtful answers.
5. I try to be helped or to learn in the group.
6. Write a sentence or two evaluating your group.

Quick feedback of this kind allows students to vent, suggest, or request, and then you can respond to the whole class, talk with particular groups about problems, or make changes. Such checks as these should be quick checks, but they are necessary to make group work productive.

One hopes that peer pressure will ameliorate the problem behavior of group members, but students often need help confronting the dominating or silent members. A private conference with a problem member may resolve the situation. However, more active measures may be required. You can add another strong extrovert to a group with a dominating member or another silently involved student to a group with a single quiet member. Unprepared students should not be punished or humiliated; such students have probably suffered with or become inured to teacher disapproval. However, they should not be allowed to interfere with the successful functioning of their groups. If students are exchanging drafts, that unprepared student is out of the loop and suffers the natural consequences of missing peer feedback. I often ask those students what would be most helpful to them—using class time to write their drafts; talking with each other to discover a starting place, if there are several; or reading additional student samples. I might also set up a private conference with a student so that I can help him or her move forward with the assignment, knowing that students are often reluctant to initiate an office conference, even when they desperately need individual help.

PROCESS AND PRODUCT

Reading and Writing Essays is a hybrid of process-oriented composition textbook and a traditional modes-as-models textbook. The processes described in Chapters 1 through 4 should be utilized throughout the course, and the essays serve as content to stimulate student talk and writing and as illustrations of ways of development that are often combined in a single piece of writing. Producing essays modeled after the readings is about as likely as producing the complicated syncopations of Gershwin's music by listening to it. Students should primarily be engaged with the content of their short written responses and essays and they should be writing for a variety of audiences and purposes, not in producing modes.

Expressive writing, when students are writing primarily for themselves, can be satisfying and useful, but students may initially see such writing as busy work. In Part 2, the sections ''Writing Before Reading'' and ''Jotting Down Your First Responses'' allow students to prepare for reading and to respond to readings. This writing should be done in the Idea Bank and should never be graded. However, it should be used regularly in a variety of ways. Early in the semester to prepare for reading their essay drafts aloud, students can read some of these in their small groups. Later a few students can read theirs aloud to the class. Even if the book doesn't ask students to read their responses to these prompts for ideas to write about, you can ask students to spend a few minutes reading their Idea Banks, thus affirming the value of writing for oneself by using class time. As a rule of thumb, writing that isn't graded usually should be used in some way.

Just as using ungraded expressive writing reinforces its importance and serves as a springboard for discussing, using class time to edit revised drafts and focus on correctness makes the same point. Correctness is important and not beyond the capability of most students, given enough time, resources, and effort. If you have marked their revised drafts with the symbols for errors and correcting, students can use the handbook on their own, which is keyed to the symbols and designed as an editing aid rather than a compendium of rules. (I caution here against the premature editing of a work-in-progress.) They can work in small groups, asking each other for help with problems they can't solve alone. If they are using a word processor with spelling and grammar checkers, they can also use them. In marking student drafts, look for patterns of error; give a brief lesson on a problem that many students have, using the transparencies and exercises in the ancillary package for this series or assign appropriate exercises to individual students. Answer any questions students have about editing their drafts.

USING THIS BOOK TO DEVELOP A COURSE

SAMPLE SYLLABI

A clear sense of course goals and one's teaching priorities must precede building a syllabus, or one (at least I do) becomes mired in the coverage trap. For instance, using readings in a composition course can make it difficult to keep the focus on composition. We want students to be engaged by the content of essays they read, yet they often need much help understanding and thinking critically about the selections. We want them to respond to the reading by writing about their experiences, yet we also want them to analyze the audience and purpose of the author and the structure of the essay. We want them to be able to do everything, yet racing through to cover the course means giving short shrift to student needs and interests or to using the writing process. There should be a balance between structure and freedom in assignments, process and product, reading and writing, whole class and small group work, concern about students' affective and cognitive states, and writing about personal experience and writing about texts. What this means for me is designing the ideal course and then ''getting real'' about the motivation, abilities, and complex lives of my students and adjusting the ideal. I find I am haunted by the coverage model of education and the myth of the ideal paper, in which each paper is compared with a mythic ideal. Focusing on course goals and continually setting priorities exorcises those ghosts.

My goals for a basic writing course and freshman composition course would be similar, but the syllabi would differ.

COURSE GOALS

Students will:

1. value reading and writing as worthwhile activities and enjoy both
2. know their own reading and writing processes and be able to adjust them for various situations
3. write for various audiences and purposes
4. collaborate effectively
5. recognize and be able to develop a point in several ways
6. make substantive revisions
7. develop editing strategies and skills
8. write sustained discourse about a main point

SAMPLE SYLLABUS FOR A BASIC WRITING COURSE

Week 1	Introduce course, get acquainted, begin the writing process: Chapter 1
Week 2	Continue with the process; begin the essay: Chapter 2
Week 3	The reading process: Chapter 4. Read one descriptive essay: Chapter 5
Week 4	Read second descriptive essay. Write a draft.
Week 5	Study revision: Chapter 3. Revise descriptive essay.
Weeks 6–7	Read two narrative essays: Chapter 7 and write narrative essay.
Weeks 8–9	Read two exemplification essays: Chapter 8 and write exemplification essay
Week 10	Revise either narrative or exemplification essay
Weeks 11–12	Read two division and classification essays; Chapter 9 and write an essay
Weeks 13–14	Read two comparison and contrast essays and write an essay
Week 15	Revise one of the last two essays
Week 16	Final exam: After reviewing the writing folder, write an evaluation of one's writing progress.

SAMPLE SYLLABUS FOR A FRESHMAN COMPOSITION COURSE

Week 1	Course introduction; getting acquainted; the writing process: Chapter 1
Week 2	The essay: Chapter 2
Week 3	Revision: Chapter 3
Week 4	The reading process: Chapter 4

Weeks 5–7	Description and narration, Chapters 5–6. Read two from each chapter. Write an essay and revise.
Weeks 8–9	Exemplification: Chapter 7. Write and revise an essay.
Weeks 10–11	Division and classification: Chapter 9. Write and revise an essay.
Weeks 12–13	Comparison and contrast: Chapter 10. Write and revise an essay.
Weeks 14–15	Cause and effect: Chapter 12. Write and revise an essay.
Week 16	Final exam: Students reread their essays and write an essay evaluating their best essay or select one they wish they could revise and describe what they would do and why.

When two weeks are relegated to a kind of essay development, the classes might be used in this way:

- Day 1—read chapter introduction and one essay, doing the pre- and post-reading writing prompts
- Day 2—read an essay, doing the pre- and post-reading writing prompts and assigned questions; begin discovery work for writing an essay in class; assign a draft
- Day 3—collaboration day in class on drafts; make plans for revising
- Day 4—read an essay, doing the pre- and post-reading writing prompts and assigned questions; receive draft with teacher's comments; make plans for revising
- Day 5—editing day on revised draft with brief lesson on grammar or punctuation
- Day 6—proofread final draft; vocabulary play

The choices about which chapters, readings, or writing assignments to make can be daunting. In writing the sample syllabi above I chose some chapters calling for lower level thinking skills (explained in the next section) and some calling for higher level skills. For the lower level skills, I chose the chapters about description and exemplification because the writing of most basic writers and weak freshman students often lacks focus and supporting details. Mina Shaughnessy noted that some basic writers write in stunning detail with no controlling ideas and that others write in generalizations with few details. What they lack is the ability to provide both consistently. The chapters on exemplification and description address focus and details.

I also chose the narration chapter because people love stories (See Robert Coles's *The Call of Stories* for the power of stories in teaching a variety of subjects in undergraduate and graduate courses), and I want students to like reading. Additionally, narration exhibits the power of focus and details in a piece of writing. Chapters 5–7 on description, narration, and exemplification elicit personal experience essays, but such writing can also provide opportunities for incorporating quotations and citing titles and authors, skills that students need much practice with for writing from sources, the major writing they do in other college courses.

For higher level thinking skills, I chose the chapters on division and classification and comparison and contrast. Students must be able to distinguish categories before they can write comparison and contrast, which is included because it too is a frequently required kind of college writing. In the freshman syllabus I added the chapter about cause and effect to sneak in some elements of argument without teaching it. (Cause and effect is often argumentation.) Cause and effect is difficult for students because it requires the linear logic expected in Western exposition and argumentation and because causal chains often mask the distinction of cause and effect.

You may wish to design your course around groups of related readings that will appeal to your students and then transport and adapt writing assignments from selections not used. The following lists may help you select.

Success in College

Burns—"How To Relax in a Crowd"
Godwin—"The Watcher at the Gates"
Holt—"Kinds of Discipline"
Jones—"Don't Press Your Luck"
Malcolm X—"A Homemade Education"
Poelman—"My Public Address"
Rose—"I Just Wanna Be Average"
Scudder—"Learning to See"
Smith—from "Learning To Read: The Never-Ending Debate" in the introduction to Chapter 11
Ueland—"Be Careless, Reckless"

Cultural Differences

Ackerman—"Notions and Nations of Sweat"
Hall—"Private Space"
McGee-Cooper—"Other Cultures, Other Times"
Mathe—"Carbon Copy"

Courage

Angelou—"Momma, the Dentist, and Me"
Cruz—"One More Foreigner, One More Stranger"
Jones—"Don't Press Your Luck"
Mathe—"Carbon Copy"

Poelman—"My Public Address"
Ragghianti—" 'I Wanted To Be Treated Like a Human Being' "
Rodriquez—"Loss of Intimacy"
Smith—"Making Amends With Mom"
Warren—"A Hard Lesson in Smoking's Danger"

Friendship

Ellerbee—"When Television Ate My Best Friend"
Goodman—"The Tapestry of Friendship"
Letich—"Do You Know Who Your Friends Are?"
Viorst—"Friends, Good Friends—and Such Good Friends"

Women

Frank—"The Liberated Woman"
Ivins—"Texas Women: True Grit and All the Rest"
Reardon—"Twits, Cookies, and Queens"

ADAPTABLE ASSIGNMENTS FOR ANALYSIS, SYNTHESIS, AND EVALUATION

Some essay assignments in "Responding by Writing" call for analysis, synthesis, and evaluation, and these can be adapted easily as assignments for various readings. I use Bloom's taxonomy of cognitive complexity as a conceptual guide for designing and ordering assignments. In Bloom's hierarchy of cognitive skills the lower levels are knowledge, comprehension, and application. Description, narration, and exemplification fit here. The higher-level thinking skills are analysis, synthesis, and evaluation. Division and classification, comparison and contrast, and cause and effect require these higher-level skills. Beginning writers can perform the higher-level thinking and writing skills using familiar material (personal experience), and they can advance to using them on unfamiliar or more difficult material.

However, students should be given many low-risk opportunities to practice. For instance, questions throughout the text in "Making Judgments and Thinking Critically" often ask students to evaluate and then explain. After the Ueland piece in Chapter 5 students are asked to evaluate Ueland as a writing teacher for themselves. Students could answer this question in a ten minute in-class writing. Then several could read their paragraphs aloud, and you could comment on the similarities or differences in the criteria used to evaluate. Such practice is necessary to tap students' experience with these higher processes in other situations and transfer them to writing for college.

Beginning synthesis assignments that ask students to combine personal experience and ideas from a reading in an essay or to use information from two or more readings are scattered throughout the text. These are bridge assignments to writing from more difficult and numerous sources.

If the analysis, synthesis, and evaluation assignments occur after readings you do not select, you can adapt them easily for the readings you do select. The following list of their occurrence may help you make choices for your course or transport and adapt writing assignments. It also shows where readings have been linked. For brevity's sake, I have referred to selections by the author's name and included the number of the assignment in "Responding by Writing." When an assignment links a reading in one chapter with one in another, I have given in parentheses the author's last name and the chapter in which the reading occurred.

Synthesis of personal experience or opinion with a reading, requiring use of quotations, essay's title, and author's name:

Chapter 5: Momaday #4, Sheehan #4 (with Ueland)
Chapter 6: Cruz #4
Chapter 7: Hoffmann #2 (with Sheehan, Ch 5) and 3; Burns #2, 3, and 4
Chapter 8: Keillor #3 (with Ueland, Ch 5), Scudder #4, Malcolm X #1, 3 (with Scudder, Ch 8)
Chapter 9: Ivins #1, #4; Viorst #3; Holt #1, 2, 3
Chapter 10: Goodman #4, Mathe #4
Chapter 11: Sarton #2, 4; Greene #4; Guilbault #4; Frank #2 (with Guilbault)
Chapter 12: Letich #4 (with Guilbault, Ch 11), Rodriquez #4 (with Mathe, Ch 10), Ellerbee #3, Poelman #3 (with Burns, Ch 7)
Chapter 13: Warren (with Sarton, Ch 11; Hall, Ch 10; Mcgee-Cooper, Ch 10; Mathe 10); Goodman #1, 2; Smith #1, 2

Evaluation of an idea from an essay, the essay, or the student's learning:

Chapter 5: Ueland #4, Kleifgen #3
Chapter 6: Ragghianti #4, Angelou #4
Chapter 7: Hoffmann #4 (with Sheehan, Ch 5), Ackerman #3
Chapter 8: Hanika #4
Chapter 9: Viorst #4, Reardon #4
Chapter 10: McGee-Cooper #3
Chapter 11: Frank #4
Chapter 12: Ellerbee #2, Letich #4
Chapter 13: Smith #4

VOCABULARY BUILDING

An increasing vocabulary comes from both attitude and habit. Students must like words, experience the need for more words to express what they want to write or say, and have pleasurable word experiences. However, many inexperienced readers and writers see unfamiliar words as a source of embarrassment and anger, a confrontation of their limitations. They ridicule speakers or writers who use "big" words; they ignore words they don't know rather than trying to say them or figure out their meanings from context. If reading aloud becomes part of your classroom, as I hope it will, you too may be surprised at the words students don't know and their eagerness to avoid them. Of course these negative feelings work against the often professed student goal to increase their vocabularies.

I believe that vocabulary building should be fun, involve word choice, and be habitual. Making vocabulary cards, as described in Chapter 4 and after the readings in Chapter 5, is one way to meet those criteria. Students choose three words they want to learn, either from the vocabulary list that precedes the reading or from the reading. They make cards (cut index cards in half and give each student ten or twelve to begin with), write the word on one side and a definition and original sentence on the other. They are encouraged to keep these in their purses or pockets and to review them briefly at odd moments—when they are waiting for a bus, for class to begin, or in line at the bookstore. Then every week or two they use the cards in class some way.

Vocabulary games in the book can be used any time and are easy to adapt. Since research reveals that laughter and fun enhance learning, allow students to interact, and offer a welcome change of pace in the classroom, these games can be very productive. Team games appear in "Using New Words" in Chapter 9, Reardon, #2; Chapter 12, Rodriquez, #2; and Chapter 13, Smith, #4.

SOME SIMPLE VOCABULARY GAMES

- Practice reading your words aloud to a partner until you are comfortable pronouncing all the words. Switch roles.
- Ask your partner to choose five of your words for you to spell. Switch roles.
- Ask a partner to choose five words from your vocabulary cards. Switch roles. Each writes a paragraph using all five of your own words in five minutes. Read your paragraphs to each other.

The vocabulary work/play in this book is intended to be easy, take little time, and be continual. A list of words and definitions appears before the readings to help students read more easily and with more comprehension. These are intended as a reference, not as a list of words to learn. Collaboration on the vocabulary exercises makes vocabulary work quick and fun.

THE WRITING FOLDER

Since I want students to see the process of writing, the volume of writing they have done by the end of the semester, and the improvements they have made, I want them to keep all their work. Because many students view daily or class work as valueless after it has been checked, don't anticipate using it again, and have no strategies for keeping and organizing their papers, they lose them or can't retrieve a particular one from a disorderly heap of paper. Some assignments in this book ask students to reread their pre- and post-reading personal responses to get ideas for their essays or to compare their answers to questions from more than one reading, so students will need to reread portions of earlier work. For these reasons I recommend you have students keep a folder of their writing.

Here's one way to set up such a folder. To keep together and organize the many pieces of writing students will do in this course, I suggest a folder with pockets and brads. Because students tend not to label papers with the information necessary for retrieving work done days or weeks earlier, train them by frequent reminders to write their names, the dates, and assignment labels for each piece of writing. Ask students to place ruled paper in the brads for their Idea Bank. They can tape to these pages any notes or ideas they write outside of class, such as those suggested in Chapter 1. They can keep essay drafts in the right-hand pocket and other written work in the left-hand pocket. All of the prewriting and revised versions of a single essay should be stapled together so both you and the student can see the development of a piece of writing. If you can, keep the folders in the classroom and have students pick them up as they enter, insert anything written for their Idea Bank, and ready their daily work for checking.

Because of the work habits and academic history of many students, daily checks on assignments are necessary, but you don't have to read or mark all of them. In a quick tour of the room you can do a visibility check and record a symbol, such as "H" by the day's date, to indicate the assigned work was done on time. Some class work or daily work you may scan and mark with a check, check plus, or check minus to indicate quality. On other work you may want to make a quick comment or question to provide helpful evaluation of students' work.

A record of daily work and attendance can be kept at the front of daily work in the left hand pocket or stapled to the front of the folder. At appropriate intervals, perhaps every four weeks, you can review the record sheet of each student and assign a letter grade. If attendance is part of the grade as designated by your syllabus, you can keep attendance on the record for daily work and include this in your periodic assessment. The record provides a frequent update on one aspect of the semester's grade and helps to make good habits of behaviors—regular attendance and preparation—students need to be successful in college.

ASSESSMENT AND EVALUATION

The definitions of assessment and evaluation in the literature fluctuate. Here I am using assessment to mean evaluative responses intended to help a student learn and evaluation to mean judging the quality of writing or students' performance in a course. The words distinguish between the two roles of teacher and judge. Assessment should be frequent, multifaceted, and tied to criteria for assignments and goals for the course. It includes responding to parts of drafts and whole drafts, assessing students' progress, and students' self-assessment. Evaluation includes grading final drafts and assigning a course grade. A qualitative evaluation of students' writing can occur on single essays or on a collection of final drafts called a portfolio.

RESPONDING TO STUDENT WRITING

Is the student doing the assignment? What are the strengths of a draft? Weaknesses? Is there a clear focus, adequate development? Does the draft address the intended audience and purpose? Responding on drafts is valuable teaching time because students are more likely to act on teacher comments when they can revise than when an essay is graded. Comments on graded papers tend to be for the purpose of justifying a grade, not teaching, and although students need some explanation of a grade, a brief comment and quick feedback methods (see suggestions below) are appropriate and adequate.

But what kinds of comments on a draft are helpful? How much should you write? I find I am helpful when I say less, think of myself as an interested reader and writing coach, and address both rhetorical and correctness concerns.

A wonderful article by Joseph Williams (see "Suggested Reading") illustrates how differently we teachers read student texts and other writing, how we tend to look for errors in one and overlook them in the other. Yet, we need to address both kinds of concerns.

I find I am more helpful when I respond as a reader instead of an omniscient critic, writing questions or making suggestions in the margins, and as a writing coach, making global comments at the end where I can comment on features of a draft, focus on the criteria of the assignment, and suggest priorities for revising. I'm reminded of Donald Murray's description of his revising process, of his going back and forth from viewing the whole to focusing on a small part of the text, and of my switching back and forth between wide angle and close-up lenses on my Canon Sure-Shot to get a good picture. Students can't make those kinds of shifts of focus; they have difficulty getting distance from a draft. We can help by doing that and telling them what we see.

Another kind of help is in editing, although I explain that I'm not a grammar cop. Research reveals that the bloody work of the editing pen (even when it's plain pencil) discourages more than it teaches. To most students symbols for errors and corrections, by which the handbook in this book is organized, are as much marks of failure as they are codes for self-help. Such symbols must be used judiciously. For instance, there's no sense in marking errors on a whole draft when a major part is unrelated to the thesis or when the student has obviously spent little time on a draft. When marking drafts with many errors, I sometimes mark everything in half a page, draw a line across the page, and write a note that I stopped marking errors here, there's such-and-so pattern of errors, and these helps are available. One colleague stops reading at that point and requires the student to edit the paper and resubmit it, an action that sends a clear message that such carelessness is not acceptable.

The idea of patterns of errors has been very helpful to me. The work of Mina Shaughnessy, David Bartholomae, and more recently of Bob Connors and Andrea Lunsford (who found, by the way, that student writing doesn't have more errors today than fifty years ago) helps identify and address these, such as a problem with pronoun reference or missing verb endings. Pointing out these patterns to students makes learning Edited Academic English less overwhelming and correcting a draft a shared venture. For instance, you might mark three of seven comma splices, and ask a student to use the handbook to review the problem and solutions for comma splices and then to find the remaining four in the draft, correcting all seven.

My own classroom research reveals how frequently my "helpful" comments are experienced as criticism that work against revision because they discourage and de-energize students from further work on their drafts. This negative response to my comments sometimes reflects my clumsiness in commenting and sometimes the students' perception. George Hillocks's research confirms that negative comments (or those perceived as negative) do not improve student writing but instead affect their attitude toward writing. Global comments are more often interpreted negatively (even though they may be accurate and tactful) than local comments that are related specifically to content. Generic comments (''awkward,'' ''word choice'') and symbols are often interpreted more negatively than content questions and suggestions are. In summary, students want specific help focused on content, some help with the global issues, and help with editing. However, too much feedback simply overwhelms them. Less is sometimes more.

SELF-ASSESSMENT

Self-assessment is another part of multifaceted evaluation. To help students recognize and claim the power they have over their own learning and to provide us with another window on their progress, ask students what they want to learn or what they have learned. I use a letter-writing strategy to get students to assess their writing. Several times during the semester I ask them to write me a letter about what they've learned from an assignment. I might ask them what problem did you have doing this kind of reading or writing, how did you or can you solve this problem, where will you use these new skills, who or what helped you make progress in some way, etc. Of course letter-writing should be a reciprocal activity, and I usually begin the semester with a letter to the class and ask them to write me a letter back. Then I jot them notes on their drafts or their letters to me. This practice creates a one-to-one conversation between me and each student and is quick besides. Further, it fosters the metacognitive awareness so important in empowering students as readers, writers, and learners.

EVALUATING FINAL DRAFTS

Evaluating a final draft is a quicker process than responding to drafts. Time should be spent responding to drafts when students can use the feedback to revise, not when they have stopped work on a paper. However, students need some feedback on the final draft. A grade and a quick comment is all that's needed, or some other quick appraisal that lists the main criteria for a particular assignment. Stating the criteria on such forms links our teaching, the assignment, and evaluation for students. Further it helps keep us grading what we taught and assigned. (See Dick Fulkerson's article.)

Evaluation: The sample on the next page is for assignment #3 after ''The Flight of Eagles'' in Chapter 5.

EVALUATION OF YOUR DESCRIPTIVE ESSAY

Criteria	Weak	Adequate	Strong
Focuses on one incident or thing			
Shows your attitude or feeling to the reader			
Uses concrete and specific nouns			
Uses sensory details			
Uses strong action verbs			
Edited for grammar and punctuation			
Proofread for spelling and typos			

Here's my overall evaluation of this assignment:

P+ = very good   P = passing   NYP = not yet passing

Evaluation: This sample is for assignment #2 after Holt's ''Kinds of Discipline'' in Chapter 9.

EVALUATION OF AN ESSAY USING DIVISION AND CLASSIFICATION

1. Your introduction has a hook for the reader and a clear thesis.

Not acceptable	poor	adequate	good	excellent
0–2.5	3	3.5	4	5

2. You make clear what area your expertise is in, how skilled you are, and how you learned.

Not acceptable	poor	adequate	good	excellent
0–5	6	7	8	9–10

3. You show how the kinds of discipline described in Holt's essay helped you develop your expertise.

Not acceptable	poor	adequate	good	excellent
0–10	11–13	14–15	16–17	18–20

4. You identify the source of the kinds of discipline, using the title of the essay, punctuated correctly, and the author's full name.

Not acceptable	poor	adequate	good	excellent
0–5	6	7	8	10

5. You use adequate details and examples to show your readers your expertise and the effects of discipline on your learning.

Not acceptable	poor	adequate	good	excellent
0–14	15–16	18–19	20–22	23–25

6. The conclusion gives readers a sense of closure.

Not acceptable	poor	adequate	good	excellent
0–2.5	3	3.5	4	5

7. Because of careful editing, there are few errors to distract a reader.

Not acceptable	poor	adequate	good	excellent
0–5	6	7	8	9–10

8. Your paper reflects careful proofreading with neat corrections for errors.

Not acceptable	poor	adequate	good	excellent
0–5	6	7	8	9–10

Your total points ______

THE PORTFOLIO

Another increasingly popular method of evaluating writing at all levels is the portfolio. Instead of grading a single piece of writing, a teacher evaluates a collection of a student's writing. Students may write more essays than they revise; they may take some of these through peer review and a middle draft. They may select three or four, according to the guidelines given, and use their accumulated semester's experience to revise further and submit these essays for their portfolio grade.

By reading several essays of a student instead of one, a teacher can form a more valid assessment of a student's ability to make a single point in a piece of writing, to provide adequate development, to write for various audiences, to write introductions, to edit for correctness, etc. The portfolio may be one part of a semester's grade or it may become the instrument by which students exit basic writing or freshman composition. If the latter, the department draws up the portfolio requirements, and a committee or teacher other than the student's evaluates the portfolio. (See Elbow and Belanoff's brief description.)

Suggested Reading

Bartholomae, David. ''The Study of Error.'' *College Composition and Communication* 31 (October 1980):253–269.

Cooper, Charles R., and Lee Odell, eds. *Evaluating Writing: Describing, Measuring, Judging*. Urbana, IL: NCTE, 1981.

Elbow, Peter, and Pat Belanoff. ''Portfolios as a Substitute for Proficiency Examinations.'' *College Composition and Communication* 37 (October 1986):336–339.

Murray, Donald M. ''The Maker's Eye: Revising Your Own Manuscripts.'' *Learning by Teaching*. Montclair, NJ: Boynton, 1982.

Shaughnessy, Mina P. *Errors and Expectations*. New York: Oxford, 1977.

Ueland, Brenda. ''Tell Me More.'' *Utne Reader* Nov./Dec. 1992:104–110.

Wiener, Harvey S. ''Collaborative Learning in the Classroom: A Guide to Evaluation.'' *College English* 48 (January 1986): 52–62.

PART 4: ANSWERS TO QUESTIONS FOR THE READINGS

CHAPTER 5 NARRATION

THE FLIGHT OF EAGLES

Checking Your Comprehension

1. to be able to watch unobserved
2. golden eagles; rattlesnake
3. mating flight
4. full grown—wings broader than a man's height
5. younger than female—slightly more than half as long
6. lets it go for the female to catch

Understanding a Writer's Patterns

1. In appreciative silence, Abel watches two eagles in flight in a beautiful mating ritual.
2. from Abel's, 3rd person
3. time organization (chronological)
4. not as smooth a flow
5. cavorting, spiraling, spinning, fanned, swerved, sailed
6. flourish, pivots, wheels

Making Predictions and Drawing Inferences

1. in flat area broken by some large rocks—''Knelt behind the rock,'' ''soared out over the plain''
2. so that the male can catch it

3. they mate and live in pairs alone
4. She's bored, finished the mating ritual
5. He's fascinated with their behavior, so perhaps he likes nature stuff. Maybe he was just taken by the novelty of it.
6. A few minutes
7. This is part of a novel, so he's setting a scene; he could be starting an analogy or extended metaphor about ''natural'' rituals vs. man-made rituals; this could be about Native American reverence for the natural world.

BE CARELESS, RECKLESS!

Checking Your Comprehension

1. criticism; overemphasis on structure, unity, etc.
2. from her students
3. closely observed details
4. They fix their attention on mistakes and repeat them.
5. praise, encouraging them to write what they know and feel, respecting their subjects as worthwhile
6. 30, Irish, unmarried, plain sad face, humble, looks Chinese
7. ''Four Days in Glacier Park''
8. ''simple, open eye,'' ''naive truthfulness,'' compared with Irish poets.

Understanding a Writer's Patterns

1. Write from your experience and your heart because everyone is talented and has something worthwhile to say
2. for a general audience who wants to write, students
3. paragraph 15—sight: big black engine, ugly bony arm, string of boxcars, tramps sitting on top, oil tanks, stove-piped caboose
   paragraph 18—touch/feel: cinders, smoke, stifling air, cool atmosphere, easy parlor chairs; sight—delicate green, silver racks, delicate lights
   paragraph 20—sight: smokestacks, tanks, houses, trees, gaudy signboards, flour mills, Mississippi River, cold blue color, shivering water, sun's face, haloed in glittering color.
   paragraphs 22–24—feel/touch: rough woodwork, ''cold, woodsy, rainy-day touch,'' wicker chair. Taste/smell: specific foods
4. chugged, rolled, shivering, mirrored
5. (a) engine with a powerful person, its movable rod connecting the wheels with an arm; (b) sun with a human face
6. both/neither—it depends on what mood I'm trying to establish.

Making Predictions and Drawing Inferences

1. In an adult class. Seems informal. Maybe a night class for working people in a city college. Like noncredit courses

2. let them discover the writer within themselves; each individual has a writer within
3. She's so ''out there'' with her philosophy (see the title) and the ''alas, to no avail'' which she says she got from her brother. Also the ten dollar bet she knows she can't lose.
4. skeptical, critical, but not negative—subtlety is conveyed with ''more easily pleased''
5. She's obviously literate. Perhaps she comes from a tradition of writing, if only privately; also she's closer in time (1935) to when a log of travels was something people kept.
6. I can't imagine she was anything but pleased and wanted to keep writing. BU offers only praise.

LOVE, BRENDA

Checking Your Comprehension

1. from Ueland's letters to him
2. flatter, deter from ''right course''; because such enthusiastic praise moves us all. As he says, who wouldn't be?
3. She did what she thought right, wouldn't follow along with convention—hair, divorce, dress.
4. too heavy, short hair, pants, shoes and socks instead of hose and heels; thinner, healthy, beat up clothes
5. to remain useful and functioning
6. wrote for a newspaper and edited; taught writing. She exercised, wrote him letters, very active and enthusiastic about life.

Understanding a Writer's Patterns

1. Brenda Ueland was a mentor and friend who lived life exuberantly and inspired me to write with her encouragement; I celebrate her life.
2. to celebrate a friend's life; hold up her example of vitality, exercise, and caring for others
3. because of her letters to him, which was the only way he knew her
4. Compares taking a dive off the high board with taking risks in life. Compares the unknown of landing in a dive with the unknown consequences of bold actions in life

Making Predictions and Drawing Inferences

1. He'll talk about her letters.
2. She read his columns and books.
3. exercise, especially running
4. determination, boldness, independence, kindness
5. Women didn't cut their hair; they wore it long and piled up. She was practical, independent, rebellious.

Making Judgments and Thinking Critically

1. Yes, it's his appraisal of her life philosophy.
2. absolutely—his laudatory remarks about her positive contrariness would turn any dead person's head

FIRST UNITED METHODIST CHURCH

Checking Your Comprehension

1. First Methodist Church in Cedar Hill, TX
2. many memories of her youth, wedding of herself and other family members; continuity
3. arches, bell tower, oak doors
4. cream walls, choir loft, recessed altar
5. sleeping in church, pillars rising forever
6. sitting in back giggling, watching woman doze
7. her grandmother; loved to sing hymns
8. getting married
9. go alone and recall
10. continuity of life; recalls pleasant memories; links her life with the spiritual

Understanding a Writer's Patterns

1. The continuity of the place reinforces her faith in God and makes her feel a part of a "line."
2. spatial—out to in
3. chronological—through various time periods
4. change in significance when connected to different memories; links two parts of the essay
5. coherence and emphasis
6. "first memory," "when I was a teenager," "now the ribbons," "like my mother and sister."
7. brisk and cool November afternoon, autumn leaves swirling
8. dance, stroke, caress
9. cascade, caress
10. ring, drape, bind, revolve, sit, feel

Making Predictions and Drawing Inferences

1. an architectural tour
2. 40+—mature, returning to school, rural community is less likely now
3. place with parents where nurtured and safe
4. paragraphs 3:5, 7:3, and 8:6
5. Others don't share her experiences or faith.

Making Judgments and Thinking Critically

1. no, then it *would* be only an architectural tour
2. what makes this effective is the suggestion of stories and her compression of them, and since her purpose is to show continuity, it helps to light on different periods for short visits.
3. neither—it's far too internal and emotional, and neither media can do that.

CHAPTER 6 NARRATION

"I WANTED TO BE TREATED LIKE A HUMAN BEING"

Checking Your Comprehension

1. to find out what she was really like; to see what Parks is doing now
2. 1st time—conference of feminists and politicians—NYC
   2nd time—Detroit
3. grandmotherly
4. that there had been another similar incident earlier
5. Driver threw her off the bus.
6. She wouldn't give up her seat or leave the bus so she was arrested.
7. boycott the city buses
8. Martin Luther King came to prominence; began the Civil Rights movement

Understanding a Writer's Patterns

1. Parks doesn't see self as hero but continues to work to help black youth.
2. insider view of real human being, remind people of the continuing struggle for civil rights and equality
3. hero and real little old lady
4. by posing questions that the writer wants to know
5. (a) the incident when Parks won't give up her seat on the bus; (b) her previous encounter with the driver
6. many possible answers
7. shows she's still relevant and still working

Making Predictions and Drawing Inferences

1. Parks' own words—this is the locus of it all—all civil rights
2. maybe found her even more heroic because so soft-spoken, unassuming, regal, etc.
3. her previous treatment; involvement with civil rights

Making Judgments and Thinking Critically

1. both—reasons vary
2. both
3. no; sticking to principles in spite of opposition.

MOMMA, THE DENTIST, AND ME

Checking Your Comprehension

1. Stamps, Georgia
2. child's painful abscess; couldn't fix it herself; doc owed her a favor
3. serious scrubbing and dressing up
4. whitefolks' country; calaboose (jail); wagonload of powhitetrash children acting snobby
5. to tell doc that Annie was there
6. reminded her he didn't treat colored people; ignored the child in pain
7. of the money she'd lent him in the Depression
8. He's repaid her loan; would "rather put his hand in a dog's mouth"
9. a thorough vanquishing of the doctor by Momma
10. Texarkana
11. Paid her $10 interest on the loan and made her sign a receipt

Understanding a Writer's Patterns

1. to recall (expressive) and tell others (communicate) about the past and racial injustice
2. the immediacy—this is *her* story
3. what is said and how it's said are important; reported speech wouldn't have impact.
4. (a) the imagined dialogue—makes for dramatic contrast
   (b) when recalling to Uncle Willie—to show how Momma explained the event
5. (a) compares the world and her pain (all she could think about or experience at the time); to show how bad the pain was
   (b) compares hunting for shells with hunting for words; to show the effort and careful choice
   (c) compares brushing off a piece of lint to pushing aside a bother; to show its insignificance

Making Predictions and Drawing Inferences

1. as a child; from "I knew then"
2. blacks used the back as was customary
3. as though not worthy of a full adult name

4. didn't want to; deliberate action
5. that he felt constrained by custom to use courteous words
6. she'd never seen her so humiliated

Making Judgments and Thinking Critically

1. the sun's light was harsh and so was her realization really
2. probably the norm
4. yes—no—certainly
5. that of being treated as inferiors

I JUST WANNA BE AVERAGE

Checking Your Comprehension

1. in biology because Rose was a Voc. Ed. kid
2. checked the school's records and discovered that Rose was misplaced
3. chemistry and math
4. quantitative (math)
5. attention wanders and quit trying after a while
6. embarrassment, frustration, and anger
7. got progressively sicker with arteriosclerosis
8. Jack MacFarland, his English teacher
9. made him feel special by using his mind
10. loved getting good grades from MacFarland, felt valued and encouraged
11. none, because he didn't expect to go
12. called his professors and admissions officer at Loyola and got Rose admitted as a probationary student; helped him get a loan

Understanding a Writer's Patterns

1. his father's decline (7–8); MacFarland's class (9–12); getting into college (14–15)
2. Rose's life was dramatically changed from being a kid without goals or much of a future to having ambition and direction by the interest of two teachers, who hooked his interest in learning and helped him go to college.
3. answers vary
4. paragraphs 3–6; paragraph 13
5. deliverance began with sophomore biology (1); through this entire period (7); J.M. couldn't have come into my life at a better time. My father was dead . . . (9); one day in the December of my senior year (14)

Making Predictions and Drawing Inferences

1. means to push on something with one's finger or an instrument; shifts from using it physically "poke in the back" to mentally "Poke: cytoplasm," learning new terms poked his brain. Used for emphasis and to show how he felt from the mental challenge
2. scientific subject matter in his biology class
3. self-blaming, as in "I ought to know this"
4. an informal literacy club where talking about books and ideas were fun
5. work and take a few courses at a local junior college

Making Judgments and Thinking Critically

1. both luck (getting placed in the two teachers' classes) and effort (his studying, reading, and thinking)
2. may have changed who he hung around with and how he spent his time outside school (doing homework and reading); changed his attitude toward school, seemed more enthusiastic and alive
3. the biology teacher's discovery that Rose was misplaced in Voc. Ed. or his placement in MacFarland's class; no, because these were such new experiences for him
4. because as a Voc. Ed. kid he didn't have any ambition or plans for the future; because he or somebody else said it

ONE MORE FOREIGNER, ONE MORE STRANGER

Checking Your Comprehension

1. repeat dirty words
2. pencil/table
3. at first she complied, then refused and avoided these people
4. panic stricken, teary
5. stayed away, sat alone during lunch
6. felt desire to learn English
7. English conversation
8. listened, tried to duplicate the sound of English ("mumbled nonsense") in pretended conversation, ESL classes
9. tried to communicate with her; silence
10. thanked her
11. language
12. made her determined to attain her goals

Understanding a Writer's Patterns

1. Although kids were sometimes cruel to Cruz, she became determined to learn English, the first step needed as a foreigner to accomplish her goals.

2. by her experience and that of Namm
3. with a scene on the playground—immediacy and poignancy
4. "Say b–i–t–c–h." "Was what I had said really that funny, or were they laughing at me?" "Can they not see the fear in my eyes, or the pain in my heart?" "Thank you, you are much kind."
5. #1: 1–3; #2: 1–3
6. #1: 4–8, 10–11; #2: 4–7
7. tongue, lips, tears, burlesque laugh
8. when, time passed, 8 month, after that, by the time, then one day

Making Predictions and Drawing Inferences

1. unsure of how to speak correctly
2. because her words sounded funny and she was shamed
3. humiliation; to show the chill of being so humiliated

CHAPTER 7 EXEMPLIFICATION

MY FRIEND, ALBERT EINSTEIN

Checking Your Comprehension

1. simplicity
2. to discuss ideas he was working on
3. asked him to go slowly because he understood things slowly
4. poor student
5. patent examiner in Berne
6. concentrate fiercely, pace, twirl a lock of hair
7. Understanding the universe is difficult, but not hopeless.
8. violin
9. stick in a lake
10. Water between the grains of sand creates surface tension making the grains work together and resist separating and sinking under the weight of a foot.
11. flee Nazi persecution of the Jews in Germany
12. theory of relativity, $E = mc^2$, and quantum theory of light
13. that they were contradictory

Understanding a Writer's Patterns

1. yes—explanations vary
2. their first meeting = utter naturalness of Einstein
   "ideas come from god" = his spirituality
   playing duets; Einstein's statement that Mozart found music = faith in the goodness and unity of the universe

3. his educational history = his seeming ordinariness
   his salary request when he came to U.S. = his modesty, simplicity
   Christmas anecdote with the carolers = his whimsy and kindness
4. "How shall I sum up?"
5. simplicity
6. Nobel Prize winner/walk on sand

Making Predictions and Drawing Inferences

1. to indicate a personal and anecdotal biography
2. looked for underlying principles, the simplicity at the heart of everything
3. that such a brain would need to go slow would seem to contradict genius; also it reveals his lack of ego.

NOTIONS AND NATIONS OF SWEAT

Checking Your Comprehension

1. cleaned itself; felt soiled by the human contact
2. to repel predators
3. diets, habits, hairiness
4. races/groups offended by differences; smells of a group are identifying features;
5. rich with smells
6. fats such as butter; oils absorb odor
7. natural oils of the hair absorb odors readily
8. joy in smelling

Understanding a Writer's Patterns

1. Humans have strong body odors which are perceived and reacted to differently in various cultures.
2. humans have odor that repels predators
3. Asiatics have less body odor than Europeans and therefore fewer find them smelly. Strong body odor in Japanese men could once exempt them from military service. There's less scenting of bodies in Asian life.
4. Gives examples: kiss means smell in several widely separated countries; New Guinea ritual to say good-bye by putting a hand in each other's armpits; greeting rituals of sniffing each other or rubbing noses

Making Predictions and Drawing Inferences

1. something about sweating and who sweats, why, etc.
2. because anthropologists study the social behaviors of various cultures

3. more hair, therefore more apocrine glands, therefore more oils which attract and retain odors
4. inherited beliefs, what people say or have said; contrasts with scientific study
5. no sweat glands, fewer body smells

HOW TO RELAX IN A CROWD

Checking Your Comprehension

1. that a practicing psychiatrist would have this fear
2. anxiety
3. fear of acting ''wrong'' in a group, worrying excessively about what other's think of you
4. He was unaccustomed to the elegance and expense of the house and its furnishings.
5. by admitting it aloud to the owner
6. that they coped with anxiety by breaking the task into small steps
7. to keep her pencil moving and not question herself
8. put the focus on someone else
9. stopped worrying about being charming and concentrated on presenting his ideas well
10. that someone else would know all about his feelings

Understanding a Writer's Patterns

1. anecdote
2. others with anxiety or social phobias
3. #1 with #2 together
4. to show how widespread the problem is, though less severe than social phobia

5–7. Remove false front—anecdote about picking up his daughter at a mansion in his jeans—personal
Tackle fears one step at a time—study of gymnasts—research
Imitate Johnny Carson—J.C. tries to learn about guests by asking them questions about themselves—gen example
Turn anxiety into energy—TV interview in which he was insulted by another speaker—personal
Stop comparing yourself—lost his journal with personal feelings and thought—personal

8. when, one night, like
9. the ''would'' tense
10. ''On one talk show''
11. ''When I was a college student''
12. whole essay

Making Predictions and Drawing Inferences

1. as a professional psychiatrist and as a person who has conquered his own anxiety with public speaking
2. laughed, stammered, awkward posture
3. Tackle your fears one step at a time.

DON'T PRESS YOUR LUCK

Checking Your Comprehension

1. trying to fit into crowd
2. start rumors about her
3. foolish pride
4. tried hard to fit in, drank to excess
5. played a drinking game called quarters; egging Rob to drink; hours and three cases of beer later
6. driver had broken arm and DWI; Matt had many cuts on his face and legs; Rob had permanent brain damage
7. don't cave in; be true to self

Understanding a Writer's Patterns

1. Don't give in to peer pressure.
2. things you don't agree with or don't want to do
3. for example, another example, another instance
4. gives a personal anecdote about her friends—used general examples about society—turns to the audience: 1st person, 3rd, 2nd
6. you

Making Predictions and Drawing Inferences

1. because it happened to her at the age of her audience
2. yes—they do experience the pressure to conform to group standards or expectations
3. because she walked away and didn't fight; didn't do what they wanted
4. to show it's a common problem, not just for young teens and not just this audience

Making Judgments and Thinking Critically

2. to make a familiar term concrete
3. her confrontation with the girl who started the rumors; the DWI story; typical, not a specific, example

CHAPTER 8 PROCESS ANALYSIS

HOW TO WRITE A PERSONAL LETTER

Checking Your Comprehension

1. shy people
2. because it isn't required; it's a gesture of caring
3. to be known by another and express themselves
4. whatever feels easy to the hand
5. visualize the person
6. say what's happening at that moment
7. work your way out of them

Understanding a Writer's Patterns

1. other shy folks afraid of writing letters/because of all the emphasis on how to overcome hangups
2. calm, informal, "you and me"
3. get over the guilt of not writing; some convenient supplies; think about the person you are writing; start by explaining what's happening at that moment; don't worry about form; don't start over—work your way out of mistakes
4. chronological; appropriate because it's a process
5. identifies with reader, puts self in same situation as readers, uses "we"
6. compares letter writing with telephoning; compares a rock star's need to be known with the letter writer's need; to make the essay funny, appealing, and personal
7. to show how onerous and intimidating largeness can seem
8. fear of grammar—don't think about it; largeness of paper—"try a smaller page and write boldly"; how to begin—start with right now

Making Predictions and Drawing Inferences

1. humorous and informal lecture on why we ought to write
2. a relic is anything no longer in use from a different time, and a letter is part of a past that no longer exists

Making Judgments and Thinking Critically

1. informal, humorous tone appropriate for the general public that doesn't like to write letters and doesn't want to be preached at
2. yes, good public relations; also promotes the use of paper and thus sales

LEARNING TO SEE

Checking Your Comprehension

1. asked about Scudder's goals, personal history, and plans for the future
2. disappointment
3. keep fish wet; keep the stopper in the bottle; to prevent the fish from ruining and the liquid from evaporating or from smelling up the room
4. 10 minutes
5. hands, eyes, fish
6. began to discover new features
7. disappointment
8. the symmetry of the fish
9. taught him the method of observing facts and their orderly arrangement
10. drew fish on the board
11. another fish of the same group, then more
12. eight months
13. observing facts and their orderly arrangement, not being content with facts until they are connected to some general law; because it prepared him for a lifetime of study

Understanding a Writer's Patterns

1. use of "I" (paragraph 1); dialogue (2–7); chronological order of his first few days through his turning to insect study eight months later; transitions (in ten minutes (9); on my return (10); the afternoon passed (16); the next morning (21); and so for three long days (25). Also verb tense: past tense was, entered, enrolled, asked, etc.
2. ten minutes, half an hour, an hour, another hour—to show just how much time had passed, to convey the endlessness of it
3. past—setting up process in context of time
4. present tense; past tense for the narrative and present tense in dialogue
5. gained, greater value
6. through chronological order

Making Predictions and Drawing Inferences

1. preserve it; keep foreign humors from contaminating it and keep the odor in the bottle
2. to figure it out on his own, if he truly wanted to learn something
3. answers vary
4. to teach him to observe closely and be self-reliant
5. You have to look closely in order to draw. Also it's like writing to find out what you know and don't know.
6. the fish, because he knows them so well

Making Judgments and Thinking Critically

1. Unconnected facts are meaningless until they're connected and made sense of by the human mind.
2. experiential learning or trial-and-error; perhaps, but he probably wouldn't have learned as much and he wouldn't have been trained to be an independent thinker

A HOMEMADE EDUCATION

Checking Your Comprehension

1. wanted to communicate with Mr. Elijah Muhammad whom he respected
2. couldn't read, couldn't express self in writing
3. eighth grade
4. stock of knowledge
5. improve vocabulary and penmanship
6. copy the dictionary and review the words
7. built a stock of general knowledge and became ''free'' through reading

Understanding a Writer's Patterns

1. to show that no matter what, someone can overcome hardships and illiteracy; inspire other blacks, especially undereducated ones
2. others like him and those who would mistreat them.
3. miniature encyclopedia; because it's a storehouse of miscellaneous information but is usually used just to check a word's spelling or meaning
4. aardvark
5. ''It had really begun'' (paragraph 4); ''I spent two days'' (6); took me a day (8); ''I woke up next morning (9); ''I copied the dictionary's next page'' (10); ''With every succeeding page (10)
6. ''I suppose it was inevitable''
7. an interpretation of being able to read as a freeing thing

Making Predictions and Drawing Inferences

1. because he did it himself
2. nothing else to do
3. usual if people want to do something that requires reading and writing, but many simply avoid situations where those skills are needed
4. running his eyes over words, but not understanding
5. didn't understand much so wasn't worth continuing to do; yes
6. Reading allows him to go many more places than just the here and now, understand more, connect with other literate people.

Making Judgments and Thinking Critically

1. Have to be more precise and explain more, show better connections and organizations in writing than talking.
4. Not motivated, not courageous or hard-working enough.

HOW TO HUNT, CLEAN AND COOK A PHEASANT

Checking Your Comprehension

1. complicated
2. dog
3. be in touch with weather
4. boots, array of clothes, clean gun, coffee
5. 8:00 am
6. run, hide, doubleback
7. 35 mph
8. marking and retrieving shot birds
9. so the meat won't be tainted or start to rot
10. don't overcook it

Understanding a Writer's Patterns

1. Pheasant hunting requires patience, perseverance, and a little luck.
2. four; without dog, can't find the birds shot down in the cornfield; because it's so important
3. weather awareness, equipment
4. yes; in fact, they might work better the other way since the equipment is something of a constant and the weather is a variable. However, discussing the less obvious first gives it emphasis.
5. prepare—dog, weather, equipment
   hunt—bird behavior, dog for marking and retrieving, cleaning
   cook—friends, chant, ingredients, time, serve with
6. now, by
7. first, second
8. trickiness of the pheasants
9. run, hide, doubleback
10. follow and watch dog, stepped on one
11. first, second, next, now

Making Predictions and Drawing Inferences

1. that's when it's legal to start hunting
2. eating grain
3. because it takes off so fast

4. a mouthful of bird, which is that colorful
5. yes, since Hanika tells him everything

CHAPTER 9 DIVISION AND CLASSIFICATION

TEXAS WOMEN: TRUE GRIT AND ALL THE REST

Checking Your Comprehension

1. because she couldn't participate
2. Texas sexism
3. southern belle, chicana sisters, rednecks, frontier
4. so deeply ingrained
5. women have become a ''bodacious bunch of overcomers'' as a result of the sexism
6. 1918, 1954, 1969, 1972
7. expected to say ''hi''
8. know how to cope

Understanding a Writer's Patterns

1. # 3-It is virulence of Texas sexism that accounts for strength of Texas women.
2. She lives in Texas so Texans must read her; among them, those who agree with her politics and find her ribbing satire amusing.
3. Uses humor and satire to combat the problems she sees or to make those who aren't aware of issues through her wit and sarcasm
4. Texas is hell on women and horses; a legislator compared women and horses.
5. # 2, also a little bit in # 9
6. ''All of these strains lead. . . .''
7. men not charged with murder one for killing an unfaithful wife; small towns named after women use first names only
8. ''That's the bad news—the good news . . .''

Making Predictions and Drawing Inferences

1. the opening indirect quotation ending in ''I don't know why they stopped''
2. because those who elected them are also fools
3. shows personal distance so she can be an observer of women; also humorists are often self-disparaging. Now she seems amused, but then she's well into middle age.

4. righteously indignant that it has taken so long
5. the kicker woman's quick and witty response to the Highland Park snob

Making Judgments and Thinking Critically

1. yes, her use of slang, made-up words such as "delightsome, jokes
2. no, she writes about the good that comes from the bad
3. maybe, but only attacks the sexist culture, not men
4. less probably, would read more like a historical account
5. yes, shows women aren't bitter or hostile in spite of their treatment
6. Bold action, not modest passivity, gets the rewards.
7. Uses one stereotype to reveal the other, although she seems to believe the snob one

FRIENDS, GOOD FRIENDS—AND SUCH GOOD FRIENDS

Checking Your Comprehension

1. totally love and support and trust one another
2. friendships are conducted at many levels of intensity
3. help out with quick favors
4. hobby or work-related friends
5. those with whom we have a shared past
6. those with whom we shared important parts of life
7. friends from different generations
8. friends only through spouses
9. women she talked with insisted she include men friends
10. defined by level of intimacy
11. don't have to agree about everything

Understanding a Writer's Patterns

1. once
2. now I believe
3. #2 "For the friendships I have and the friendships I see. . . ."
4. primarily adult women—all examples are female and "over 21" and the issue of men is brought up separately
5. ". . . but now I see that's a narrow point of view."
6. classification
7. office, yoga, tennis
8. second grade, flat in Brooklyn, dad out of work, etc.
9. Evelyn's friend, JV's own friend
10. returns to her definition of best of friends; uses same words in slightly different context—no longer all friends, but best

Making Predictions and Drawing Inferences

1. classification of kinds of friends; yes, to a degree—I hadn't anticipated it'd be all female
2. talked to friends and coworkers
3. because it's about the different kinds of friends: kinds, types, categories. The subject is naturally classification.

Making Judgments and Thinking Critically

1. yes, shows the subject and that she's going to write about kinds of friends
2. paragraphs 7, 10, 11, 16, 20, 26; yes, puts people in the essay and makes it more interesting and clear
3. only first names to protect her sources, to let these selected but real women represent other women; use the full name when you first refer to a person and then just the last name
4. yes, to include quotations from men
5. that we're polite as with strangers, not intimate
6. the idea that thoughtful women shouldn't care about such things; to ridicule that idea

KINDS OF DISCIPLINE

Checking Your Comprehension

1. learn from them
2. nature/reality—laws of nature/instant response; culture/society—what people really do/social rules; superior force—following rules of power
3. because reality is the best teacher
4. instant results, points out needed correction, giver of answer is indifferent
5. from being around habitually courteous adults
6. superior force
7. when children would otherwise be hurt; when the child can understand danger
8. locked into babyhood
9. their experience and competence
10. no, because they willingly devote themselves to learning what they care about

Understanding a Writer's Patterns

1. kinds of discipline—that a child may meet and learn from three kinds of discipline

2. first and most important, the next discipline, the third discipline, ‘‘there are places where all three’’
3. If he . . .
4. building blocks, musical keys, hitting a nail
5. behavior in church, concerts, and opera
6. Mexican drivers—‘‘In Mexico, for example . . .’’
7. ballet training

Making Predictions and Drawing Inferences

1. quick feedback/clarity/impartiality
2. he’d probably advocate it—to teach discipline of society
3. to teach

Making Judgments and Thinking Critically

1. strict, but not harsh because he believes in it
2. to protect children or things they can hurt

TWITS, COOKIES, AND QUEENS

Checking Your Comprehension

1. tough cookies, twits, fashion queens
2. by what they wear
3. sex, drugs, rock and roll
4. slink, strut
5. guys’ bodies
6. easily pressured
7. glide, sway
8. as status symbols
9. stable, mature, herself

Understanding a Writer’s Patterns

1. ‘‘There are three main sects in the clique world,’’ and they are sickening.
2. to show the silliness of high school cliques
3. ridiculous, sickening
4. how they treat guys, how they walk, who their heroes are
5. Twisted Sister, Menudo, Rolling Stones, and Beatles
6. Love Connection, Teen Beat, National Enquirer, Michael J. Fox
7. the non-group individualists who can think for themselves

Making Predictions and Drawing Inferences

1. cynical—ridiculous, cynical; yes, all examples are negative
2. to make themselves feel superior and turn on the guys
3. live in a fantasy world of romance; interested in sex but hide their interest
4. no, because of conclusion; she's obviously on the outside observing these groups

Making Judgments and Thinking Critically

1. even, all critical examples
2. just out of high school so the subject is still interesting to her
3. use of details

CHAPTER 10 COMPARISON AND CONTRAST

THE TAPESTRY OF FRIENDSHIP

Checking Your Comprehension

1. *Girlfriends*, *Turning Point*, *Julia*; underline them
2. male friendship
3. from ''buddies'' to ''friends''
4. buddies; friends
5. bond vs. love, do things together vs. be together, face adversity vs. face each other, categories vs. ''special'' category, hang tough vs. hang on to each other
6. men call themselves true friends, but women are better friends
7. movies
8. female

Understanding a Writer's Patterns

1. to show that women are and have been better friends and to value women's friendships; those who don't value female friendships and all who value friendship
2. paragraphs 1–6
3. movies because so many people love movies and third person ''she,'' probably herself but makes you wonder
4. The public's definition of friendship has shifted from buddies to friends.
5. point by point
6. she = I; to objectify, to distance herself from ''her self'' and make more universal

7. but—6 times
8. on the other hand
9. semicolon; paragraph 8
10. how much a female friend will reveal
11. superior—each example seems to put men down, though she says things are changing
12. yet
13. a quotation

Making Predictions and Drawing Inferences

1. that movies are realistic; that life changes to reflect what's in the movies
2. all those female friendships
3. the female version was being shown as the superior goal; for once it wasn't the male version

Making Judgments and Thinking Critically

1. defines friendship by showing the contrast of buddies and real friends
2. yes, since a woman's writing it though that doesn't mean there's no truth in it

PRIVATE SPACE

Checking Your Comprehension

1. as an undergraduate
2. entered a room where others were talking
3. invisible boundary around two or three in conversation; boundary of having entered a room
4. entering a room and making eye contact
5. personal observation and research when subjects photographed people together in different situations
6. created barriers in their prison for personal space
7. started killing each other
8. double/soundproof; privacy
9. German—closed; American—open
10. obey them; love of order, value obedience, respect for authority
11. American—each situation different; German/Italian—7 feet
12. so it would remain at a proper distance

Understanding a Writer's Patterns

1. American definitions of space differ from others', especially from German's

2. American, because most information is about how different other cultures are from and how American habits are interpreted by others
3. to make Americans aware of differences
4. point by point
5. paragraph 3
6. first, second
7. intimate, personal, social, public
8. reported observation of soldiers
9. reported an observer's account of Germans having to share kitchens after WW II
10. doors and the need or lack of to be heavy, soundproof, and closed. Differences in doors show different concepts of what sort of privacy is important.
11. however

Making Predictions and Drawing Inferences

1. mostly a discussion of German concepts of space, with comparison to other cultures, but not exclusively German and American
2. He's referring to Hitler's insistence that Germany needed more space, hence their policy of conquest and taking what was ''rightfully theirs.''
3. when companies merge or employees work in foreign countries or for foreign bosses
4. with all the emphasis on the global village and the increasing need to interact with other cultures

Making Judgments and Thinking Critically

1. I prefer the personal narrative as an opener; less intimidating than a technical discussion about an unfamiliar subject
2. alternates examples with information and explanations

OTHER CULTURES, OTHER TIMES

Checking Your Comprehension

1. Socrates, Lincoln
2. a few hours, otherwise not considered worth hearing
3. pressing the highest number of things into the smallest number of minutes—monochronic
4. promptness, speed, brevity, punctuality
5. flexibility, intuition, dedication, inspiration, imagination

6. predictable tasks—how long to dress for work, boil an egg, word process six pages
7. not predictable in advance—fall in love, gain trust, solve a computer problem, gain support
8. West is monochronic; East is polychronic.
9. Airline employees, assembly line workers, cab and bus drivers, cashiers
10. teaching, counseling, sales, arts

Understanding a Writer's Patterns

1. Two opposite ways of viewing time are valuable in different cultures and in different jobs.
2. to make people aware of the differences, to help them appreciate others' view of time, and develop flexibility by having both views
3. American with a monochronic view: because it's written in English and the author works with American businesses which generally have a monochronic view of time
4. uses two historical anecdotes
5. . . . in fact, we may be lessening the quality of our work . . .
6. sentences 2 and 5
7. when you . . .
8. on the other hand
9. some, other
10. In our society and . . ./business, on the other hand
11. asks a question about significance

Making Predictions and Drawing Inferences

1. neither is superior; both are given equal time and are shown to be important in different situations
2. still clung to old tradition, for entertainment because little else to do
3. if the individual isn't flexible, trouble arises because he/she will have monochronic expectations
4. their entire profit sense is based on production; time is money; value of the industrial revolution

Making Judgments and Thinking Critically

1. monochronic, because short answers are expected and you can predict fairly closely how much time answering will take
2. polychronic, because figuring out what to write can't be done in a strict time frame; writing isn't a linear project.

CARBON COPY

Checking Your Comprehension

1. tortilla sandwich
2. laugh and say it wasn't food
3. to fit in and do exactly as the anglos did
4. moved from barrio, sent daughter to parochial school
5. style of dress, eliminate laid-back attitude, stop using hand gestures
6. changed spelling of name, sisters emphasized conformity
7. became best model of conformity, excelled in academics; lost sense of authentic self

Understanding a Writer's Patterns

1. That day I learned to hide my ethnic difference and to assimilate into the accepted white culture.
2. the anglos who would will the creating of carbon copies; other hispanics feeling similar pressure
3. specific, personal, immediate, poignant
4. changing of name, Apache grandmother
5. dress—4; behavior—5, 6; speech—7, 8
6. implies that being ''not just good'' isn't good enough; loses the emphasis of contrast
7. sets up expectations of contrast; dramatic emphasis

Making Predictions and Drawing Inferences

1. yes; she effectively sets up the tone of how insensitively she'd been treated and what effect this had
2. no, because that day she would make the trip back home only once
3. mother recognized chicano values would always leave daughters second class, wanted more and better
4. feels sad; from the conclusion
5. could go either way—strength of will to use system, weakness to give in
6. that she gained from it (strict disciplinarians and excellent educators) and that she lost her heritage; she says so

Making Judgments and Thinking Critically

1. a carbon sheet used to be placed between two sheets of typing paper to make a copy, before copy machines and word processors; now seen mostly in charge tickets; something that is exactly like the original; yes, because it's a concrete image of her changes
2. seems regretful but realizes the positive outcomes too

CHAPTER 11 DEFINITION

THE REWARDS OF LIVING A SOLITARY LIFE

Checking Your Comprehension

1. living alone with no other humans
2. in shock to learn how much he could enjoy himself
3. might discover he bored himself or no self there to meet
4. launched into inner space; getting to know himself
5. 20 years
6. with other people, when there's a lack of intimacy
7. knowing yourself, personal exploration and growth
8. being overtired, working too long without a break, returning home after lecture trip
9. water plants, feed cat, cook meal
10. self slowly reemerges and loneliness leaves

Understanding a Writer's Patterns

1. anecdote
2. the focus moves from her friend to herself; ''we'' includes the reader; moves from the opening anecdote to an exploration of the subject
3. A solitary life is rewarding.
4. the opening anecdote about her friend; contrast appears in the discussion of music heard with another person and alone; examples of rewards (watch the sun rise over the ocean, uninterrupted day, take a walk with my dog, etc.)
5. the enjoyment of being alone with falling in love
6. as astronaut—on mission to find self; seeing self with naked eye—without aid of others' vision
7. explains the naked eye metaphor
8. explains the astronaut/adventurer metaphor
9. probably that there's something wrong with it
10. to defend the choice of such a life and to recommend it

Making Predictions and Drawing Inferences

1. into doing things alone
2. one's own thoughts, feelings, observations, perceptions, etc.
3. because others' feelings and perceptions color the experience
4. feels out of touch with her own feelings
5. when outside world recedes from prominence in her thoughts

Making Judgments and Thinking Critically

1. yes, unknown with few familiar landmarks and so scary
2. defines the term by giving an anecdote and quotations
3. yes, leads up to it; effective for a disbelieving audience
4. being out of touch with yourself

PERMANENT RECORD

Checking Your Comprehension

1. the death of the permanent record
2. screw-ups in school
3. fear that the transgression would appear on the permanent record
4. people believe they'll be forgiven for anything and laugh at the concept; sins became ''interesting''
5. how people have ''sinned''
6. rejuvenate their careers
7. deduced any kind of behavior was permissible
8. in ''heaven''

Understanding a Writer's Patterns

1. begins with a generalization
2. adults who grew up on the concept of a permanent record
3. mostly to entertain, also on declining standards of behavior
4. past in paragraphs 2–5; more recent past to present in paragraphs 6–12; present in paragraph 13–14; future in paragraph 15
5. people felt the threat of the permanent record
6. people have deduced any behavior is acceptable
7. people should behave because there may be a permanent record after life
8. informal, humorous—it rambles and is only mildly cautionary

Making Predictions and Drawing Inferences

1. that he would talk about the good old days
2. that we might need to be careful after all
4. authority and a sense of justice
5. Freedom of Information Act, hackers could get in and change
6. St. Peter at the gates of heaven

Making Judgments and Thinking Critically

1. yes, for humor
2. for coherence and for emphasis of it's omnipresence in people's minds

4. humorous throughout; nostalgia with an edge, makes fun of our unrealistic fear in the past but sees the good of it

AMERICANIZATION IS TOUGH ON 'MACHO'

Checking Your Comprehension

1. manly, responsible, hardworking, in charge, patriarchal
2. chauvinistic, brutish, uncouth, selfish, loud, abrasive, etc.
3. Stallone, Schwarzenegger, Bronson
4. Stewart, Connery, Olivier
5. good provider, kept problems to self, let others blow his horn; yes
6. nonassertive, unambitious, ignorant, weak
7. drink, gamble, fool around
8. Because of the feminist movement *macho* came to have negative meanings.

Understanding a Writer's Patterns

1. Anglo Americans—to make them aware of the hispanic definition of the term
2. the anglo negative image of macho
3. in paragraph 4 contrast of hispanic and anglo use of *macho* and paragraphs 5 and 6 which describe the American *Macho* and the hispanic macho
4. brutish, selfish, uncouth, etc. from previous paragraph
5. hispanic concept of strength through silence
6. as an admirable example of hispanic *macho*
7. father struggled with cultural ambiguities: worked farm 20 years, worked 20-hour days laying pipe and plowing; didn't defend himself or complain about unjust criticism
8. because it results in a stereotype of the Latin male and stereotypes distort the truth; not entirely successful because it tries to do too much and fails to take into account the fluidity of definition; she was better before she got preachy

Making Predictions and Drawing Inferences

1. they feel they've been mischaracterized and their values are misunderstood and not appreciated
2. she can see him from an American value system
3. ruled by men, women subservient; most cultures
4. rules are firmly established, no ambiguity about choices or right and wrong—all is settled; lack of respect for women, their values, perceptions, and experiences

5. misunderstanding of each other's values; devaluing of the qualities in men valued by hispanics

Making Judgments and Thinking Critically

1. creates a values conflict and cultural misunderstandings

THE LIBERATED WOMAN

Checking Your Comprehension

1. chic women with college degrees and careers
2. to set free from involuntary servitude
3. financial independence
4. freedom of choice
5. responsibilities to others in the family
6. a highly efficient program of cleaning, shopping, and laundering by designating specific days for each
7. an article in *Dallas Morning News*
8. schedule of work and home
9. wake at 7:00, fix breakfast and lunch for family, relax with paper and snack
10. balanced meals, varied menus
11. few childhood diseases, regular health maintenance
12. homemaker

Understanding a Writer's Patterns

1. describes society's liberated career woman
2. She and a working friend were debating who was more liberated.
3. According to her definition of having choice how she spends her time, she is truly liberated.
4. freedom of choice to organize her time
5. what she doesn't contend with
6. process, narration, description, comparison/contrast

Making Predictions and Drawing Inferences

1. laundry, meal-planning, housekeeping, caring for her children; no—she made the choice and decides about her time
2. work and family; yes, comparison made in paragraph 8.
3. Frank—no; friend—yes
4. the day-to-day aspects of her children's lives

Making Judgments and Thinking Critically

1. yes, there are others like her; to defend her decision to stay at home
2. because she chooses to do these activities and can decide how to organize her time
3. after paragraph 7; these two aspects do not need to be in a particular sequence; better as is because paragraphs 5 and 6 are about life now and 7 sounds like time when the children were small
4. not if she feels she is still making choices about her own life but she may look for new interests to replace her diminishing responsibilities with the children

CHAPTER 12 CAUSE AND EFFECT

DO YOU KNOW WHO YOUR FRIENDS ARE?

Checking Your Comprehension

1. colleagues and work buddies, golf partners, members of couples
2. homophobia, men are biologically competitive, culture discourages it
3. idealized in the abstract
4. He eliminates them.
5. male bonding
6. limited number of jobs leads to competition
7. leaves little passion for anything
8. passion, capacity for intimacy
9. with his wife and children
10. willingness to recognize one is going against the grain, courage to do so, and effort

Understanding a Writer's Patterns

1. ''But the major reason for the shortage of true friendship among men in America is that our culture discourages it.'' (paragraph 3)
2. persuade men to ''brave'' a friendship and ''others'' to accept
3. adults—men and women—over 30; he mentions that age specifically
4. a quotation—a line from a song
5. causes
6. ''Why is this so?''
7. ''The most obvious time this [pressure] happens is when a man gets married. . . .''
8. this—refers to sniggering at male friendship in paragraph 5

9. decline of blue collar worker, increase of great white collar jobs, more job competition to move up the ladder, decreasing trust (paragraph 7)
10. encouragement that male friendships are possible if men want them

Making Predictions and Drawing Inferences

1. As a man, he's particularly knowledgeable about and interested in the issue of male friendship.
2. more along typically ''feminine'' lines, after Viorst and Goodman
3. The lover in him, the passionate side necessary for intimacy is destroyed by ruthless competition on the career ladder.

Making Judgments and Thinking Critically

1. yes, he really seems to articulate the pressures
2. yes, at that age, but young men are still advised to be careful because of homophobia
3. potential for mischief and destruction
4. because passion means the ability to love life and to feel

LOSS OF INTIMACY

Checking Your Comprehension

1. at school—words directed to general audience, meaningfully ordered, purpose to be understood
2. half a year
3. speak English at home
4. practicing English like a game after dinner, a year's special attention from teachers to keep him from straying, and his parents' speaking English at home
5. One day he heard his parent's voices change when switching from Spanish to English when they saw him.
6. that it was unremarkable that the whole class understood
7. no longer listened to how strangers sounded
8. his identity as an American citizen
9. the special feeling of closeness at home
10. grew alert to their accented English
11. a Mexican farmworker who asked him questions; an old lady who murmured in Spanish as she got on the bus

Understanding a Writer's Patterns

1. the effect; it's the result of learning to speak English
2. paragraphs 5, 6, 7

3. paragraphs 8, 9, 10, 11
4. but—to emphasize the loss and to show all wasn't positive
5. teacher visit, speaking up in class, overhearing parents
6. hears another family speaking and momentarily feels the old feelings of intimacy until he see them as strangers
7. change of rhythm; for emphasis
8. to show how they mixed Spanish words in with English; to emphasize the sounds he heard
9. to stress differences in his ''names'' and his identity
10. sound

Making Predictions and Drawing Inferences

1. parochial
2. good and docile
3. thought he wasn't getting reinforcement at home
4. the more immersed in English, the further he was distanced from his Spanish identity and his home life
5. denying their true nature for his sake; knowing they were forcing him away for his sake and feeling the loss
6. knew his English was easily understood by others

Making Judgments and Thinking Critically

1. yes, he selects details from the child's perspective
2. very typical—unsure what to say or how to say it, so he's silent; could have acted out, caused trouble
3. native speakers can't read assignments, fear being wrong, don't know what's expected
4. easy to make—wanted to help son succeed in Anglo world, but difficult to follow through on because of their limited English and lack of education
5. yes, he's discussing at all times how he felt and how he continues to feel. It recaptures his intense feeling of intimacy and loss.

WHEN TELEVISION ATE MY BEST FRIEND

Checking Your Comprehension

1. eight
2. Lucy
3. swinging
4. fell/jumped out of the swing
5. She could have flown if she'd done it right.
6. waiting for her arm to heal

7. became too busy to play
8. afraid it'd eat her since Lucy had disappeared after getting a television
9. stopped eating in dining room, dinner served on TV trays, no talking, went to sleep with TV on, dad stopped reading

Understanding a Writer's Patterns

1. adult—indicates many more to follow
2. paragraphs 1–6, the swing incident
3. months, seasons, holidays
4. thumbs up; the pilot's okay signal
5. slammed the screen door, bang, knocked, called; emphasizes it with the child's logic that Lucy's disappearance must mean she's dead
6. Time rolled on, marked by the seasons and holidays—no excitement
7. "Television changes people."
8. use of stopped, didn't, and time words
9. never, best friend, fly, television eats people

Making Predictions and Drawing Inferences

1. ball hit so hard it imprinted the brand name on her leg; exaggeration
2. a theory arrived at to explain a variety of results through hypothesis; capitalized to show how serious it was to them
3. typical behavior in summer, what they considered was the norm
4. end of friendship
5. "up" is an affirmative symbol
6. for emphasis
7. TV show about a kid and his or her horse

Making Judgments and Thinking Critically

1. Both serve a purpose: the text gives the overview; the personal essay gives the specific, concrete evidence.
2. Child's point of view in the June and August swing stories and her child's perception that television eats people. The rest is from adult point of view, explaining and filling in the narrative.
3. to evoke a child's feelings and perception and reflect as an adult about the events and their effects; yes
4. she has completely disappeared

MY PUBLIC ADDRESS

Checking Your Comprehension

1. first grade, age 6, to say a three-line poem
2. eight years later in her freshman English class

3. after that miserable experience in high school
4. rehearsed presentations, practiced dealing with distractions and mistakes, practiced in front of the mirror on the morning of the speech, changed thinking
5. about roller figure skating
6. no butterflies, no shaking, natural breathing, better memory, no search for witty remarks, voice projection
7. become more relaxed and receptive

Understanding a Writer's Patterns

1. uses 3rd person to tell the narrative
2. with description of the child, short ''She'' sentences
3. describes the physical and visible symptoms
4. shows how that ''inner child'' still has needs to be met
5. shifts to 3rd person to show application to the audience

Making Predictions and Drawing Inferences

1. serious and determined, goal-oriented
2. yes, she could not remember anything
3. figurative; when nervous or unprepared, moments can seem to last forever.

Making Judgments and Thinking Critically

1. Problem: fear of public speaking. Solution: intense preparations. Effect: confident feelings and behavior.
2. Problem: paragraphs 1–8. Solution: paragraphs 9–11. Effects: paragraphs 12–13.
3. problem—so the reader can identify, since it's a common problem; also, her solution is relatively simple.
4. Paragraphs 4 and 5, 6 and 7. Neither of the one-sentence paragraphs is dramatic; both are traditional topic sentences for the details that follow.

CHAPTER 13 ARGUMENTATION

THE CASE FOR OFFENSIVE HUMOR

Checking Your Comprehension

1. public writing, education, and comedy
2. *Airplane* and *Naked Gun* $2^1/_2$; 1980 and 1991
3. the federal deficit; nobody supports it or demands its return
4. It died.

5. because it defuses tensions, educates, disarms, undermines prejudices, and is funny
6. insulting everyone takes the sting out
7. When taboo subject matter becomes entertainment, the unknown becomes known and fear and prejudice fade.
8. Spoofing sensitive subjects rather than avoiding them raises the subjects issues and avoids patronizing them.
9. Making fun of yourself or reversing the humor (minorities making fun of majorities) ridicules stereotypes.
10. violent slapstick

Understanding a Writer's Patterns

1. contrasts humor in two movies made ten years apart
2. There are several reasons to lament the death of offensive humor.
3. people interested in comedy, especially those who oppose it
4. gives reasons (ways); five
5. reasons, examples, anecdotes, contrast (paragraph 8) movies
6. stand-up comedy, TV sitcoms, musical
7. ''As we've pushed the risque off stage''
8. between violence in *Home Alone* and old slapstick like the Three Stooges and *Animal House*
9. offensive humor as support, not threat to society; contrast of cruelty in jest with cruelty in seriousness
10. by claiming the value of offensive humor to a multicultural society such as ours—ending offensive humor may add to racial and social tensions

Making Predictions and Drawing Inferences

1. reasons, the ways
2. thoughtful when it looks at close observation of the foibles of humankind
3. yes; Jewish and black humor; more references to them—paragraphs 1, all of 4, 7 for Jewish and paragraphs 1, 3, 5, 7.
4. all types; mentions gays, ethnic, drug gags, frontal nudity, obscenities, Jewish, women and men, handicapped
5. bad; less talk may lead to more violence in life

Making Judgments and Thinking Critically

3. The source of the clerk's snicker was the stereotype of blacks liking fried chicken; the black man responded by evoking two other stereotypes of blacks and their fondness for watermelon and their skill in tap dancing. When the one being ridiculed can play with the stereotypes, the tables are turned.

6. Prejudicial jokes are often told because the teller assumes the hearer will share the teller's disparaging opinion about the subject. However, such jokes in comedy usually arise out of recognition of the stereotype and using it to ridicule it, not the subject of the joke.

A HARD LESSON IN SMOKING'S DANGER

Checking Your Comprehension

1. One-fourth of deaths in Oregon in 1989 were smoking-related.
2. the norm and the movies
3. stopped vacationing in the mountains, started smoking filtered cigarettes, and finally quit smoking
4. 35 years
5. had to rest a lot; progressed to a motorized scooter and oxygen; finally on oxygen all day and too weak to go from room to room
6. much medicine
7. fishing, go to his daughter's graduation and wedding
8. full of regrets and sadness

Understanding a Writer's Patterns

1. probably smokers and families of smokers: paragraph 2 and 17, use of "you"
2. Smoking can kill you; don't do it. It is an opinion because many smokers don't really believe smoking will harm them.
3. uses a recent statistic about smoking-related deaths
4. draws on personal experience to narrate and describe the effects of smoking
5. reports her present feelings and states her thesis in the last sentence
6. makes me notice them, dramatic
7. grew up (3), were married (4), years went by (5), finally (6), for a while (7), when he took retirement (8), through the years (12), in the last month of his life (14), when I returned (15)
8. one morning
9. from the norm and movies to specific stars, Bogart and Davis

Making Predictions and Drawing Inferences

1. Paul shrugged aside my concern about his chronic cough (5)
2. thought about quitting and changed to filtered cigarettes (6)
3. early retirement, maybe 55–60
4. because of his disability—emphysema
5. because he kept his interest in politics and world events throughout his illness

6. paragraph 14 describes the last month of his life
7. to get his wife out of the house to pick up the mail
8. Her life was changed by his illness too—things they couldn't do, places they couldn't go, and her caretaking of him as he grew weaker. Also perhaps less money because of early retirement and medical expenses made her life different than it might have been.

Making Judgments and Thinking Critically

1. to show the seriousness of smoking, to get the reader's attention; few stats such as those available so she had to use Oregon stats
2. yes, shows the problem is widespread, not just a personal story. No, more statistics would probably slow the reader down. She made her point.
3. forceful, concerned, reasonable. She doesn't want to "ding-dong" smokers and use scare tactics, but wants them to have the "opportunity" to understand the dangers of smoking (2). Doesn't exaggerate or give gory details, doesn't talk about its effect on her life.

REWRITING HISTORY

Checking Your Comprehension

1. the Japanese's rewriting history textbooks to whitewash their role in WW II
2. changes in emphasis, wordings, and in the way they were telling their children about WW II
3. because it's difficult to tell their children about their historical acts of aggression and brutality
4. changed "invasions" of China, etc. to "advanced"; changed "killed and assaulted" 200,000 Chinese willfully to "in the midst of the confusion . . ."
5. Egyptians, U.S., Argentina, and Great Britain
6. called the slaves who built the pyramids "volunteer labor"; to soften a cruel part of their history
7. to explain, judge, justify
8. because nations and parents want respect from the young
9. we are tainted by it and commit the ultimate assault on our victims
10. by admitting their wrongdoing

Understanding a Writer's Patterns

1. no, just gives the subject—rewriting history
2. compares history with math, foreign languages, biographies, memory, truth, and politics

3. History must not be rewritten to hide or soften the mistakes of the past; honesty the only way to pay for the wrongs.
4. general public, especially those who might favor a heroic and spotless rendition of our history in textbooks
5. paragraphs 3–7
6. paragraph 8
7. paragraphs 9–13
8. Germany
9. parents; because both have the young they want to influence
10. applauds the past honesty of the Japanese and shows the good effect of Japan's admitting its wrongs and its defeat. Says there's an end for guilt, but not for needing to know the truth

Making Predictions and Drawing Inferences

1. no, because its facts are complex
2. that history is selective like memory, that perception is involved
3. those who have suffered as a result of the other's actions
4. Cowboys and Indians have been romanticized or mythologized, stereotyped, made simplistically bad or good.
5. slavery: treatment of Native Americans, Chinese, others
6. because it was so shameful a part of their history

Making Judgments and Thinking Critically

1. examples, short paragraphs, having some knowledge of history
2. not knowing much world history, the incidents she uses
3. probably justification
4. grades 1–4 explanation, after that judgment (showing good and bad); never as justification because that's another version of "rewriting" history and it's dishonest

MAKING AMENDS WITH MOM

Checking Your Comprehension

1. during adolescence, the transition from childhood to womanhood
2. changes of shifting roles
3. from personal experience and research
4. the daughter
5. that they are stuck in the old relationship with their mothers
6. improves other relationships, especially those with guys
7. from their mothers
8. Her mother was diagnosed with chronic diabetes and was hospitalized in intensive care several times.
9. immaturity, not being able to consider the mother's feelings

Understanding a Writer's Patterns

1. Young women with troubled relationships with their mothers should take steps to mend the relationship.
2. personal experience and research
3. because she understands the problem, her part in it, and something about solving it; connects her with the audience
4. paragraph 2
5. first, secondly, furthermore
6. paragraph 5
7. to address the possible feelings of her audience and their resistance to taking action to improve the relationship; sets up the thesis
8. in quotation marks because it is the title of a magazine article; underlined because it is the title of a book

Making Predictions and Drawing Inferences

1. about 20 because she's in college and sounds more mature than 18; sounds like she might have been on her own for a while because she says she didn't talk to her mother for a year and she mentions her mother's hospitalization with diabetes over a period of time
2. probably six months or so because she mentions her realization of her mother's not being around forever and her problems with her ego and pride
3. about creating an adult relationship between mother and daughter after adolescence; examples of problems with her mother and ways she overcame them; possible surprise may be information from sources

Making Judgments and Thinking Critically

2. because she has more in common (shared ground) with daughters and will likely have more credibility with them; because they often have the power to change their relationships with their mothers
5. yes, emotional subject; not emotional writing although the writer has obviously felt great conflict and pain to be motivated to address this subject